T0352942

The Canary Code

The
Canary
Code

A GUIDE TO NEURODIVERSITY, DIGNITY, AND INTERSECTIONAL BELONGING AT WORK

Ludmila N. Praslova, PhD

Berrett–Koehler Publishers, Inc.

Berrett-Koehler Publishers, Inc.
1333 Broadway, Suite 1000
Oakland, CA 94612-1921
Tel: (510) 817-2277
Fax: (510) 817-2278
www.bkconnection.com

ORDERING INFORMATION

Quantity sales. Special discounts are available on quantity purchases by corporations, associations, and others. For details, contact the "Special Sales Department" at the Berrett-Koehler address above.
Individual sales. Berrett-Koehler publications are available through most bookstores. They can also be ordered directly from Berrett-Koehler: Tel: (800) 929-2929; Fax: (802) 864-7626; www.bkconnection .com.
Orders for college textbook/course adoption use. Please contact Berrett-Koehler:
Tel: (800) 929-2929; Fax: (802) 864-7626.

Distributed to the US trade and internationally by Penguin Random House Publisher Services.

Berrett-Koehler and the BK logo are registered trademarks of Berrett-Koehler Publishers, Inc.

Printed in the United States of America

Berrett-Koehler books are printed on long-lasting acid-free paper. When it is available, we choose paper that has been manufactured by environmentally responsible processes. These may include using trees grown in sustainable forests, incorporating recycled paper, minimizing chlorine in bleaching, or recycling the energy produced at the paper mill.

Library of Congress Cataloging-in-Publication Data

Names: Praslova, Ludmila N., author.
Title: The canary code : a guide to neurodiversity, dignity, and intersectional belonging at work / Ludmila N. Praslova, PhD.
Description: First edition. | Oakland, CA : Berrett-Koehler Publishers, Inc., [2024] | Includes bibliographical references and index.
Identifiers: LCCN 2023046667 (print) | LCCN 2023046668 (ebook) | ISBN 9781523005840 (hardcover) | ISBN 9781523005857 (pdf) | ISBN 9781523005864 (epub)
Subjects: LCSH: People with disabilities—Employment—United States. | Neurodiversity—United States. | Intersectionality (Sociology)—United States.
Classification: LCC HD7256.U6 P737 2024 (print) | LCC HD7256.U6 (ebook) | DDC 658.30087/4—dc23/eng/20240116
LC record available at https://lccn.loc.gov/2023046667
LC ebook record available at https://lccn.loc.gov/2023046668

First Edition

32 31 30 29 28 27 26 25 24   10 9 8 7 6 5 4 3 2 1

Book production: Westchester Publishing Services
Cover design: Ashley Ingram

CONTENTS

PRELUDE AND DEDICATION

People have more change-making power than we give ourselves credit for.

In late June 2023, this book was nearly finished. Four years of research, almost eight months of writing, and one month to the deadline. But the last few steps of major projects—even passion projects—tend to be the hardest.

Despite all the examples of inclusive companies, despite all the business case research, advancing neuroinclusion at work is hard. Excruciatingly hard. Just a few weeks earlier, many members of neurodivergent communities voted strongly against using the word "included" in one of the proposed titles of my book—because many of us have never felt included in the world of work and in the larger society.

I worried, "Will all my work make a difference? Will enough people care?"

Then I witnessed something that renewed my faith in humanity and hopes for acceptance and belonging for everyone.

On June 24, a crowd of more than 100,000 gathered at the Glastonbury Festival of Contemporary Performance, an outdoor event held in Somerset in the southwest of England, to see Lewis Capaldi, a Scottish singer-songwriter. Capaldi is known for his chart-topping hit "Someone You Loved" and his unpretentious style, humor, and candid disclosures about his diagnosis of Tourette Syndrome. Tourette Syndrome causes involuntary tics that vary between individuals and are often intensified by stress and anxiety.

As he performed his hit song, Capaldi's tics became increasingly pronounced. His shoulder moved in ways he did not intend. His voice faltered. His struggle was visible to all. When Capaldi stumbled over the words to "Someone You Loved," the audience joined in, finishing the song as he tried to sing a few words here and there.

There were no boos, no complaining. Just empathy and support.

There was no mockery or impatience. Just love.

Those fans did not buy festival tickets because they intended to make a difference. But when a difference-making moment happened, they rose to the occasion.

I was one of many neurodivergent people who watched this moment and felt hope. Hope to see this type of support and acceptance in their lives.[1,2] For many people with Tourette Syndrome, as well as for autistic, dyslexic and dyspraxic people; ADHDers; and others whose neurobiology differs from the typical, the Glastonbury crowd showed what might be possible. Acceptance. Support. Inclusion. All denied to too many, for too long.

What would it take to replicate the Glastonbury effect—the acceptance and support for neurodivergence—in our workplaces?

In this book, I explore strategies for cultivating a more empathetic and inclusive, "Glastonbury-like" organizational environment. Systemic factors within workplaces can bring out the best or the worst in humans. This book shows how to bring out the best.

For now, much research documents the worst. A UK study published in 2020 reported that 30 percent of managers would not want to hire someone with Tourette Syndrome. About half of the respondents would not want to hire or manage someone with at least one of the conditions typically associated with neurodivergence.[3]

The Glastonbury crowd showed there is more caring in the world than these dire statistics suggest. Their humanity was enough inspiration to help me push through the final hurdles of finishing my work. I saw an example of people showing love and support to those who are different from them, and becoming changemakers just by opening their hearts. I want to contribute to building a world where more people are loved and supported. Regardless of differences.

This book is dedicated to everyone who struggles with being different, bullied, rejected, and told to try harder to fit in.

And to every changemaker who helps show that kindness and humanity can triumph.

July 11, 2023

PREFACE

I stepped out of the women's inclusion conference reception into the hotel garden. Ahh, the quiet, the cool evening air. Except there was someone who seemed to be struggling to breathe. The person was vaguely familiar—we might have been in some sessions together. Anne? I thought her name might have been Anne.

I approached her, and she held up her EpiPen. I hung near just in case. When she finally caught her breath, Anne said she was sure she had mentioned her food allergies on the sign-up form. But evidently, the reception options had not been safe. Ah, yes, one of the main dishes filled the room with the smell of peanuts, but I did not pay attention. I don't have allergies. Perhaps the organizers also did not have allergies. We humans are rarely good at noticing issues that don't directly affect us.

I did pay attention to the fact that the music in the hotel lobby was tortuous—a loud, pulsating, painful assault to my senses. I had to walk around the building to the back entrance to get to the conference meeting rooms. Noise makes me physically sick. That is also why I had to escape the reception. I brought up the music issue. But the organizers must not have had sensory sensitivities either.

Anne and I commiserated about the deep irony of being excluded at an inclusion conference. And I added another thing to my list of factors to solve for when creating inclusive environments—allergies. My list was getting very, very long. Many experiences, many decades long.

I started working in global diversity when I was 19.

Nobody told me it was supposed to be hard, so I thought it was great fun. I got to figure out how to help people work with colleagues from drastically different countries, even when the countries weren't on the best terms, historically or currently. It didn't make sense to me to choose one culture and force everyone to fit into it. Why give up our cultures when we can share and enjoy many different traditions? This is how I stumbled on the "culture-add" approach—

creating an environment that incorporates many cultural ways of being and creates new ones. Instead of requiring people to conform or assimilate, the environment itself could flex, adapt, and be enriched by the diversity.

By age 25, I was running international relations for a large global not-for-profit focused on the post-Soviet areas of Eurasia. Our cafeteria served mashed potatoes with kimchi, and everyone knew basic phrases in multiple languages. I loved my job, with all its challenges. Despite tensions and historical adversities within larger cultures, we created a safe, productive, and inclusive environment—at least when it came to national-level cultures.

Gender inclusion was a different matter. I pushed it further than anyone ever had—but it was not far enough. Yes, I was a department head by 25, but I was also told point-blank that was as far as I was ever going to go. People in the organization could get professional development and advancement, one of my bosses informed me, but "a person" was "a brother." Or, in the words of another boss, "A girl should not be smarter than her boss."

Honestly, I tried being a "good girl" by making myself small—for a time. But it was not going to work. I wanted to grow. I wanted to figure out how to make organizations fully inclusive. Not along just one dimension of human differences but along all of them. So I left and moved continents to go to a PhD program in industrial-organizational psychology. Then I moved states, time zones, and climate zones for jobs in my "second career" in academia.

I learned a lot about organizational workings and organizational change. I also kept learning about human differences—often the hard way. In escaping blatant sexism, I ran straight into blatant xenophobia and classism and into a few less blatant, systemic ism-s.

I don't recommend experiencing xenophobic hate crime as a creativity booster, but somehow every knock made me think ever deeper about comprehensive inclusion. Running is not the answer to exclusion. Improving organizations is.

Every organization I encountered had diversity initiatives, inclusion statements, and some great people. And yet, someone was always excluded—be it from professional development or from basic human dignity. Someone was always on the margin. Women. Black women, Asian women, single women, tall women, short women. Caregivers. Disabled people. First-generation college graduates. People with kids and people without kids. Class migrants. Immigrants. Older people. Younger people. Quiet people and modest people. People with the "wrong" kinds of names. People with accents. People with allergies. People with a funky fashion sense. Really, just people.

Exclusion does not need a reason—just an excuse.

I eventually found a home in a good organization with great colleagues. I taught graduate students how to create organizational environments based on fairness. I managed departments and initiatives, hired people, and wrote policies. I was doing meaningful, rewarding work, the kind of work I was very good at. It was a good life. Challenging, but good.

Then, a rapid succession of bosses led to increased political jousting and changed the emotional climate of my job. Soon after that, my office relocated, and my commute became much more stressful. After enduring that commute, I sat shivering in a space where I was too cold to think straight—even when I was not getting interrupted, which was often. The work I'd been happily doing for many years turned into something I could not do. Something that made me physically sick and mentally miserable.

At first, I was mad at myself. Just how pathetic was I to let an office move, an extra bit of driving, and some office politics get to me? I wrote a dissertation while living at a poverty level. This should be nothing. It did not make any sense that I would be this miserable.

When something does not make sense, I research until it does.

There was a reason I had chosen to pay extra to live close to the (old) office: driving in traffic always left me drained. So did politics. Driving and politics felt unnatural to me. And then there were other things I never quite mastered. Dealing with interruptions, multitasking, tolerating loud music and synthetic clothes . . . It's almost as if I were autistic, except I love words and writing . . . Oh wait, many autistic people love writing.[1,2] And that research on autistic women sounds so, so much like me.[3]

The diagnostic tests showed I was autistic after all. And the current version of my work environment was not inclusive of autistic people. Mystery solved.

Workplaces, in general, are not designed for autistic talent. If they were, autistic people with college degrees would not have an 80–85 percent unemployment rate in the United States;[4,5] reports from some other countries, like Australia and Germany, indicate lower but still concerning rates.[6,7]

Discovering the horrifying US statistic—just before the misfortunate conference experience—got me out of my head. It added fuel to my mission of finding a way to create organizations that welcome all differences and intersectionalities.

In that statistic was also the answer. If organizations could learn how to welcome people as excluded as autistic talent, surely they could welcome all differences, all the time. By including the most marginalized, we can include everyone.

And that is when a picture formed in my mind: a complete model for making organizations radically inclusive across the entire cycle of employment. From designing jobs to professional development. From access to jobs to success in jobs. The key was to design for the canaries in the coal mine—the ones who struggle to breathe before anyone else is affected.

The way to prevent or heal toxic work environments is to start at the margins, to create systems that support the people most sensitive to toxic problems in the workplace, who are the most excluded. That model—the Canary Code for intersectional inclusion—is the core of this book.

The model is centered on six core principles embedded across all talent processes in organizations. By practicing employee participation, focusing on outcomes, promoting flexibility, ensuring organizational justice, enhancing transparency, and using valid tools in decision making, organizations can support the well-being of all employees. More than that, they can help create a more inclusive, thriving society.

Since 2019, I've been refining my approach to systemic inclusion, researching and helping organizations develop systems for neurodiversity and intersectional inclusion. I threw myself into neuroinclusion work. My consulting, speaking, and writing help leaders break free of myths and stereotypes so they can develop a systemic and comprehensive approach to inclusion. I spoke at companies like Amazon, IBM, and the Bank of America; healthcare systems; and universities; I wrote academic papers and published business articles in *Harvard Business Review* and *Fast Company*.

But more questions were coming my way than I could possibly answer one at a time. My LinkedIn box was exploding. And when a Berrett-Kohler editor invited me to submit a book proposal, I was thrilled to write it.

This is that book.

The Canary Code

UNINCLUDABLE TALENT

A bad system will beat a good person every time.

—W. Edwards Deming

THE CANARY CODE: METAPHOR, MODEL, AND METHOD

Exclusion robs people of opportunities, and it robs organizations of talent. In the long run, exclusionary systems are lose-lose.

The Canary Code is a guide to building win-win organizational systems. It outlines specific steps to embedding inclusion across the entire talent cycle and creating fair, outcomes-focused cultures in which everyone can participate and belong.

The model's goal is to provide organizations with a framework and tools for creating fair and flexible talent processes (figure 1). Fairness and flexibility are essential for supporting marginalized and forgotten humans—and unlocking their often-remarkable talents. Better yet, applying the same principles improves work for everyone. Although the primary focus of this model is identifying and removing barriers to the employment and success of dyslexic, autistic, ADHD, and other neurominority communities, the same barriers exclude many aspects of humanity, from physical disabilities to cultural differences.

The book's title, *The Canary Code*, stems from the metaphor of people particularly impacted by dysfunctional organizational environments and injustices as canaries in the coal mine. The "canary in the coal mine" is not a myth or a literary device. For most of the twentieth century, each coal mining pit in the United Kingdom employed two canary birds.[1,2] They went underground with the miners as living, breathing carbon-monoxide detectors. Canaries' intense breathing allows them to fly—but it also makes them sensitive to airborne poisons, and their distress was an indication that miners should evacuate.

After serving that warning function, the canaries were given oxygen and revived. The Museum of Science and Industry in Manchester, England, showcases a canary-resuscitation device: a bird-sized box with a metal frame, glass walls, and an oxygen cylinder with some tubing.[3]

In 1986, electronic carbon monoxide detectors replaced the birds. But the imagery remains a part of many cultures.

The canary metaphor is popular in Autistic culture, as well as in chronic illness and disability communities. The Autistic Doctors International group adopted the canary as its symbol because of the belief that "*if a workplace is manageable for us as autistic doctors, then it is likely manageable for most others. If we 'fall off our perch,' others are likely to follow.*"[4] Organizational problems like the lack of fairness, bullying, and toxic cultures impact people with more intense senses and nervous systems before affecting others. Sensitive does not mean broken: it means processing the experience more fully, and intensely, just like birds process the air—the oxygen and the pollutants—more fully.

A dramatic illustration of the impact of broken and toxic systems on the "canaries" is the high unemployment rate of 30–40 percent among all neurominorities in the United States and an even higher rate for autistic college graduates.[5] However, if organizational problems are not addressed, not only the "canaries" but everyone in the organization will eventually be overcome by stress and burnout.

Just like fresh air benefits all, work environments that welcome human cognitive and emotional differences—including the acute sensitivity to the world associated with many forms of neurodivergence—benefit all. Creating organizations where canaries can thrive, create, and innovate also means creating healthier, stronger organizations.

Although neurominority experiences and research focused on autism, ADHD, dyslexia, dyspraxia, Tourette Syndrome, and other developmental differences inform much of this book, most of the advice is applicable to many forms of neurodivergence, including mental health differences, psychological trauma, and acquired neurodivergence due to brain surgery or long COVID. People from much larger groups—for example, those who identify as highly sensitive, introverts, people from disability and chronic illness communities, and many others—also often find environments that support neurominorities helpful. Flexibility and fairness at work help everyone thrive.

You don't need to be a neurodiversity expert to get insights from this book. In the first set of chapters, we will build the foundational knowledge together. In addition, a glossary provides definitions for some of the key terms.

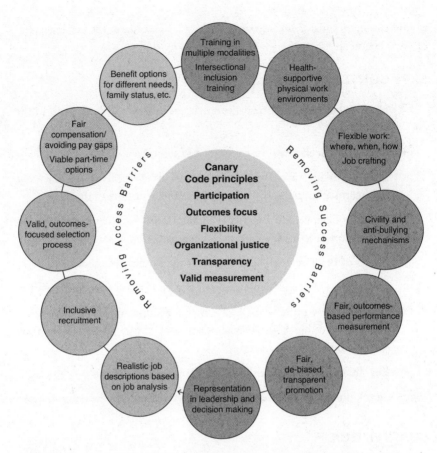

FIGURE 1: The Canary Code for Building a More Inclusive Workplace (Originally published in *Harvard Business Review*, Ludmila N. Praslova, "An Intersectional Approach to Inclusion at Work," *Harvard Business Review*, June 21, 2022, https://hbr.org/2022/06/an-intersectional-approach-to-inclusion-at-work.)

HOW TO GET THE MOST OUT OF THIS BOOK: DESIGN YOUR OWN ADVENTURE

To support different types of readers—practical and artsy, detail loving and summary seeking—most chapters include multiple types of content. With this book, you can build your own experience. As when visiting a park, you could take the "ultimate experience" path and follow the book in its entirety. Or you could take the "key points" path; then, if you wish, you can return and do "the story path" or "the deep dive" path. Most chapters can also be read independently, although I recommend reading the book in order. For those who prefer to read summaries first, Appendix A, "Spoiler Alert," contains the key takeaways of every chapter.

EASY CONTENT GUIDE

Human Happenings—real-life stories of individuals from around the world

Employer Excellence—case studies and interviews with employers

Neurodiversity Narratives—cultural-level observations on the place and the treatment of neurodiversity within the larger human diversity

Bridging Science and Practice—explorations of academic studies with application to creating neuroinclusive organizations

Points of Practice—application points for a quick reference

Deep Dive—a deeper exploration of key points, research, and theories

Deeper Dive—a further exploration of key points, including new, original, and possibly controversial ideas—for those who enjoy getting (closer) to the bottom of things!

Key Takeaways—chapter bullet points for busy readers

Developmental Questions—chapter reflection and application questions

CHAPTER GUIDE

Part 1 is focused on the foundations of neuroinclusion. **Chapter 1** provides a neurodiversity primer, a terminology review, and explores the origins of neurodiversity as a scientific concept and a social movement. It challenges common myths and misunderstandings that perpetuate neurodiversity exclusion in the workplace. **Chapter 2** explores stories of neurodivergent people at work, the human need to belong, and the holistic approach to inclusion. **Chapter 3** discusses the key idea of the Canary Code framework: contexts that support the most vulnerable support everyone.

The applications portion of the book is split into three parts. First, we discuss removing access barriers to work by improving recruitment, selection, onboarding, and accommodations. Then, we focus on removing success barriers by making the work environment, performance management, and organizational culture neuroinclusive. We conclude with an in-depth exploration of inclusive leadership and neurodivergent leadership. Each chapter contains case studies of organizational success and stories of neurodivergent individuals navigating work.

In Part 2, **Chapter 4** discusses the hiring process, starting with job descriptions and recruitment, and focuses on removing selection barriers irrelevant to the job but nevertheless faced by job seekers. **Chapter 5** examines training, onboarding, and accommodations and tackles pay, the elephant in the room of inclusion.

In Part 3, **Chapter 6** considers how the work is done and provides recommendations for optimizing physical work environments. **Chapter 7** offers tips for better work organization and scheduling to maximize both inclusion and productivity. Humans now have the opportunity to create much more flexible and inclusive work, and it is our responsibility not to squander this opportunity. **Chapter 8** explores psychological work environments that are so crucial to our well-being and outlines the principles of detoxifying organizational cultures and facilitating psychologically healthy work.

One of the key determinants of psychological health at work is performance management. **Chapter 9** outlines the principles of inclusive performance management that focuses accountability on outcomes and the substance of performance—not the surface characteristics that often bias evaluators.

Part 4 explores leadership in the context of neuroinclusion. **Chapter 10** focuses on the WHY of inclusive leadership, and **Chapter 11** provides tips for inclusive HOW. **Chapter 12** takes on a rarely discussed topic that is long overdue for some attention: neurodivergent individuals as leaders and the role of organizations in creating neuroinclusive leadership pathways. **Chapter 13** considers leadership from the perspective of neurodivergent leaders and provides advice for overcoming the deep stigma they face.

Finally, the **Conclusion** outlines the ways for everyone to lead and participate in changemaking and creating an inclusive future of work.

Let's build systems where good people can be good, and nobody feels unincludable. History suggests that so far, such systems have been possible but rare.

 HUMAN HAPPENINGS

THE DITCH DIGGER SPOKE EIGHT LANGUAGES

The ditch digger spoke eight languages. He was a lean, tall man obsessed with cleanliness and accustomed to wearing elegant suits. Yet there he was, shoveling New York City dirt mixed with horse manure—this was 1886—and who knows what else.

It did not help that he had dozens of engineering patents, most of them for groundbreaking inventions that could improve the lives of all people. All he got from them so far were the heavy shovel, dirt, and betrayal.

His last employer promised him a sizable bonus for solving issues with the company's vital technology. He delivered the work, but the employer never paid. He quit and started his own company, producing more inventions and patents—until his partners pushed him out and kept his patents.

And so, he dug ditches to survive. Dealing with dirt was unpleasant. Digging a trench to support technology that was not nearly as advanced as his own was worse. But the worst part was not working on inventions that could make the world much more comfortable and everyone's labor much more efficient. "*My high education in various branches of science, mechanics and literature seemed to me like a mockery,*" he wrote about that time.[6]

 DEEP DIVE

BRAINS BEYOND BOUNDARIES

If you are reading this book as an ebook, bought it online, or are using electrical lighting from the grid to read it, you are benefiting from this ditch digger's work. When you plug your gadgets into an outlet, use remote control, or rely on other types of wireless technology, you are benefiting from Nikola Tesla's world-reshaping inventions.[7] The alternating electric current (AC) he learned to harness powers most of our homes, and the Tesla coil is the forerunner of all wireless transmission. But we will never know how much more he could have accomplished if he could have spent more time doing the work most aligned with his talents. Perhaps we would have had cell phones and the internet much earlier—both were envisioned by Tesla in 1926.[8]

By all accounts, Nikola Tesla was quite an unusual person. In modern terms, he would be considered a "neurodivergent": someone whose thinking and way of being were quite different from the expectations of the day. He thought in pictures, visualizing and testing his inventions in his mind until he perfected them without the need for drawings or models.[7] That thinking was undoubtedly aided by his photographic and eidetic memory and the ability to perform complex calculations in his mind. Most of his life was centered around his work and intellectual pursuits, to the exclusion of any romantic partnership. His elaborate daily routine included working, walking, and dining on a precise schedule, which made some suggest that he had obsessive-compulsive disorder (OCD).[9,10]

However, OCD does not explain Tesla's complaints about noise—such as the "deafening" sound of the train 30 miles away—and his other peculiar characteristics.[11] Of course, diagnosing based on historical records is always a guess, but all his "eccentricities," as was the term of the time, seem to align with autistic traits. Autism can explain sensory sensitivities, a single-minded commitment to one's work, a trusting nature, and thinking in pictures—Temple Grandin, another autistic inventor, describes that last quality as her way of thinking.[12]

The story of Nikola Tesla, Thomas Edison, and the race to provide electricity to the US and the world, known as the "War of the Currents," is one of the most fascinating and dramatic chapters in the history of innovation and business. It is also a story of neurodivergent minds, bias, ethics, leadership, and organizational talent systems.

 DEEP DIVE

ELECTRICITY AND ETHICS

In the 1880s, electricity was just becoming a viable source of power for homes and businesses. In 1882, Thomas Edison opened the first power plant in lower Manhattan to electrify wealthy New Yorkers' homes using his preferred direct current (DC) technology. In 1884, Nikola Tesla arrived in New York with four cents in his pocket and offered Edison his services.[6] Instead of the direct current, which could only travel about a mile, he proposed developing motors to harness alternating current (AC) that could deliver electricity between cities and states. Edison was not interested. Instead, he reportedly offered Tesla a $50,000 bonus if he could improve DC generators. When Tesla did so, Edison told him the offer was a joke and that Tesla, as a new immigrant, did not understand American humor.[6] At the time, American-born descendants of Western and Northern Europeans looked at Slavic and Southern European immigrants with contempt and suspicion.[13] It was unlikely that Tesla, born in modern-day Croatia and a son of a Serbian small-town priest, would have any recourse against Edison or the other partners who defrauded him.

Yet, even while supporting himself with manual labor, Tesla kept envisioning ways to transmit electricity over long distances without having a coal power plant every mile. This would make it available to all people, rather than only to those in rich urban centers. Eventually, George Westinghouse, an industrialist and inventor in his own right, saw the potential in Tesla's work and partnered with him to power the US—and the world—with AC using Tesla's system of AC distribution.

Westinghouse-backed AC was a threat to Edison's DC enterprise, and Edison fought against it in every way he could think of. In the War of the Currents, Edison's tactics included using newspaper articles to spread fear and misinformation; publicly electrocuting dogs, calves, and horses with AC to demonstrate its dangers; and eventually procuring a secondhand Westinghouse generator to power an electric chair for the first human execution by electricity. Edison termed it "westinghousing."[14]

But despite anti-AC propaganda, Tesla/Westinghouse technology was versatile, effective, economical, and preferred by most customers. Westinghouse's company won the contracts to light up the Chicago World's Fair in 1893 and to install AC generators at Niagara Falls.

AC, Tesla, and Westinghouse clearly won the War of the Currents. Edison's board sidelined him and switched the company to AC, effectively putting Edison out of the electricity business. Edison's connections with the media helped, in part, to protect his reputation. Many biographers gloss over his ruthless tactics and his treatment of Tesla and other employees, who were expected to work from morning until the next morning, without holidays, for low pay and with little acknowledgment of their efforts.[15] Nonetheless, historical records did note Edison's questionable business practices including the appropriation of others' work—at least part of the credit for the lasting incandescent lightbulb is due to Lewis Latimer, a Black inventor—and his prejudices.[16,17]

Of course, neither Tesla nor Westinghouse were saints. To complicate the matter, there are conflicting accounts about many of the events surrounding the War of the Currents. Nevertheless, the records of Westinghouse's management show a clear pattern of practices that were well ahead of its time. The victory in the War of the Currents was not just a fluke of luck or even the work of a singular genius creating a better technological system—however exceptional. It was, in many ways, a reflection of a better talent system.

 EMPLOYER EXCELLENCE

WESTINGHOUSE: MINDFUL INVESTMENTS, HEARTFELT RETURNS

Possibly the largest private employer in the world at the peak of his business success, George Westinghouse was viewed with suspicion by his industrialist peers for being "too good" to his people.[18,19] He shortened the workweek to 5½ days—

unheard of at the time when weekends in a modern sense did not exist. He was determined to attract the best talent—and paid better wages than his competitors. He invested in state-of-the-art work facilities and provided his employees with low-cost and high-quality housing—homes with nice yards, indoor plumbing, and electricity.[20] He also helped break gender biases by employing Bertha Lamme, America's first woman electrical engineer.[15,21]

A positive organizational culture leads to employee commitment, and Westinghouse's employees were fiercely dedicated to his company.[22] During a banking crisis, when credit dried up they offered to work for half-pay, which Westinghouse rejected.[15,23] He did, however, approach Tesla for relief on his substantial royalty payments. Tesla went beyond what was asked, giving up or tearing up his royalty contract altogether to save the business.[24] Westinghouse might have invested in Tesla's brilliance, but it's the loyalty return on investment (ROI) that was priceless. And it was not just Tesla's loyalty—many of Westinghouse's employees felt the same because Westinghouse also invested in them. Individual decisions and acts of betrayal versus loyalty matter.

The War of the Currents victory was not just a victory of more efficient technology. It was a victory of an organizational system built to attract and support talent—including the talent others discarded, excluded, or drove out. The War of the Currents exemplifies the impact of the talent-focused, human-focused, difference-welcoming system developed by Westinghouse. Edison's error was not just his stubborn investment in DC technology. It was his stubborn investment in only one type of talent—his own—and his choice to use his power to hold down the different types of talent.

 DEEP DIVE

MODERN WORK: SYSTEMIC STRUGGLES

Many of us like to think that with our fancy inclusion vocabulary and antibias training, we are much more progressive than people of the Gilded Age. But how inclusive are we really? Would Nikola Tesla's job application pass the automated Applicant Tracking System (ATS) screening in most of our organizations? What about the "culture fit" interview?

Let's be honest. Modern employment practices keep 30–85 percent of neurominorities unemployed or underemployed, "digging ditches" rather than using their best strengths.[5,25,26,27,28] And this is not for the lack of "business case" evidence. There are findings from the autism hiring program at JP Morgan that autistic employees can be up to 140 percent more productive than the average employee.[29] There is the success of the Israeli Army's Roim Rachok program that recruits autistic analysts.[30] There are findings from the BBC study that 40 percent of self-made millionaires are dyslexic.[31] There are studies demonstrating the strengths of divergent thinking and creativity in ADHD.[32]

Still, all the business case arguments touting neurodivergent talents have yet to make a significant dent in the widespread prejudice against neurodivergent people. In some ways, by trying to counterbalance the "lack of ability" stereotype, the business case created the "superhuman" stereotype—but the everyday humanity of neurodivergent people is lost in the gap between these stereotypes.

In the UK 50 percent of surveyed managers do not wish to hire and work with neurodivergent individuals.[33] Hiring agents in the US discriminate against autistic candidates with derogatory language and stereotypes, expecting them—us—to be "shitbirds."[34] Autistic people are still cheated out of their pay, excluded from employment, and discriminated against.[35,36,37]

How many brilliant inventors, loyal employees, and simply humans who should have the basic dignity of work but are denied it are struggling against modern biases?

If you are thinking, "It's not just neurodivergent people; workplaces are a mess for everyone," you are correct. Work is not working for most people, and multiple parts of the system are broken.

Toxic cultures are driving employees out.[38] Communication is not working—80 percent of US workers report being stressed due to ineffective company communication, and 63 percent of employees are so frustrated that they're ready to quit.[39]

People are not functioning at their best: more than 50 percent of workers are disengaged because of stress. But it's not just stress—34 percent would not tell their boss about their stress out of fear of repercussions.[40] Worse, for 35 percent, the boss IS the main source of stress.[41] But managers are not OK either: 40 percent of C-suite employees say they will likely quit within the year because of work-related stress, and 25 percent of middle managers say they are burned out.[42,43]

Talent systems in most workplaces appear to be broken. There are *access* barriers that eliminate many talented people from hiring considerations. And those who are hired face *success* barriers because of poor work organization, understaffing, and various forms of bias.[44] Many talent systems seem to be working against talent: high performers are bullied and driven away, faced with ever-increasing workloads until they break and burn out, and are required to work in inefficient ways because of institutional inertia.

Systemic problems like these require systemic solutions.

> This book is about creating better systems of work—systems that measure talent objectively, reward results and commitment fairly, and support everyone in working with their strengths.

Most systems are built around a set of assumptions. An important part of systemic change—whether in technological or human systems—is challenging and changing these limiting assumptions. But challenging assumptions is tricky because they feel familiar. They feel to us as natural and even wise.

 DEEP DIVE

EDISON'S ERRORS—AND OURS

In the War of the Currents, Edison made two errors stemming from limiting beliefs. First, he believed that AC was too powerful and so could not be managed effectively. Second, he believed that his iterative, perspiration-based, trial-and-error approach was THE way to invent. Tesla's theory-driven, boundary-pushing, leapfrogging, inspiration-based thinking clashed with this style.[15] Edison did not recognize Tesla's talent because it was unlike his own.

I can't help thinking that decision makers in many modern organizations do not know how to manage the power of neurodivergent talent. They prefer to stick with the familiar cultural narrative of the "ideal worker"—where the ideal is often defined as "similar to me"—and the "ideal work."

But the familiar is so very limiting.

In 2019, disabled and neurodivergent employees were routinely denied the opportunity to work from home as an accommodation. It was not considered reasonable.

You know how this story goes. In early 2020, most office workers rapidly transitioned to working from home. After a few months of stressful transition, the majority came to love it and did not want to go back. A stressful tug-of-war between employees and employers over the return to the office ensued.[45]

Ultranauts, a tech company founded by Rajesh Anandan and Art Shectman in 2013, did not have to deal with all that stress. The company was designed with autistic talent in mind from the start, and 75 percent of employees are neurodivergent. Remote working was the norm, and so the company avoided the disruptions of the COVID-19 pandemic and revenue continued to grow by 50 percent a year.[46] The quality of work that Ultranauts' employees delivered was exceptional. As a result, Fortune 100 companies have chosen their services over the global firms they were previously using. Discarding limiting cultural beliefs and cultivating an openness to a different type of talent and a different way of working were foundations of the company's resilience and thriving in a changing environment.

But working from home in knowledge jobs was possible even earlier—much earlier. Around the mid-1990s I obtained my first laptop, a wonder of science with a black-and-white screen. I could have never afforded it, but one of my side gig employers gave it to me as an advance for translating a textbook.

And thus, I invented work from home. OK, I did not invent it—but I did start working in a hybrid manner and suggesting the same to organizations. The technology was there in the 1990s. Yet, until 2020, limiting beliefs kept millions of people—an entire generation—in daily traffic in their cars, or on trains and buses, or walking in the heat and the sleet so they could sit in cubicles doing the work that could have been done from anywhere. Inertia kept the old ways of working alive for decades longer than necessary. And it kept millions of disabled and neurodivergent people unemployed and excluded entirely.

Preventing people from exercising their talents not only harms these people, **it harms everyone**. Research shows that when potential inventors and innovators are held back by a lack of opportunity, society as a whole falls behind. In contrast, when a higher proportion of people in society have opportunities to develop their talents, society is more likely to innovate and thrive.[47] Thriving is not a zero-sum game; it is a win-win game.

Of course, everyone has limiting beliefs. It is painful when these beliefs limit our own lives. It is unfair when these beliefs, combined with power, limit other people's opportunities. Take disability employment—it ticked up during the pandemic and in a few months was yet again threatened by return-to-office mandates.[48]

When some people's limiting beliefs about others limit other people's opportunities, we call these beliefs "stereotypes," and the resulting behavior is called "discrimination." But people and organizations do not necessarily see their own bias. We all like to consider ourselves good people. And most of us are good in some ways—but not in others.

I mentioned that one of my early-career organizations was wonderfully inclusive when it came to national cultural differences but not in terms of gender.

Other organizations can be inclusive of gender but not ethnicity, ethnicity but not disability, physical disability but not mental health. In one of my other jobs, a boss topped off saying that I was not allowed to go to my father's funeral with xenophobic rhetoric. Another boss explained not paying me for completed work with "single women don't need the money." My high education in various branches of psychology, management, and inclusion felt very much like a mockery.

I had to invent a word to describe how I felt at that time—"unincludable." In various contexts, some aspects of who I am, be it gender, culture, or economic distance traveled, had others classifying me as not fully human.

 DEEP DIVE

INCLUSION BY DESIGN

The typical set of assumptions on "how to do inclusion" is limiting—and so are the systems based on these assumptions. As long as inclusion is thought of as something slowly doled out by the "born included" based on a limited set of characteristics they choose to include, some people will remain unincludable. Half-measures do not work. Sequential interventions to fix one "ism" without fixing all others leave people out. True inclusion is systemic inclusion.

The *entire* organizational system must become inclusive—by design.[2,49,50]

Systemic inclusion must be **intersectional**. An intersectional approach considers multiple identities and characteristics that may create additional exclusionary barriers—and addresses them all. If a woman is invited to a gender-focused event but cannot attend because the venue is not accessible, disability exclusion nullifies the attempted gender inclusion. The lack of an intersectional approach excludes those facing multiple barriers: Black women, as in Kimberlé Crenshaw's original work,[51] disabled women, or neurodivergent immigrants.

Systemic inclusion must be **comprehensive**. It must address all elements of talent management, from job descriptions to work organization, succession planning, and leadership development. Noncomprehensive approaches create bottlenecks and ceilings—people from certain groups might be hired but do not advance or are not retained.

Inclusion by design must be **embedded**. It must be reflected in processes and procedures, personnel forms, and workplace norms. Embedding inclusion in organizational functioning means *removing* barriers—for example, revising the promotion process to make it more transparent and based on objective, measurable criteria—helps those who would be left behind by subjective evaluations of "fit." Embedding inclusion into organizational functioning makes it sustainable.

Finally, inclusion by design must start **from the margin.** Creating systems that remove barriers for the most marginalized and multiply marginalized is the fastest way to remove all barriers.[52] When organizational systems are designed to support the most excluded, removing barriers addresses the specific needs of those groups and supports broader inclusivity. The classic example is curb cuts. Curb cuts, one of the accomplishments of the disability rights movement, remove barriers for wheelchair users. They also make getting around easier for everyone, from parents with strollers to delivery people with heavy loads.

Consulting the most marginalized among us about what would be helpful for them is likely to lead to innovative solutions and a more human-centric design for all. In the context of neurodiversity, optimizing the environment for neurodivergent people by providing flexible schedules, quieter workplaces, lower stress, clear communication, and training designed for a broader range of learning needs—the psychological curb-cut effect—will create an environment where everyone can thrive. The air quality that keeps canaries healthy will keep everyone healthy. And that is the essence of the Canary Code.

KEY TAKEAWAYS

- *The Canary Code model is designed to help organizations remove barriers to work and success faced by neurodivergent talent.*
- *As canaries in the coal mine, many neurodivergent people are affected by unhealthy work environments before others are.*
- *The key Canary Code principles—participation, focusing on outcomes, flexibility, organizational justice, transparency, and using valid tools in decision making—can help improve the work experience for everyone.*
- *Unlocking neurodivergent abilities calls for developing inclusive talent systems that recognize different types of talent and can support everyone in working with their strengths.*
- *Designing inclusive systems requires an intersectional, comprehensive, and embedded approach informed by the perspective of the marginalized.*

DEVELOPMENTAL QUESTIONS

- Have you participated in interactions where some people (canaries) were more attuned to the environment with its potential dangers or changes than others? How can differences in sensitivity result in misunderstandings?
- How can misunderstanding or discounting of the "canaries'" experience be prevented?
- How could changes to organizational systems and practices help make interactions between people with different thinking styles more effective, fair, and equitable?
- Have you experienced an "inclusion fail" because an intervention was not systemic? How could an intersectional, comprehensive, embedded, and participatory approach have prevented the "fail"?
- Have you worked (or perhaps studied) in an environment that was supportive of different types of talent? What factors helped make this environment inclusive? What lessons from this experience could you use for improving other environments?

PART I

FOUNDATIONS

CHAPTER ONE

NEURODIVERSITY PRIMER

A Treasure in around Your Head

Being different is difficult in a world that tells us there is a "normal."

—Sonya Renee Taylor

 NEURODIVERSITY NARRATIVES

THE LANGUAGE OF ENRICHMENT

In 2020, in Aotearoa (New Zealand), a not-for-profit organization Te Pou launched an online dictionary of Te Reo Hāpai—the "language of enrichment" in Māori.[1] This project of creating a nonstigmatizing language for neurodiversity, mental health, and disability was funded by the Ministry of Health and the Māori Language Commission. For several years, linguists, clinicians, and, most importantly, community representatives worked to develop a positive, strengths-based language aligned with the community perspective and Māori culture. They replaced words evoking stigma and discrimination with words focused on humanity and dignity.

For example, the Te Reo Hāpai word for ADHD is *aroreretini*—"attention goes to many things."[2] Compare the meaning of "attention deficit hyperactivity disorder" with "attention goes to many things." In many situations, such as when looking for food sources in the wild or working in a busy ER, attention to many things can be a benefit—not a deficit or disorder. This word is an example of both a more accurate and intentionally nonstigmatizing, nonjudgmental language.

Aroreretini may not be a perfect word—it is not possible to capture the many manifestations of ADHD and the unique forms it can take in every individual.

But a nondeficit perspective is a major departure from the traditional medical approach.

Like any attempt at developing terminology, creating the Te Reo Hāpai involved negotiating alternative opinions and settling debates stemming from both the multiple dialects of Maori and differences in perspectives. For example, the Te Reo Hāpai word for autism is *takiwātanga*—"in his/her own time and space."[2] However, there is an alternative Maori term for autism—*kura urupare*, which is often translated as "treasure in around your head."[3,4] This latter term has many interpretations, and there are likely to be shades of meaning only a native speaker would pick up on.

Still, I find these terms irresistibly beautiful. They are examples of looking at differences in human psychological functioning as just that—differences, rather than deficiencies or pathologies. And that is the very heart of the neurodiversity approach.

KEY CONCEPTS

Neurodiversity-related terminology is still developing and there are disagreements regarding language within neurodivergent communities.[5,6] Here are some key neuro-terms as envisioned by those who developed them, which may help clarify often-encountered misunderstandings:

- **Neurodiversity:** A biological fact that there is a limitless variety in human neurodevelopment across the lifespan, with many neurotypes and individual differences.[7,8,9] Neurodiversity as *a concept* refers to the full range of variations in human cognition, emotion, and perception.
- **Neurodiversity paradigm:** A *perspective* on neurodiversity that sees it as an essential aspect of human diversity; a view that there is not one "correct" type of brain or mind, although some types of minds have been societally privileged and others have been shunned or disadvantaged.[7,8,10]
- **Neurodiversity movement:** A social justice *movement* born in the 1990s to counteract the medical model of autism (also known as a deficit or pathology model) and soon expanded to include other developmental differences (e.g., ADHD, learning differences, Tourette Syndrome) and neurobiological variations. Its goal is to promote the interests of individuals and groups that have been disadvantaged and denied opportunities due to their neurobiology.[7,8]
- **Neurotypical:** A person or people whose neurodevelopment falls within the range conventionally seen as typical by prevailing cultural standards and is enabled by their society for a given period. [10,11]

- **Allistic:** A nonautistic person who may be either neurotypical or neuro-divergent (this more accurate term replaced the earlier/original use of "neurotypical").[12]
- **Neuronormative:** A set of ideals, actions, and functions seen as "normal" by prevailing cultural and societal standards.[13]
- **Neurodivergent:** A person or people whose neurological development or functioning diverges from the range conventionally seen as typical (e.g., a dyslexic or dyspraxic person may refer to themselves as a neuro-divergent person; a group of ADHDers or people with a specific phobia are groups of "neurodivergent" people). Some use "neurodistinct," "neu-rospicy," and other creative variations of this term, while others prefer "neuroatypical."[7,10] Many prefer identity-first language.[6,10]
- **Neurodiverse:** A *collective* term for groups including mixed neurotypes (e.g., a group of dyspraxic, autistic, and neurotypical people is a "neuro-diverse" group).[7,10,13] This term and the term "diverse" should not be ap-plied to individuals.[14]
- **A neurominority group:** A population of neurodivergent people who (1) share a similar form of neurodivergence that is (2) largely innate and inseparable from who they are. These people also (3) experience some degree of prejudice from the neurotypical majority/larger society, are disadvantaged by societal norms and systems, or both.[13]

Heated arguments and misunderstandings often occur within neurodiver-gent communities and in communication between neurodivergent communi-ties and larger societal cultures because neurodiversity as a fact, the neurodiversity paradigm, and the neurodiversity movement are all sometimes referred to as "neurodiversity." Hence, it is important to clarify these distinctions.

Although some degree of neurodiversity is generally found in most organizations, people of some neurotypes (for example, those more sensitive to the environment or more inclined to focus on tasks rather than office politics) experience more barriers to workplace access and success. The movement for **neu-roinclusion in the workplace** can be seen as a specific form of the neurodiver-sity movement and neurominority justice. Ensuring fair opportunities for those who have been excluded from and disadvantaged in traditional work environ-ments can be accomplished by creating more flexible organizational systems that include and support a wider range of talent and productivity styles.

For example, the use of selection methods that have little or no relevance to essential job responsibilities and instead focus on neuronormative expression (such as maintaining eye contact or not fidgeting) adversely affects certain neurominority groups. Hence, one of the approaches to workplace neuroinclusion is identifying and correcting organizational practices that unfairly exclude or disadvantage neurodivergent individuals in pursuing work for which they are otherwise qualified.

Workplace improvements associated with neuroinclusion benefit individuals of many different neurotypes—including those who are neurotypical. A more accurate measurement of skills and work outcomes, along with increased flexibility and transparency, not only creates truly neurodiverse workplaces but also improves the overall work environment and strengthens organizations.

If you are wondering whether you need to identify with any specific form of neurodivergence to benefit from this book, the answer is *absolutely not*.

> If you are a human who can benefit from working in a more ethical, transparent, participatory, just, and outcomes-focused environment, where decisions are made based on valid data, this book will show you how these principles can be implemented across all aspects of employment.

 DEEP DIVE

IF NEURODIVERSITY APPLIES TO EVERYONE, IS ANYONE AT ALL NEUROTYPICAL?

There are some who believe that neurotypical does not exist—that everyone is in some way neurodivergent.[15] However, according to an autistic psychologist and thought leader Nick Walker, this argument stems from the false assumption that "neurotypical is just a synonym for normal."[13] The belief in "normal" minds and brains is associated with the medical/pathology paradigm and does not make sense from the neurodiversity perspective. "Neurotypicality" is socially and culturally constructed. Dominant cultures operating within the "normal" versus "pathological" paradigm create cultural expectations of normativity: hence, children and adults are repeatedly told to "act normal" and not be "weird."

The collective belief in "normal" creates an image to which people are expected to conform—or else. In my paraphrasing of Walker's[13] work, a neurotypical person is (1) able to convincingly and reliably perform according to expectations of neuronormative functioning throughout one's life, without unbearable suffering, and (2) chooses to maintain that performance and comply with the standards of the dominant culture. The reward for compliance with dominant standards, or neuronormativity, is the perception of "normality" and, consequently, neurotypical privilege.

For example, in many modern cultures, teenagers are expected to enjoy dance parties, and adults are expected to enjoy lively lunches with colleagues. Those are "things to do." Both of these things are also stimulating. However, optimizing the functioning of some people's nervous systems requires relaxation, not revving up. Research indicates that the brains of autistic youth at rest produce 42 percent more information than the average.[16] This elevated resting state results in higher neurological excitation for autistic youths compared to allistics exposed to the same stimulation and likely triggers the need for protective withdrawal. Thus, some nervous systems are naturally more active and become more easily overwhelmed with additional external stimulation.[16,17,18,19]

There is nothing inherently wrong with having a nervous system that is more active at rest. There is also nothing inherently wrong with being highly responsive to environmental signals in the form of sounds, smells, and other sensations. Being highly attuned to sensory environments is likely an advantage in the wild, but it can be torture in revved-up human-built environments like bars or clubs.

 HUMAN HAPPENINGS

SENSES AND SOCIETY

As an undiagnosed autistic teenager, I tried to meet neuronormative expectations of enjoying dance parties—heavy music, flashing lights, and all. And every time, I would end up sobbing uncontrollably and feeling physically sick. I could not convincingly perform the socially sanctioned role of a "normal teenager," which meant that I would never be particularly popular in high school.

It's a good thing I did not care about popularity all that much.

But I did care about my career—a lot. Neuronormative work expectations, however, are often concerned with neuronormative performance more than with objective outcome performance. Most workplaces have an expectation of lunchtime socializing. For me, that usually meant a choice between experiencing the sensory overwhelm of lunch in a busy cafeteria and the resulting shutdown, or being able to do the "work work" in the afternoon. After trying for some time, I largely chose to work and take walks instead of socializing. The penalty was the loss of the neurotypical privilege of access to organizational power.

In traditional workplaces, neurotypical privilege often takes the form of rewards for neuronormative social performance, rather than for objectively measured work performance. Neuronormative social performance should not be confused with social skills. Regardless of social skills, this performance often occurs in environments that are overstimulating for people whose brains are naturally more active, taxing their neurological capacity. In effect, the socially constructed "neurotypicality norm" favors those who prefer, or at least can tolerate, the levels of stimulation preferred by those who are neurotypical. The "neurotypical brain" may not exist, but the neurotypical privilege of conforming to neuronormative expectations without making oneself sick certainly does.

 BRIDGING SCIENCE AND PRACTICE

TRICKY TERMINOLOGY

What kind of people would you rather hire?

A. People who behave ethically, regardless of whether they are observed or not, or

B. People who are likely to behave ethically when observed, but less ethically when not observed?

One may think that, at the very least, if people were doing the right thing when not observed, managers' jobs would be much easier, right? Surveillance would not be needed, which would free up time and resources to focus on other aspects of work. If you were hiring a CFO, wouldn't you want someone who is less corruptible?

During the decade leading up to 2020, researchers conducted experiments focused on moral choices. In many studies, participants had to decide whether to be charitable or greedy in two situations: when they thought they were observed and when they thought they had privacy. Researchers were interested in exploring differences between groups in how they behave publicly versus privately.

In 2020, an online-first publication appeared in the *Journal of Neuroscience*.[20] It described an experimental study of moral behavior in which privacy manipulation was complemented by monitoring brain activity patterns in people from group A as compared to people from group B. The results illuminated the same between-group differences as were observed in earlier studies:

- People in group A financially supported a good cause (children's education) and refused to support a bad cause (killing street animals) consistently, even if doing the right thing cost them some money, whether they were observed or not.
- People in group B acted ethically when they were observed. But, when not observed, and when helping a bad cause resulted in personal gain, people from group B were more likely to be self-serving. They were more willing to financially support killing the animals if that also meant more money in their own pockets.

As researchers predicted, noted differences in moral behavior were also accompanied by differences in brain activity detected with functional magnetic resonance imaging (fMRI). After analyzing the results, the research team proceeded to explain how dysfunction of the right temporoparietal junction (rTPJ) leads to higher concerns about ill-gotten gains and a lack of moral flexibility in group A individuals.

That's right. The purpose of the study was to better understand the *dysfunction* and *pathology* in moral judgment in group A. You see, group A consisted of the "atypical": autistic people or, in the language of the original article, "Autism Spectrum Disorder" patients. Their more consistent moral behavior was interpreted as a *symptom* of that disorder.

In contrast, group B was made up of "healthy controls." The allistics—the "healthy controls"—tended to do the right thing when monitored. But they were more self-serving than autistics when left to their own devices. Following the tradition of prior studies, the researchers interpreted the more hypocritical behavior of people in group B as *normal* and explained it in terms of a *healthy* concern for their reputation. The lack of hypocrisy in autistic individuals was described as a *deficit* attributable to lower reputational concern.

By no means was this study particularly egregious or ill intended. It simply reflected the state of the discipline—the decades of teaching and mentoring steeped in assumptions about autistic "pathology." Many other researchers studied the "lack of reputational concern" among autistic people in a similar way.

Back in 2011 prominent neuroscientists Uta and Chris Frith of the University College London pointed out that obliviousness to others and a lack of hypocrisy are not the same thing.[21,22] They deduced that autistic people demonstrate not a deficiency of reputational concern but a lack of hypocrisy—or, in other words, "transparent trustworthiness." At that time, the Friths' gentle correction was largely ignored, and studies continued to investigate autistic "deficits."

However, as the neurodiversity movement strengthened, pathologizing interpretations of research results became increasingly likely to be called out by the public. The 2020 *Journal of Neuroscience* publication was met with an outcry from the autistic community, in the form of a Twitter campaign and letters to the journal editor, one of which was published along with the article when it appeared in print.[23,24] The authors quickly revised their work to address some of the concerns and remove stigmatizing language. It is difficult, however, to fully reinterpret a study stemming from a certain set of assumptions. And, unfortunately, assumptions behind a significant portion of autism studies to date have been influenced by a highly stigmatizing perspective on autism.

Research on psychological and developmental differences has been dominated by the deficit perspective for so long that this paradigm was the only way of thinking that entire generations of researchers and clinicians ever encountered. Consequently, a large part of autism research is based on the expectation that autistic reasoning and behavior are "inferior" and "deficient" by virtue of the label. For example, research findings have also been interpreted to mean that autistic people are abnormally logical, resistant to cognitive bias, and deficient in deception.[25,26]

Monique Botha and Eilidh Cage from the University of Stirling described a pattern of ableist assumptions in autism research, including the use of dehumanizing language such as comparisons to apes.[27,28] They also found evidence of objectification: treating autistic people like objects whose presence within humanity must be justified by their usefulness to others. Assumptions that guide the design of studies, methodologies, and the interpretation of findings become a part of the self-perpetuating cycle of stigmatizing and pathologizing that is only starting to be challenged.[28]

Words used to frame human differences have consequences far beyond research. The choice to call one group of people "lacking in moral flexibility" and "disordered" rather than "morally principled" and "transparently trustworthy" creates very different consequences for this group's well-being, position in society, and access to jobs. Likewise, the choice to call people from another group "healthy" and "morally flexible" rather than "hypocritical" creates very different opportunities for them. And there are consequences for the larger society as well. The wording and framing of research contribute to the cocreation of societal norms and the acceptability of honest versus dishonest behavior.

Let's try the question from the introduction to this section again. Would you change your initial answer?

What kind of people would you rather hire?

A. The autism spectrum disorder patients, or

B. Healthy people?

Despite understanding the results of research on moral behavior, many would think twice about hiring "ASD patients." Despite their best intentions and a desire to be inclusive. Despite the evidence of outstanding productivity, such as the JP Morgan findings that individuals in their autism hiring program learn much faster and are 140 percent more productive than the typical employee. In many people, the words "ASD patient" conjure visceral fears that are hard to override.[29,30] Until there is an internationally accepted nonstigmatizing language for differences associated with neurodivergence, workplace neuroinclusion advocacy remains very much an uphill battle against stigma and stereotypes.

 DEEP DIVE

FLAW OR FLOW?

Deficit labeling is so powerful that people and organizations would pay to obtain certain neurodivergent advantages for themselves while simultaneously trying to cure neurodivergent people of the same characteristics. For example, there are leadership programs that help leaders be more honest. But would the same organizations that wish to increase honesty hire autistic people and promote them to leadership positions? Considering autistic unemployment rates and the thorny paths of autistic leaders, this does not seem to be the case.

However, there does exist research focused on finding the most effective ways to teach autistic children how to lie.[31,32,33]

In response to the many instances of ethical failures, business ethicists call for increasing the ability of employees to see their responsibility for the outcomes of their actions and consider how their behavior, if scaled, would affect the world.[34] This is, paradoxically, the very type of moral reasoning that researchers deemed *dysfunctional* in autistic people[20]—the most excluded group in the workplace.

As another example, in search of productivity advantages, many people seek focus gurus to help them get into a flow or hyperfocus.[35] However, in autistics and ADHDers, hyperfocus is seen as a deficit and a symptom of the disorder in need of correction.[36,37] This is the essence of the medical model and its biasing impact on thinking. Without an "autism" or "ADHD" label, hyperfocus is framed as a highly desired state of flow, associated with people working on tasks that interest them with a level of challenge that is just right—stretching, yet within reach.[38] With a label attached, however, the flow becomes a *flaw*—something to break rather than nurture.

The stigma associated with all types of neurodivergence is hard to override—dyslexic doctors find themselves stigmatized, bullied in medical school, and not heard by medical administrative bodies.[39] Dyspraxic medical students are worried about the stigma.[40] People in the ADHD community are stereotyped as deficient in character.[41] People with depression and anxiety face a lack of acceptance and support in the workplace.[42,43] Media representations of neurodivergence make us seem either scary or laughable.[44] The widespread prejudice is reflected in the fact that half of surveyed UK managers stated that *they do not want to hire neurodivergent people.*[45]

If we want to live in a more just world and if we want more trust, less corruption, and higher productivity, we must override fears of the different and challenge negative assumptions. And that is the point of the neurodiversity movement.

 NEURODIVERSITY NARRATIVES

THE ROOTS AND BRANCHES OF THE NEURODIVERSITY MOVEMENT

The neurodiversity movement is a social justice movement challenging the traditional medical model's view of neurodivergent individuals as disordered and in need of cure or "normalization."[46,47] Instead, it seeks to recognize the value and diverse strengths of all neurotypes and advocates for equal rights and opportunities for neurodivergent people.

An influential forerunner of the neurodiversity movement was Michael (Mike) Oliver, a disabled British sociologist and a disability rights activist credited with developing the social model of disability in a 1983 book.[48] Oliver strongly critiqued the positioning of disability *within individuals* and instead pointed out that people are disabled by unaccommodating *environments*. Rejecting the medical focus on "fixing" disabled people—regardless of how painful that "fixing" might be—Oliver emphasized the need for creating accessible environments.

Oliver's social model of disability stresses the importance of removing barriers and creating an inclusive society that accommodates the needs of all individuals, regardless of their impairments. Or, in the case of neurodivergence, perceived impairments such as having strong ethical principles and the tendency to hyper-focus. Instead of prescribing the fixing of neurodivergent honesty and flow, the logic of the social model calls for creating environments where honesty is wel-comed and productivity that comes from the flow is supported.

Oliver's work was inspired by the disability rights movement of the 1970s and, in turn, inspired the early autism rights movement in the 1990s. Then, in 1993, Jim Sinclair published a "manifesto" of this emergent movement, now con-sidered a classic of autism acceptance and possibly the first example of identity-first language as applied to autism.[49] Sinclair also organized autistic gatherings, what he called "Autreats"—an important step in developing an autism acceptance community and Autistic culture.

Another important element in building a community was the internet. Au-tistic listservs and early web spaces of the 1990s allowed for unprecedented ex-perience sharing along with cocreating the Autistic culture—and the early language of neurodiversity. The term "neurotypical" was born in Autistic cul-ture in the early 1990s and made prominent, in a satirical context, by Laura Ti-soncik, an autistic advocate. In 1998, Tisoncik launched a website named the "Institute for the Study of the Neurologically Typical" (ISNT). It was a parody exposing the biases and assumptions underlying research on autism and other neurodivergent conditions. The symptoms of "neurotypical syndrome" included preoccupation with social concerns, a lack of interest in trains, and "a denial that there's something wrong with them."[50]

Initially used to refer to nonautistic individuals, the term "neurotypical" caught on in online communities. It quickly became part of the vocabulary of both Autistic culture and the emerging neurodiversity movement used to high-light the social power and privilege differences that made neurotypicality a per-ceived "norm" and neurodivergence a "pathology."

Today, "neurotypical" is meant to be a neutral and descriptive term. It ac-knowledges the diversity of human neurobiology and of social and cultural factors shaping the experiences of people with different neurological predisposi-tions; for example, the much higher likelihood of harsh criticism, rejection, abuse and bullying faced by neurodivergent individuals, starting in early child-hood.[51,52,53]

The late 1990s were an eventful time for the neurodiversity movement. Judy Singer, an Australian researcher, wrote a sociology thesis that defined the term "neurodiversity" and contextualized it within a critique of the medical model and recognition of the diversity of human minds.[8] Harvey Blume, an American jour-nalist, published a widely read 1998 essay on positive aspects of neurodiversity in

The Atlantic magazine.[54] Judy Singer's work was more extensive and academic, and although Blume's essay was published first, Singer is credited with coining the term "neurodiversity." Harvey Blume and Judy Singer also corresponded with each other and participated in autistic online spaces.[8,55] It is likely that both expressed the zeitgeist and the community's desire for a cultural rather than medical framing of the autistic experience.

The late 1990s autism acceptance discussions—including both Singer's and Blume's work—were generally focused on Asperger's Syndrome.[8,54] At the time, it was an accepted diagnosis that did not have negative associations with Hans Asperger's Nazi ties or the "high functioning" superiority it acquired in the early 2000s.[56,57] However, neurodiversity thought leadership and terminology use continued to develop rapidly, leaving this narrow use behind.

In 2000, Kassiane Asasumasu, an autistic/multiply neurodivergent writer and activist, coined the terms "neurodivergent" and "neurodivergence," which were meant to apply to a wide range of human neurological differences, from genetic to acquired.[16] Soon after, in 2004, Nick Walker coined the term "neurominority" to refer more specifically to groups of people who share similar forms of innate developmental neurodivergence for which they might encounter discrimination (e.g., autistic or dyslexic people).

Damien Milton, an autistic British academic, led neurodiversity-related discussions in education and the workplace by advancing the concepts of the double empathy problem and of a "spiky profile" of abilities.[58] The double empathy perspective counteracts the notion that autistic people are deficient in empathy and suggests that autistic and allistic people struggle to empathize and communicate with each other.[59] A spiky profile signifies that neurodivergent people are more likely than the general population to have pronounced capabilities in some areas, such as math, reading, and creativity, and struggles in other areas like multitasking or task switching. Many people have since found this approach useful for explaining neurodiversity to those used to the relatively flat profile of abilities considered average or typical.

The neurodiversity movement is still young, and ideas and terminology are developing rapidly. Moreover, this movement is not represented by a single organization. Rather, it is a collection of thought leaders who take the core of the work done before them and push it forward based on new research, analysis, and their lived experience. The neurodiversity movement is a changing, organic phenomenon.

DEEPER DIVE

DEBATES AND MISUNDERSTANDINGS

The heterogeneous nature of the movement results in much debate and misunderstanding. One of the critical areas of contention is the relationship between the neurodiversity perspective and seeking help and treatment. Some believe the neurodiversity perspective is incompatible with seeking medical treatment or any form of therapy for distressing psychological symptoms, but the issue is more nuanced.

True, for a long time, society pathologized harmless or positive neurodivergent characteristics like left-handedness, strong emotions, or the lack of hypocrisy. Some earlier and even current treatments hurt more than the neurodivergent condition. Schools "treated" dyspraxic handwriting and other motor issues by humiliating students in gym class or beating someone's hands (in my case, hand beating came from a music teacher). Relentless societal shaming of ADHD characteristics resulted in a range of negative psychological consequences.[60] Electrical shock "treatments" for autistic children remain a focus of a debate between US legislatures and autistic advocates.[61]

The medical and educational establishment profoundly failed people like the nonspeaking autistic accessibility professional, Jordyn Zimmerman, who was not expected to be able to learn anything beyond repetitive tasks and was frequently restrained and secluded at school. But what she needed was a communication device and a bit of patience from people. With these, she went on to earn a master's degree.[62,63]

Some mistrust from the neurodivergent community toward the "cure and treatment" establishment is expected. But it is also true that it is important to address personal distress, self-harm, or harm to others, including addressing them medically. It is also true that people who need care or disability support should have access to that care and support. And while neurodivergent people may not wish to be "cured" of their ability to hyperfocus, we may need help in dealing with the consequences of lifelong bullying. Any good theoretical framework must be flexible enough to accommodate life's complexity and compatible with common sense.

Addressing a person's distress also does not preclude investigating whether the concerning behavior is, in part, a form of communication—and whether something in the environment might be the trigger. When it comes to adults, for example, feelings of unease in unsafe or unethical work environments are to be expected. Humans are complex, as discussed in the next chapter, and intellectual honesty requires consideration of multiple perspectives.

As I write this book, I do not claim that I will always be right. Moreover, *I hope* that my own understanding of neurodiversity in the workplace will further develop between the time of this writing and the time when this book will be published and in your hands.

What I can promise is my best effort to identify the most relevant and the least biased research and to provide honest and practical applications. I also promise to draw on my decades of experience and curate the most outstanding examples of inclusive organizations worldwide to inform this book.

More than anything, I will not pathologize normal human reactions to stress, overwork, and mistreatment as individual deficits. And I will aim to uphold the view of neuro-differences as *kura urupare*—"treasure in around your head."[4]

 KEY TAKEAWAYS

- *The neurodiversity perspective was born in the 1990s from the desire to reframe differences in neurobiology and their psychological expression (e.g., dyslexic or ADHD thinking, autistic focus, sensory differences) as an essential aspect of human diversity rather than a pathology.*
- *It was informed by the disability rights movement and the social model of disability, focused on fixing the environment rather than the person.*
- *The dominance of the pathology perspective still affects the everyday experience of neurodivergent people, including work opportunities. It is reflected in the language used to describe neurodivergent experiences and people, which can sometimes be dehumanizing.*
- *The movement toward neuroinclusion in the workplace aims to create flexible organizational systems that can support a wide range of talent and productivity styles.*

DEVELOPMENTAL QUESTIONS

- Did anything in this chapter surprise you?
- What does your surprise tell you about your own perspective and how it was formed?
- How can our choice of words affect the life outcomes of other individuals?
- How can you support marginalized and misunderstood populations by being more intentional in your word choices?
- What is your personal experience with neurodivergence? In what ways can it broaden or narrow your perspective on neuroinclusion?

CHAPTER TWO

HOLISTIC INCLUSION

The Key to Belonging

I've learned that people will forget what you said, people will forget what you did, but people will never forget how you made them feel.

—Maya Angelou

 HUMAN HAPPENINGS

AN INTERSECTIONAL IMPASSE

Mary McConner, founder of Inclusive Excellence Consulting, has a PhD in higher education administration and substantial leadership experience. But as a job applicant, she never advanced to the interview stage when she indicated a need for reasonable accommodation. Never. "Zero interviews. Not a single callback."[1]

Like many other neurodivergent and disabled people, she stopped disclosing her need for reasonable accommodation on applications. But disclosing later in the employment process was not ideal either. When she informed organizational representatives that she was a part of the Deaf/Hard of Hearing community and was dyslexic, and therefore needed computer applications that read the text aloud and a quiet office to hear what was being read, she was typically met with blank stares.

Organizations seemed to have a hard time including all of Dr. Mary McConner. She found the best application of her talents as a consultant and speaker, educating organizations on the importance of disability and neurodiversity inclusion, along with gender, race, and other aspects of our humanity. This allows her to work as a whole person, drawing on the entirety of her human experience—mind, body, soul, and spirit.[1]

Mary McConner needs holistic inclusion to flourish fully.

So does Jessica Jahns.

HUMAN HAPPENINGS

DEFINITIONS OF DESIRABLE DIFFER

Jessica Jahns is an ace data analyst; her mind excels at seeing connections that others miss. For many years, she delivered outstanding work and supported her company with system improvement suggestions. And then her work life crumbled—along with the walls of her cubicle, which the company decided to take down.

"It will be wonderful," her boss insisted. "It will be light and bright and open and collaborative."

No. Not wonderful, not for Jessica.

For one thing, Jessica has congenital cataracts. Fighting and avoiding glare is a lifelong exercise, and although "light and bright" might be desirable for others, it is detrimental to her health.

But her vision difficulties were just a part of the problem. She is sensitive to many aspects of her environment. The sensation of the forced air from the industrial office vents is both unpleasant and distracting: it makes her unable to pay attention. The walls of the cubicle protected her from the worst of it. In the open office, that protection would be lost.

And then there was the horror of having her back exposed. Jessica had always been "jumpy," easily startled. Arranging her desk in her cubicle to face the entrance helped her feel safe. With the sense of physical safety gone, how would her glorious, data-attuned brain produce the exceptional work it had delivered for so many years?

Managers brushed Jessica's concerns off with comments like "Oh, you will come to like it." She did not. Her well-being and productivity suffered in an open office. *She* suffered in the open office, physically and emotionally, needing to hide just to breathe. Still, managers denied her requests to work from home as much as some of her colleagues could.

After emotionally struggling for a while and ready to quit, Jessica broke down in her therapist's office. Fortunately, the therapist connected the dots. She left the office with a diagnosis of autism and an accommodations letter.[2]

Soon after that, the COVID pandemic exposed just how outdated in-office work had become. Jessica—mind and body—could now deliver her outstanding work from home. She also discovered her autistic pride and a passion for neuroinclusion, becoming a founding member of the neurodiversity-focused Umbrella Alliance and an advocate for others.

Jessica's employer at that time welcomed some of the aspects of Jessica's autistic mind—or rather the results it produced. But our minds work best when the needs of our bodies for accommodating physical environments are met. They work best when our emotions are acknowledged and respected, not dismissed with generic platitudes.

We are whole people. And every aspect of us matters.

 DEEP DIVE

WE FEEL BELONGING IN OUR BODIES

Neurodiversity is sometimes referred to as cognitive diversity, brain differences, or information-processing differences. But that is a limiting definition, especially if by "cognitive" we only mean thought patterns, ideas, problem-solving methods, and intellectual perspectives—mental manifestations that can be explained in words and diagrams. Neurodiversity also encompasses our emotions and our bodies, which are intertwined.

Dyspraxia may interfere with the intended movement, and Tourette Syndrome may result in movements that are not desired. People with sensory sensitivities respond to environmental stimuli more intensely than others.[3,4] We can be overwhelmed to the point of shutting down by what others would perceive as "normal" noise levels or "hardly noticeable" smells. On the positive side, research shows that ADHDers can use physical activity and body movement to effectively improve attention and emotional regulation, and the lived experience of people describing other forms of developmental or acquired neurodivergence suggests the same.[5,6]

The mind–body distinction is, in many ways, artificial. Our information processing and our cognition are very much embodied. For example, have you tried to think logically—or remember where you've put your keys—in the midst of major personal events? Our thinking is tied to our emotions. Have you tried to think logically—or relax emotionally—in a freezing wind or in sticky, suffocating heat? Our thinking and our emotions are tied to our bodies.

We are whole people. Our work experience, too, involves the whole person—and whole people require a holistic approach to inclusion. We can't experience belonging at work when our bodies do not feel safe.

Jessica Jahns and Mary McConner need **holistic belonging** to flourish fully. So does Jerry Gidner.

HUMAN HAPPENINGS

TICS AND TAUNTS

Jerry Gidner is a government official in Washington, DC, a world traveler, and a writer; one might call him a "conventionally successful" person. And yet condescending attitudes and insults are a part of his daily life.

Jerry has Tourette Syndrome. His brain and body are wired differently, which sometimes produces tics. Many people respond to this manifestation of having a different brain by pretending that he is invisible. Others respond with hostility.

As Jerry shares:

> Let's face it, many Diversity, Equity, Inclusion, and Accessibility initiatives don't even recognize or include neurodiversity at all. The preferred management approach seems to be that if they pretend we don't exist, we won't. But we do, of course. And we bring such wonderful gifts to the workplace. Resilience, creativity, empathy, humor, vulnerability. Every one of us is different of course. From the mainstream, but also from each other.[7]

Yes, we are all different. And we are whole people. Our intertwined minds and bodies require holistic inclusion because if any aspect of us is not included—whether our emotional lives, our brains' productivity needs, our sensory needs, or respect for our bodies—we do not experience belonging.

> In this chapter, I develop the idea of holistic neuroinclusion that normalizes and welcomes differences in how humans think, feel, relate, and experience our physical environments. We all need social, cognitive, emotional, and physical/sensory neuroinclusion to feel and be our best. Holistic inclusion supports holistic belonging.

 EMPLOYER EXCELLENCE

ULTRANAUTS

Holistic inclusion may seem like a big ask—and it is. But it is possible. Ultranauts, a technology company where the majority of employees are autistic, exemplifies many elements of holistic inclusion.[8]

The company is remote first, with flexible scheduling built into the work-flow. Everyone's uniqueness is normalized, welcomed, and celebrated. To communicate their inclusion needs, employees fill out a Biodex—a user manual for each individual that helps colleagues interact with everyone according to their needs.[9] It lists their preferred learning and work styles, productivity habits, and preferences for social interaction, as well as what could trigger or distract them.

The Biodex helps normalize cognitive style diversity and reduces the possibility of miscommunication and conflict. Emotions are not forgotten: by asking what can trigger or upset employees, Ultranauts also demonstrates attention to emotional inclusion. The company's philosophy removes as many barriers to employees' sense of inclusion and belonging as possible. Not just because it maximizes performance but because well-being is a value in itself.

 DEEP DIVE

HOLISTIC NEUROINCLUSION

The complexity of neurodiversity and its manifestations defies simplistic inclusion solutions. Unlocking neurodivergent—and, overall, human—potential requires supporting a sense of holistic belonging. This means a deep respect for differences in how our thinking, emotions, bodies, and relationships work best.

It also means that organizations can't be truly inclusive without holistic inclusion. Flexibly aligning work's social, cognitive, emotional, and physical/sensory aspects with how different humans experience life best also means supporting their ability to perform their best.

 DEEP DIVE

SOCIAL (NEURO)INCLUSION

When people refer to inclusion in the workplace, often the focus is on social inclusion—being invited to participate in the actual or metaphorical party, meeting, conversation, and decision-making process. Of course, social inclusion is vital. Equitable access to social interaction and support is essential to inclusive environments. Social exclusion is processed as physical pain.[10]

However, forms of human social needs differ. If social inclusion is approached as a one-size-fits-all issue, it can turn into mandatory fun, collaboration overload, and pressure to fit in gratefully.

The social inclusion of neurodivergent people in the workplace requires rethinking traditional neuronormative expectations of workplace socialization. Inclusion efforts must aim to create environments where people wired to need different levels and forms of social interaction feel accepted and valued. Here are some key considerations for social aspects of neuroinclusion:

- Although some employees enjoy parties or small talk, others feel included when colleagues respect their privacy, and enjoy fewer but deeper interactions. Large group gatherings or social events energize some. The same events might be physically draining or anxiety-provoking for others, who are more likely to feel included when in smaller or task-focused settings.
- A neuroinclusive social environment means that employees should be welcomed but never pressured to participate in social activities. The ability to opt out of social events without fear of judgment or repercussions is as essential as being invited to social events.
- The forms of communication also matter to effective social inclusion. Some are comfortable expressing their thoughts verbally and on the spot; others communicate best in writing. Social inclusion should normalize a wider range of communication styles and modes of participation in organizational life.
- To fully participate in organizational life, many people also need direct, straightforward communication and transparency. If social participation relies on implicit cues and mind reading, it is bound to be exclusionary.
- Recognizing and valuing different social needs are key to social inclusion at work. It's essential that neurodivergent individuals participate in shaping more neuroinclusive social norms and cultures. This may involve their participation in decision-making processes and ensuring their accomplishments are recognized in a way that respects their comfort levels. Not everyone enjoys surprise parties.
- Understanding that engagement and commitment can be expressed in different ways can expand social inclusion and the valuing of different personality styles. Hosting parties might be one way of expressing engagement at work. Quietly developing groundbreaking products communicates engagement at least as much.
- Neuroinclusion training can also foster more welcoming social environments. This training can involve workshops or seminars on neurodiversity,

dispelling stereotypes, and teaching social and communication skills to help neurotypical employees interact respectfully with their neurodivergent colleagues.

For too long, social inclusion at work was conditional on individuals changing themselves or being actively trained to "fit in"—think of assertiveness training for women or accent reduction programs for immigrants. The key to true social inclusion in the workplace is ditching the idea of making everyone fit into a rigid social mold. It is about reshaping the culture to allow for different ways of being and participating in the community. For example, Twilio, a tech company committed to the idea that supporting diversity means supporting people in being themselves, banned the use of the phrase "culture fit."[11]

 DEEP DIVE

COGNITIVE (NEURO)INCLUSION

Cognitive diversity is often defined as diversity in knowledge processing and perspectives. This diversity enhances team performance and helps build more innovative, productive, and successful organizations.[12] But ensuring these rewards takes some work. To unlock productivity that comes from the diversity of thinking, working, and decision-making styles, with their underlying experiential and neurobiological bases, organizations must change some prevalent practices to ensure cognitive (neuro)inclusion.

- Removing access barriers requires hiring for *culture-add* and creating environments that support multiple thinking and productivity styles. This enriches organizations by introducing additional perspectives and lived experiences.

For example, people with more contextual and systemic thinking can balance groups of individual-focused thinkers. Without having that balance, groups are prone to making decisions shaped by the fundamental attribution error, such as trying to "fix" people when systems change is required.

People intuitively see their way of thinking as "right," which may lead to hiring bias—often in the name of "culture fit"—that limits cognitive diversity. Hence, developing transparent and intentional processes for culture-add and thinking-add hiring is crucial for overcoming neurodiversity hiring gaps[13] and ensuring the diversity in thinking styles essential to quality decision making.[14]

- Removing success barriers requires respect for diversity in productivity styles. Productivity gurus often sell one-size-fits-all approaches, but cognitive diversity means there is no one best way to work.[15] Some people work best in the morning, others at night. Some need at least 3–4 hours of uninterrupted deep work, while others thrive on 25-minute Pomodoro productivity sprints. Respecting the need for different schedules, communication mechanisms, and work environments is the key to unlocking neurodivergent—and, overall, human—productivity.

Cognitive diversity and inclusion in leadership teams might be particularly important to developing lasting and systemic solutions to the problems of systemic and intersectional neurodiversity exclusion. Organizations must systemically guard against overrepresenting one thinking style—for example, Western or linear—in their leadership and decision making.[14] This calls for changes to multiple organizational processes, such as making communication inclusive and accessible by supporting multiple communication modalities. Leadership development and promotion mechanisms should also be aligned with the goal of neurocognitive diversity.

 DEEP DIVE

EMOTIONAL (NEURO)INCLUSION

Neurodiversity is, to a large extent, a diversity in the intensity of emotions and in the types of emotions we are likely to experience more often. I cry more than most others—but rarely get angry. Many neurodivergent people feel a range of emotions with amplified intensity. Hence, neurodiversity inclusion requires emotional inclusion. Moreover, human well-being, in general, requires emotional inclusion.[16]

Suppressing and masking our feelings is taxing and stressful,[17] and the outdated norms of professionalism interfere with normal human emotional expression, including compassion and empathy, and with emotional well-being. Those who are culturally marginalized or disabled pay extra for each stigmatized identity.

Human feelings are an essential part of our makeup; they are a driving force behind our motivations, effort, and innovation. Our sense of justice has an emotional as well as cognitive component.[18,19,20] Yet, few organizations practice emotional inclusion by normalizing authentic emotional expression at work. In traditional business environments, showing harmless emotion can cost the person a job. Or at least a promotion. I once cried at a large organizational gathering out of love for my colleagues, which might have cost me a long-promised promotion. But I also know other women who have been penalized for "not showing enough emotion" according to gendered expectations. Neither is fair. People wear their emotional energy in different ways, and any nonharmful way is perfectly fine.

Removing access barriers associated with emotional diversity requires reconsidering capricious expectations of emotional expression based on cultural biases and pop psychology. I've met people who proudly declared they would never hire someone with "flat affect." However, what is perceived as flat affect or lower-than-typical outward emotional expressiveness could reflect neurodivergence, an idiosyncratic reaction to interview anxiety, or the effect of taking medication to counteract the interview anxiety. There are also cultural differences in habitually exaggerating or moderating emotional expression. Some hiring managers believe that showing "too much enthusiasm" is a sign of faking, whereas it could simply be enthusiasm.

Emotional homogeneity in the workplace is not a justifiable goal—few jobs require a specific emotional profile that can be empirically supported as a valid job requirement.[21] Arbitrarily applying the old-fashioned emotion-focused "professionalism" criteria is exclusionary and often ableist.

- Creating emotionally inclusive systems requires ensuring that cultural and personal views on emotional expression held by those in power are not embedded in systems for high-stakes decisions.
- To remove success barriers related to emotional exclusion, organizations need to normalize emotion. Rather than judge others' feelings, organizational norms should encourage employees to check their cultural and personal biases.
- In workplace design, emotional inclusion means creating physical spaces where employees can process their emotions. Private and soundproof workspaces that allow for emotional processing are generally better for our performance and well-being,[22] but some organizations support emotional inclusion by providing rage rooms or crying rooms.[23,24]

Of course, some behavioral expressions of emotions can be destructive. For example, envy that turns into bullying and sabotage, harming another individual, is not the same as acknowledging that sometimes people experience envy.[25] **Entitlements should end where harm to others begins.**[26] Organizations are responsible for developing mechanisms that maximally prevent and address harm to employee well-being caused by other employees or customers.

Emotional inclusion also requires preventing emotional harm caused by the organizational system itself. A frequently expressed argument is that organizations cannot be responsible for employee happiness. A fair point: not all aspects of individual happiness are within the employer's control. Organizations are, however, responsible for not inflicting harm.

Under the US Surgeon General's *Framework for Workplace Mental Health & Well-Being*, this means ensuring that organizational systems and work organization are designed to prevent harm—be it from overwork, economic precarity, or discrimination.[27] Organizations are responsible for making use of the empirical data that show which organizational conditions (such as disrespect and being pushed into unpaid overtime) cause mental health harm to employees and prevent such conditions from occurring.

In other words, protecting employee emotional well-being means supporting *social safety*, such as protection from harm due to bullying, ostracism, and abusive supervision. It also means supporting *economic safety* by providing fair and equitable pay, ensuring a "predictable living wage before overtime, tips, and commission," and preventing wage theft.[27]

 DEEP DIVE

PHYSICAL AND SENSORY (NEURO)INCLUSION, ACCESSIBILITY, AND SENSORY SAFETY

In the most general sense, physical inclusion means removing barriers to work for people whose bodies function differently from the typical. These barriers can be associated with employees' physical injuries and conditions. They might also be associated with psychological differences, as well as with brain–body relationships (epilepsy, tremors, dyspraxia, or effects of brain injuries).

The term "inclusion," when applied to various disabilities or neurodivergence, is broader than "accessibility" and "accommodation" (see Appendix F for more detail). Inclusion has a crucial element of nondiscrimination, whereas with accessibility and accommodation, various forms of discrimination may still occur.[28] Many workers can testify that compliance with minimal legal accessibility requirements or the grudging provision of accommodations does not ensure a welcoming environment or prevent social exclusion and bullying. Going beyond accommodations and ending neurodiversity and disability discrimination require a systemic revision of all aspects of employment, including cultural norms and leadership development processes.

Workplaces that support physical aspects of neuroinclusion are accessible, safe, and supportive of diverse sensory needs. Here are some ways organizations can practice physical inclusion:

- **To remove** *access* **barriers,** organizations should ensure that their job announcements and application systems are both accessible and nondiscriminatory. Physical environments should also be accessible to all individuals, regardless of ability. This may involve providing wheelchair ramps, elevators, and accessible restrooms and designing spaces that are easy to navigate for individuals with visual, hearing, balance, and other differences. It is also important to create welcoming environments for people who have sensory sensitivities and those who might feel sick in overstimulating environments. Ignoring sensory needs means excluding neurodivergent talent. Because our needs differ greatly, systems and spaces must be flexible.
- **Removing** *success* **barriers** also requires flexibility. Even people within the same "label" have different needs. For example, Jessica Jahns and I are both autistic women, but she needs to avoid glare, and I need all the sunlight I can get to prevent depression. Workplaces and work organization should be flexible enough to support health and maximize the productivity of people with different needs through either supportive and adjustable spaces, adjustable schedules, or remote work.

Going beyond neuroinclusion, physical inclusion applies to the ergonomics of creating environments well suited to users' needs. It may mean providing adjustable desks and chairs to accommodate individuals of different heights and body types. It may also require designing spaces that reduce physical strain and fatigue, such as by minimizing the need for repetitive motions or heavy lifting.

Humans experience the world through their senses. We rely on them to navigate our environments, receive information, and interact with others. However, traditional workplace design often fails to account for the diversity of sensory needs. This can lead to discomfort, distraction, illness, injuries, exclusion, and disabling, in the sense of the social model of disability, for those who do not fit the "norm."[29,30,31]

The experience of sensory-sensitive people in busy and overwhelming environments is often described as sensory assault—in my case, hearing music can feel like being beaten on the head with a heavy bat, with an added full-body torture of vibration, and it shuts down my ability to function. Feeling safe in noisy environments is physically impossible for me.

At the same time, sensory-seeking individuals need stimulation to perform their best. Barbara Ruth Saunders, a neurodivergent writer and editor, describes that without sufficient sensory stimulation, *"My body can't tell I'm alive and is just shutting down."*[32] Ironically, understimulation primes her for the worst kind of overstimulation and makes her hypersensitive, which illustrates the complexity of sensory experience. To be at their best, those who need stimulation should have options for adding movement, colors, or sounds. The trick is to provide workplaces or flexible arrangements that will allow them to do this without disabling those who are sensory-avoidant.

Although, technically, sensory inclusion is physical inclusion, I emphasize it separately for these two reasons:

1. Sensory inclusion is particularly relevant to neurodivergent people and is the foundation of social, cognitive, and emotional inclusion.
2. Sensory inclusion needs are often nonapparent and—partly for this reason—are not seen as real and are consequently denied and disregarded, as in Jessica's and many other examples. We can't belong if we are not believed.

Sensory inclusion means designing workplaces supportive of diverse sensory needs. Lighting, noise, temperature, and smell greatly affect our ability to focus and think, our emotions, productivity, and well-being. Because of a heightened sensitivity, an inability to filter sensory stimuli, a more intense reaction to stimuli, or all the above, neurodivergent people can even become physically ill in response to environments that others may not find particularly aversive.

Designing spaces that allow individuals to control their sensory environments, reduce distraction and discomfort, and maximize well-being helps neurodivergent talent thrive.

The bottom line is that attention to sensory inclusion and safety is not just a workplace nicety but a *necessity* for neuroinclusion. It also benefits all employees. When we create spaces that support well-being by removing the auditory, visual, and other stimuli that might be distressing or even painful for neurodivergent employees and provide opportunities for stimulation that are not distracting to others, we improve work environments for everyone.

Moreover, practicing holistic inclusion and welcoming differences in how humans think, feel, and experience our physical environments might be the key to belonging—the component of diversity, equity, inclusion, and belonging (DEIB) work that has been difficult to achieve for many organizations. This chapter ends with a deeper dive that connects the science of holistic inclusion to the science of belonging.

 A DEEPER DIVE

EMBODIED BELONGING

Belonging is crucial to organizational performance.[33] According to Deloitte, it can help increase job performance by 56 percent and the employer net promoter score by 167 percent while decreasing sick days by 75 percent and turnover risk by 50 percent. Yet 40 percent of employees feel lonely and disconnected.[34]

A sense of belonging remains elusive at many organizations, likely because inclusion efforts are often signaled with diversity statements and speeches from leaders.[35,36] However, humans have multiple systems for fact-checking whether these statements are true, with different lengths of time for processing. A sense of belonging or rejection could be triggered by any of these systems.

Our conscious, logical minds that interpret PR statements are just one information-processing system; it is highly reliant on language. However, our sense of belonging and safety is largely determined by our emotions and sensory information processing distributed throughout our body. Interpreting language-based input requires deliberate attention and effort and takes longer than emotional and bodily reactions.

Researchers have identified several interrelated systems that enable us to sense our social and relational environments. Slow, symbolic, word-based processing generally corresponds to Daniel Kahneman's System 2 thinking.[37] The fast-acting System 1 can be subdivided into **connectionist**, **emotional**, and **embodied** systems of knowing, which differ in neurological foundation and processing speeds.[38] System 1 involves automatic processing that operates primarily outside our conscious awareness yet significantly influences our decisions.[39,40,41]

Connectionist processing, or intuition, is based on neuronal networks that learn associations between different elements of our environments. It is fast and automatic, such as when a job applicant makes an association between the workspace arrangement or the website accessibility and whether they will be included. **Emotional** processing, largely relying on subcortical structures deep in the brain, is even faster and alerts us to potential environmental benefits or dangers. **Embodied** reactions to the temperature, textures, or smell are the quickest and can produce physical responses to the environment, such as goosebumps. These reactions can significantly affect our social judgments and decisions.[41,42]

Research on the levels of information processing explains how people implicitly know whether they belong long before their conscious attention will process the words in an organizational inclusion statement. Organizations do not need a sign saying "AUTISTICS KEEP OUT": blaring music in the lobby immediately tells me I am excluded, loud and clear.

Website accessibility and the physical accessibility of the premises send an unambiguous signal about whether disabled people are included. This means organizations can't declare themselves inclusive and expect people to feel it. Inclusion must encompass all signals an organization sends out, not just symbolic ones. Mixed signals do not work.

> Information processing speeds of different systems: symbolic, 500 milliseconds to 10 seconds. Connectionist, 200–500 milliseconds. Emotional, under 10 milliseconds. Embodied, under 5 milliseconds.[38]

Creating environments for belonging requires developing systems that are deeply and holistically inclusive—in ways that people can experience and sense with their entire being.

 KEY TAKEAWAYS

- *People do their best work when they are supported in feeling and being their best.*
- *Holistic neuroinclusion means social, cognitive, emotional, and physical/sensory inclusion.*
- *A holistic approach to inclusion is likely to be the key to belonging for everyone—and belonging is the key to retention, productivity, and engagement.*
- *Organizational statements and PR cannot "create" belonging because it is processed on deep emotional and embodied levels.*

DEVELOPMENTAL QUESTIONS

- Have you ever been surprised by your own reaction to a situation and later realized that your body was reacting before your mind? How does this align with the stories and the research reviewed in this chapter?
- Have you ever experienced a workplace disagreement because your definition of a desirable and productive work environment was very different from how other people defined desirable and productive? What lessons could be learned from that disagreement?
- People with nonapparent differences, such as sensory sensitivities, can't belong if they are not believed. Have you encountered a situation in which you doubted other people's accounts of sensitivities or considered them mere wants, rather than needs? How could you better support the nonapparent needs of others?

CHAPTER THREE

THE CANARY CODE

Radical Inclusion for Holistic Belonging

Inclusion is not bringing people into what already exists; it is making a new space, a better space for everyone.

—George Dei

 DEEP DIVE

HOLISTIC BELONGING REQUIRES RADICALLY INCLUSIVE SYSTEMS

In many organizations, inclusion programs take the form of sequential interventions focusing on specific aspects of diversity for a year or two—maybe starting with gender or race and then moving onto disability and neurodiversity . . . well, someday. Only about 5 percent of organizations include disability in their diversity programs,[1] and most organizations vastly underestimate how many employees might be disabled.[2] The "someday" that never comes harms many people's lives. In the previous chapter, we saw how multiple barriers impact the lives of those at the intersection of several differences. We learned how important it is to support every aspect of who we are whether someone is a Black, dyslexic, hard-of-hearing woman like Mary McConner; or a Native American man with Tourette's like Jerry Gidner; or a white autistic woman with congenital cataracts like Jessica Jahns. Any person who happens to have some attributes that aren't "currently includable" faces exclusion and bias. With sequential inclusion approaches, intersectionally marginalized people may remain unincludable for a lifetime.[3]

Sequential inclusion that is slowly expanded from the circle of power out does not work.

Truly radically inclusive organizations are designed from the margins. Meeting the needs of those most excluded—and most sensitive to problematic aspects of the environment—will help create systems where everyone can thrive.

 NEURODIVERSITY NARRATIVES

SYSTEMS FOR THRIVING

An elementary school teacher from New York, Karen Blacher wanted to support her students in the best way she could. So she created a decorated "calm corner" where students could relax and self-regulate in a fantasy-like tent. She brought in sensory toys and taught emotional literacy. She also abandoned some of the standard practices that can be anxiety-provoking, like clip charts and token economies.[4]

In essence, in her regular classroom, she created an environment that is typically found in special education classrooms. As a result, her neurotypical students flourished.

Then, her Facebook post about this approach went viral, leading to her appearance on *Good Morning America*.[5]

Karen Blacher did not think her teaching methods were all that unusual. She was using what she learned from nurturing her own neurodivergent children and assumed that others knew what she had learned: "*When we treat autistic children the way the world tells us to treat neurotypical children, they suffer.*" Yet, when we treat neurotypical students as autistic students should be treated—"*with open communication, adaptive expectations, and respect for self-advocacy and self-regulation*"—neurotypical students and every human being treated in this way will thrive.

"Special" needs—like the prevention of unnecessary anxiety and the provision of flexible support—are in fact human needs, at any age. And perhaps neurodivergent people are "*not the only ones who've been misunderstood and mistreated all this time. . . . They're just the ones who feel it most, and the ones who finally got the message through to the rest of humanity that there's a better way to be.*"[5]

 DEEP DIVE

TOXIC SYSTEMS, NEURODIVERGENT CANARIES

Like canaries in the coal mine, neurodivergent people are the first to feel the mistreatment and effects of poorly designed systems, whether at school or work. A systemic approach to improvement is essential because fixing just one negative workplace factor, be it the inaccessible, stress-inducing design of physical work environments or a lack of flexibility, will not be enough. But fixing *all* these factors will make a difference not just for neurodivergent people but for many others. Fixing unwelcoming spaces supports disability inclusion and is enjoyed by all. And flexible work supports caregivers, working students, and many others.

Consider the problem of the unemployment and underemployment of autistic professionals. It is not created by only one barrier; rather, a *combination* of numerous workplace barriers adds up to dramatic levels of exclusion. These barriers may affect many people, although they could be more detrimental to autistic job candidates and employees.

For example, unstructured interview questions about culture-specific leisure activities might be an access barrier for immigrants or class migrants, who are likely to be rated lower than candidates from cultural backgrounds similar to that of the interviewer.[6] Many autistic people faced with such questions may feel reluctant to discuss their personal life with strangers and may be confused about the relevance of such questions to job responsibilities, and so they also "lose points." As another example, when rewards are based on self-promotion rather than objective outcomes, autistic employees are likely to be negatively affected—along with others who are less likely to self-promote, including class migrants, many women, and people from cultures that value modesty.[7,8,9,10]

On the job, a major workplace problem that strongly affects autistic people and may result in job loss is workplace bullying.[11] Autistic people are more likely to be targeted, and their emotional resources are likely to be already stretched by trauma from prior bullying and other adverse experiences.[12,13] However, the same double whammy could be faced by those with depression, PTSD, chronic illness, or a generational vulnerability to stress.[14] More generally, bullying harms all targets, regardless of neurotype, even if some are more vulnerable. Workplace bullying is often a symptom of systemic organizational toxicity.[15] If the targets' concerns are ignored, as is often the case, bullying behavior will likely spread across units and departments.

The canaries sense the increasing toxicity and sound the alarm in whatever ways they can.

Sometimes, the alarm can come in the form of the **absence** of neurodivergent people in the organization. At other times, it comes in the form of neurodivergent people actively **warning** others of danger.

When organizations function on the assumption that sensitivity is a deficit and employees must be "tough" enough to withstand cutthroat, disrespectful, exclusionary, abusive, and unethical—in other words, toxic—environments, canaries are seen as "deficient" and are not welcomed.[16,17] Excluding canaries leaves organizations without a toxic culture alarm.[17] Over time, however, organizations' toxicity levels can become so high that even the "tough" employees feel the effects. Then, a major event, such as the COVID-19 pandemic, can become "the last straw" and result in a mass exodus. Studies indicate that toxic organizational cultures were the critical factor driving employee exit from their organizations during the Great Resignation.[16] Making organizational air healthier not only allows canaries to return but also prevents costly resignations, reputational damage, and, in some cases, corporate demise, like in the case of the infamously toxic Enron scandal.[18]

When canaries sound the alarm but are ignored, inefficiencies continue, challenges are unresolved, and opportunities are missed. Overlooking the concerns of neurodivergent people often means missing out on crucial insights about systemic problems that may threaten everyone's well-being.[19]

Many neurominority people are wired to notice problems and to speak up. For example, ADHD is associated with an elevated sensitivity to injustice.[20,21] And, despite the "unfeeling autistic" stereotypes, research shows that autistic people experience the world more intensely than the average person.[22] We can feel elevated empathy, notice patterns that others miss, are more attuned to justice, and are committed to telling the truth.[23,24,25]

Prominent examples of neurodivergent canaries include the dyslexic Erin Brockovich and autistic Greta Thunberg, who focus on environmental issues.[26] Simone Biles has been open and outspoken in fighting the stigma associated with ADHD and in exposing the sexual abuse of the US Olympic gymnasts and the cover-up of this abuse.[27,28]

There are many stories about neurodivergent canaries detecting problematic patterns in an organizational environment long before others and trying to sound the alarm while others stay quiet. Often, canary warnings are not welcomed. Here is one of those stories.

 HUMAN HAPPENINGS

THE COVID CANARY

Five months into the COVID pandemic, a neurodivergent young professional who chose to identify here as Evie Adam, got a job at a care facility for troubled youth. There were no COVID policies in place—no masking, no social distancing.

Many employees worried about their older colleagues and clients with preexisting conditions, but most felt helpless in effecting change.

Evie was compelled to do something and say something. She tried to advocate for policies that would keep everyone safer and reduce organizational liability. Her efforts were unwelcome, however; she was warned that she should toe the line. Evie got into even more trouble for trying to challenge the belief that COVID was not dangerous and was a political ploy. She did succeed in getting a staff masking policy—before getting fired from that job.

But at least when COVID came through the facility after she left, the damage was somewhat contained.

Many neurodivergent canaries have "told you so" stories. But most of us would rather have been heard and the damage to organizations prevented. What would it take to create organizations where canaries thrive and help everyone succeed?

 DEEP DIVE

OXYGEN FOR CANARIES, OXYGEN FOR ALL

Organizational cultures interact with national-level cultures, regional differences, and societal trends to create specific sets of barriers that employees encounter. Yet, there is a general logic in how those the least similar to power holders are kept out or pushed out. I observed the same power dynamic all over the world and in different types of organizations, even when specifics of culture and power distribution differ. Organizations must be very deliberate about being culture-add and personality-add not to create such barriers.

When I realized that I was autistic, something else occurred to me. All the different types of systemic bias I had experienced at various points of my career—sexism and family status discrimination, classism, and xenophobia—could have been prevented by implementing the same organizational practices that would support neuroinclusion.

Moreover, most of these organizational practices are best talent practices established by organizational psychology, management, and human resources research. Unfortunately, these practices, such as using valid instruments for decision making and ensuring organizational justice, are not always implemented.[29,30,31] Additional analysis of the experiences of neurodivergent job seekers and employees reviewed in this book, as well as practices used by neurodivergence-inclusive and disability-inclusive organizations, converges on the same themes. Just as the universal design of buildings improves physical accessibility for all, the inclusive talent systems design improves the well-being and productivity for all.[32]

The Canary Code model is focused on six key principles for organizational practice that can help remove barriers to neuroinclusion, improve the well-being of all employees, and support organizational outcomes. These principles are embedding employee **participation, focus on outcomes, flexibility, organizational justice, transparency,** and the use of **valid decision-making tools** in organizational systems.[3]

 DEEP DIVE

PARTICIPATION

Meaningfully involving employees, specifically marginalized employees, in decisions that influence their work distinguishes the Canary Code approach from traditional interventions that "benevolent includers" design on behalf of those "to be included."[31]

The participation principle addresses the important drawbacks of design methods that call for empathy toward the marginalized but not participation of the marginalized, such as the many variations of universal design and design thinking approaches.[17,33,34] Direct participation of those most affected by the design is consistent with the crucial call of disability rights advocacy—"Nothing about Us without Us" or, more recently, simply "Nothing without Us." Exclusion from any aspect of life is unacceptable.

Individuals are the experts on their inner experience, and designing work for neurodivergent people without their input often results in less-than-optimal solutions. For all employees, participation supports the sense of belonging and boosts organizational outcomes.[35,36]

 EMPLOYER EXCELLENCE

DELOITTE

David Martinez, an autistic and multiply neurodivergent/disabled army veteran from Colorado, in the US, had a rough start in the working world. Then he was hired via Deloitte's neurodiversity program as a data analyst.[37]

But he was not "just" an analyst. He was invited to provide input on neuro-diversity hiring and other programs and welcomed to explore various leadership opportunities. A year after joining Deloitte, he ran an updated version of the hiring and onboarding process—improved according to his and others' input.

David considers Deloitte to be a distinctively inclusive environment that helps employees engage and create unique niches that maximize their talents. He and his colleagues feel valued—even those who may not have felt valued before.

 DEEP DIVE

FOCUS ON OUTCOMES

Organizational outcomes are maximized when people do their best work. And people do their best work when they work with their strengths. Outcomes suffer when the performance focus is lost, and attention is directed toward a subjectively defined personality "fit" or "being seen by the bosses." A focus on personality and "being seen" often excludes neurodivergent talent.

I mentioned earlier my struggle to choose whether to quietly recharge during lunch to ensure I would have the energy to work in the afternoon or to fulfill the social expectation of engaging in lunchtime chatter. When organizational norms label people who quietly recharge to make sure they excel in their work a "bad fit," many autistic people, introverts, or people with chronic illnesses who need a physical break can be viewed negatively and lose out on rewards despite delivering outcomes.[38]

Likewise, when employees can deliver outstanding work by using dictation software instead of typing or need flexible hours because they do their best work at night, why not let them work the way they work best? Focusing work on outcomes gives all employees a much-desired sense of autonomy and empowerment and supports inclusion, higher performance, and morale.[17,39,40] Focus on outcomes, however, should not be confused with "outcomes at any cost" or the pursuit of strictly individual outcomes. It simply deals with supporting people in contributing to collective results in ways that maximize their strengths, and evaluating outcomes without bias.

EMPLOYER EXCELLENCE

INFINITE FLOW

Let's do an experiment. Think of a few key requirements you would include in a position announcement for a dancer. Write these down before reading on.

Infinite Flow dancers glide across the floor, lift each other with incredible athleticism, and create dramatic group shapes perfectly in sync with the music. Their joy and energy are contagious.

But would you have hired them?

Many Infinite Flow dancers are wheelchair users; some are deaf. Most dance companies would not give them one look. They would not fit a typical "dancer job description."

Why though?

A dancer's job, in its essence, is to use body movements in aesthetically pleasing and interesting ways to evoke an intended emotional reaction in the observer. The outcome is the viewer's experience of beauty, wonder, or a specific emotional response.

If a deaf dancer can accomplish the outcome, why require hearing? If a wheelchair user can accomplish this outcome, why should they not have an opportunity to do so? If wheelchair tricks achieve the same viewer outcomes as some of the more traditional dance moves, why not focus on outcomes and what the person *can* do?

The founder of the Los Angeles–based dance company Infinite Flow, Marisa Hamamoto, is a dancer and a choreographer with a will to bring the healing power of dance to the world. She is also a stroke survivor diagnosed with PTSD and autism.

Marisa's path to creating Infinite Flow was anything but easy or certain. Dance was her passion, yet she was repeatedly told that her body type and even her ethnicity were all wrong. And then, when it looked like her efforts were starting to pay off, a spinal stroke left her paralyzed.

After recovering her ability to move, Marisa wanted to share the healing power of dance with the world. So she started an inclusive dance company, Infinite Flow, in 2015 and has been creating beauty and promoting healing ever since.[41,42,43]

What would the world be like if all organizations choreographed work like Marisa Hamamoto choreographs performances, focusing on achieving the outcome of beauty and wonder in an infinite number of ways?

DEEP DIVE

FLEXIBILITY

Rigid requirements based on time, place, and style of work rather than outcomes can exclude neurodivergent and marginalized talent.[3] Conversely, expanding flexibility even more, including aligning jobs with people's unique strengths, can make seemingly impossible levels of employee thriving and organizational performance possible.

Let's say that each person in an organization spends one-third of their time working with their top strengths, one-third of their time doing things at which they're average, and one-third of the time doing things at which they're weak. This is a recipe for mediocre productivity—and in many organizations, the picture is even worse, because only 35 percent of US employees report doing what they do best every day at all.[44] Now, let's say we helped people trade their responsibilities so that two-thirds of their time is focused on their top strengths and one-third on average areas. The cumulative effect of the increased productivity would be game-changing.

Sometimes providing the flexibility that neurodivergent employees need is approached as an issue of accommodations. Accommodations certainly help, but they also have two important drawbacks.

1. Accommodations often require disclosure and documentation. Not everyone is comfortable disclosing or even can provide the requested documentation, however. Disclosure can result in discrimination, and for many, healthcare options are limited.
2. Accommodations for nonapparent disabilities, such as flexible schedules or working from home, are desired by most employees and may result in envy and bullying from coworkers who see accommodations as privileges.

Making flexibility a rule rather than an exception addresses the problems of disclosure, discrimination, and bullying. It also helps support all employees with a wide range of needs.

EMPLOYER EXCELLENCE

LEGALITE

A career in law, flexibility, and life-work balance? Sounds like fiction, but Marianne Marchesi made it possible—for herself and for others. Designing work with flexibility in mind based on the holistically flexible Work by Design™ approach made Legalite, a commercial law firm specializing in franchising and property law, the winner of the 2022 Australian Business Employer of Choice Award. Its flexibility also made a difference in the lives and careers of many employees. All work is centered around individuals' needs and talents; gone are the days of asking all employees to fit into an outdated job description. Although there are core requirements for a role (qualifications, certifications, key skills), the rest of the job is up for codesign.

- Disabled employees can access their dream job and build their dream careers using their unique skills and talents.
- Working parents can balance caring responsibilities with their ideal role and continue progressing in their careers. There is no need to take a demotion in exchange for flexible work.
- Pregnant employees and adoptive and surrogate parents can attend appointments and flex their working arrangements to support this special time in their lives.
- Employees can integrate their personal lives and work—attending their kids' awards ceremony at school, participating in important family and cultural events, taking working holidays, or getting out in the fresh air.

Not only are schedules flexible but the firm has also introduced new practice areas aligned with staff members' unique skills and expertise. This flexibility allowed Legalite to deliver unique offerings for its clients and effectively serve the legal needs of some of the best-loved Australian brands. A true win-win![45]

 DEEP DIVE

FOCUS ON ORGANIZATIONAL JUSTICE

Justice in hiring, pay, benefits, promotion, and the entire talent cycle is a foundation of strong cultures that retain talent. Fair treatment and equitable processes build confidence in organizational leadership. Across cultural contexts, organizational justice increases collaboration and productivity.

Workplace justice comes in several forms.[46] Early research focused on the fairness of outcomes (*distributive* justice, such as fair hiring decisions) and procedures (*procedural* justice).

Leventhal's six procedural justice criteria can also be used as a checklist for key inclusion practices in the workplace.[47]

Just procedures should meet the following criteria:

- Consistent application across individuals and time
- Absence of bias
- Accurate information as a foundation of decision making
- Mechanism to revise incorrect decisions
- Adherence to ethical standards
- Inclusion of the perspectives of various groups affected by the decisions

Later models added considerations of interpersonal treatment, dignity, and providing sufficient information to employees (*interpersonal* and *informational* justice). The most recent addition is *contributive* justice: opportunities for employees to fully and meaningfully participate at work,[30] which can increase the sense of belonging.[30,31] All types of justice affect employee well-being, morale, and, ultimately, the sense of belonging in the organization.

 EMPLOYER EXCELLENCE

CALL YACHOL

Call Yachol, a call center and the largest private disability employer in Israel, has been proving since 2008 that it is possible to focus on justice and be a successful business. The founder, Gil Winch, designed the company to help right societal wrongs and include those previously excluded from the world of work—people he calls the underdogs. The majority of employees are disabled people and others rejected by society: seniors, the shy and anxious, or ex-convicts.

The company is focused on ensuring justice by providing job opportunities, supporting employee well-being, and building belonging.

For example, the hiring process is designed to provoke as little anxiety as possible and support candidates' success. Workplace characteristics that other employers consider accommodations, such as wheelchair access, exist by design.

Management principles are focused on supporting emotional well-being. As a result, employees' souls feel healed. And by all objective measures, they deliver outstanding performance.[48]

 DEEP DIVE

TRANSPARENCY AND CLEAR COMMUNICATION

The lack of clear communication in the workplace often excludes neurodivergent people. Class migrants and immigrants are also particularly disadvantaged by insider politics governed by secret handshakes. Transparency, in contrast, supports psychological safety, trust, and organizational performance. In addition, it can help restore trust eroded by previous injustices and nurture a sense of belonging.[31]

Making transparency universal can also support organizational outcomes. Suppose the innovation proposal process needs to be adapted for autistic employees because it's a Byzantine maze of contradictions and unspoken assumptions. In that case, that process likely stifles the innovation of all employees. A more transparent process will help both employees and the organization thrive.[32]

 EMPLOYER EXCELLENCE

ULTRANAUTS

Ultranauts, a US-based software company with a 75 percent neurodivergent workforce, was designed to be flexible, focused on well-being, and founded on principles of transparency and collaboration. It invites the active involvement of neurodivergent employees in designing systems that work for them, making the company both resilient and successful.

For example, the promotion criteria and the application process are made clear to every employee. The process is also transparently implemented, minimizing the potential for bias and favoritism. As another mechanism for ensuring transparency, Ultranauts also posts minutes of all weekly management meetings. The public management dashboard makes company performance indicators and priorities visible to all team members. A company-wide culture of learning encourages knowledge sharing and collaboration across different areas.[49,50]

DEEP DIVE

VALID TOOLS FOR DECISION MAKING

Selection and promotion practices based on a subjectively defined "fit" often exclude neurodivergent and marginalized talent and limit organizational talent pools.[3,51] For instance, research shows that hiring agents reject even exceptionally qualified autistic applicants. This happens partly because selection processes allow subjectivity and bias to influence hiring decisions.[52]

Another common problem is using selection instruments that may appear objective but are not relevant to the job. Unnecessary written tests can limit employment opportunities for dyslexic people and second-language job seekers: both groups would benefit from valid selection practices that can support inclusion and ensure that organizational decision making is backed by work-related and valid measurements.

Valid decision-making instruments are based on a thorough job analysis and require ensuring inclusivity during the job analysis process itself. They should incorporate an understanding of how the same job might be done and experienced differently by people from different groups.[53]

 EMPLOYER EXCELLENCE

DELL

Traditional job interviews are meant to assess the employee's potential to do the job. Unfortunately, they often assess the mastery of small talk, charisma, and the similarity with the interviewer. Not great for expanding diversity and often exclusionary for autistic candidates.

Dell's neurodiversity program designed skills-focused interviews with questions provided in advance to help give the interviewee control of the conversation. Projects and portfolios are used to demonstrate candidates' performance. When not pelted with vague questions like "Tell me about yourself" and "What fruit would you be," autistic people can showcase their skills relevant to the job.[54] A more accurate measurement of the candidate's ability benefits neurodivergent candidates and allows Dell to hire the right talent.

POINTS OF PRACTICE

KEY DO'S (AND DON'TS) OF NEUROINCLUSION

The key ingredients in the success of organizations in all my examples are pushing the boundaries of inclusion beyond what others consider possible and even breaking those boundaries. There are many ways, however, to welcome neurodivergent talent and create organizations where all can thrive.

Many organizations start small with one or two neurodivergent hires in particularly welcoming departments, evaluate their experiences, and then expand. In addition to Deloitte and Dell, successful neurodiversity hiring programs exist in SAP, JPMorgan, Microsoft, and many other major companies. Alternatively, others create fully neurodiversity-friendly companies like Ultranauts, disability-friendly companies like Call Yachol, or holistically flexible companies like Legalite. This comprehensive approach expands inclusion by developing organizational processes that work for people from different backgrounds and with various talents and struggles.

My passion is creating fully inclusive and integrated organizations where neurodivergent and neurotypical people expertly cocreate and collaborate on all levels of the organization. The fundamental principles of the Canary Code extend what works for neuroinclusion to supporting holistic belonging for all. Going beyond sequential inclusion is challenging at first, but it will save much effort and frustration in the long run. Here are some key principles of this work, which reflect the advice I typically give to organizations:[55]

1. **Don't just design a neurodivergent-friendly (or any other group-friendly) hiring system. Design a valid one.** It should be based on thorough job analysis and selection methods aligned with core job responsibilities. Everyone who may face bias in hiring will benefit, as will organizational performance.

2. **Don't just design a neuroinclusive workplace. Design a flexible one.** Most employees will benefit from and support this work.

3. **Don't just design a neurodivergent-friendly communication system. Design a transparent one.** First-generation college students, veterans, and refugees pulling themselves up by the bootstraps will thank you.

4. **Don't just design a neurodivergent-friendly work culture. Design a trauma-informed one.** Those with depression, anxiety, or PTSD might need this safe environment the most, and autistic people are more likely

to be targeted by bullying. Still, we all need supportive environments to be our most productive, creative selves.

5. **Don't just design a neurodivergent-friendly organization. Design a human-centric and a talent-friendly one.** When Karen Blacher designed an autism-friendly classroom for all, all students thrived. At Ultranauts, a full range of employees and the business itself thrive.

6. **Don't try to make people "fit" by assimilating and suppressing their individuality.** Hire for values-fit and celebrate culture-add and personality-add.

7. **And finally, don't just design a neurodiversity hiring program because you've read about "amazing dyslexic thinking" or "amazing autistic productivity."** These characteristics only apply to a segment of the population, but all humans should have an opportunity to maximize their potential—without being expected to do the work of two people. The business case is important, but human dignity is essential.

POINTS OF PRACTICE

INTERSECTIONAL INCLUSION: RADICALLY PRACTICAL TOOL FOR INCLUSION PROFESSIONALS

The work of diversity professionals and advocates can be frustrating. It is hard to get support. The progress is slow, and sometimes gains are lost. It is difficult to score "wins" that would inspire others to keep going.

The Canary Code approach can help reduce these frustrations. It can help diversity professionals create earlier and more lasting "wins" for systemic inclusion.

As a result, the comprehensive, intersectional approach to inclusion is not just radical but also practical.

Here are a few steps for assessing how the Canary Code approach can help in our work:

1. **Reevaluate Your Past and Current Strategies:** Like any change, the Canary Code framework should be implemented based on accurate data and careful reflection. What are your inclusion pain points? Is it perhaps a difficulty in retaining new hires? Diversity fatigue and cynicism? Have abandoned initiatives left people bitter? I often encounter this problem in my practice: gender-focused, veterans-focused, and other initiatives that

are abandoned because of personnel turnover, changing priorities, or a loss of funding are remembered for a long time, leaving people cynical about all organizational inclusion initiatives.

Your organization might have launched numerous initiatives with the best intentions. And even if they did not go as planned, there are lessons to be learned. What could have been more effective in supporting the diversity of talent? What could have made the change effort more effective? And what pains do people across the organization express in focus groups or surveys *now*? Can you help address these pains using the Canary Code principles? Perhaps people across the organization are craving more flexibility or transparency—if so, you have a ready-made support coalition.

2. **Recognize the Derailers:** The typical inclusion work challenges are fear, fragmentation, and fatigue.[32] By acknowledging these pitfalls head-on, you position yourself to craft effective solutions.

   - **Fear** of the unknown and the fear of making mistakes may lead to postponing the seemingly "complex" disability and neurodiversity inclusion or intersectional approaches. However, tackling a *complex* problem might be the radical solution for *multiple* connected problems.

   - **Fragmentation** of diversity and inclusion work stems from separate, often reactive, and compliance-driven programs that are focused on specific dimensions of diversity. Reactive programs leave people disappointed, especially when the next reactive program comes along. For some, fragmentation leads to the sense of "my time will never come." Worse yet, fragmented efforts may result in cynicism toward diversity work in general, along with diversity fatigue.

   - **Fatigue** can be specific to diversity programs, especially when they are stop-and-go, a reflection of the more general organizational change fatigue, or an expression of individual exhaustion and burnout. Multiple sources of fatigue combine to make people more self-protective and less compassionate. This makes it particularly important to tackle challenges by working smarter, not harder.

3. **Make a Plan for Working Smarter.**

   - **Holistic Integration:** Integrating the Canary Code principles across all talent processes—from recruitment to leadership development—ensures that inclusive practices become an organic part of operations, not an add-on that could be easily taken away. You could address each topic in order, from recruitment and hiring to leadership development, as reflected in the order of this book. However, if institutional data show a major pain point—such as the lack of flexibility in work organization, pay disparities, or the Byzantine promotion system—it could make sense to tackle this area first.

- **Focus on Functions within the Talent Cycle,** not just on specific groups. This strategy has several significant advantages. Addressing the needs of all who can benefit from increasing flexibility, or ensuring transparency in promotion systems, can create a strong support for effecting change. This, in turn, makes an early win more likely.[56] And early wins create more support and decrease cynicism.
- **Repurpose Existing Tools:** Don't reinvent the wheel unless you have to. Sometimes, organizational hiring practices or leadership development systems are so biased it is necessary to build from scratch. In other cases, existing and familiar frameworks can be adapted to reinforce inclusion principles, making the shift both intuitive and efficient. For example, I have seen great success with integrating new questions into existing employee surveys, rather than creating additional ones. I love designing surveys, but that does not always make sense. Likewise, if your onboarding programs are relatively robust, integrating additional flexibility to accommodate neurodivergence and introducing neurodiversity topics might be an efficient way to score a valuable win. Here is another tip: working with your organization's stated values might be an effective way to craft your communication.

The following chapters focus on removing barriers at all stages of the talent cycle, from recruitment and staffing to leadership development. Making organizations neuroinclusive is about creating barrier-free environments to improve people's work lives, period.

 KEY TAKEAWAYS

- *Organizations that exemplify key principles of the Canary Code— participation, focusing on outcomes, flexibility, organizational justice, transparency, and the use of valid tools in decision making—push inclusion boundaries in ways previously thought impossible.*
- *Neuroinclusion principles help all employees thrive and support organizational outcomes.*
- *Organizations can start implementing neuroinclusion in many ways, from baby steps to system-wide.*

- *Companies such as Call Yachol, Legalite, and Ultranauts illustrate the win-win nature of systemic intersectional inclusion and the consideration of different employee needs for individuals and organizations.*
- *Using the Canary Code approach may also help develop broader support for inclusive practices and systemic change.*

 ## DEVELOPMENTAL QUESTIONS

- Have you experienced organizational or social change that was developed to support one group of people but ended up serving the interests of people from many other groups? How could this experience inform other changes you may want to see introduced?
- What type of neuroinclusive change might be particularly welcomed by most people in your organization (or perhaps your/your child's school, gym, neighborhood, and so on)?
- Which example of an inclusive company discussed in the chapter (Dell, Deloitte, Call Yachol, Legalite, Infinite Fusion, or Ultranauts) particularly resonated with you? Which lessons could you learn from their practices? How could these lessons transfer into your life/work?
- If you are involved in inclusion work professionally or as an advocate, which principles or suggestions from this chapter could help you work more efficiently and overcome obstacles more effectively?

REMOVING BARRIERS TO EMPLOYMENT ACCESS

THE HIRING PROCESS

On Bias, Barriers, and Doing Better

The candidate is not the Enemy.

—Gil Winch

 NEURODIVERSITY NARRATIVES

GUT FEELINGS AND GATEKEEPING

Sometimes, recruiters feel heartbroken for applicants.

After her "first career" in marketing with Virgin and Sony and learning the ins and outs of corporate life, Caroline Stokes, a UK native living in Canada, pivoted into her "second career" as an external headhunter and recruitment consultant—and did that work on a global scale for more than a decade. For much of that time, neurodiversity in the workplace was just emerging as a significant area of interest, and Caroline had yet to discover her own ADHD. When searching for and helping select talent for her mostly neurotypical clients, she detected a clear pattern that she suspected had been present during her corporate marketing years: decision makers liked hiring people like them. Often, they even physically looked alike. Many times, she observed either an uncanny facial resemblance, political resemblance, or mindset resemblance between the hiring manager and the new recruit.

She also observed people who demonstrated genius-level intelligence, responsible attitudes, and work ethics and performance outcomes being rejected with the classic "we don't think they'll be a fit." Some managers assumed that a candidate different from them might be "difficult," "awkward," or unable to "influence." Others speculated that a candidate would turn out to be "not a team player" or "troublesome" or would not "tow the company line." Many hiring managers would make such assumptions during behavioral interviews; some went as far as seeking informal references from other similar-to-them people who knew the candidate—without approval by the candidate.

Even before Caroline became interested in neuroinclusion, she was troubled by those search outcomes. She could see the talent of rejected candidates. She was heartbroken for them and the fact that organizations weren't adapting fast enough to bring in people of all backgrounds to create products, services, and solutions that would make a difference to a broader humanity.

When Caroline discovered her own neurodivergence and the neurodiversity movement, she better understood why someone "similar to me" may seem like the best possible hire in the world of risk avoidance. And why, in the long term, the lack of diverse perspectives is a true threat to organizational survival.[1]

 DEEP DIVE

EVERYBODY LIES?

Hiring is a form of matchmaking. We even use the language of "applicant attraction" and "making yourself an attractive candidate." But matchmaking only works if both parties are honest and know what is actually important to them—and in hiring, that rarely seems to be the case.

Most organizations seek "collaborative, optimistic, and ambitious go-getters" while promising a "people-first environment with the potential for advancement." Yet these same organizations often try to trip up and stress out applicants to catch them in a lie. Expert liars, however, are unlikely to be tripped or stressed out in response to these interviewer tactics; it is honest people who are much more likely to become stressed or flustered when an interviewer is attempting to unnerve them. Neurodivergent people are particularly vulnerable to being labeled as liars while telling the truth and to be disproportionately negatively affected by such tactics.[2,3]

Potential applicants do not trust organizations either.[4,5] Both neurotypical and neurodivergent job seekers are increasingly wary of organizational promises and scour online employer review sites for the real scoop on what's going on. Meanwhile, organizations might be posting fake positive reviews.[6]

No wonder organizational divorce rates are so high. According to some reports, more than 80 percent of new hires fail.[7]

There are many signs that something is very wrong with organizational matchmaking. Instead of true matches, organizations end up with false positives (hires who don't live up to expectations) and false negatives (rejecting talented people who would have been outstanding).[8] Both errors have financial, morale, and ethical costs. A wrong hire costs *at least* 30 percent of the hire's annual salary in the form of lost productivity, potential need to rehire, and other expenses.[9,42] Often, the cost is much higher, as occurs when a poor management hire hurts the retention and morale of the most productive and committed employees or damages the organizational reputation.

For applicants, selecting the wrong employer based on false promises or the façade of inclusion can have devastating career, financial, and health consequences. Experiencing xenophobic hate in an organization presenting as globally inclusive (true story) and neuroexclusion toward employees in an organization claiming to be neurodiversity-serving (also a true story) is particularly injurious.

Human and organizational costs of "everybody lies" hiring are enormous, and the ethical imperative for honest hiring is compelling. So is the economic imperative. The Canary Code principles of transparency, focus on outcomes, and valid measurement are crucial in creating hiring systems that work for both employees and employers.

 DEEP DIVE

STYLE AND SUBSTANCE: HIRING PRACTICES AND NEURODIVERSITY ACCESS BARRIERS

Current hiring practices often rely on style over substance.[10,11] Style-based hiring presents barriers for many neurodivergent job seekers and leads to shockingly high levels of unemployment. The need to improve employment opportunities has given rise to specialized recruiting agencies, such as Specialisterne, that help connect organizations with autistic and, more recently, other neurodivergent talent.

However, to make a substantial difference in unemployment rates, recruitment practices in all organizations need to become more inclusive of neurodivergent and other marginalized job seekers.

Inclusive recruitment to attract neurodivergent applicants is one of the first steps toward creating neuroinclusive organizations. It typically involves de-biasing job descriptions and ensuring fair and equitable talent search strategies. The next steps require de-biased screening and selection. Of course, recruiters always must truthfully represent the state of inclusive practices in the organization.

POINTS OF PRACTICE

APPLICANT ATTRACTION: DE-BIASING JOB DESCRIPTIONS

Exclusion starts long before the selection process: it begins with job descriptions and position announcements. Making the content of job descriptions inclusive is crucially important for attracting and hiring neurodivergent job seekers.

Unfortunately, job descriptions are often based on generic templates and may include skills or personal characteristics of little or no relevance to specific positions. Another common problem is centering job descriptions on preferred workstyles or personality buzzwords—for example, "collaborative yet competitive high-energy activator"—rather than essential outcomes.

Research demonstrates that carelessly developed job descriptions are detrimental to hiring autistic talent.[12,13] The requirements included, regardless of job analysis, are usually neuronormative social expectations and personality characteristics, such as being outgoing. This practice is likely to do the following:

1. Discourage neurodivergent job seekers from applying to positions even though they are highly qualified to perform all core tasks of the job.
2. Be used to justify hiring procedures that lack validity and adversely affect neurodivergent populations; for example, using high-stress, large-panel interviews for positions that require focused data analysis and minimal social interaction.

To improve job descriptions and overall job design, organizations should follow established best practices:

1. Conduct a thorough job analysis to ensure that the job description accurately reflects the position's requirements. The job analysis itself must be examined to ensure inclusivity. It should account for the fact that employees from different demographic groups may experience the same job differently[14] and that employees with different abilities can perform the same job in dissimilar but equally effective ways.[15] Neuroinclusive job analysis, similar to the disability-inclusive approach to job analysis, considers essential functions while being focused on outcomes rather than methods.[15,16] Essential functions specify desired outcomes of employee actions, not the specifics of how each employee must achieve them. This

type of outcomes-focused job analysis can also help establish individual accommodations. If it is possible to achieve the same essential performance outcomes via different processes, limiting the ways in which outcomes can be achieved—via phone communication or via written communication; from the office or from home; sitting in a wheelchair, regular chair, or standing; using voice-to-text or text-to-voice—is likely to be unnecessary. As long as actions are safe and legal, it is reasonable to allow people to achieve outcomes in the way that is most efficient for them.

2. Clearly separate required qualifications essential for performing the job— the key skills—from desirable qualifications such as specific experiences: previous jobs or internships are just some of the ways to develop such skills. Focus on minimal core qualifications and clearly indicate that desirable qualifications are just that—desirable. This will help avoid discouraging qualified candidates from marginalized groups,[17] including neurodivergent candidates,[18] from applying.

3. Evaluate job descriptions for unnecessary, generic, and cut-and-paste requirements. Some organizations use job descriptions with very general skill requirements that can apply to multiple settings, such as "strong communication skills." Ask whether the position truly calls for outstanding communication skills. And if it does, what type of skills? Be specific: "can effectively present technical information in a written and visual format in quarterly reports" is not the same as doing "engaging public speaking to community organizations 2–3 times per week." Catch-all descriptions can make some neurodivergent people apprehensive about applying for a position. Employers should clarify whether qualifications or tasks are essential to accomplishing the job. Simply omitting nonessential qualifications and tasks may be even better.

4. Avoid references to personality or possible neurodivergent and mental health differences. Does your technical writer really need to be "dynamic" or "upbeat"? Does it mean that a person with dysthymia (a chronic low-grade depression) or anxiety, coupled with world-class writing skills that are unaffected or even sharpened by a somewhat gloomy mood, should not apply? As another example, do your quality control specialist and AI ethicist really need to be "fun" and "optimistic"?

5. Avoid biased language like the ageist "digital native" and masculine-coded "hard-charging." With neurodivergent candidates, consider what you actually mean by "resilient" and "adaptable" and whether you need those qualities. If it means "able to work with an abusive manager," perhaps selecting

employees for "resilience" is not the right solution. Resist including the likes of "thrives in a bustling and energetic environment." If your office is overcrowded and frenetic, don't try to make it sound positive. This phrase may be in the job description just because someone saw it in other job announcements, but it will be a turnoff for many candidates.

6. Avoid asking for anything that is not indeed required but may limit the applicant pool. For example, do not ask for a driver's license when you only need proof of identity. Some people do not drive but are still perfectly qualified to do the job.

In addition, neuroinclusive job advertisements must use plain language, avoid jargon, and provide clear and precise information about the job content. These same characteristics will support job seekers from other marginalized groups, such as people from underrepresented or underestimated cultural and socioeconomic backgrounds, and are likely to be appreciated by all applicants.

 DEEP DIVE

APPLICANT ATTRACTION: INCLUSION STATEMENTS

Many modern position announcements have inclusion statements that range from detailed lists of specific groups and reasons for inclusion to single-line nondiscrimination statements. If a company specifies welcomed demographic categories but does not include neurodiversity, neurodivergent applicants may not apply. Because most organizations traditionally excluded neurodivergent employees, clarifying whether your organization is neuroinclusive might be helpful.

Alternatively, organizations may simply indicate their commitment to fair and inclusive treatment of all applicants and employees.

Organizations also often specify the reasons underlying their commitment to inclusion directly in position announcements or on their websites. Research suggests that specifying the business case backfires and results in lower attraction to organizations among applicants to whom it is applied.[19] It communicates an instrumental, commodifying view of marginalized employees. Using the fairness-based explanation reduces such concerns. However, the best applicant reaction is achieved when organizations simply state that they value diversity without trying to explain or justify it. There is no need to justify fairness.

POINTS OF PRACTICE

APPLICANT ATTRACTION: TARGETED RECRUITMENT

Where and how jobs are advertised matter for all types of diversity—ethnic, class, cultural, or neurodiversity. For example, recruiting from local community colleges, Ivy League universities, and historically Black colleges and universities (HBCUs) will result in different demographic profiles of applicants. Organizations aiming to appeal to neurodivergent candidates also often use targeted recruitment strategies.

There are an increasing number of options for employers interested in recruiting neurodivergent talent. *Immediate recruiting approaches* include advertising in media serving specific ethnic, neurodiversity, or disability communities.[20] Specialized organizations such as Specialisterne or Disability:IN reach many neurodivergent groups. Not-for-profit organizations like the Colorado Neurodiversity Chamber of Commerce and TACT (Teaching the Autism Community Trades) help neurodivergent youth with job preparation and internships and partner with a wide range of employers. Additionally, national and regional services in many countries support workplace transitions of neurodivergent workers who are also considered disabled. In the US, vocational rehabilitation (VR) agencies in each state facilitate employee matching and support services to help neurodivergent people transition into the position successfully. Access to Work programs in the UK can provide preemployment and employment support.

Campus recruiting can be extended to schools focused on serving neurodivergent students, such as Beacon College and Landmark College in the US, and to many other colleges and universities that offer neurodiversity-focused programs.

Another option, the *long-term talent pipeline strategy*, requires forming relationships with colleges and community organizations to support the pipeline of employees by providing internships, apprenticeships, and other educational programs. Such programs can introduce people from underserved populations to career options they otherwise would not have considered.

POINTS OF PRACTICE

APPLICANT ATTRACTION: NAVIGATING THE APPLICATION PROCESS

To ensure neuroinclusion, organizations should carefully evaluate whether their application process is user-friendly. How many clicks does it take to navigate to

position announcements on your website? Is the process unnecessarily complicated? Are there distracting video pop-ups and dizzying moving pictures? Do
transcripts accompany welcome videos? Are your fonts and colors dyslexia-
friendly? In addition to following the standard accessibility guidelines, it is
helpful to invite members of various disabled and neurodivergent communities
to evaluate how inclusive your HR webpages are.

Many job applicants complain about the burden of entering information that
is already in their resume into long, clunky online application forms that tend
to freeze, log applicants out, and not save the data. Multiply that by the number of applications job seekers need to submit, and many disabled and neurodivergent people will be eliminated because the process will drain all their available
"spoons" of energy and keep demanding more. Companies that accept applications in user-friendly ways, such as by pulling information from the resume without the need to retype it, are much more disability and neurodiversity inclusive.

 DEEP DIVE

APPLICANT SCREENING: BEWARE OF BIASES

In most organizations, receipt of the candidate's application signifies the move
to the next stage of the hiring process: candidate screening. Screening typically
refers to the initial round of "selecting out" applicants who are the least qualified
or not qualified. Traditionally, it was accomplished based on resume review.
Now organizations increasingly rely on automated systems to perform the screening. Regardless of the specific screening approach, checking for biases—human
or algorithmic—is essential.

 DEEP DIVE

APPLICANT SCREENING: CREDENTIAL AND RESUME REVIEWS

On the surface, job experience and educational requirements may appear unbiased. However, people from marginalized groups with high unemployment rates
may become locked in the cycle of a lack of formal job experience and of opportunities to obtain such experience.[21,22,23] Moreover, although education may
serve as a proxy for skills, directly measuring skills relevant to the job is the most
valid approach to ensuring that applicants indeed have the skills.

Autism employment programs in companies such as IBM and many others show that hiring based on skills, rather than credentials, allows organizations to bring in extraordinary talent.[21] Organizations committed to closing neurodiversity employment gaps can also help develop talent by creating positions that provide training or time-limited paid internships leading to jobs. This can both increase the candidate pool and help ameliorate the lack of job opportunities for stigmatized talent.[21,22,24]

Credential and resume reviews are not the most valid predictors of job performance. According to Eric Sydell, PhD, executive vice president for innovation at Modern Hire, several decades of research into how candidate assessments do (and do not) predict new hire job success indicate that the "conventional wisdom" of hiring is deeply flawed.[25] Simplistic notions of what makes an employee successful are often incorrect. It seems *"obvious,"* for example, that *"the more experience a person has doing a certain job, the better they'll be able to do it for a new company. But this is often not the case—people get burned out and set in the ways of the old company, and are often less likely to succeed in a new environment doing the same basic job. Skills and capabilities transfer, but the amount of time spent doing them often does not."*

 DEEPER DIVE

APPLICANT SCREENING: AUTOMATED SYSTEMS

The automated screening process is frequently met with applicant suspicion. In many cases, the process is indeed fraught with bias.[26,27] As one example, there is now a proliferation of advice on outsmarting ageist bias, which appears to be built into many automated applicant screening systems, by removing or condensing information on earlier experience and education.[28,29]

But what about neuroexclusion? Most basic automated screening systems often replicate the same biases as manual resume screening. However, expanded versions of automated screening may include additional barriers. Systems that have built-in assessments, such as personality testing, are rarely validated for neurodivergent candidates.[30] These assessments may also not sufficiently correspond to the specific position.

In evaluating automated screening, let's consider Temple Grandin, the famous autistic author and professor. For much of her early career, she used portfolios of her work to impress hiring managers and sidestep the likely discrimination based on her autistic differences.[31] But at that time, Temple Grandin was not dealing with automated screening systems and could show her drawings and photos of completed projects to hiring managers. Would she have made it through and been able to show her portfolio in today's world? Or would she have been automatically screened out?

Most automated systems are trained on data that historically predicted employee success. But data-based is not the same as fair: data quality and the way it was collected matter. Because of the long-term exclusion, current applicant screening systems are **not trained** on neurodivergent employee data. They are also **not trained** on data that would apply to neuroinclusive environments.

The long-standing exclusion in what data are used to predict success presents a fairness concern that may take a long time to address. A cycle of exclusion that keeps neurodivergent people out of work may contribute to a lack of information on whether existing screening and selection procedures are valid— can accurately predict their success in the workplace. In turn, the lack of validated screening approaches may perpetuate the cycle of unemployment.

Here's an example of using typically available data to train automated systems. Imagine that we are predicting the success of individuals in doing cooking tasks. We give them all an opportunity to cook in a kitchen and measure their speed and accuracy in the food prep. Sounds fair, right?

On further examination, let's say the kitchen is built for people who are around 5½ feet (168 cm) tall with no disabilities. We use that same kitchen to test the success of everyone: average-height people, those who are 4 feet tall, those who are 7 feet tall, and wheelchair users. Although the people who do not "fit" the kitchen show incredible ingenuity to accomplish their task, their success requires extra time and effort. Very few pass the test and are hired. Even fewer become master chefs. Over time, we have enough data to justify that being 5½ feet tall is a valid predictor of an aspiring chef's success. Which it is—*but only because the kitchen is built for these people.*

Should we continue hiring 5½-feet-tall chefs, allowing the automated screening to exclude applicants who don't meet the height requirement because it is technically "predictive?" Or should we make kitchens more flexible and accessible and avoid automatically screening out a wider pool of applicants?

By the same logic, what makes more sense: Should organizations continue to exclude neurodivergent people based on the data that come from exclusionary environments? Or should we make organizations neuroinclusive and collect better data?

DEEP DIVE

APPLICANT SELECTION

In many hiring systems, there is a distinction between "screening out" a large number of applicants and "selecting in" from the smaller pool after the screening.[32] This stage of the process can be experienced as both more competitive and more personal than screening. Because of its both personal and high-stakes nature, the selection process can be particularly anxiety-provoking for all. However, this anxiety can be higher for marginalized candidates, including neurodivergent applicants, because they may feel the pressure of bias and the burden of prior rejections. For neurodivergent applicants, the pressure placed on them by unemployment statistics can also be intense.[30,33]

 DEEPER DIVE

APPLICANT SELECTION: INTERVIEWS

Many people outside HR use the word "interview" interchangeably with "hiring" or "selection process." This illustrates just how ubiquitous interviews are in the workplace. An interview, however, is just one tool of the selection process, and technically, it is not even necessary. It is possible to hire, for example, based on test scores, work samples, or portfolios of work—without the interview. In fact, the unstructured interview that has no formal question set or scoring is one of the least valid selection tools. However, many people—like Caroline Stokes's clients in the opening example in this chapter—believe in their power of intuition to choose the "right" candidate via an interview.[10,34]

Unfortunately for many job seekers, interviews have become tools of exclusion and social disablement. These effects are particularly drastic for autistic job seekers.[30]

Many autistic individuals have high levels of educational attainment and skills and are more than capable of performing the work.[35,36,37] However, few excel at making small talk with strangers. For many jobs—algorithmic bias auditing, writing, programming, or precision manufacturing, just to name a few—small talk is in no way essential. However, being hired for most of these jobs still requires an interview. Neuronormative small talk expectations in the interview subject autistic applicants to "style over substance" negative judgments made by evaluators quickly and largely outside their awareness that are then justified by the "poor fit" statement.[37,38]

In effect, interviews in their current form "disable" autistic people and prevent them from entering jobs for which they are fully qualified: they become the "false negatives" of the interview-focused selection process. The traditional interview also has a significant potential for leading to "false-positive" decisions. Because many interviewers are attracted to charisma and confidence, they often decide in favor of dangerously overconfident yet incompetent individuals.[11]

Those who are not overconfident are often hampered in their interview performance by anxiety, which is extremely common: 92 percent of all people report having interview anxiety. Traditional job interviews are really stress tests, which means they are not neuroinclusive because many neurodivergent people are more susceptible to stress and its effects on executive function.[30,39,40] And because most people are not interviewing to be secret agents, interviews are not representative of their actual job responsibilities.

When I mention to hiring managers that stress test interviews are unnecessary, I often hear some variation of the line, "That's how we got our jobs; people just need to toughen up." But just because the stress interview and other forms of organizational hazing have "always been there" (and I've been around long enough to have been through a good deal of that) does not mean we can't do better.

We can eliminate interviews and rely on skills tests instead. Or we can reimagine the interview the way Gil Winch did.

 EMPLOYER EXCELLENCE

CALL YACHOL: THE CANDIDATE IS NOT THE ENEMY

Gil Winch started his company, Call Yachol, with the ambitious goal to hire disabled people and other marginalized workers. He completely redesigned the interview experience and called it reverse screening. It is a two-way chat in a comfortable place resembling a living room. Why? Because *"the candidate is not the enemy."*[41] If organizations want to create workplaces where people can flourish, why not start at the initial screening stage?

The reverse screening does not include tricky questions. On the contrary, it includes questions and examples tied to the candidates' daily experiences. The goal is to determine not whether the candidate will fit with the organization's way of training and managing but how training and management can be adapted to the candidate's needs. The focus is not on the immediate "hit the ground running" performance but on the potential to learn over time. To address interview anxiety, the company allows applicants to come with companions and pets and have interview do-overs. Since Call Yachol was founded in 2008, these practices have helped many people obtain a much-needed opportunity; in turn, these people have helped the company thrive.

Many other companies have tried modifying interviews for neurodivergent people by providing questions in advance and making the situation as comfortable as possible. Others have done away with interviews altogether. The latter approach is well aligned with the trend toward skills-based hiring.

 POINTS OF PRACTICE

APPLICANT SELECTION: SKILL ASSESSMENT

There are many systems of skills assessments in neurodiversity hiring. Some organizations use workshop-type experiences that last several days or even two to three weeks where candidates complete actual work projects. Although generally effective as assessments, these workshops limit participation to candidates who can afford the lengthy and typically unpaid process.

A potentially more promising approach is the minimally viable demonstrations of competence (MVDC) approach that focuses on assessing essential job-related skills through simple and brief tests designed to evaluate a candidate's performance in core job functions.[42] By using MVDC, hiring managers can better understand candidates' potential to succeed in a specific role, regardless of their background or previous work experience.

Although this approach is designed for general use, MVDC can be especially beneficial in neuroinclusive hiring. As noted, traditional hiring processes, such as interviews and personality tests, might not accurately assess the abilities of neurodivergent candidates. These methods can also introduce bias or discrimination based on other characteristics, such as race, gender, or national origin. By focusing on the core competencies required for the job, MVDC and other skills-based methods offer a more equitable and inclusive approach to hiring.

Here are some ways to apply MVDC to neuroinclusive hiring:

1. Train hiring managers and HR professionals: Educate hiring managers and HR staff on neurodiversity and how to adapt the recruitment process to be more inclusive. Encourage them to look beyond traditional qualifications and to focus on the essential skills required for the job.

2. Customized assessments: Design minimally viable demonstrations relevant to the job.

3. Accessible assessments: Consider the unique needs and abilities of neurodivergent candidates. Ensure that the assessments are accessible and provide reasonable accommodations if needed.

4. Use scenario planning and AI-enabled VR tools: For roles that require physical movement or adaptability, technology can increasingly simulate real-life situations.[42] This allows you to observe how candidates respond to various challenges without putting them in actual high-stakes scenarios. However, make sure to adjust for accessibility and check proposed tools for validity and possible bias.

5. Monitor and improve the process: Continuously assess the effectiveness of the MVDC approach in your organization. Solicit feedback from candidates and employees, and make adjustments as needed to ensure the process remains inclusive, fair, and effective.

As automated skill assessments become more valid, sophisticated, and equitably accessible with proper disability and neuroinclusion safeguards, it might make sense to increasingly rely on them as a screening tool earlier in the hiring process, rather than as a selection tool. However, even the most ardent proponents of assessments agree that a follow-up discussion that debriefs the exercise can be a powerful tool for finding highly qualified candidates that AI tools might have passed over.[42]

Overall, using multiple and different evaluation methods (rather than multiple interviews) can create a more comprehensive understanding of each candidate's potential. It can also be a more inclusive practice if those struggling with interviews could compensate with their performance on skills tests—and vice versa. Of course, assessments must always be job-related and not excessive. The next section provides more insight into using multiple assessments.

 DEEP DIVE

HOLISTIC HIRING FOR SPIKY PROFILES

Selection systems can generally be divided into *compensatory systems* (those in which the candidate can make up for a low score in one category with a high score in another category) and *noncompensatory/multiple cutoff systems* (those in which a person cannot compensate for a lower speed with higher accuracy or for a lower math score with a higher writing score).

A small number of jobs require hard, noncompensatory cutoffs. For example, an applicant for a school bus driver position should not be able to compensate for below cutoff driving skills with a pleasant personality. A pleasant personality is highly desirable, but driving skills are not negotiable. Most work and life tasks, however, are quite compensatory.

Eric Sydell points out that we tend to overestimate the importance of isolated candidate characteristics. For example, *"We think a person who is generally quiet can't be a good salesperson. Or a person who is creative can't be a good manager of detail work. Or an individual who lacks some specific technical expertise can't rise to lead others who have it. But in believing these things, we overlook a fundamental aspect of being human, which is our ability to find a way."* We are much more than the sum of our parts, our additive scores on a personality test, or our list of skills. When we are interested in some outcome, we bring together the holistic totality of our being to achieve it. *"If an introvert wants to sell something, they will find a way to sell it. If a creative person realizes they need to manage a detailed project plan to bring their idea to life, they will immerse themselves in spreadsheets."*[25]

Human beings are holistic embodiments of learning, experience, and motivation. The hiring process should also be holistic. In the world of selection, this means creating compensatory systems in which lower scores in some category of skills and experiences can be compensated for by an outstanding score in another category. This aligns with Damian Milton's idea of the value of our spiky neurodivergent profiles and the different ways in which we can achieve and thrive.[43]

As Eric Sydell clarifies, *"Individual characteristics, such as conscientiousness, are often predictive of job success, but it is really the candidate's entire profile that matters most. This is why the assessments and simulations we have built focus on the whole person—a candidate can always compensate for a low score if they are motivated to do so."*[25]

 EMPLOYER EXCELLENCE

DEVELOPING AT DELOITTE

Most organizations with specialized neurodiversity hiring initiatives traditionally use a multiday skills assessment process. Sometimes, the process is even longer.

However, this excludes candidates who can't afford to go through such a process.[44] Deloitte used a participatory methodology of improving their approach to hiring: the company invited neurodivergent employees to help envision and codesign an improved process. For example, soon after David Martinez, an autistic and multiple neurodivergent data analyst, started his job at Deloitte, the company asked for his input on neurodiversity-focused hiring and onboarding. The process was streamlined according to David's and others' input. Not only that but David also took on a leadership role in facilitating the updated program.[45]

Workplaces need all kinds of minds,[31] and selection systems should be fair and valid for all kinds of minds. Often, making systems fair requires a commitment to continuous improvement and the participation of those the system has previously not served well, as demonstrated by Deloitte.

 DEEP DIVE

STRENGTH-BASED STAFFING

Traditional methods of hiring, focused on finding people who "fit" jobs, exclude some of the most marginalized job seekers. A more radical and effective way to provide opportunities to those who need them most while supporting organizational goals is *creating jobs that fit people*. Pioneering companies create such jobs in two ways: redesigning entire types of positions and individual-level job crafting.

1. Lemon Tree Hotels, a successful hotel chain in India, divided the standard job of a restaurant steward into two parts. The highly social and interactive set of tasks, which most typical stewards enjoyed, remained with employees ordinarily hired for such roles. The precision-demanding set of tasks such as setting tables, seen by typical stewards as tedious, became a separate job. Then, Lemon Tree developed a program of hiring people with Down Syndrome who enjoy setting tables and excel at this work. Many other jobs can be redesigned to fit specific patterns of strengths.

2. Legalite, an Australian law firm, helps employees craft portfolios of work aligned with their unique expertise rather than old-fashioned job descriptions. This is an excellent example of succeeding with job crafting—redesigning employee work to make it more personal and meaningful while also ensuring alignment with team and organizational goals.

Traditional approaches to staffing fall short of the goal of inclusion. Making work fit people is a practical way to create a future of work where both employees and organizations thrive.[46]

KEY TAKEAWAYS

- *Selection practices are rapidly evolving. On the one hand, there is a promise that AI will help eliminate human bias in selection. On the other hand, automated screening systems may instead multiply this bias.*
- *Technology and data are no guarantee of unbiased evaluations—especially for groups that had been excluded from the workplace to the extent that there is not enough data on their performance to train the AI.*
- *Most of the data we currently have predicts success in organizations that are not neuroinclusive, which limits the usefulness of that data.*
- *Some of the most promising instruments for creating neuroinclusive selection are mini-work samples and skills tests tailored to specific positions.*

DEVELOPMENTAL QUESTIONS

For employees/job seekers:
- Do you have a list of needs/best ways to support you in the hiring process that you could provide to a potential employer? If not, how can this chapter help you develop a few key suggestions?
- Interviewing is also an opportunity for you to ask questions. What questions can you ask to decide whether the employer is a good match? Design your top three questions and run them by a trusted person or a group.

For managers/direct supervisors:
- What is your approach to developing the list of requirements for job descriptions? Using what you learned from this chapter, how could you make job descriptions fairer to all applicants, as well as more neuroinclusive?
- Are the candidates likely to experience the hiring process in your unit as supportive and as a realistic preview of a positive work environment?
- How could you make the candidate experience more neuroinclusive?

For HR and upper management:

- How (neuro)inclusive is your hiring system? Using what you learned from this chapter, could you make it fairer to all applicants, as well as more neuroinclusive?
- Are the candidates likely to experience the hiring process in your organization as supportive and as a realistic preview of a positive work environment? Could it be improved?
- How could you make the candidate experience more neuroinclusive?
- What kind of training or support could help your recruiters and hiring managers create a more neuroinclusive candidate experience?

CHAPTER FIVE

STARTING OFF RIGHT

Onboarding, Training, Accommodations, and Compensation

Highly specialized work calls for highly specialized minds. For these programs to work, we need to understand that accommodations are not special favors.

—Temple Grandin

 HUMAN HAPPENINGS

SLEEPLESS AT THE INTERSECTION

If I were just autistic or just broke, I would have been fine. But I was both, so I was starting my new job sleep deprived.

I was finishing my dissertation and had just moved across the US for a full-time academic job. With the unexpected luxury of three offers in three states, I made sure to pick a fully walkable town as my new home.

I wish I could say I wanted to walk for health reasons, but in truth, I did not have a car or a driver's license. In grad school, I was able to get around by bus, despite the infrequent and sometimes unreliable service. My new town had no public transportation, but I thought I had it all planned out—walking should have worked.

What I did not know when making my move was that the academic year kickoff would be held out of town. In a kids' summer camp in the woods. Only accessible by car.

This was long before Uber, Lyft, and similar ridesharing services. And in any case, I only had $90 in the bank, which had to last until I got my first paycheck—in two weeks or so.

This was not good.

Another thing that was not good is that most of my summer camp experiences involved being bullied, getting sick, and leaving early. I am extremely sensitive to noise and the presence of strangers. And there was no way I would be able to sleep in a room with several new coworkers.

There was an option to stay in a town a few miles from the camp, but that required having money and a car, and I had neither.

Finding good colleagues to give the newbie a ride was not difficult. Getting the powers in charge to understand that I really, honestly, can't sleep in a room with strangers was a no-go. Admittedly, my self-advocacy was limited to a very meek inquiry. That was many years before I knew I was autistic or spoke the language of accommodations—and even if I did, I don't know if I would have brought it up in a new job.

At that time, I was still trying to fit in.

Except I did not fit. Or, rather, the experience did not fit me.

The event was clearly not designed for autistic people, but money could have provided a workaround. In fact, if I had the money for transportation and a motel room, I would have enjoyed the beautiful natural setting, as others did.

The event also was not designed for first-generation academics with tight budgets. But at least the sleeping arrangements would have been more manageable for a neurotypical.

Money can buffer some of the challenges of neurodivergence, and neurotypicality can make poverty a little less painful. Conversely, disadvantages stack up and beget more disadvantages. And this is why I started my new job sleep-deprived.

This is also why inclusion must be intersectional.

> This chapter provides recommendations for building a foundation for belonging at work through better onboarding and training—both for neurodivergent employees and their peers. It also addresses accommodations and compensation.

Onboarding is the process of integrating a new employee into an organization. It is much more than a new employee orientation. The onboarding process is often defined as the first 90 days of employment, but it can be much shorter if an organization defines it largely as task training. Yet, it can also last up to a year or longer, especially in organizations highly committed to culture-building.

The significance of onboarding and organizational socialization cannot be overstated. This critical period of the employment relationship shapes employees' enthusiasm and commitment to their role and is a foundation of future performance.

Early employee turnover can be a great challenge. Up to 20 percent of new hires may leave within the first 45 days, and about one-third of new employees do not make it past their first 90 days.[1,2,3] Reasons for this turnover include unmet job expectations, negative incidents, ineffective training, and a hostile or toxic company culture. Onboarding can present additional challenges for employees who come from different cultures, marginalized demographic groups, or stigmatized populations like disabled or neurodivergent employees. In contrast, an inclusively designed onboarding process can set the tone for a welcoming and fair environment and contribute to the process of continuous organizational improvement and nurturing a positive culture.

 POINTS OF PRACTICE

PREBOARDING

One way to improve onboarding is to design a quality *preboarding* (also known as pre-boarding or pre-onboarding) experience. Preboarding refers to the period between the job offer and the first day at work. It is often focused on filling out forms, which can allow onboarding to focus on the social and cultural experience.[4] However, to support the best possible employee transition—in particular, for neurodivergent employees—preboarding can be much more than a time to fill out forms. Here are a few ways in which leaders in organizations can enhance preboarding and support a smooth employee transition:

1. **Understand Individual Needs:** Engage in a dialogue to understand specific needs, strengths, and potential areas in which an employee may need extra support.
2. **Ease the Paperwork Burden:** Make the process as user-friendly and straightforward as possible. Ensure that forms are accessible. Electronic forms and signatures typically speed up the process, but organizations should offer alternatives and human support to those who may need it.
3. **Provide Clear Information:** Share detailed information about the workplace, expectations, culture, routines, and daily tasks. Include maps, pictures, or videos of the workspace to help people visualize the environment. Develop a welcome packet tailored to various learning styles with options for text, visual, or audio guides, and use step-by-step instructions.

4. **Mantain Ongoing Communication:** Stay in touch throughout the pre-boarding period, offering opportunities for new employees to ask questions, provide feedback, or express concerns.

5. **Offer a Mentor or Buddy System Early:** Pairing the new hire with a seasoned employee can provide a much-needed personal connection and an additional layer of support. Some managers or new colleagues voluntarily and informally take on this role. In other cases, a more formal assignment would serve the goal better, such as offering to connect an employee with someone from a relevant Employee Resource Group, if appropriate and if an employee expressed an interest in such an arrangement.

6. **Offer a "Preview" Option:** Offer an option to visit the workplace before the first day to meet colleagues and ask questions. This option might be invaluable to those who feel anxious or need some extra time to learn the physical "lay of the land."

7. **Provide Accommodations:** If an employee disclosed a need for accommodations, such as specialized equipment, a quiet workspace, or adjusted work hours, arranging these as early as possible can support a smooth transition.

8. **Develop a Support Network:** With employee consent, ensure that their team and immediate supervisors are prepared to welcome them in a way that aligns with their neurodivergent needs. For example, not everyone appreciates surprise parties, scavenger hunts, or re-creating childhood camp experiences.

By designing a thoughtful preboarding process, organizations can cultivate a supportive environment that is likely to translate into better retention and morale. Robust and flexible preboarding supports a culture of inclusion and a sense of belonging.

 POINTS OF PRACTICE

INTERSECTIONALLY INCLUSIVE TRAINING AND ONBOARDING

Foundational elements of a quality first-day experience, such as meeting a new employee and guiding them to a well-prepared workspace—or the virtual equivalent of a well-organized first-day orientation and technology kit—are the minimal courtesies that should be extended to all employees. Consideration and adjustments to the process based on various factors that may affect the employee experience, such as neurodivergence, disability, or socioeconomic background, make the process truly inclusive. One-size-fits-none is as applicable to onboarding as it is to all aspects of the employee experience.

For example, as organizations increasingly expect employees to bring their own technology, it is important to consider that this requirement could be a barrier to work for some of the most vulnerable populations. At the very least, provide an option of borrowing equipment for a transitional period. As eventful as my sleepless employee orientation had been, I was most grateful that I was provided a laptop—a standard university practice. Otherwise, I would not have been able to do my job.

Here are other examples of considerations for intersectional inclusion:

- Provide transportation assistance, carpooling options, or information about public transportation for those who might find commuting to be a financial, physical, or psychological challenge.
- Respect the diverse cultural backgrounds of your new hires by considering different customs, traditions, and communication styles in the onboarding process. For example, scheduling required events that conflict with religious holidays might be a major barrier for some employees. Requiring attendance at weekend and evening events can also be disproportionately taxing for neurodivergent and disabled employees.

Individual needs based on disability, caregiving, immigration, long-distance moves, and many other factors may influence an employee's transition, experience, and retention. Specific language needs such as translation are also important, including spoken language, sign language, or the use of communication devices. Not everyone is comfortable sharing their requests early in organizational entry, and the most disadvantaged might be the least likely to self-advocate.[5] Providing a menu of available support options to all employees might be particularly important to those dealing with multiple challenges.

 EMPLOYER EXCELLENCE

THE BBC

Harry Badger, an autistic aspiring journalist in the UK, loved his postgraduate journalism courses. Still, the messages presented by some guest speakers left him disheartened. They conveyed that, as someone shy and not particularly well connected, he probably would have little chance of success in the world of media. Harry felt that he was "doomed from the start."[6]

His training with the BBC as a part of the BBC Next Gen Scheme, in contrast, was most uplifting. He found journalists to be most welcoming and understanding of trainees' backgrounds, experiences, and skills/weaknesses. Everyone was supportive and reassuring, and their *"empathy and support for all of us didn't seem in any way to be for show; it came across as entirely authentic."*

Even though Harry did not reveal his autism diagnosis, his colleagues and mentors met him where he was, acknowledging his anxieties about learning new skills. They guided him toward mastering skills through hands-on training and learning exercises, providing patient instruction and constructive feedback. The effect of the training was far beyond learning new skills—the experience restored Harry's confidence that he could succeed as a journalist.

 POINTS OF PRACTICE

NEURODIVERSITY-AFFIRMING TRAINING

The key to training neurodivergent employees is to not make assumptions about the specific learning needs of individuals. Some neurodivergent people may not need any accommodations and will learn much faster than the typical employee.[7] Others may need more structured instruction, visually presented guidelines such as charts, or step-by-step directions—for some, these should be written and, for others, verbal. If training relies on instructional videos, it is crucial to provide a transcript and written quizzes because autistic people often find videos overstimulating and many others find reading more efficient.

Overall, inclusive organizational practices require that all training be offered in multiple modalities. Learning differences are common and should be considered in planning all training. Other common differences, such as introversion and extraversion, are associated with different optimal learning environments: settings and methods preferred by extroverts, such as long sessions of group-based learning in a packed and busy room, will leave introverts exhausted and overstimulated.[8] Providing training resources in multiple formats including discussion and reflection time, preventing sensory overload, and regularly assessing training effectiveness will help facilitate effective learning for all employees.

Another way to support inclusivity is to invite neurodivergent employees with different learning styles to participate in planning training and onboarding, as Deloitte did when revising its programs.[9] Adult learners, in general, benefit from taking an active part in determining their educational experiences.[10]

Even for those somewhat familiar with neurodivergence, it is easy to fall into the trap of overgeneralization and forget that there are tremendous differences even within specific neurodivergent populations. Labels such as ADHD provide very little information about an individual. Assumptions about lesser-known differences, such as nonverbal learning disability/difference (NVLD)—which involves motor, visual, or, in some cases, social difficulties but often no trouble with verbal communication—can be particularly misleading.[11]

 HUMAN HAPPENINGS

NAVIGATING NVLD

Anna L. tells her NVLD story:

Throughout my life I have been treated as if I had challenges that occur in more common neurotypes. . . .

I've been given visuals to learn things, or been left to learn by doing, when I need words to learn. This has confused me and made it harder to backtrack and learn processes after I learned the wrong way.

I've been assumed to have challenges with cognitive empathy despite actually having a skill in that area. This assumption, and having people who made this assumption frequently tell me I was not being empathetic enough, has left me to struggle with the feeling that I don't matter as much as all other people and put others first far too often, which has been harmful to me.[12]

Even Anna's therapist assumed that she would be nervous about crowds and socializing, while her concerns are with doing motor and physical tasks.

———

It is crucial to always ask how individuals process information and learn, and not rely on assumptions.

Here are a few best practices for onboarding all employees, although neurodivergent people particularly benefit from some of these:

1. **Do Not Make Assumptions.** This is the key to training neurodivergent employees. It's important to take time to understand the specific learning

styles of each individual and each one's unique patterns of abilities. Being aware of spiky ability profiles is a must. For example, a dyspraxic person can wow instructors by mastering complex concepts and arriving at creative solutions in record time and then puzzle them by struggling to learn how to operate basic (to others) machinery. Such struggles, without the awareness of spiky profiles, may lead to unfair accusations of laziness or bad attitude—"How come you can do X, but you cannot do Y?" Of course, different abilities, such as visual, motor, and analytical skills, are not necessarily related. I was reading college textbooks for fun when I was eight years old, but I never learned to write legibly by hand or to drive on freeways.

2. **Be Flexible in the Choice of Instructional Methods.** Learning differences are common[13] and should be considered in planning all learning activities. Onboarding methods should be flexible and adaptive to support the diverse needs of employees. For instance, if instructional videos are a part of the onboarding process, ensure that transcripts or other nonvideo-based resources are provided. If your onboarding materials are text-heavy, provide options for those who struggle with too much text.

3. **Pace the Learning Options and Support Tailored Pacing.** Carefully organize your content to prevent cognitive overload.[14,15] For example, if elearning courses are part of the onboarding process, divide the learning content into shorter, manageable chunks, and let employees engage with the material in a logical sequence at their preferred pace.[16]

   Although "snackable"/bite-sized learning in the form of segments lasting just a few minutes is popular and enjoyed by many, be aware that this option does not necessarily work for everyone. Some prefer learning in short bursts, while others would rather master a significant amount of material in one focused sitting without interruptions and having to refocus. Learning systems that "lock" the next bits of content can be extremely frustrating to hyperfocused learners in the flow who want to connect all the dots for systemic comprehension. Do not assume such learners are "cramming"—rather, ensure comprehension via assessments.

4. **Give Employees an Opportunity to Practice.** Regardless of learning styles, training design should allow employees enough time to learn foundational information and skills in a deep and meaningful way. Practicing integrating and building these skills in an applied context over time facilitates true mastery.

POINTS OF PRACTICE

SOCIALIZATION AND RELATIONSHIP BUILDING

Regardless of learning style, however, it is likely that most employees will benefit from mentoring and having an orientation to the social environment, including any unwritten rules and organization-specific norms.

Effective training and onboarding for neurodivergent employees should go beyond simply providing information about the job role. The onboarding period should be a supportive and welcoming introduction to the organization's culture and social environment. Even employees naturally drawn to and at ease with building relationships are likely to appreciate some introductions and support during their organizational entry. For those who are more reserved or unsure about social rules, providing help is crucial.

1. **Orientation to the Social Environment:** Providing clear information about the organization's social environment is essential. Communicate details about the workplace culture, the dynamics among teams, expectations for interactions and communication, and so on. Clarifying such unwritten rules can help neurodivergent individuals navigate social situations in the workplace more effectively.

2. **Mentorship Programs:** Mentors can help new neurodivergent employees understand the nuances of the workplace; they provide guidance on unwritten rules, organizational norms, and social cues that might not be immediately apparent.

3. **Optional Events:** Some organizations and teams have specific socialization traditions, ranging from dining at favorite restaurants to sports activities, potlucks in the park, or taking turns hosting parties at home. It is always a good idea to give the new person a choice of a shared "welcome" activity and clarify that engaging in no activity at all is also an acceptable choice. Some people might be comfortable with one-on-one coffees but not necessarily large gatherings, and definitely not with hosting parties. Invite the individual into relationship building, but let them guide the pace.

Tailored support that considers individual social needs and comfort levels can make or break the onboarding experience. Considerate and respectful socialization provides opportunities for every new hire, regardless of their neurotype, to feel a welcomed part of the organizational culture.

POINTS OF PRACTICE

CONTINUOUS FEEDBACK

Regular feedback is crucial during the onboarding process. It helps neurodivergent employees understand their performance, areas for improvement, and progress toward goals. When implemented correctly, it should also give them the opportunity to voice concerns or request additional support.

Unfortunately, the experience can take a wrong turn when the focus of feedback is on personal characteristics and neurodivergent traits, rather than performance.

HUMAN HAPPENINGS

FEEDBACK FAIL

Amanda Gibson from Idaho, in the US, is a highly successful strategist and business consultant with an MBA degree and significant experience in building organizations. But earlier in her career, she had several experiences with onboarding and "employee development" that illustrate quite a few things that are wrong with traditional employee feedback and employee development systems.

At her 90-day review in one of her early jobs, Amanda was told that she "wasn't funny enough and that group needed more humor to work with her."

She adjusted to inject humor.

In the next review, she was written up as rude and insubordinate, with her attempts at humor used as examples.

In that same role, she noticed that some rules, policies, and procedures were inconsistent and not necessarily followed. When she asked whether she should follow the written rules or what the managers were doing, managers became so irritated that actual things were thrown.

To top it all off, in a later role with similar disconnects, Amanda also received this gem of career advice: "You need to care less and drink more."[17]

Do you see the trend? None of this feedback reflected Amanda's performance, respect for her as an individual, or inclusive leadership.

POINTS OF PRACTICE

FEEDBACK THAT FITS

Neurodiversity-affirming feedback during employee onboarding and beyond requires an understanding and respect for individual differences, a commitment to creating a supportive and inclusive environment, and the willingness to adapt traditional practices to meet the needs of neurodivergent employees. Investing in doing this right also helps build a richer, add-on culture with a repertoire of communication styles and ways of working that include a wider range of individuals.

Providing quality feedback for the successful onboarding of neurodivergent employees requires a thoughtful and inclusive approach. Here are some crucial considerations to keep in mind:

1. **Invite Participation:** Encourage employees to share their thoughts on the best way to provide feedback and what they hope to gain from it. Their input can guide the process and make it more meaningful. Neurodivergent people may have unique communication preferences and needs. Take the time to understand these, and tailor your feedback accordingly.

2. **Offer Choices:** If possible, provide options for how feedback is delivered. Some individuals may prefer written feedback, while others might appreciate face-to-face conversations.

3. **Create a Safe Environment:** Ensure that the feedback occurs in an environment where the employee feels comfortable. This might involve choosing a quiet space or allowing them to have a support person present. Remember, in addition to differences in preexisting anxiety levels, many people experienced poorly delivered feedback and worked with supervisors who yelled, threw items, and were otherwise abusive, heightening subsequent anxiety.

4. **Focus on Specific Behaviors and Goals:** Make corrective feedback about specific skills, not the individual as a person. Link skill development to organizational goals to provide a big-picture context for your suggestions.

5. **Be Clear and Specific:** Use clear language and provide specific examples. Vague or generalized comments, hints, and veiled messages are confusing and unhelpful. Where there are areas for growth or improvement, provide practical, actionable suggestions that align with the individual's abilities.

6. **Use Growth Focus:** Focus on strengths and accomplishments, and frame areas for growth in a positive and constructive way. Acknowledge effort and progress, not just results.

7. **Avoid Overload:** Be mindful of the amount of information and the number of suggestions you provide at one time. Too much feedback can be overwhelming.

8. **Follow Up:** Check in after the feedback session to see if there are any questions or additional support needed. Offer ongoing opportunities for dialogue and reflection, as well as for adjusting your feedback style if needed.

Taking these steps can help organizations create a feedback process that is much more effective than what Amanda experienced. And infinitely more inclusive.

 DEEP DIVE

NEUROINCLUSION TRAINING

Traditional methods of integrating neurodivergent (with most research focused on autistic) employees into the workplace have often been rooted in the medical model, focusing on teaching individuals to adapt to neurotypical standards. But as research has shown, this approach falls short.[18,19] Autistic people do develop work skills but remain excluded; "fixing" people doesn't work when the environment remains exclusionary.[20]

The social model of disability offers a different perspective on making an effective transition to work. Instead of trying to force neurodivergent individuals to fit a neuronormative "box," organizations need to develop neuroinclusive environments and provide all employees neuroinclusion training, helping them embrace neurodiversity. Such a shift in the focus from "correction" to "connection" requires training that would cover at least the following:

1. **Recognizing Individual Uniqueness.** Neurodivergent individuals are not monolithic. The wide variability of individual characteristics calls for getting to know and respecting the uniqueness of each person.

2. **Addressing Both the Denial of Abilities and the Denial of Difficulties:** Prevalent stereotypes lead many people to see neurodivergent individuals as either extremely limited in their abilities or as superhuman and expected

to perform the work of two people.[21] This results in (a) *the denial of abilities*—for example, the assumption that limited verbal communication is always a sign of impaired intellectual functioning, and (b) *the denial of difficulties*—for example, the assumption that those with notable abilities in some areas do not struggle and are "not really autistic."[22] Training must help coworkers develop a more nuanced understanding of both neurodivergent strengths and struggles to avoid the extremes of infantilization or the lack of compassion.[23]

3. **Understanding Accommodations:** Accommodations are not about catering to preferences or providing "unfair advantages." They are about creating an equitable environment where everyone has the opportunity to thrive.

Effective training, whether in-person, virtual, or hybrid, should involve ample opportunities to ask questions, both openly and anonymously, and clarify misconceptions. Ideally, training should include multiple perspectives of individuals with lived experiences to illustrate the breadth of the neurodiversity umbrella; for example, I often partner with colleagues whose neurodivergent experience complements mine. Participants are also likely to appreciate having access to quality additional resources for continuous learning.

To create lasting change and embed neuroinclusion in organizational norms, training can't be "one-and-done." It should be reinforced by continuous opportunities to practice inclusive behaviors, with leaders providing an example. Neuroinclusion is a journey of continuous learning.

 DEEP DIVE

NAVIGATING NEEDS: UNDERSTANDING ACCOMMODATIONS

A significant challenge faced by many neurodivergent individuals is the nonapparent nature of their struggles and disabilities. This invisibility often leads to misconceptions and judgments about the need for and validity of accommodations/adjustments. There may be an assumption that accommodations are preferential treatment or afford some "unfair advantage." This could not be further from the truth. Accommodations for nonapparent disabilities are not different from people who need help seeing wearing eyeglasses or those who need a ramp to access a building using one. They simply level the playing field, enabling productivity. Accommodations are essential tools for inclusion, allowing neurodivergent employees to perform at their best and contribute fully to the organization.

For example, autistic, sensory-sensitive, and introverted people do not simply "dislike" noise; it severely interferes with our performance. Experimental research demonstrates that noise levels that do not bother extroverts can reduce the ability of introverts to perform cognitive tasks—due to the higher baseline activation in introverts' brains—which makes additional stimulation overwhelming.[24,25,26] For sensory-avoidant autistic people, the effects of noise can be extreme and painful and have been described as "falling apart."[27,28,29] In my case, noise causes my brain to shut down, and I can't function. If the noise is inescapable, I become physically ill. The noise level I am talking about is what others find pleasurable, like chit-chat exceeding a few minutes or most music. To my ear, these sound like a leaf blower. How fair is it to hold a leaf blower to someone's head?

Here is how Marian Schembari, an autistic author of *A LITTLE LESS BROKEN*, describes her experience:[30]

> *The offices were open from the ground floor to the fourth—"To keep our creativity flowing," said the . . . CEO. There wasn't a single rug or curtain, just hardwood and glass, so you could hear each and every sound that each and every human made in that building: the chatter of customer support; the loud, bro-ey laughter from the sales department; the blenders and timers and food processors in the kitchen. I was on the second floor, sandwiched between it all.*
>
> *Every day went the same. For the first few hours, I was a machine, knocking out tasks left and right. But every few minutes, even with my headphones blasting Brown Noise Playlist #3, I felt a thud downstairs as someone new walked into the building. As my coworkers and deskmates trickled in, I said hi and answered questions. The sound and interruptions chipped away at my capacity until there was nothing left.*
>
> *By eleven a.m., the words on my screen blurred. I could no longer piece them into any coherent meaning. While I'd finished the bulk of my work, there were still hours left in the day. I needed to get ahead, right? The expectations were never clear to me, only that I needed to remain in this building until five o'clock. The thought of this discomfort lasting six more hours felt like a boulder on my chest.*

Then, Marian's husband suggested that she ask whether she could work from home.

> *This was 2014. Pre-pandemic, pre-Slack, pre-Zoom. . . . But I was clawing out of my skin, scrabbling at the cage, desperate for relief from the noise and*

the chaos and the confusion. The next job wouldn't be better; I knew that. I was on a hamster wheel of attrition, going nowhere. I could work from home or quit. I had nothing left to lose.

The next day, before I had the chance to overthink it, I approached my boss, tentative and stumbling.

"Sure, let's try it," the boss shrugged. He suggested two days a week to start, then we could reevaluate.

And just like that, I could breathe again. . . . My productivity skyrocketed. I did my best, most thoughtful work. . . . For the first time, my career made sense. In this small way I learned to stop forcing myself to perform in an environment that wasn't built for me. It was the kindest thing I had ever done for myself.

All Marian needed was a quiet place to work. Nevertheless, for decades the requests for quiet workspaces or work from home were rejected as "unreasonable" or "frivolous" by so many organizations.

And then, the COVID-19 pandemic sent most office workers home and demonstrated just how easy it was to provide those "unreasonable" accommodations. To many people, this was a life-changing discovery of how effective and productive they can be.[31,32,33]

Many accommodations that make or break neurodivergents' work experience—like quiet spaces and flexible work hours—could simply be a part of good work design, available to all, rather than accommodations requiring disclosure and paperwork. It just makes sense to allow people to work in ways that best support their productivity. Even more specific accommodations, like software that helps employees be more organized, can often benefit the majority of their colleagues. But when people need more tailored accommodations, managers who understand the importance of supporting people in doing their best, and systems designed to provide this support, can make a life-defining difference.

 HUMAN HAPPENINGS

DYSLEXIC AND SUPPORTED

In 2023, Charles Freeman was awarded an honorary doctorate in media from Solent University in the UK. As a media professional and executive director of Culture, Southeast—a nongovernmental entity supporting the UK Government's

Department for Culture, Media and Sport—he worked to ensure the legacy of some of the most exciting, high-stakes sports and cultural events in the UK, such as the 2012 London Olympics, heritage film, and arts.[34]

But in 1998, he had a crisis of confidence. After a year of working for Sport England and coming up with creative ways to fund underserved communities, he was promoted to the position of senior regional development manager. Around that very time, senior management introduced a new requirement of submitting detailed notes of all meetings. Simultaneously, secretarial/administrative assistant positions were eliminated, which meant managers had to generate the notes themselves.

Charles Freeman is dyslexic, and this requirement—and the resulting need to seek support and to get a new dyslexia assessment—reawakened his feelings of childhood trauma and struggling at school.

However, Charles's boss David was very supportive. And when a new assessment confirmed that Charles was dyslexic, he received funding from the UK Access to Work program to pay for a support worker. This was a major win-win, because this funding also allowed Charles's administrative assistant to keep her job and continue supporting him for the next 12 years through three jobs. And Charles could focus on the creative work he does best.

In addition, David also encouraged Charles to engage in job crafting and build his career on his strengths. A major part of this was getting a master's degree in public policy at Birmingham University, for which Charles received a year of unpaid leave. His support—both the funding and the encouragement for job crafting—laid a foundation for a productive and successful career, including his promotion to the executive director role at Culture, South East.

 HUMAN HAPPENINGS

DYSLEXIC AND STIGMATIZED

Salomon Chiquiar-Rabinovich is the founder and cochair of the Boston Bar Association (BBA) Committee for Attorneys with Disabilities, the chair of the Attorneys with Disabilities Section of the Hispanic National Bar Association, and a member of the BBA Diversity and Inclusion Section Steering Committee. He also served as president of the Massachusetts Association of Hispanic Attorneys.[35]

Salomon is a highly skilled attorney who was diagnosed with dyslexia as a child and was not expected to complete school. Nevertheless, he persisted and obtained a law degree from Georgetown University through hard work and academic accommodations. Throughout his 30-year career, Chiquiar-Rabinovich succeeded as a lawyer with creativity and committed concentration. And yet he also faced stigma and discrimination.

Salomon needed the same type of administrative support that Charles Freeman received—yet Salomon was repeatedly refused this support, even though attorneys with other types of disabilities were provided administrative help. Eventually, Salomon hired his own support worker for a few hours a week—for which he was punished by first having his permission to work remotely suspended and later being fired.[36]

Salomon continued practicing law at a different firm, but he also developed an even stronger passion for inclusion advocacy. He earned an additional masters's degree in leadership with a focus on DEI from Boston College.

The contrast between Charles's and Salomon's stories underscores the importance of accommodations and the role of national-level differences in approaches to supporting neurodivergent and disabled workers. As Salomon put it,

> *From the academic literature and my colleagues in the labor employment legal field in the UK, it is clear that they are much more advanced in their DEI achievements and strategies. Language differences are significant. For example, in the UK, they use "reasonable adjustments" instead of "reasonable accommodations." The difference is not subtle and should not be lost in semantics.*

An adjustment could be compared to drivers adjusting their rearview mirrors or car seats. You adjust *"simply because we're all different, and you want to make your drive for your work comfortable so you can be productive."*

 DEEP DIVE

ACCOMMODATIONS AND LEADERSHIP

In some organizations, the limited perspective on accommodations might be due to the absence of neurodivergent and disabled people in leadership positions. People with lived experience of needing accommodations are likely to have more context for understanding how these work. Anne M., an autistic manager from the US, shares her story:[37]

I create a lot of structure for my own survival. The people I supervise (my direct reports) have regularly scheduled one-on-one meetings in part to reduce my daily interruptions but also to allow me the time to develop scripts for what I want to say.

I was recently meeting with one of my neurodivergent direct reports when I noticed that they were struggling to answer some of my questions. This isn't the first time this happened. Being autistic, I cannot only relate to this struggle, but I've also got experience with related accommodations. In the moment, I asked if it would help if I sent my questions to them before our meetings and explained that I always type up my questions before our meetings, so it wouldn't be a burden. They agreed to this accommodation, and now I can proudly say that my accommodation supports theirs.

Christina Ryan, the founder of the Disability Leadership Institute in Australia, echoes this perspective: *"The way we [disabled leaders] put it: 'We'll make it happen; we just have to work out how.' Whether that is accessibility measures (in a really broad sense, so alternative formats, hearing loops, signing interpreters, timing, sensory awareness, etc.), or doing things differently like flexible working conditions or reframing conversations. No excuses, no explanations or justifications required—just getting on with it and making it happen for everyone."*[38]

While lived experience does not translate into the commitment to helping others in every case, often it does. This is yet another illustration of why representation in leadership matters to neuroinclusion and disability inclusion.

Of course, it is also important for all managers and human resources professionals to build their understanding of accommodations and flexibility. Disabled and neurodivergent leaders should not be the token experts on accommodations.

 DEEPER DIVE

INCLUSIVE COMPENSATION: DEMYSTIFYING PAY

Pay gaps are the elephant in the room of inclusion. In neurodiversity employment, pay is a controversial topic shrouded in mystery, half-truths, incomplete statistics, and uncomfortable silence. The three elements of the Canary Code—transparency, justice, and accurate measurement of performance—might be particularly relevant to addressing this problem.

According to the UK's Office for National Statistics, in 2021 the UK had a 13.8 percent disability pay gap, with disabled employees paid less than their nondisabled colleagues. Autistic employees had the widest gap, being paid 33.5 percent less than nondisabled employees, while those with learning difficulties were paid 29.7 percent less and those with a mental illness 22.1 percent less.[39,40] The US data from 2019 indicated that as a group, full-time, year-round workers with a disability earn 87 cents for every dollar earned by those with no disability. However, these data are hard to interpret because of the effects of the occupational mix and age. Disabled employees are more likely to work in lower-wage jobs, while among professionals, disabled workers tend to be older and might be earning more as a function of age or experience.[41]

Most countries do not provide granular enough data on neurodivergence pay gaps. The lack of disclosure further complicates our understating of the complete picture. However, there are several statistics about autism employment, in particular, that suggest a likely disconnect between what autistic employees offer to organizations and what they get in return.

Data from around the world indicate that autistic people are often employed in positions well below their level of educational achievement.[42,43,44,45] Notably, their level of educational achievement in some countries is significantly higher than that of the general population.[43,46] Additional research should explore whether a significant percentage of underemployed neurodivergent people might be de facto performing work above their title and pay.

A popular business case argument for hiring autistic people is that they are 90 to 140 percent more productive than typical employees, make fewer errors, and do "two people's work."[47] I have spoken to quite a few autistic employees who tell me that they are doing the work of two or even three people. Sadly, I have yet to meet one who has financially benefited from that productivity. Moreover, elevated productivity is not some "free bonus magic"—it comes at least in part from the extra effort and time that autistic employees invest in their work, such as not taking breaks.[48,49] Of course, extraordinary levels of productivity should not be expected from every autistic person, nor should such "superpowers" be a requirement for hiring. Nevertheless, in cases where such productivity does occur, as indicated by objective performance measurement, it is the ethical responsibility of organizations to provide commensurate compensation.

Another worrisome issue in pay fairness is subminimal wage laws. This legislation allows employers in some places to pay disabled individuals much less than a livable wage, regardless of the work they do.[50,51]

To support fairness in pay in the context of neurodiversity, it is crucial to implement pay transparency and equality measurements and interventions, similar to those typically applied to gender and race.[52,53,54] Ensuring fair pay for all employees, regardless of their neurotype, is vital for creating an inclusive work environment.

KEY TAKEAWAYS

- *To create a strong foundation for belonging, organizational preboarding and onboarding practices should consider individual differences and intersectional inclusion needs. One size does not fit all.*
- *New employee training should include multiple instructional methods and pacing options. Do not make assumptions about employee learning needs; ask whether any accommodations are needed, and support all with flexible learning systems.*
- *Mentorship and support in navigating the new social environment might be appreciated even by the most outgoing employees.*
- *Provide new employees with performance-focused, clear, actionable feedback. Do not try to change their personalities.*
- *Creating neuroinclusive environments requires training for all employees. This training should help dispel myths and stereotypes.*
- *Accommodations for nonapparent differences are not "catering to preferences." They are essential for providing individuals with a fair opportunity to succeed.*
- *Neurodivergence-related pay gaps should be addressed in the same data-informed ways as gender or race pay gaps.*

DEVELOPMENTAL QUESTIONS

For employees/job seekers:

- Have you been in a situation where an organization has not considered your transition needs?
- How could you use this chapter to better advocate for yourself?

For employees:

- Which ideas from this chapter might be helpful in supporting transitions in your organization? Did you learn something that you could suggest to others or implement in your team/department?

For managers, HR, and other organizational professionals:

- Do you have data on employee reactions to your current onboarding processes? Are there any pain points that could be addressed by implementing suggestions from this chapter?
- How (neuro)inclusive is your onboarding process? Using what you learned from this chapter, could you make it more welcoming for all employees, as well as more neuroinclusive?
- Have there been conflicts, misunderstandings, or turnover in your organization that could have been prevented by neuroinclusion training? What type of education might be particularly useful for preventing the same problems from recurring?

PART III

REMOVING BARRIERS TO SUCCESS

CHAPTER SIX

WORK ENVIRONMENT

Flexible Spaces

By reclaiming silence in the workplace, we can create the conditions for reducing burnout and enhancing creative problem solving.

—Justin Zorn and Leigh Marz

Planning physical spaces for inclusion and flexibility is, undeniably, a challenge. How do we balance the needs of those with low vision or who are hard of hearing, the needs of those who are sensory sensitive and experience incapacitating sensory overload, and those who seek extra stimulation?

The Canary Code principles of participation and flexibility suggest an answer. Developing spaces that can support many different people can only be accomplished with the participation and engagement of many different people.

 EMPLOYER EXCELLENCE

BUILDING FOR BELONGING

One example of such participation was the planning of the BBC Cymru Wales New Broadcasting House in Cardiff, Wales, which opened in 2019 and was designed with neuroinclusion in mind. During the design stage, neurodivergent employees with different sensory needs provided feedback on whether the design and layout would be comfortable. The resulting building uses a neutral color palette, which is less likely to be overstimulating, with pops of color to help wayfinding. A variety of textures—from fabric to wood—provide sensory interest. The building also has large windows to let in natural light, which many find essential to their well-being. In addition, there are a variety of quiet spaces, including private meeting rooms and relaxation areas, to provide a refuge for those who need a break from the bustle for quiet focus or rejuvenation.[1,2]

Perhaps most importantly, the BBC Cardiff building was designed with the understanding that *everyone's needs and optimal working conditions are different.* The designers created a flexible workspace that can be adapted to accommodate a variety of sensitivities, capacities, and requirements, whether that means providing extra lighting in certain areas or soundproofing in others.

Physical work environments affect inclusion and belonging. And yet, the BBC is in many ways a pioneer with its Cardiff building: typically, conversations about inclusion still rarely consider the physical work environment.

The BBC Cardiff building was designed in 2015. Since then, the research has provided much more knowledge on how to build for productivity and inclusion. Awareness of the need to build with neuroinclusion in mind is also growing. As of summer 2023, Philips, a healthcare technology company headquartered in Amsterdam, is actively collaborating with members of its neurodiversity Employee Resource Group and other employees in planning the design and day-to-day use of its new head office.[3] Welcoming neurodivergent employees' input in the early stages of planning is an excellent example of inclusion through participation.

> This chapter focuses on applying the knowledge of how to design inclusive spaces for productivity to a variety of work settings, from factories to offices and from retail spaces to warehouses. It also provides some ideas for how working from home can support the well-being of employees across occupational groups, including frontline workers.

 DEEP DIVE

MENTAL FRAMEWORKS FRAME THE WORK

In consulting with organizations, I have observed three levels of understanding of how the design of the physical environment influences inclusion.

1. **The expense focus.** Many organizations approach workspaces largely from the perspective of cost and look for the cheapest solutions, whether

in the form of cube farms, industrial-style open spaces, or, more recently, minimally supported remote work. Spaces for upper management may reflect attention to both comfort and aesthetics, and customer-facing areas may be pleasing, but most employees are "housed" as cheaply as possible. This approach is not necessarily dictated by the funds available: I have seen leaders with very limited resources find ways to support their employees with the best workspaces possible. Others prioritize minimizing expenses over providing a supportive environment for employees. This approach tends to send the message that employees are disposable and interchangeable.

2. **The investment focus.** These organizations understand the value created when workspaces support high performance. They invest in comfort and aesthetics, seeking to maximize productivity. However, their approach may be one-size-fits-all, based on trends and fads, and lacking in flexibility to accommodate the diverse needs of their employees. Stories of investing in beautiful furniture unusable for disabled people—sleek-looking but ability-height-age-and-size-exclusionary high tables and chairs—or providing stand-up desks when employees ask for dual monitors illustrate the drawbacks of this approach. It tends to send the message that employees (at least some of them) might be a form of investment—perhaps *human capital*—but they are still seen as rather homogeneous and not as unique and valuable humans with diverse needs.

3. **The inclusion focus.** These leading organizations understand that maximizing productivity requires a flexible approach to organizing workspaces rather than one-size-fits-all solutions. They focus on creating environments that reflect a human-centric perspective, accommodating the unique needs of their employees. This approach sends the message that employees are valued not only as contributors but also, more than that, as *unique and valuable human beings.*

Sometimes, posh or sleek environments reflective of organizational means are confused with human-centric environments. But *cash* and *caring* do not necessarily go together. One of the most caring environments I ever encountered was a small not-for-profit organization in a lower-GDP country that invested in ensuring that employees in portable offices (aka trailers) were able to regulate the temperature to their comfort. Compare that to gleaming offices of wealthy organizations that use a single control to cool the building according to the preferences of those with the most power—and forbids employees who are cold to use "unsightly" cover-ups, typing gloves, or heated footstools.

Overcooling, especially prevalent in the warmer areas of the US, has disparate effects on different groups of employees.[4] For example, multiple studies show that women function best at higher temperatures than men. Because most positions of power are still held by men who, *on average*, prefer colder settings, most women and others who need warmer temperatures are left not only shivering but also unable to perform at their best.[5,6] Neurodivergent people who are sensitive to temperature, as well as to the sensation of air blowing from air conditioners, also struggle in this type of environment. Of course, the same logic applies to supporting those who need cooler workplaces. Optimal functioning and best performance do not occur in one-size-fits-all conditions.

> Holistic belonging applied to the work environment means understanding that our performance, health, and well-being are significantly influenced by workspaces. In some cases, inaccessible or sensorily unwelcoming physical work environments exclude certain groups of individuals altogether.

 HUMAN HAPPENINGS

ED DUPREE'S DISAPPEARING DISABILITIES

Ed Dupree, a business data analyst from Drinkstone in the UK spent much of his working life in an office without understanding what it was doing to him. As a very late-diagnosed autistic (at age 48), and dyslexic and dyspraxic (at age 53) person with very few sensory filters, he had been expending a great deal of energy just to block out sensory stimuli. But he assumed everyone felt this way. Struggling—and failing—to block out bright lights, constant noise, movement, temperature changes, strong scents, and interfering people every working day for nearly 25 years left him chronically depressed, anxious, sick, and morbidly obese. Even his autism diagnosis at age 48 made little difference, because working in an "office" was his only option. After his second breakdown, he was being forced back to the office when COVID hit.

It took a global pandemic, and finally the opportunity to work from home, for Ed to realize that he could live a healthy and happy life and still be productive. Far more productive, in fact.

His chronic illnesses and excess weight just went away. As did depression and anxiety. There was only one explanation: the demands of the neurotypical world had turned his neurological differences into disabilities. In a more sensory-friendly environment, they were disabilities no longer. After the pandemic, the one thing that still provokes anxiety for Ed is the possibility of having to return to the sensory nightmare of the office.[7]

BRIDGING SCIENCE AND PRACTICE

THE OFFICE SPACE: WARS ON WALLS, WARS FOR WALLS, AND WARS ON HUMAN NATURE

Research on open offices produced extensive evidence that (1) their expected benefits of face-to-face collaboration did not materialize, and (2) they have significant negative effects on employee communication, productivity, health, and well-being. These effects were found in studies conducted across cultural and organizational settings, from Southeast Asia to Western Europe.[8,9,10] Improvements to collaboration resulting from open offices appear to be elusive at best and mythical at worst. The negative outcomes for employee health and performance, in contrast, are very real and well documented.

- An extensive review of prior studies established that workers in open offices complain about a lack of personal privacy and personal space, as well as high noise levels and interruptions of their work.[11]
- Up to 95 percent of workers are annoyed by noise in open offices. But the effects extend beyond annoyance: the noise in open offices increases employee stress and causes physiological (cardiovascular and respiratory) reactions that harm their long-term health and productivity.[12]
- Field studies conducted just prior to the COVID-19 pandemic in the global headquarters of two Fortune 500 multinational companies showed that the "war on walls" waged to increase face-to-face collaboration and collective intelligence was actually waged against the foundational human desire for psychological privacy. Human nature won. Removing the office walls had the outcome opposite to the intended one. Face-to-face interaction *decreased* significantly—by approximately 70 percent—while electronic interaction increased. Instead of the envisioned vibrant face-to-face collaboration, the war on walls triggered a social withdrawal from officemates and an increase in email and instant messaging. In one of the companies in the study, the executive team also acknowledged that productivity had declined after the "war on walls" redesign.[8]

- A practice of hot desking—not having workspaces assigned to employees at all but instead requiring employees to find a spot to work every day—adds to the stress of open offices and is often detrimental to both employee health and collaboration.[13]

Over time, the stress of open offices wears on everyone. However, people who tend to be highly absorbed by work tasks—such as autistic and other neurodivergent people with a natural tendency to hyperfocus—suffer more immediate and severe effects on concentration and performance.[14,15] A unique combination of sensory sensitivities and the physiological tendency to hyperarousal make autistic people especially susceptible to negative health effects associated with such designs.[16,17] Providing employees with more control and addressing the problematic aspects of open offices can reduce barriers to autistic employment and will benefit the majority of employees.

 NEURODIVERSITY NARRATIVES

FRONTLINE FOCUS

As a teenager, I worked at a knitwear factory. Being highly sensory-sensitive autistic and dyspraxic (of course, I was not diagnosed until decades later), I was terrified I was going to faint from the noise, fall right into the industrial knitting machine, and die. So I know full well that offices are not the most sensory-challenging environments for work. Those working in factories or warehouses are often subjected to immense sensory assaults.

And yet, it is possible to improve industrial environments as well. Openly communicating with and regularly soliciting feedback from neurodivergent and neurotypical employees to identify areas for improvement and make necessary adjustments can yield ideas for humanizing all work environments, even those traditionally seen as harsh by default.

 POINTS OF PRACTICE

FACTORIES AND WAREHOUSES

Factories and warehouses may be filled with noisy machinery, but these workplaces can become less taxing on the human ability to cope. Ethically led organizations will seek to eliminate harm and minimize discomfort; here are some ideas that can help.

1. Noise-reducing measures, like installing soundproof barriers and acoustic panels, and ensuring machinery is well maintained, can help reduce the level of sensory assault.

2. Going beyond minimum safety requirements helps protect people better. Although workplace safety guidelines are based on the physical aspects of hearing protection, the effects of noise are also psychological and can include depression and suicidal ideation.[18] Meeting employees' needs for psychological protection needs may require going above and beyond the minimal requirements for preventing physical hearing damage. The line between physical and psychological harm may be further blurred by the fact that the psychological effects of noise also increase the likelihood of physical injuries.[18,19] More protection can save more lives.

3. Normalizing sound protection as a part of the workplace culture through training and modeling can go a long way in supporting well-being. This cultural aspect is crucial: without a culture of safety, employees may experience peer pressure to disregard safety regulations from those who see protection as a sign of weakness.

4. Providing employees with their preferred form of protection, such as noise-canceling headphones or earbuds, can further help normalize safety.

5. Including signage reminding employees to use hearing protection may help prevent exposure due to forgetfulness.

6. Thoughtful use of signage has additional benefits. Using clear signage and visual or tactile aids throughout the workspace can help employees navigate their environment more easily, reducing confusion and frustration. This includes labeling equipment, posting safety instructions, and providing visual cues for work processes. Although these aids are necessary for some neurodivergent people, they can help alleviate stress for all employees, as well as reduce errors and injuries associated with fatigue.

7. Lighting adjustments can also improve employee well-being across occupational groups and work settings. Fluorescent and flickering lights can cause discomfort and sensory overload. Using natural or adjustable LED lighting in the daylight spectrum that can be dimmed to accommodate individual preferences can make spaces more inclusive. Offering adjustable task lighting or providing individual lamps can also help accommodate employees' varying needs.

8. Opting for neutral color schemes in all large shared spaces and introducing pleasing textures—wood elements to soften and warm concrete, steel, or brick expanses of space or exposing warm-colored brick to break up the gray monotony of concrete—can have a regulating, calming effect. Employers can consider using soft, muted colors in complementary shades for walls, floors, and workstations to create more human-centric environments, even in industrial buildings.

9. Sensory-friendly zones can help employees rest and recharge. Creating quiet lunch spaces and designating additional quiet or low-stimulation areas can help employees who work in busy environments take breaks and recharge.[20] Having minimal noise, sound-absorbing materials, soft lighting, and comfortable seating in such areas can help employees feel supported, regardless of their line of work.

   Elements of nature can greatly enhance indoor environments. Of course, not every employer can afford a giant aquarium room with recliner massage chairs where employees can drift off and nap while watching fish, like the one unveiled by Zappos in 2017.[21] However, even small aquariums and plants have documented restorative effects. While dogs, cats, birds, and other animals can also have calming effects, they may create multiple safety and allergy problems to consider. Larger organizations can have a few themed break rooms. Options include areas with low stimulation, positive stimulation spaces like cat cafes made popular in Japan, and brightly colored spaces that allow for playing music for those who are sensory-seeking.

   Whenever possible, access to outdoor relaxation can be especially beneficial. Plant-filled courtyards and outdoor spaces can turn even taking a brief walk, eating lunch outdoors, or relaxing on a bench into a micro-vacation.

10. Offering employees flexible shift and schedule options, including shorter shifts or shorter weeks, may also help minimize the negative effects of sensory-challenging environments. Additional accommodations could include more frequent work breaks and providing opportunities for hybrid work for those whose jobs include elements that can be performed remotely.

EMPLOYER EXCELLENCE

A RECHARGE ROOM FOR FRONTLINE WORKERS

Working in frontline healthcare settings in New York at the height of the COVID-19 pandemic was extremely taxing. Long shifts, the lack of personal protective equipment, uncertainty, and anxiety combined to create extremely stressful environments.[22] To help relieve strain, a New York City hospital repurposed a neuroscience laboratory as a recharge room.

The room created multisensory, nature-inspired experiences. Elements to engage and revive the senses included "silk imitation plants, projected scenes of soothing natural landscapes, low lighting that is tailored in color to match the projected landscapes, high-definition audio recordings of nature sounds paired with relaxing music, and an infusion of essential oils and calming scents using an essential oil diffuser."[22] Frontline healthcare workers could book 15-minute experiences before, during, or after their shifts. The data revealed that a single experience significantly lowered stress levels. Satisfaction, measured as a willingness to recommend the experience to others, was 99.3 percent.[22] Multisensory relaxation rooms of this kind can be invaluable to frontline workers across industries.

 POINTS OF PRACTICE

RETAIL RESCUE

Another example of a sensory-taxing industry is retail; its environments can be exclusionary to both neurodivergent customers and potential employees. Yet the sensory stress caused by retail work environments can be minimized by using several strategies.

1. Noise reduction: Retail environments can be very noisy, with employer-determined music, customer chatter, and announcements. Similarly to the strategies for industrial spaces, implementing noise-reducing measures such as playing music at a lower volume, offering noise-canceling headphones for the times when an employee is not directly interacting with customers, and providing quiet break areas for employees can go a long way in improving employee well-being.

2. Lighting adjustments: Just like in offices or factories, harsh or flickering lights can cause sensory overload. Using natural lighting or adjustable lights that can be dimmed benefits both employees and customers.

3. Flexibility in scheduling: Some stores have designated quiet shopping times for neurodivergent customers. Expanding these one-hour windows to, for example, half-days can allow employers to schedule shifts of sensory-sensitive employees to coincide with sensory-friendly times. Additional options include assigning these employees to work during quieter times or in less busy sections of the store. Of course, it might be worth considering designating all times as sensory-friendly times.

Even environments that traditionally have not been sensory-inclusive can be improved. Consulting with experts specializing in a specific occupational niche, along with inviting employee participation, can provide solutions that will support both productivity and well-being.

The general rule is that every on-site work environment could benefit from quiet rooms/sensory rooms/chill rooms. Creatives can use such spaces to help with ideation, manufacturing workers to take a break from the harsh sensory environment, and middle school teachers to recharge from extreme social demands, along with the sensory overwhelm caused by the bustle and the bells. Sensory rooms already exist in many schools for students, and quiet hours exist in retail for customers. Employees have the same sensory needs as students and customers.

 DEEP DIVE

NO PLACE LIKE HOME

BBC and other leaders in creating welcoming workplaces have done much to improve on-site spaces. And yet, when it comes to disability inclusion, neurodiversity inclusion, and supporting workers with caregiving needs, **there is often no place like home**. For people who must preserve their "spoons" of energy,[23] such as those with many chronic illnesses or long COVID, or for people with intense sensory sensitivities and some mental health conditions, working from home all or much of the time is the only way to work because a commute can deplete their entire energy allowance for the day.

For decades, working from home was restricted to the privileged few, or it was grudgingly and skeptically doled out through a grueling process of accommodation requests. Neurodivergent and disabled people often had their needs denied because of employers' notion that flexibility is not a reasonable accommodation.[24] The pandemic exposed the charade of the fake scarcity surrounding flexibility. Working from home was not only perfectly possible and reasonable for many workers like Ed Dupree but often it was also more effective than face-to-face work.[25,26] Flexibility increased productivity and the long overdue justice for disabled employees,[27] for whom unemployment decreased because of remote and hybrid work opportunities.

But these gains are threatened in the post-pandemic work environment.[28] One argument for the return-to-office mandates is that they are "better for productivity and organizational culture." However, research has demonstrated the power of remote and flexible work to attract and retain top talent, boost productivity,[29] and increase employee engagement[30] and satisfaction.[31] Work cultures do not need to suffer either.[32] On the contrary, remote opportunities can improve cultures and make organizations more diverse, supportive, and human-centric.[33]

Still, some decision makers appear to be holding onto the scarcity mindset that pervaded flexible and hybrid work before the COVID-19 pandemic. One of the arguments is that office workers must be on-site because, otherwise, those who can't work from home become resentful.[34] This argument is based on limiting assumptions. First, as demonstrated by Amazon and Starbucks frontline workers who supported remote opportunities for office workers, people are not that petty.[35] And, importantly, there are opportunities for many categories of frontline workers to work from home at least some of the time.[36] These workers can also benefit from other forms of flexibility, such as flexible scheduling, leaves, and more. There are many ways employers can support employees in various positions.

 EMPLOYER EXCELLENCE

FRONTLINE FLEXIBILITY

Organizational consultant Gleb Tsipursky describes several cases of successfully introducing hybrid work in healthcare and retail organizations that bust the myth of frontline work as in-person only.[37]

For example, many retail employees spend a significant amount of time on administrative tasks that don't involve interacting with customers. Enabling them to complete some of these tasks remotely can improve job satisfaction, productivity, and employee retention. Two large retail chains implemented this approach by allowing store managers and department heads to work from home on administrative tasks, while also giving customer service representatives and inventory managers the option to work remotely for a portion of their work-week. This flexibility increased productivity because workers could better focus on customer-facing tasks while in-store. Job satisfaction and retention also improved, and recruitment became easier.

Healthcare work is also much more conducive to hybrid arrangements than many realize. A recent study revealed that physicians spend about half their time on electronic health records and desk work.[38] Nurses also devote much time to paperwork, logistics, and administrative work.[39] Remote work, in the form of work-from-home days dedicated to administrative tasks, can save healthcare workers time and energy that would be spent on commuting. In another way to introduce flexibility, some hospitals that previously required that doctors conduct follow-up telehealth appointments from the office successfully shifted their schedules to support hybrid work. A hybrid model allowing for completing paperwork and taking telehealth calls remotely resulted in improved job satisfaction, reduced stress levels, higher retention rates, and better recruitment efforts.[37] Although telehealth still represents a relatively small percentage of the healthcare workload, the COVID-19 pandemic facilitated its growth.[40]

Hybrid work improves healthcare workers' life–work balance by reducing commuting stress and time. Today, when many healthcare workers are leaving the field due to burnout[41] and organizations struggle with personnel shortages, this is a true win-win solution.

Supporting frontline workers with flexibility also makes these jobs more accessible for some neurodivergent employees who otherwise might have been excluded, thereby increasing and diversifying the talent pool available to organizations. In the next chapter, we discuss additional approaches to flexibility that make work more inclusive. But first, let's address one concern that may limit the inclusion benefits of remote and hybrid work: the proximity bias.

 DEEP DIVE

PROXIMITY BIAS

Proximity bias refers to the preference for people who are familiar to us due to physical proximity and the resulting familiarity. Even when all the work is done on-site, those who seek ways to be seen by the management and spend time by the watercooler are likely to benefit from this exposure, while those who focus on heads-down work from a quiet corner miss out on rewards. In the context of remote or hybrid work, managers favor employees who are physically present or located nearby (including being in the same time zone) as opposed to those who work remotely or are geographically distant.[42,43,44]

Remote and hybrid work offer disabled and neurodivergent people access to work they otherwise would not have. The same flexibility also supports caretakers and many others with flexibility and better life–work balance. But does this mechanism for more inclusive work come with an exclusionary "progression tax"? If we do not monitor for the effects of the proximity bias, it might.[42,43,44]

This potential threat to careers is not the problem with remote work per se: the problem is bias. The solution is not forcing everyone into the office. It is embedding fairness mechanisms into the work organization.

Proximity bias harms employee advancement opportunities when managers make implicit inferences that those who put in the face time are dependable—regardless of their actual work output.[45] Research shows that although remote workers are likely to be more productive than in-office workers,[46,47,48] they are less likely to receive equitable pay, promotions, high-visibility assignments, raises, and bonuses.[46,49,50] Neurodivergent people, disabled people, women, BIPOC, and others who traditionally have less power in typical Western organizations are more likely to need remote work arrangements.[43,51] This means the negative effects of the proximity bias are often compounded by the effects of other biases, resulting in significant losses of opportunity and pay for already marginalized workers.

Inclusion means it is truly OK to close one's office door, work from the focus room on-site, or work from home without missing the watercooler wages or proximity perks. Otherwise, disabled employees, neurodivergent employees, and solo caregivers contributing from home are, at best, "included-ish" but not really included.

Managers need to be aware of proximity bias and ensure that all employees, regardless of their location, have equal opportunities and are treated fairly. Otherwise, remote employees are likely to be left out of stretch assignments and rewards, feel undervalued and unfairly treated, and may ultimately resign. For organizations, this means the loss of valuable talent and higher turnover costs, which, conservatively, could be between half and more than double the employee's annual salary.[52]

To monitor and ameliorate proximity bias, managers can take several steps, including the following:

1. Encourage equal participation by explicitly inviting remote or geographically distant employees to contribute to discussions, meetings, and decision-making processes (we discuss this in more detail in the next chapter).
2. Provide equal opportunities to take on new projects or assignments, job craft, or participate in learning and career development programs.
3. Recognize and reward remote contributions through promotions, bonuses, or other forms of recognition.
4. Get to know remote employees via alternative methods of communication.

The crucial factor in preventing the negative impacts of proximity bias is outcome-focused work. It can help shift the focus away from face time and toward measurable performance and progress toward clearly defined goals. When managers and team members prioritize outcomes, they can better recognize the contributions and value of remote or geographically distant workers. Ensuring productivity in hybrid and remote environments often means using collaborative technology that can (1) support flexible and asynchronous work, (2) make outcomes transparent, and (3) facilitate valid recording and measurement of employee contributions. Using this data to make decisions supports fairness and helps create a culture of inclusive productivity.

In the next chapter, we discuss how work can be organized more flexibly and inclusively with a focus not only on where we work but also on when and how we work.

 KEY TAKEAWAYS

- *Physical work environments significantly affect well-being and productivity.*
- *Some inflexible aspects of the environment disadvantage or even exclude neurodivergent people.*
- *Inclusion requires flexible workspaces designed with substantial participation from employees.*
- *The "open office collaboration advantage" is a myth. Research shows that open offices undermine collaboration and overall productivity for all employees. They are particularly exclusionary to neurodivergent employees.*

- *It is a myth that supporting frontline workers with good spaces and flexibility is not possible. Remote and hybrid work is more available to frontline workers than many believe.*

 DEVELOPMENTAL QUESTIONS

For employees:
- How (neuro)inclusive are the spaces in your organization? What works and what does not?
- How could you communicate both the appreciation for what works and ideas for improving what does not work? Is there an ERG that could help advocate for improvement? Allies?
- What can you do to suggest win-win solutions that will benefit both employees and the organization?

For managers/direct supervisors:
- How does your physical organization support individuals in doing their best work? Is it flexible enough to be neuroinclusive?
- Which ideas from this chapter could you implement or adapt to better support employees?

For HR and upper management:
- Do you have a strategy for making spaces neuroinclusive and conducive to everyone's best work?
- How can examples in this chapter be adapted to your organizational culture to improve retention and facilitate recruitment?
- What training or systemic improvements, such as systems for asynchronous work, can help your people leaders support inclusive productivity?

CHAPTER SEVEN

WORK ORGANIZATION

Productivity and Purpose

*People can mistake the perception of maximum effort with what
actually produces maximum results.*

—Greg McKeown

 HUMAN HAPPENINGS

FROM BUSTLE TO BLISS: A HYPERFOCUS STORY

Caroline Stokes started her corporate career with all the external signs of success—
she was employee number nine in the European division of Sony and one of
the first employees at Virgin. People thought she was an overachiever. A worka-
holic. Some applauded her "dedication" as they observed her stay at her desk
late into the evening hours.[1]

In reality, she *had* to work nights to get her job done. She had to compensate
for not being able to do her work between 9 and 5 like everyone else. Distractions, meetings, watercooler moments, constant noise, and conversations made
her unable to focus. So, she had to work at her desk after hours and on weekends.

These struggles happened long before work-from-home became a norm and
long before she knew that she was gifted with an ADHD brain.

Caroline burned out a lot during that time. It did not help that she could
see the ineffectiveness of the system, the politics, the favoritism, the games. She
did not have time for any of that. She just wanted to do her job.

But she was also determined to succeed—and, conventionally, she did succeed. During her five years at Sony, she rose through the ranks and departments,
worked in two countries, and led crucial projects to introduce Sony's PlaySta-
tion to the world's markets.

And all along, she had to work weekends and evenings to get the job done. But when she could work, wow, did she deliver. People said she had an amazing ability to get work done three times faster than any of her colleagues. Her secret weapon was hyperfocus—but it was only useful when there was silence.

Caroline's solution to the ineffectiveness of office life took shape when her eldest son—now grown—was born. She started her own company and discovered working from home. She no longer needed 100-hour weeks. *All her hours were now productive hours.*

Since then, she tried working from the office again a few times. Every time the result was the same: she needed the silence to do the work, to ideate, and to finish the job. So, she made peace with her brain, which thrives on delivering client value via consulting work done productively and efficiently—from home and in her own way.

 DEEP DIVE

PRODUCTIVITY THROUGH PURPOSE

Caroline's story offers several lessons for how work is best organized—in a way that fits people and enables true productivity. It also offers lessons for understanding what productivity is and is not.

Many companies still focus on the number of hours worked, bodies in seats, faces seen, and words typed. Many systems still reward productivity theater in the form of meetings called, colleagues interrupted with pretend urgent communications, and much-trumpeted short-term wins that come at the expense of long-term losses. Rewards based on "looking productive" encourage doing whatever it takes to "look productive."

The illusion of productivity often hurts true productivity, which is inseparable from a long-term focus on quality and requires creating well-designed systems that support employees to do their best and take pride in their work.[2]

Intuitively, many of us know that inputs are a poor proxy for evaluating whether quality outcomes are accomplished. Whether outcomes are aligned with objectives. And whether value is delivered. Genuine productivity—creating quality and value—often suffers in systems focused on quantity and visibility. But many of us often feel swept along by the torrent of frantic activity that prevents people and entire organizations from aligning their activities with a purpose.

The constant gasping for breath is not productivity. This chapter is meant to be a rope to pull you out of the deluge of business, to help you catch your breath and plan a more deliberate approach to work.

 DEEP DIVE

ONE SIZE FITS NONE: FORMS OF FLEXIBILITY

Caroline Stokes always worked extremely hard. Unfortunately, the typical work organization was working *against* her rather than with her. This is a recurring theme when I talk to employees—not only neurodivergent but also neurotypical ones. Many share the struggle of having to work in ways that do not allow for their productivity; they are tied down by outdated, industrial age models.

If the goal of work organization is maximizing human talent, then one-size-fits-all is a counterproductive approach. Uniformity for the sake of uniformity sacrifices productivity. In mechanical jobs, the equipment may need to be aligned to fit each employee. The best creative work comes in many forms, from long stretches of hyperfocus to quick creativity spurts, from early morning flow to late-night inspiration. Forcing us to fit someone else's "ideal" work will not help us do our best. Worse yet, trying to "make us fit work" could break us.

It makes a lot more sense to make the work fit us. And there are more ways to accomplish this than many people realize.

In the previous chapter, we discussed how flexibility in where we work helps create productive, neuroinclusive, and generally more inclusive organizations. But *place* (working from home, office, or the coffee shop) and *mode* (different forms of hybrid, remote, or face-to-face work) are just two of the aspects of flexibility that can make or break the employee experience. Ellen Ernst Kossek, a leading researcher of flexibility in the workplace, and her colleagues describe **schedule, workload, and continuity** as other ways to make work more flexible.[3]

Maximizing the productivity and well-being of differently wired people across different occupations calls for using all forms of flexibility. In the first part of this chapter, we explore how schedule, continuity, and workload flexibility can support neurodivergent employees and help create inclusive organizations. In the second part, we discuss how other aspects of both face-to-face and remote work organization can make work inclusive—or exclusionary.[4]

POINTS OF PRACTICE

SCHEDULE FLEXIBILITY

Adjusting work hours to fit an employee's needs is a major facilitator of inclusion. Schedule flexibility can make working possible for some employees and greatly support productivity for others. For example, what if Caroline could have officially worked at least a portion of her "paid" day during the early or late quiet hours, rather than fighting a losing battle for focus amidst the office bustle and then having to put in extra hours to get the work done? It would have been a win-win for her well-being and for maximizing her talents in the service to the organization.

There are many ways flexibility can help employees:

- Parents may use flexibility to align their schedule with their child's school schedule. Many countries such as Argentina and Sweden have passed legislation that supports flexible scheduling for employees who care for children or adults.[5]
- Dyspraxic, autistic, or physically disabled employees may need a later start time to avoid rush-hour traffic with its overwhelm and, in some cases, significant danger of physical harm from being forcefully pushed by other commuters in a busy city or becoming a target of road rage.
- Sleep differences, unique circadian patterns, caretaking responsibilities, school schedules, and other aspects of life can conflict with traditional work hours, so people would benefit from the ability to choose their shifts or trade shifts with others.

In short, schedule flexibility can support the needs of neurodivergent employees and benefit those dealing with multiple and intersectional challenges.

Schedule modifications do not need to come in the form of individual accommodations. Around the world, entire countries embrace schedule flexibility as a rule rather than an exception. For example, in 1996, Finland's legislation gave most employees the right to adjust their working hours by starting or finishing up to three hours earlier or later.[6] In 2020, this legislation expanded to give full-time employees the option to work when and where they want for half their working time.[7]

Many organizations have experimented with adapting schedules for all employees. Initially, some tried a compressed week—working fewer but longer days

(4 days × 10 hours) to keep the 40-hour week—which saved commute time but in some cases increased fatigue. Still, compressed schemas are often well received by employees and used by organizations of different types, including departments within the US government,[8] increasingly, in combination with remote work.

In a creative schema that earned it many glowing Glassdoor reviews from employees,[9] Lockheed Martin, a defense technology company, offers a "4XFlex" schedule.[10] This flexible approach is based on working 75 hours over 8 or 9 days in a two-week period, allowing for longer weekends. This scheduling flexibility is often combined with remote work.

Increasingly popular modifications to the workweek include shorter weeks at the same pay as a 40-hour week. A 32-hour (4 days × 8 hours) week with full pay has been successfully tested around the world.[11] After Microsoft offices in Japan adopted this schedule, productivity improved by 40 percent and electricity costs fell by 23 percent.[12] Wide-scale trials by multiple organizations in Iceland, the UK, Portugal, and many other countries led to many organizations adopting the 32-hour week permanently.[11] A 30-hour (5 days × 6 hours) week with full pay also produced positive results.[13,14] People are more productive when they are less tired. Working more efficiently, such as by minimizing meetings, allows teams to complete their work faster and earn the same income.

Although not every role in all organizations can operate on shorter week schedules, shift choice, as a specific form of schedule flexibility, is possible for all occupational groups. It can support people in industries that are sometimes excluded from the benefits of flexible work, such as manufacturing workers, some agriculture workers, and security and medical personnel. With the help of scheduling software, such flexibility is also increasingly easy to implement.

 POINTS OF PRACTICE

WORKLOAD FLEXIBILITY

Many employees value **workload** flexibility options, such as working full-time, part-time, or sharing a job with another part-time employee. For example, Ultranauts, with its majority autistic workforce, has used a variety of full-time and part-time options as an effective neuroinclusion tool since the earliest days of the company. Employees appreciate the option to tailor their workload to their energy patterns and life circumstances, says the CEO, Rajesh Anandan.[15]

Traditionally favored by women and caretakers,[16] job sharing can be an excellent option for neurodivergent employees. It can also be effectively combined with job crafting to create win-win arrangements in which employees work with their strengths and advance organizational outcomes using the "spikes" of their talent profiles.[17] In one win-win arrangement I helped negotiate, an autistic and dyslexic duo, each working a three-quarter schedule, used their unique combination of writing, analytic, graphic design, and relational skills to drastically improve the effectiveness of a small organization's marketing. Flexible working is essential for neurodivergent workers,[18] 50 percent of whom say that they are willing to quit when they do not feel supported.[19]

For organizations, part-time work is also a fantastic recruitment and diversity tool that provides access to talent who otherwise would not apply. As an illustration, when Zurich, a global insurance company, added the words "part-time," "job share," or "flexible working" to all its UK job advertisements, applications from women increased by 16 percent.[20] Combined with the use of gender-neutral language in job postings, the focus on flexibility resulted in nearly 20 percent more women applying for management roles, and the number of women hired for senior positions also rose by one-third.[21]

With planning, workload flexibility is possible across all types of occupations. Moreover, it can be combined with continuity flexibility to accommodate a wide range of circumstances, goals, and needs.

 POINTS OF PRACTICE

CONTINUITY FLEXIBILITY

Continuity flexibility allows employees to take a leave of absence without losing their jobs and, in many cases, while retaining all or most of their salary. Most countries provide paid maternity leaves,[22] and there is increasing support for paternity leaves as well. Other valuable types of leaves that can support inclusion and employee well-being include family, sick, mental health, education, sabbaticals,[23] and adult gap years.[24] All forms of leaves support organizational engagement and commitment—especially if used as a *proactive* tool to *prevent* burnout or bore-out. Using leaves *reactively* as a last resort for already burnt-out employees should be secondary to their proactive use.[23]

Continuity flexibility can help employees handle their care responsibilities or their health conditions, ranging from autoimmune disorder flare-ups and long COVID to mental health challenges such as seasonal depression or bipolar depression. For example, Germany has a provision for burnout recovery leave that can last several months.[25] Leaves can support the infinite number of intersections of neurodivergence with various life challenges. For autistic employees, the pro active use of leaves could make a difference in preventing autistic burnout, a particularly debilitating and long-lasting form of burnout.[26,27]

EMPLOYER EXCELLENCE

LEGALITE: A HUMAN-CENTRIC LAW FIRM

The legal profession is not known for flexible work. But even in this traditional industry, it is possible to create a different type of law firm. When Marianne Marchesi started Legalite in 2017, she was able to design a business and a job that worked for her lifestyle, and she found herself loving work again for the first time in a long time. Then she thought, "*Why can't I extend this to my employees?*"

She could and she did—with a tremendous impact on her future employees who have opportunities to work flexibly, remotely, and tailor their careers to their strengths. For example, Shevonne Joyce, head of Business Strategy & Innovation at Legalite, a disabled and neurodivergent working parent of two disabled and neurodivergent children, always felt like a misfit. Professionally, not fitting into a prescribed box was a challenge. As Shevonne shares, "*While some organizations saw the opportunity and benefit in everything I had to offer, others were preoccupied with trying to squeeze me into the box they understood.*"[28]

Legalite's Work by Design™ approach has given Shevonne "*the kind of exciting and fulfilling career that wouldn't be possible at many traditional firms.*" It helped her to build her own "box" and fully shine.[27]

DEEP DIVE

FINER POINTS OF FLEXIBILITY

Even though hybrid and remote work can greatly benefit employees, they are only truly effective when inclusively implemented. Several aspects of poorly organized remote work can be stressful for employees, and particularly detrimental for neurodivergent people.

- A common threat to employee well-being and inclusion in remote environments is excessive or inappropriate use of videoconferencing. It results in what became infamously known during the COVID-19 pandemic as "Zoom fatigue" and, more generally, elevated stress levels.[29,30,31]

- Remote, hybrid, and even face-to-face teams overuse asynchronous tools as synchronous ones. The expectation of immediate email or message board responses results in interruptions, frustration, and the loss of productivity.[32]
- Meetings of all kinds and formats consume employee time. According to some reports, knowledge workers spend more than 85 percent of their time in meetings, drastically cutting into actual productivity and creative work.[33] The stress of outdated, performative, and counterproductive requirements, such as excessive meetings, harms employees' psychological, physical, and mental well-being.[34] The lack of control, constant social pressure, and chronic stress in workplaces harm the brain's ability to deliver much-needed creativity.[35] Because 35 percent of neurodivergent employees report struggling with focus, they are particularly likely to become overwhelmed by poor work organization.[36] For autistic individuals who also have an intense reaction to stress[37] and are wired to need focused time,[38] the cost of interruptions is much higher than average.
- One-size-fits-all requirements ignore variability in how individuals work best. Equality is not equity. Supporting different people in doing their best work means considering their individual productivity needs with accountability based on outcomes rather than personal style.

Using neuroinclusive practices of work organization can improve both virtual and face-to-face work. Because neuroinclusive practices are flexible practices, they are likely to benefit all employees.

 BRIDGING SCIENCE AND PRACTICE

VIDEOCONFERENCING GUIDELINES

Videoconferencing can be a wonderfully helpful, time-saving tool. Yet, it can contribute to burnout if not used correctly and inclusively. Stanford professor Jeremy Bailenson outlined four possible explanations for Zoom fatigue:[29]

1. Excessive amount of close-up eye gazing, which simulates interaction at a distance that is normally reserved for intimate encounters
2. High cognitive load of remote social-cues processing
3. Increased self-evaluation from staring at a video of oneself
4. Constraints on physical mobility

Of these, the first three are likely to be particularly anxiety-provoking and exhausting for autistic employees who already must work extra hard to process social cues and handle the stress of eye contact. For many ADHDers, the constraints on physical mobility are likely to be extremely taxing. Of course, various intersectionalities can create double- or triple-whammy effects.

Bailenson's analysis suggests limiting self-view, allowing audio-only calls, and generally reducing the number of meetings as best practices for videoconferencing. Other studies suggest that audio-only calls can help us focus on listening because there is limited video distraction. In essence, visual "presenteeism" is just as unproductive as old-fashioned office presenteeism. Flexibility in choosing a mode of communication is especially vital for neurodivergent individuals who are more likely to suffer from Zoom overwhelm.[30,31]

 POINTS OF PRACTICE

ASYNCHRONOUS COMMUNICATION AND COLLABORATION

Email is not inherently evil, although some may disagree. However, the *misuse* of email and other asynchronous tools, such as message boards, as synchronous tools—when coupled with the culture of immediate response—can make us feel stressed, overwhelmed, and like we are drowning in a seemingly endless deluge of messages interfering with our essential work.[32,39] In "immediate response" cultures, managers and coworkers impatiently send follow-ups, and email threads explode with multiple people making sure they are being perceived as working. Under the pressure of shallow work, employees check their messages every six minutes,[39] leaving no time for deep work that requires concentration.[40]

Collaboration is not inherently evil. Yet, under the guise of collaboration, the average employee is interrupted 50–60 times per day,[41] and 80 percent of these interruptions are unimportant.[42]

To support focus and productivity and reduce burnout, leaders need to protect employee ability to concentrate. Some of the ways to do this include:[39]

- Ensuring that asynchronous communication tools are used as such. Leaders must demonstrate that it is *really okay* not to respond to messages in real time, decline meeting requests, turn off notifications, and not be online all day.

- Encouraging the use of shared documents to empower people to work on the same document asynchronously without the burden of version control.
- Encouraging the use of task boards to show a clear and definitive state of team projects.
- Supporting employees in blocking time for focused work and aligning work calendars with their biological times for best work.

These suggestions are not specific to neuroinclusion—in fact, they were developed to support all employees in doing their best work. Efficient work organization truly benefits everyone. However, for those neurodivergent employees who need extended time for concentration and struggle with attention switching and multitasking, these suggestions could make a positive difference in their overall ability to work.[43]

 DEEP DIVE

DEFENDING THE DEEP WORK

Cal Newport defines deep work as the ability to focus without distraction on a cognitively demanding task—usually at least for three to four uninterrupted hours.[44] Having time for deep work can help employees achieve flow: an enjoyable state of focusing on mastering a challenge.[45] In flow, we do our best, most creative work. Support for focusing on work that really matters without getting interrupted is vital for many neurodivergent people.[31,38]

A useful approach to preventing overpacked calendars is *timeboxing*, a technique that sets aside blocks of time for focused work. Those of us who need considerable time stretches to get into our best productivity mode particularly appreciate this scheduling approach. Individual employees can use timeboxing by reserving specific blocks of time—for example, three hours in the morning— for deep work and then making colleagues and managers aware that they are not to be interrupted during this time. Of course, timeboxing requires an environment that promotes true productivity and psychological safety. Despite the fact that timeboxing can increase productivity, workplaces favoring productivity theater are likely to punish it.

Collective timeboxing, where entire teams designate distraction-free periods, can multiply the benefits of focused work.[46] However, just as individuals need the support of their teams to facilitate deep work, team efforts must be supported by organizational cultures, policies, and procedures.[47]

A growing number of organizations are unlocking the benefits of deeper work by introducing no-meetings days or half-days.[33] Shopify, for example, canceled all meetings for a month in early 2023, relying instead on asynchronous communication.[48] This helped increase productivity. Organizations committed to deep work can take the no-meetings philosophy further by fully embracing a "do not disturb" approach. This practice involves creating time blocks with no-message, no-call, no-email, and no-dropping-by rules when everyone can focus on heads-down work. Knowing that they will have, say, Monday afternoons and Wednesday and Thursday mornings designated for deep work can be a major stress relief for neurodivergent employees and, likely, for most of their colleagues as well.

> The big picture of productive and neuroinclusive work organization calls for two cultural shifts:
>
> - Shift from rewarding productivity theater to rewarding quality of outcomes and long-term value
> - Shift from reactive work to proactive work

 POINTS OF PRACTICE

FROM PRODUCTIVITY THEATER TO OUTCOMES

Productivity is not about getting more done in less time. It's about getting the work that matters done well, in a minimal amount of time without sacrificing value and quality. To support true productivity, many organizations may need to move away from the cultures of "looking busy" and embrace outcomes-based work.[49,50] This transition will likely require training managers and supervisors in outcomes-focused ways of thinking and working. These four strategies for creating a more focused organization can help smooth this transition.[47]

1. Ensure that reward systems are based on outcomes, quality, and long-term value. When organizations shift the focus from visible activities to long-term value, they show that high-quality work, continuous system improvement, and positive impact are rewarded and celebrated.

2. Educate managers about the benefits of deep work and its advantages for productivity, focus, and well-being, as well as for neuroinclusion. Focus time also benefits managers, regardless of neurobiology/neurotype.[51]

3. Educate managers not just on time management but also on energy management—working in ways that honor our neurobiology. This can help managers support employees in finding their own rhythm to achieve their best work. Normalize involving employees in structuring their work to maximize their energy and supporting them in working with their natural productivity cycles. For too long, employees had to work against their brains and bodies to fit themselves to rigid expectations. This energy is much better used for ensuring true performance.

4. Invite employees and teams to share their success stories about producing high-quality work using deep work techniques and tailored energy management. It is easier for managers and supervisors to understand the value of deep work if they are shown real-life examples.

One of the reasons for productivity theater is likely employers' expectations that every second of employee time should be filled with activity and with giving 100 percent. According to top productivity expert Greg McKeown, giving 100 percent effort all the time will only lead to burnout and, eventually, lower performance.[52] Giving 85 percent is much more sustainable. Normalizing some slack—and thinking about it as necessary recovery time—allows for a much more realistic and, over time, more productive rhythm of work.

Another root of the culture of "busy" is reactive rather than proactive, well-planned work. Transitioning to a more proactive and methodical mindset can help everyone work with less anxiety and more purpose.

 HUMAN HAPPENINGS

SHIFTING PRIORITIES: SINKHOLES OF EMPLOYEE ENGAGEMENT

Elena Mendez (name changed) was thrilled to join a not-for-profit focused on helping children and youth in need. The work was aligned with her values, and she invested many extra hours into developing a program that would provide STEM learning opportunities for economically disadvantaged teenagers. For this project, she created infographics illustrating the need for and the effectiveness of the proposed methodology based on interventions in other countries. Impressed, one of her managers soon wanted her to design similar materials for a project focused on teaching dental hygiene. Elena put much work into researching this additional assignment while also trying to fully support the STEM project. Then another manager came with an urgent research request related to another project. Then someone else came with another urgent request.

As a people pleaser with complex PTSD, Elena worked extra hard to support others, as well as her "baby," the STEM project. Yet, feeling incoming burnout, she offered to teach someone to do the infographics while focusing on her original work. Instead, the organization gave the STEM project to someone who was not invested in it while assigning Elena to work on always seemingly urgent promotional materials, research briefs, board pitches, blog posts, and the like— what seemed like a completely disconnected portfolio of activities. Some of the work she produced was shelved before it was completed in favor of a different request. For several months she dealt with ever-shifting "urgent" priorities and initiatives. During that time, she also watched her beloved STEM project fizzle and die from the lack of attention. Distraught and depressed, she "tore her heart away," torturously disengaging from the organization she loved.

When she left, it took two people to replace her.

 POINTS OF PRACTICE

FROM REACTIVE TO PROACTIVE WORK

Uncovering and eliminating reactive business patterns and developing a culture of proactive and purposeful work are vital for maximizing productivity and achieving long-term goals. In burnout cultures, employees are constantly trying to reactively deal with the most immediate problems, often without time or opportunity to consider whether the immediate task is, in fact, *important*. Clear goals and well-planned pacing and procedures can free up energy that is consumed by the anxiety and stress characteristic of reactive work environments and instead direct it toward performance, creativity, and innovation.

However, the transition from a burnout culture may be challenging for some managers. The following strategies for creating a proactive work environment can help teams focus on achieving long-term goals and proactively addressing challenges:

1. Set clear, realistic, and resource-supported goals.[53] Employees burn out when "visioning" turns into unsupported dreams and mandates without

resources. Resource-aligned planning can significantly improve morale and productivity.

2. Develop proactive prioritizing decision trees and criteria. Clear criteria for assessing specifying importance and urgency should determine the priority of tasks. In our stress-filled and decision-fatigued organizations, it is all too common to react to every new request or issue as soon as it arises, resulting in the tyranny of the urgent and the neglect of the important. With proactive prioritizing, we can ensure that the most critical tasks are addressed first. Investing time into developing clear decision trees and criteria for prioritizing work is likely to be appreciated by many neurodivergent employees, and it can help reduce everyone's anxiety. In addition, it will boost morale and save managers' time in the long run.

3. Develop transparent processes and systems. Predictable workflows can essentially automate the routine and allow everyone to focus on more creative, forward-focused work. Using digital systems for asynchronous collaboration has the additional benefits of increasing transparency, lowering employee stress, and supporting creativity and inclusion.[39,54]

4. Consider whether a results-only work environment model (ROWE) might be right for your organization. With a results-only approach, supervisors manage work—not people—and people manage themselves.[55,56,57] ROWE works best for environments with highly skilled employees who are self-disciplined and self-motivated.

5. You can experiment with improvements and continue fine-tuning them based on data.

It is essential to note that even though managers and line supervisors can do a lot to support their employees, without organizational-level change they will be hard–pressed to maintain outcomes-focused and proactive work environments.[58] To be fully effective, those with the most leverage in organizations must model and nurture cultures that support purposeful, focused work; strategic and goal-oriented operations; and neuroinclusion.

 DEEP DIVE

COLLABORATION: MAGIC OR MISERY?

Collaboration and teamwork are fantastic tools for accomplishing work that one individual could not have done. And even though individuals have different social needs, positive workplace relationships benefit everyone: some just need less social time than others. However, because teamwork and collaboration are often poorly managed, employees can suffer from "collaboration overload": many people spend around 80–85 percent of their time in meetings or answering requests for information or help, leaving little time for their own work.[33,59] Collaboration strain is also unevenly distributed, with 3–5 percent of people responsible for 20–35 percent of value-added collaborations. These super-collaborators are likely to eventually burn out and leave.[33,34,59]

Most of us have teamwork nightmare stories; just think of those collaborators who demand credit even though their only contribution was irrecoverably deleting everyone's work.

Collaboration fiascoes reflect issues much deeper than individual contributors' errors. Rather than being tools used as needed and when appropriate, collaboration and teamwork became pseudo-sacred, idolized for their own sake, whether they are the best tools for the task or not. That uncritical take on collaboration, coupled with inefficient collaboration methods, results in a proliferation of meetings, messages, and misery.

There are additional reasons for teamwork trauma. Sometimes teams are asked to do the impossible with the resources given. Alas, teamwork is not a magic cure for chronic underresourcing, regardless of how many times someone says "synergy" or "give it 110 percent" while waving a pen.

In other situations, a teamwork approach simply does not fit the task, and the work could be better handled individually. Teamwork is a fine hammer, but not every project is a nail.

Teams and managers can use the following guidelines to support successful collaborative work that is also neuroinclusive.

Eliminate Unnecessary Collaboration Demands

1. Develop clear links between organizational values, specific goals, and team projects. Approach collaboration as a tool, not a cult.
2. Prioritize tasks and projects based on key values and goals. Say "no" to projects that lack clear alignment. This clarity of purpose will help both frame and motivate team efforts.
3. Use project management tools and techniques to streamline workflows and set realistic deadlines.
4. Avoid collaboration overload. Not all projects require collaboration.
5. Avoid using collaboration in an attempt to make up for chronic underresourcing.

Make the Necessary Work Efficient and Fair

1. Make sure the right people, and only the right people, with the needed set of skills are on the team. Smaller teams can be more efficient than larger ones.

2. Monitor workloads. Regularly assess employee workloads and redistribute tasks if necessary to prevent individuals from becoming overwhelmed by too many projects or too large portions of work on projects. Use workload management tools to track and balance work distribution, with special attention to collaborative contributions that often remain invisible and unrewarded.

3. Align specific assignments on the team with what energizes specific employees. A highly social individual may appreciate handling the calls and contacts portion of the project, and a more introverted person may relish the deep work of doing the research.

4. Foster a culture of productive respect. Encourage employees to honor each others' time and boundaries. Considerate behavior includes avoiding unnecessary meetings, respecting "Do Not Disturb" statuses, and understanding when colleagues need focused work time—or a social break. Nonemergency availability can be provided through regular office hours. What matters is the outcome.

5. Enable team creativity and flexibility in determining how to reach project goals. Support teams in the strength-based distribution of work and finding a balance of synchronous and asynchronous collaboration that works best for the team and the task.

6. Use collaboration tools that support transparency and accountability by design (such as online collaboration tools with contribution history) without invasive monitoring and disruptive check-ins.

Poorly organized and excessive collaborations are taxing for most employees, but those naturally wired for deep work, such as many autistic people and introverts, suffer the most.[43,60] However, suffering from the overload of poorly thought-through boondoggles is not the same as an inability to collaborate.

One of the pernicious myths used as an excuse for the workplace exclusion of autistic people is the myth that they are "not team players." In fact, autistic people can and do collaborate. However, it is important that collaborations and teamwork are meaningful, well organized, and equitable.

EMPLOYER EXCELLENCE

AUTISTIC TEAMWORK

The Spectrum Fusion media team consists of several autistic young adults who produce videos and commercials for organizations while learning what it takes to become media professionals.[61] They also help bust the myth that autistic people don't do teamwork. When Dr. Heidi Stieglitz Ham established the team, she made sure to follow the best practice recommendations for supporting autistic employees: providing spaces for focused work, avoiding social overload, and not insisting on hanging out. But the team surprised her. They *wanted* to work as a team, to be together in the same space, and to hang out after work.

The key to creating an inclusive team environment for autistic individuals is understanding their unique needs and strengths and accepting them for who they are. But these are also universal needs.

Spectrum Fusion created a successful team environment for autistic people that helps create a positive team atmosphere for all:

1. Participation and psychological safety: It's important to create a team environment where ideas are welcomed, not discouraged.[48]
2. Socializing is available but not required: Autistic people *may* struggle with forced socializing after work, especially if it occurs in overstimulating, loud environments.[62] But that does not mean we don't want to socialize when the environment and the company are safe and welcoming.
3. Authenticity is welcomed: Most people thrive in environments where authenticity is appreciated. Masking, or camouflaging, is exhausting and leads to burnout.[63] Being able to express our true selves in the workplace frees up our energy for performance and creativity.
4. Clear aim: When the team has a clear purpose, autistic people enjoy using their unique strengths and expertise to contribute to the team's success.
5. Roles match skills: When the roles on the team match the talents of contributors (and not the group-based stereotypes), they are empowered to contribute to the team's success.[16]
6. Transparency in communication: Autistic individuals, in particular, thrive in transparent environments where information is communicated clearly and openly.[49] Transparency is also vital for organizational productivity overall.

7. Fair play: Sometimes, organizations ask for collaboration while secretly rewarding competition and hidden agendas. Such environments are morally injurious for employees.[64] Because autistic team members tend to consistently follow a set of ethical rules,[66] they are likely to be deeply injured by duplicity and betrayal.[65]

 DEEP DIVE

DIVERSITY OF DELIVERABLES

The Spectrum Fusion media team demonstrates the classic definition of teamwork. Increasingly, however, teamwork doesn't mean brainstorming face-to-face or even working simultaneously in the same space. Virtual collaborations create new opportunities for meaningful participation. Brainwriting and other forms of asynchronous ideation have been shown to be more inclusive, because they allow more people to express themselves. They are also more likely to produce more creative ideas because domineering personalities are not able to talk over quieter thinkers or culturally modest people.[54,67,68,69,70,71,72,73]

The language of teamwork creates a mental association with sports teams, but there are important differences between sports and work. Work teams do not require people to play at the same time with the same ball. The complexity of most knowledge work projects calls for multiple balls—including deep, heads-down work. Individual contributions of this kind are essential and can often be made asynchronously. Hence, teamwork should not be confused with boisterous face-to-face interactions that may or may not be productive. People can deliver exceptional individual work that benefits the team as a whole—and it should count as teamwork. Pioneering management thinker Edwards W. Deming puts it this way: *"There are abundant examples of people that cannot work well in a team, but who demonstrate unquestionable achievement in the form of respect of colleagues and of peers, through inventions and publications in scientific journals. . . . The company must recognize the contributions of such people, and provide assistance to them."*[74]

Focusing on contributions can help us avoid judging people based on their work style or personality style, which often leads to exclusion. Nevertheless, for all kinds of personalities to thrive, flexible and efficient work organization is necessary but not sufficient. People also need safe, transparent, ethical environments. And that is the focus of the next chapter.

KEY TAKEAWAYS

- *Purposeful planning of work is essential for ensuring that all activity is productive.*
- *Productivity is best facilitated by flexibility; a focus on outcomes helps eliminate "productivity theater."*
- *Schedule, workload, and continuity flexibility are increasingly used around the world to support employee productivity and well-being. These are also vital for neuroinclusion.*
- *To support productivity, organizations should monitor for and eliminate collaboration overload, such as unnecessary meetings.*
- *The use of asynchronous collaboration tools can help track contributions for fair performance evaluation without invasive monitoring.*

 DEVELOPMENTAL QUESTIONS

For employees:
- How purposeful and proactive is your current workload?
- How well do you understand your own performance needs? Are you able to communicate these needs?
- Can employees in your organization advocate for a more flexible and inclusive approach?
- Who could you collaborate with in promoting best productivity practices?

For managers/direct supervisors:
- Are there productivity assumptions in your organization that might be harming rather than supporting employee productivity?
- Do you know the productivity needs of your employees?
- How could you get to know those needs better and incorporate that knowledge into creating a more purposeful and productive workflow?

For HR and upper management:
- How (neuro)inclusive is your system of work organization?

- Are there productivity assumptions in your organization that might be harming rather than supporting employee productivity?
- How can examples in this chapter help you rethink or redesign your organization's approach to ensuring high and sustainable performance?

CHAPTER EIGHT

PSYCHOLOGICAL WORK ENVIRONMENT

Detoxifying Work

Never doubt that a small group of thoughtful, concerned citizens can change the world. Indeed it is the only thing that ever has.

—Margaret Mead

 NEURODIVERSITY NARRATIVES

THE OPPOSITE OF TOXIC

In the prelude and dedication of this book, I told a story about a good concert crowd. More than 100,000 people were gathered at the Glastonbury Festival of Contemporary Performance in England on June 24, 2023. They came to a concert—but ended up giving hope of inclusion to many neurodivergent people. When the performance of Lewis Capaldi, a Scottish singer-songwriter, was interrupted by tics associated with Tourette Syndrome, the crowd showed no impatience or mockery. Instead, the fans displayed their love and support and finished Capaldi's hit song "Someone You Loved" for him.[1,2] It was a show of kindness and humanity that many neurodivergent people long for.

These fans also helped reenergize my work as I was finishing this book in California, halfway around the world from England.

In effect, the Glastonbury crowd was the opposite of a toxic organizational culture, which is disrespectful, noninclusive, unethical, cutthroat, and abusive.[3] The Glastonbury crowd was respectful, inclusive, ethical, collaborative, and supportive. What if organizations could create a Glastonbury-like psychological environment? It would likely support not only neuroinclusion but also overall human and organizational thriving.

In this chapter, we explore what makes organizations toxic and what can help clean up unhealthy psychological environments.

 BRIDGING SCIENCE AND PRACTICE

WHAT EXACTLY IS A TOXIC CULTURE?

A study of more than 1.3 million employee reviews on Glassdoor—an anonymous review site on which employees or former employees can rate their organizations—revealed the five attributes of toxic cultures—noninclusive, disrespectful, unethical, cutthroat, and abusive.[3] These attributes play a major role in employee turnover. They also can perpetuate neuroexclusion.

1. **Noninclusive:** This factor combines a lack of inclusion based on key human attributes such as race or disability and the generally noninclusive culture. A generally noninclusive environment may have elements of nepotism, managerial favoritism toward those most similar to them, cliques/clubs/in-crowds, and an overall exclusionary atmosphere. The lack of inclusion is the most potent predictor of whether employees perceive a company's culture as toxic.

2. **Disrespectful:** Employees describe environments where they feel disrespected as "soul crushing." Respect had the most impact on how employees rated the corporate culture.

3. **Unethical:** The ethics factor captures comments about a company's integrity, covering behaviors from dishonesty to disregarding important regulations, such as those supporting health and safety or privacy. Lying, misleading, making false promises, and hiding the truth by using "smoke and mirrors" and "sugarcoating" are also associated with this factor.

4. **Cutthroat:** Coworker backstabbing, "throwing people under the bus," and sabotaging behaviors characteristic of unhealthy competition are among the key factors leading employees to perceive their organizational cultures as toxic.

5. **Abusive:** This involves a pattern of hostile behavior by managers toward employees. Bullying, yelling, belittling, condescending, and talking down to employees and other aggressive behaviors fall under this category.

No person of any neurotype should work in an abusive environment. Safety from abuse must be a basic right for all employees. It is also essential for neuro-inclusion. Unfortunately, many stories illustrate the prevalence and the impact of unhealthy environments.

 HUMAN HAPPENINGS

READ MY MIND

Janice Mandel, a marketing and branding professional from Toronto, Canada, recalls working for a bully. The bullying took the form of giving the silent treatment, making belittling comments, lecturing, and providing unwarranted performance feedback.[4]

There was also an expectation that she would be a mind reader. Once, Janice gave her boss a final draft of a time-sensitive report for review. He threw it on the floor of his office and refused to look at it for a month. That was a "punishment" for something she said that he didn't like. He refused to tell Janice what that was, informing her that she should know what he was thinking without him having to tell her.

Janice, a neurotypical, found such interactions hard to cope with, although she was determined not to let the toxic environment get the better of her. But she also noticed that a colleague with a diagnosed mental health condition struggled even more and had to take leaves to cope with the stress.

Managerial behavior can make or break the employee experience; research shows that managers have as much influence on employee mental health as their spouses.[5] In the case of many neurodivergent employees, breaking is a heightened risk because of prior trauma, hereditary vulnerability, or both.[6] Expecting employees to guess and fulfill unspoken wishes is not fair to anyone. Yet, many neurodivergent employees might not only have difficulty reading veiled signals but also may have been repeatedly abused, called names, or punished for not "reading the minds" of those with power over them and for being different since they were children. The history of abuse may produce a much stronger, retraumatizing reaction to workplace mistreatment.

HUMAN HAPPENINGS

TRAUMA AND TOXICITY

Linda Roloff, a disabled and neurodivergent (migraines + ADHD) direct support professional from St. Paul, Minnesota, in the US, explains how early trauma affected her work experience and has likely increased the likelihood of workplace trauma:[7]

> *Being different since birth, has caused a lot of trauma. In school, I was often bullied. I also had difficulty maintaining friendships because communication is so difficult. I don't hear some consonant sounds, and my speech is a little hard for others to understand. . . . I have a lot of trauma, which only makes things worse in terms of communication and causes chronic pain.*

Unfortunately, many of her early work environments added to Linda's trauma:

> *Coworkers and even some managers would make jokes about me that they thought I wasn't smart enough to understand. They were wrong. Communication problems do not indicate intelligence. One thing that I do know is that I am smart. I did understand the snide comments and also when being frozen out.*

Eventually, Linda went to college as an adult and made her way up in the workplace. For many years, she worked for a large not-for-profit that was supportive. Although she did *"sometimes encounter coworkers who just didn't get it when it comes to respect and inclusion"* their bad behavior wasn't tolerated. Linda's manager made sure she had the accommodations to be successful. In her first nine years there, she never had a negative review—only praise from clients and coworkers.

Unfortunately, when Linda returned to the company after taking some family time, it was under new management, and her experience was not the same: *"There was a very popular employee who made jokes (that I fully understood) at my expense in front of team members and HR. They laughed at her 'jokes' . . . The focus changed from person-centered to just . . . mak[ing] money for our non-profit."* Most of Linda's coworkers would not talk to her or even answer her questions. She was pushed out, and the HR person announced her termination at a meeting while smiling broadly.

The bullying Linda had experienced was blamed entirely on her, *"with excuses for how I had done things wrong to deserve that treatment. Bad actors were not held accountable. There's so many things that I have repeatedly gone to therapy to cope with that can't be undone."*

Linda moved on to other jobs and plans to retire in a few years.

Linda's story illustrates multiple aspects of toxic organizational environments—exclusion, disrespect, and abuse. It also demonstrates that management can strongly impact cultures and the employee experience—for better or worse. Toxic or anti-toxic work environments often reflect choices made by organizational decision makers.

Extensive research shows that how leaders behave, the social norms they establish through behavior they reward and tolerate, and the work design they mandate can create or clean up toxic cultures.[8] Organizational systems, procedures, and expectations typically determine whether bullying is permissible, cutthroat behavior is encouraged, and ethical violations are overlooked.[9,10,11]

As Becca Lory Hector, an autistic founder of the Truly Inclusive Leadership consulting company has put it,

> *The responsibility for creating psychologically safe workplaces falls on the shoulders of a company's leadership. Leaders who understand the importance of psychological safety, actively and successfully create, and maintain, nontoxic culture in their companies by: encouraging creativity, initiative, and autonomy, being sensitive, respectful, and responsive to employees' needs, supporting continued professional learning and development, being available for mentoring and resources, and by modeling accountability and sharing credit.[12]*

How can leaders use organizational science and the Canary Code principles to detoxify work environments?

 DEEP DIVE

MAKING ENVIRONMENTS INCLUSIVE

Every Canary Code principle is vital to building inclusive workplaces Organizational justice in particular, however, is an essential lever for making systems more inclusive.

For example, one of the companies I worked with had much lower levels of promotion for people from marginalized groups, leading to lower morale, high turnover, and loss of talent. Using the levers of organizational justice, we were able to create a fairer system that helps retain talent and diversify a leadership pipeline. Specifically, two systemic changes helped support organizational justice: (1) revising promotion forms to align evaluations with explicit, detailed criteria and (2) adding a mechanism for an optional supplementary review of decisions via an impartial ombudsperson office.[13] Ensuring transparency and developing systems for procedural justice can help support equity and inclusion on the organizational level, even if unconscious or conscious biases are present to some extent on the individual level.

Here is an in-a-nutshell view of how each Canary Code principle provides valuable tools for detoxifying cultures and making them more inclusive.

1. **Participation:** Making everyone's perspectives heard can help create a sense of shared agency and break down siloes and hierarchical barriers that provide opportunities and excuses for exclusion.

2. **Focus on Outcomes:** Work outcomes are not just individual but also collective. To maximize the positive impact of an outcomes focus on inclusivity, teams and departments must balance independence and interdependence, autonomy and unity, and individual and team projects. The pursuit of common goals helps cultivate a sense of unity.[14,15] At the same time, research shows that independence also supports inclusive cultures, and giving employees autonomy in determining how best to accomplish goals improves morale.[8,16,17] For example, people who have protected time allocated for focused work on individual projects are less likely to suffer from collaboration overload and the lack of autonomy. At the same time, a connection to a healthy and inclusive team can support a sense of belonging and shared achievement.

3. **Flexibility:** Rigid work environments hinder inclusion. Implementing flexible work practices, from job crafting to offering adaptable benefits, can help attract and retain a broader range of talent.

4. **Transparency and Clear Communication:** Honest communication is incompatible with cliquish behavior, and transparency makes nepotism and favoritism much harder to pull off.[18] Transparency also levels the playing field for employees from less privileged backgrounds.

5. **Focus on Organizational Justice:** Justice ensures that all employees experience fairness in outcomes, processes, interpersonal treatment, access to information, and the ability to contribute. Fairness in processes supports equity in hiring, pay, benefits, and promotions.

Moreover, procedural justice helps establish organization wide social norms and behavioral examples of fairness. Research indicates that changing social norms and expectations is a more effective form of ameliorating the effects of implicit biases than individual-level interventions.[19,20]

6. **Valid Tools for Decision Making:** Evidence-based decisions are a foundation of fairness and set an environment for inclusion.

In most organizations, neuroinclusion is likely to require additional education because an understanding of neurodiversity is still lacking. However, much learning comes from taking action, and a combination of action and continuous data-informed improvement helps organizations refine their systems.

 DEEP DIVE

RESTORING RESPECT

A classic example of transforming the culture of a major company from being infamously brutal, hostile, and backstabbing into one much more respectful and inclusive is Satya Nadella's work with Microsoft.[21] After taking over in 2014, Nadella focused on developing empathy and compassion by encouraging the leadership team to practice nonviolent communication (NVC).[22] In a simplified form, the four components of NVC are nonjudgmental observation and stating one's feelings, needs, and requests without demanding or blaming.[22] In the context of neuroinclusion, alternatives to NVC that focus more on facts than on feelings might be more considerate of people with alexithymia, a difficulty in labeling feelings.[23] Nevertheless, Nadella's approach and NVC helped make Microsoft's culture significantly more respectful.[21]

In addition to considerate communication, all principles of the Canary Code are relevant to building respect:

1. **Participation:** By involving employees from all backgrounds in decision making, organizations demonstrate respect for the value of diverse perspectives and set behavioral norms for all organizational members.

2. **Focus on Outcomes:** A focus on outcomes communicates and strengthens respect for individual needs and working styles, supporting an overall culture of embracing human differences.

3. **Flexibility:** Providing flexibility acknowledges that a one-size-fits-all approach doesn't work. It shows respect for individual circumstances and

strengths and recognizes that different people have different paths to achievement.

4. **Organizational Justice:** Employees feel valued and respected when there's a clear commitment to fairness in all organizational processes. They are also more likely to follow the norms of respect.[8]

5. **Transparency and Clear Communication:** Open, multiple communication channels demonstrate respect for differences in communication needs and reduce the chances of misunderstandings or misinterpretations. Making respect an explicit principle of communication, as Nadella did at Microsoft, can significantly change the tone of organizational culture.

6. **Valid Tools for Decision Making:** Making decisions based on clear, unbiased criteria demonstrates respect for the abilities and contributions of all employees. It also helps develop employee trust in the system.

 DEEP DIVE

ENSURING ETHICAL BEHAVIOR

Unethical organizational practices result in one of the most insidious types of workplace harm—moral injury. This concept was developed by Jonathan Shay, a psychiatrist working with military veterans.[24] Moral injury is caused by a threat to one's *morality*, such as harming others or failing to prevent harm, and observing leadership's betrayal in high-stakes situations.[25]

The potential for moral injury exists in most jobs. For example, making products with unsafe ingredients, manipulating vulnerable customers, or enforcing discriminatory organizational policies can all result in moral distress. Over time, moral distress can develop into a moral injury that may cause a resignation or an illness. For example, a recruiter instructed only to move forward applications from younger people may experience a moral injury from enacting ageism. An HR manager ordered to make the process of requesting and receiving disability accommodations as cumbersome and exhausting as possible may be distressed by being an instrument of systemic ableism.

In other work, I defined moral injury across occupations as a "trauma response to witnessing or participating in workplace behaviors that contradict one's moral beliefs in high-stakes situations with the potential of physical, psychological, social, or economic harm to others."[26] Although the experience of distress is subjective, focusing on high-stakes situations and significant harm helps preserve the gravity of the concept and its military, life-and-death roots.

The elevated sense of justice that often occurs among neurominorities, along with a history of trauma, could make these employees particularly vulnerable to moral injury and even exclude them from some jobs.[27,28,29] The best way to prevent moral injury is to ensure transparent and ethical organizational operations. For example, organizations should provide multiple ways for employees to voice their ethical concerns and ensure transparent follow-up. Making ethics a non-negotiable element of hiring, promotion, and leadership training is also crucial for maintaining healthy cultures.[26]

Where moral injury has occurred, reestablishing trust between organizations and employees and between organizations and the community requires systemic, radical transparency. Organizations may need to make amends to the community and transparently address prior ethical violations. Volkswagen's recovery after the 2015 scandal involving fake diesel emissions measurements provides examples of making amends to the community and increasing organizational transparency.[30]

Transparency and clear communication is the key Canary Code principle in combating the questionable ethics element of organizational toxicity. But all its principles can play a role:

1. **Participation:** Shared agency emphasizes collective responsibility, fostering and rewarding ethical behaviors and cooperation.
2. **Focus on Outcomes:** It is important to ensure that results do not justify an ethical compromise. Achieving outcomes in values-aligned ways should be one of the key criteria for evaluating results. Moreover, maintaining the alignment with values is an *outcome in itself*. One example of a values-focused organization is the outdoor clothing manufacturer Patagonia, which consistently demonstrated its commitment to providing safe and planet-friendly products and even suggested that customers only buy Patagonia products they truly need—and not more.[31]
3. **Flexibility:** Research findings suggest that flexibility in the form of working from home is strongly associated with ethical behavior among finance professionals.[32] One possible explanation is that employees working from home might be better rested, and prior research established a positive connection between sleep and moral awareness.[33] It is also possible that trusting employees to work from home creates a positive self-fulfilling prophecy.
4. **Transparency and Clear Communication:** Transparency is nonnegotiable for ensuring ethical behavior.[34]

5. **Focus on Organizational Justice:** In a culture that systemically scaffolds fairness, ethical behavior becomes the norm.
6. **Valid Tools for Decision Making:** Evidence-based decisions inherently uphold fairness, setting a high standard for ethics.

 DEEP DIVE

CLEANING UP CUTTHROAT CULTURES

When writing this chapter, I played the devil's advocate with myself and tried to think of objections to using the Glastonbury crowd as an example for the workplace. It occurred to me that some could say that attending a concert is not a competitive activity and working at a job is supposed to be a competition. But is competition the best way to think about work?

Jeffrey Pfeffer and Robert Sutton in *The Knowing-Doing Gap* make a crucial distinction: competition *within* companies is not the same as competition *between* them.[35] One of the critical management mistakes that result in toxic cultures is the assumption that external competitiveness requires internal competition among employees. Nothing could be further from the truth. Management practices encouraging zero-sum internal competition, such as forced-distributions performance evaluations that pit employees against each other, can be harmful to individuals and units and counterproductive to organizations.

Encouraging internal competition fails to take into account the importance of collective organizational outcomes and the likely consequences of unethical behavior, such as normalizing sabotage and backstabbing. Organizational performance suffers when internal competition results in cruel and cutthroat behavior toward colleagues.

In addition, the practice of encouraging competition misses the critical distinction between routine physical tasks and the novel intellectual tasks of knowledge work. Unlike physical contests such as sports, complex intellectual work suffers under scrutiny, constant evaluation, and the pressure of competition.[35]

To overcome cutthroat cultures, organizations should reward collaboration while preventing and curtailing the pursuit of self-interest above organizational goals. People's energy is best used to overcome external threats, not infighting.

There are several ways in which implementing the Canary Code principles can help reduce unhealthy and unnecessary competition among coworkers:

1. **Participation:** Engaging all voices can direct energy toward collaborative performance. It makes fighting to be heard unnecessary.
2. **Focus on Outcomes:** Stressing ethically achieved and collectively defined deliverables in a transparent environment can help reduce unhealthy rivalries.
3. **Flexibility:** Offering individualized paths to success allows everyone to shine, reducing the temptation to use cutthroat tactics.
4. **Transparency and Clear Communication:** Transparency safeguards against unhealthy competition and underhanded behaviors.
5. **Valid Tools for Decision Making:** Objective evaluation metrics emphasize genuine merit and contributions to organizational goals.
6. **Focus on Organizational Justice:** Clear and fair procedures reduce the desire and the opportunity to compete unfairly.

 DEEP DIVE

ADDRESSING THE ABUSE

Similarly to competition, abusive behaviors are often misunderstood and seen as personality conflicts or "management" or simply as "not a big deal." However, bullying can be highly detrimental to people and organizations.[10,36] "Management" by bullying does not result in positive outcomes. For example, Rosa Breen, an ADHDer/dyslexic/dyspraxic professional from Belfast in Northern Ireland, tells a story of being humiliated in front of coworkers and chastised like a child with these repeated comments: *"What aren't you getting, Rosa?! How many times do you need to be told!"* Shaming and humiliating are not management. Rosa describes the effects as *"a karate chop to the gut,"* leading to a physical reaction of shutting down. She had to work hard not to let this abuse define her.

Unfortunately, stories like Rosa's are not rare. Neurominority individuals are especially likely to be bullied. As one example, autistic people are more often abused at home and school and targeted by bullies at work than the general population.[37,38] In the UK, half of autistic employees report bullying, harassment, other discrimination, or unfair treatment at work.[39]

In some cases, bullying might be due to the "get smarty pants" phenomenon when top performers are bullied and victimized as a reflection of cutthroat environments.[40] Often, managers in cutthroat cultures assume that bullies are star performers and that their high-level performance justifies abusive behavior. However, true star performers are more likely to be targets than bullies.[41] Typical bullies are mediocre performers who may appear to be stars by stealing credit for the work of others.[44] Bullies are also not motivated by organizational goals: instead, they're driven by self-interest and often victimize organization-focused high performers who are particularly capable, caring, and conscientious.[41,42] Not only are bullies not the stars but one toxic employee also negates the gains of the performance of two superstars and likely causes additional costs.[43,44]

An autistic board and management professional, Justin Donne, tells the story of a CEO who had tried to accuse two board chairs of bullying, while in fact, he was bullying them because he did not like their ethical stance—particularly that of the chair who was a neurodivergent woman.[45] The organizational fallout from this management style has been very high levels of turnover.

This CEO's behavior is also an example of a rarely discussed form of bullying— upward bullying. It includes bullying of managers by their reports and bullying of board chairs by executives. Although it is rarely discussed, upward bullying is not rare, constituting 14 percent of all bullying.[11,46] Unfortunately, many neurodivergent and disabled leaders have experienced this form of bullying.

Christina Ryan, CEO of the Disability Leadership Institute, tells her story:[47]

> *I found out the hard way that some people are really confronted by finding out that their new boss is a disabled woman. The worst bullying I ever experienced was from a younger male . . . who was threatened by me turning up at the same level as him . . . and when I was rapidly promoted to supervise others he started bullying me in horrific ways, belittling me in front of half the floor, undermining my decision making, the whole box and dice. . . . Disabled women aren't supposed to be competent, and we certainly aren't supposed to end up in positions of leadership and responsibility, apparently.*

From the research perspective, bullying behavior involves a complex interplay among multiple social identities and power; biases such as ableism, ageism, and sexism; individual differences; and context. No aspect of identity should be automatically associated with bullying, and no bullying report should be discounted on the basis of social identity or organizational position alone. For example, research shows that 33 percent of bullies are women, who mostly bully other women. Men, in contrast, bully both women and men, but other men are the more likely targets. This makes men slightly more likely targets of bullying overall.[46]

Traditional methods of addressing bullying fail for several key reasons:

- They reactively attempt to address the harm that has already occurred and rarely focus on prevention.
- They place the burden of proof and anti-bullying work on traumatized targets who may not have the coping resources.
- They try to "fix "the personalities of targets and bullies, ignoring the stability of personality and the importance of the environment.
- They ignore differences in the types of bullying, such as overt and hostile ("screamer," likely driven by anger or other emotions) versus covert and instrumental ("schemer," driven by gain and calculated strategy) bullying.[11]

Bullying is largely an opportunistic behavior enabled by dysfunctional environments. A more effective way to address bullying—and detoxify organizations—is to fix systemic issues that make bullying possible and permissible. It is also crucial to focus on prevention. Here is how systemically addressing bullying maps onto the Canary Code principles:

1. **Participation:** Ensuring participation gives everyone a voice and reduces the risk that silence the target will allow bullying to fester. Feeling heard may also reduce negative emotions and possibly prevent some hostile, emotion-driven bullying.
2. **Flexibility:** Asynchronous work tools that support flexibility also document performance and contributions.[48] Tracking contributions can help prevent instrumental bullying, such as stealing credit or making unfair evaluations.
3. **Focus on Organizational Justice:** Just processes reduce the rewards and the utility of instrumental bullying.
4. **Transparency and Clear Communication:** Transparency leaves little room for covert tactics and scheming. Clear communication may also reduce misunderstandings that could result in hostility.
5. **Focus on Outcomes:** Recognizing ethically achieved contributions ensures that all constructive efforts are valued, diminishing the utility of undercutting or undermining.
6. **Valid Tools for Decision Making:** Valid selection and talent-management tools focus on skills and results and can help prevent the hiring and promotion of exploitive and incompetent individuals.

DEEP DIVE

ORGANIZATIONAL POLITICS

In addition to the five factors of organizational toxicity identified by the study of Glassdoor comments,[3] neurodivergent individuals often mention organizational politics as an important factor in their perception of organizations as toxic. It is a major source of work stress.[49] Research also indicates that organizational politics harms the morale of all employees.[50]

Some scholars of organizational politics make a distinction between positive and negative politics.[51] In this view, political skills are neutral and can be used in honest and prosocial ways, not just in dirty, selfish, and dishonest ways:

- **Positive politics** can create networks that boost output and help achieve organizational objectives.
- **Negative politics**, which is what most people think of when organizational politics is mentioned, may involve favoritism, backroom deals, backstabbing, gaslighting, envy-driven bullying, and pushing out of high performers.[44]

Although this distinction is helpful, even some "positive politics" may fall into a gray area of ethics. For example, positively focused networks can still be exclusionary, shutting out voices and individuals who aren't part of the "in-group." This can lead to a lack of diverse perspectives and marginalize some contributors. Networks may also end up being echo chambers where everyone has similar views. Although "being on the same page" might feel great for members of the in-circle, it can stifle innovation and prevent the organization from noticing potential threats or alternative, more effective strategies.

Studies show that morale suffers when employees perceive that organizational politics benefits the most self-serving individuals. Anxiety, burnout, turnover, and disengagement are among the typical effects of highly political environments.[50,52] People who observe others' political behavior are also likely to have significantly lower job satisfaction, task performance, and organizational citizenship behavior.[50]

Long-term organizational harm can also come when politics clogs organizational talent pipelines with mediocre performers and aggressive, incompetent, and overconfident climbers, while preventing the most talented employees from advancement.[53]

Many neurominority employees express frustration with organizational politics. In particular, autistic people find the required impression management to be inauthentic.[54] Politicized environments can also be a direct cause of job loss for autistic people, contributing to high levels of unemployment.[49] However, highly political workplaces do not just exclude autistic people but also put talented employees from many nondominant cultural backgrounds, women, and class migrants at a disadvantage.[55,56,57] And even when women and BIPOC individuals demonstrate political skills, engaging in politics can still backfire.[58] Political behaviors seen as *positive* in members of traditionally dominant groups are seen as *negative* in others ("politics is a white man's game" effect).[58] This means that "training" people from disadvantaged groups in political skills may not necessarily help them.

A more equitable solution might be creating organizational systems characterized by justice and transparency. For example, Legalite, an Australian law firm, uses the tools of "two-way feedback" and "two-way trust and respect" to facilitate safe, transparent, and compassionate communication as an essential part of its inclusive work strategy.[59]

Justice mechanisms can help ensure that organizational members adhere to procedures that apply to all, and transparency supports the development of trust, psychological safety, and organizational performance.[60,61] It is essential for those neurodivergent people who are excluded when they have to decipher vague messages and "read minds." Transparency also supports inclusive and productive cultures.[62]

Creating healthy psychological environments is a part of neuroinclusion and a responsibility of all leaders. Nevertheless, leaders themselves are part of systems that can be harsh, traumatizing, and stress-inducing. Everyone in the organization—sometimes, especially leaders—can benefit from the trauma-informed approach to organizational cultures.

 EMPLOYER EXCELLENCE

A TRAUMA-INFORMED CULTURE: ULTRANAUTS

In its commitment to being a neuroinclusive organization, Ultranauts explicitly embedded trauma-informed interaction principles and individualized consideration of employee psychological needs into all its human resources and management practices. Minimizing stress and anxiety is one of the company's guiding principles. For example, Ultranauts developed a system for providing corrective feedback in a minimally upsetting way tailored to each employee's triggers and anxieties. This tailored approach helps employees with PTSD, anxiety, and sensitivities associated with neurodivergence do their best work—in a safe environment. The company demonstrates the depths of its commitment to supporting psychological health by tracking well-being metrics such as team loneliness scores and psychological safety assessments with the same attention as financial indicators.[63]

 DEEP DIVE

TRAUMA-INFORMED APPROACH TO PSYCHOLOGICAL ENVIRONMENTS

Emotional inclusion means creating work environments in which negative emotions are acknowledged and processed in ways that are healing, rather than suppressed until they cause extreme damage. Emotional reactions are a part of life. Some of us tend to internalize such emotions and may become incapacitated by sadness or shame. For others, externalized emotions may show up as anger and blame, made clear by slamming doors or irate emails.[64] We humans are tempted to tear someone down when it feels like the world is intent on keeping us down. Understanding the human reality of stress and trauma is a part of emotional and holistic inclusion.

Skills for dealing with anger and fear without spreading the pain have long been taught to those in helping and first-respondent professions. Human resources professionals, managers, and all coworkers could benefit from a better understanding of a trauma-informed approach. Using this approach does not mean that everyone must become a mental health professional—but it does mean listening and responding in ways that support human dignity.

Organizations are more likely to thrive if they universally adopt a trauma-informed mindset. According to the CDC, the fundamental principles of the trauma-informed approach are safety, transparency, peer support, collaboration, empowerment, and understanding of diversity.[65] These core principles are transferable to any workplace:[64]

1. **Safety.** In the context of working together, safety also means supporting psychologically nonviolent environments and reducing the likelihood of escalating the tension. It does NOT mean suppressing how we feel—it means communicating in productive and considerate ways, consistent with supporting emotional inclusion for all.

2. **Trustworthiness and transparency.** The sense of the unknown is stressful and sometimes unavoidable. However, it is possible to avoid intentional secrecy in organizational procedures. Decision makers and managers who cannot communicate outcomes can still communicate processes.

3. **Peer support.** Even for those of us on the more independent side, having understanding and supporting team members are sources of inspiration and drive. Humans need each other. The Glastonbury crowd clearly demonstrated the power and contagious joy of support.

4. **Collaboration and mutuality.** There are no victors in destruction. Organizations can establish social norms that encourage taking steps toward creating and, if needed, restoring mutual understanding.

5. **Empowerment and choice.** Agency and control are our core needs, and being cornered precludes true collaboration. Respecting the autonomy of others, and allowing people to make their own decisions without coercion, makes most interactions much more effective.

6. **Diversity awareness.** In most workplaces, people differ along multiple dimensions, including neurodivergence and disability, and these differences may manifest in processing emotions. For example, historical and lived injustices and discrimination create an amplified stress response. So do many physical and mental health conditions—visible or not. This means we should check our assumptions in interpreting other's behavior and reactions. Negative assumptions can result in negative self-fulfilling prophesies, creating highly destructive workplace environments.

Trauma-informed collaboration and communication may require some changes to the existing work culture. However, the alternative is being stuck in the endless cycle of "hurt people, hurt people." Breaking this cycle through considerate and courageous communication and genuine change can heal organizational cultures.

The Glastonbury crowd intuitively demonstrated the key features and power of the trauma-informed approach and anti-toxic community by embracing diversity through collaboration, support, and flexibility. Organizations can deliberately build these values into structures and processes, and leaders—both positional and grassroots—can model anti-toxic behavior and not just abstain from harm by actively bringing kindness, care, and ethics into work environments and the larger society.

KEY TAKEAWAYS

- *Research revealed the five main attributes of toxic cultures—disrespectful, noninclusive, unethical, cutthroat, and abusive. All of these also threaten neuroinclusion.*
- *In addition, neuroinclusion is often hindered by highly political work environments.*
- *Unethical organizational practices may result in moral injury. Organizational recovery after moral breaches may require amends.*
- *Bullying is a behavior of opportunity, and much of it could be prevented by systemic safeguards.*
- *Applying the Canary Code principles and developing trauma-informed cultures can help prevent and address toxic buildup in organizations.*

 DEVELOPMENTAL QUESTIONS

Personal processing (you may want to skip this if the idea of toxic work environments is personally triggering):

- Have you experienced working in a toxic environment? What was the key reason for the toxicity?
- Was there perhaps a "hurt people, hurt people" dynamic in play?
- Have you been able to process that experience in ways that make you determined not to be the source of toxicity to others? How could ideas and examples from this chapter help you model anti-toxic behavior?

For employees:

- Have you used employee review sites such as Glassdoor to find out whether a prospective work environment might be toxic? Was it effective? How about other ways, such as talking to current or former employees?
- How healthy is your current work environment? If it could use some improvement, who could be your allies in helping make it happen?
- What resources could you share with these potential allies?

For managers/direct supervisors:

- How do you ensure that your team environment brings out the best in people?
- Which suggestions from this chapter can help you build a healthy and anti-toxic environment?

For HR and upper management:

- Which systems, structures, or cultural norms might be creating aspects of toxicity in your organization?
- How can ideas from this chapter help you create mechanisms that reduce toxicity and support safe and productive environments?
- What support might you need to accomplish this, such as internal allies or external resources? Are there perhaps people in your organization you may collaborate with even if you have not collaborated before; for example, ERGs or other employee organizations?

CHAPTER NINE

I JUST WANT TO BE MYSELF

Performance Evaluation and Performance Management

Autists are the ultimate square pegs, and the problem with pounding a square peg into a round hole is not that the hammering is hard work. It's that you're destroying the peg.

—Paul Collins

 HUMAN HAPPENINGS

CHIPPING AT SQUARE PEGS

For a few years after school, Charlie Hart struggled with finding a career that interested her. Then she discovered HR data analytics—and finally, she was in her element! She passed with flying colors her Certificate in Personnel Practice and Postgraduate Certificate in HR Management from Coventry University in England.

Working as an HR systems analyst was her definition of a fun job. She had zero inclination or interest in managing people but, as it happens, eventually had to cover for her manager while she was on maternity leave. Suddenly, she had two direct reports and had to represent the HR systems and admin team at HR business partner meetings. She tried her best—but felt like an imposter.

Charlie often received positive feedback about her productivity (*"eats workload for breakfast"*) and the quality of her work (*"meticulous attention to detail,"* *"painstaking"*), yet she never got anything above "achieved" in her performance reviews. She was striving for the "exceed expectations" rating, however, and asked

the HR director what she needed to do to earn it. The director pointed to behaviors she needed to change:

> *Your output is great, but you fall down on the building and maintaining rela-*
> *tionships aspect of the role.*
> *Your meeting behaviors really let you down.*

At this time, Charlie was not aware that her autistic neurobiology was the
underlying reason why she received this performance feedback and was perceived
this way—despite her best intention to behave as others expected. Still, she argued
that what was described as "behavioral development needs" was her fundamental
personality and was not linked to performance. Despite Charlie's objections, her
boss included interpersonal skills coaching in her personal development plan.

As Charlie recalls,

> *A jovial chap of a learning and development consultant was assigned the task*
> *of helping me develop my interpersonal skills. He would bestow upon me the*
> *importance of small talk, breaking the ice, gentle banter, showing an interest*
> *in other people's holidays, kids, pets etc. This to me felt quite unnatural and*
> *uncomfortable. Then he went on to talk about nonverbal communication such*
> *as eye contact and body language. In a nutshell, without knowing I was autis-*
> *tic, he was trying to teach me how to pass for neurotypical—unhelpful to me,*
> *as it made me self-conscious about my social and communication differences.*
> *Previous struggles in relationships and social situations preyed on my mind, my*
> *inner demons were woken, and I was taken out by depression for months.*[1]

A few years later, after her eldest child was identified as autistic, Charlie was
also recognized as autistic at the age of 42. In another couple of years, she was
also identified as an ADHDer.

Trying to hammer Charlie into a round hole of neuronormativity meant
chipping at and splintering her human core. She was never going to be a round
peg. Just a battered square peg.

Understanding her neurodivergent psyche helped Charlie do much inner repair. She is now using her HR expertise to advocate for other square pegs.

We square pegs need all the help we can get.

This chapter outlines the principles of inclusive performance management
that focus accountability on outcomes and the substance of performance
—not on the surface characteristics that often bias evaluators.

BRIDGING SCIENCE AND PRACTICE

I JUST WANT TO BE MYSELF

A study of career aspirations of autistic women in Australia showed that one of the key desires of study participants was to just be themselves.[2] Yes, they wanted professional growth, meaningful work, and stable income—like most people. Yet, their heart's cry was the desire to be their authentic selves. Here is what some of the study participants said:

> *"To be valued for my natural abilities in logical thinking and creative ingenuity . . . I hope to one day be allowed to be myself at 100% and accepted, appreciated and respected for it"* (autistic woman, aged 44; hospitality or trades).

> *"I want to realize my dream of being a full-time field botanist. I have the qualifications and experience. . . . My work is my overwhelming obsession and passion"* (autistic woman, aged 45; resource and environmental protection).

> *"Although I know how to 'pretend' in order to pass interviews, I would love to just be myself and get the job because [I] am ME"* (autistic woman, aged 34; self-employed).

Sadly, many managers seem determined to deny neurodivergent employees the basic human need to be themselves. Neurodivergent employees often receive personality-focused comments on performance evaluations implying that who they are as humans is not acceptable. Sometimes, those comments do more than imply.

HUMAN HAPPENINGS

"JUST DON'T BE JACQUI"

Dr. Jacqui Wilmshurst from Beverley, England, is a health and environmental psychologist. She is also someone who just wants to be herself.

As with many neurodivergent women, Jacqui's autism and ADHD were not identified until later in life. For much of her career, she was a square peg being pounded into a round hole and not knowing why she was being pounded.

In one of her jobs, she was told that if she could challenge the status quo and develop an innovative program, her temporary role could turn into long-term employment. At performance evaluation time, her manager told her that her outputs were exactly what they needed. In fact, she achieved far more than they expected in a relatively short time.

But, while the manager wanted her to continue to produce the work as before, she was also asked if she could "*just not be Jacqui.*"

When Jacqui asked what that meant, she was told that she needed to start "playing the game," be less wedded to her values, do less straight talking, and be aware that upsetting powerful senior managers could cost her. Jacqui didn't have a diagnosis back then, but she knew that her work outputs, drive, and innovation flowed from who she was. And she told that to her manager.

Later that year when her contract was up for renewal, the company said that they had run out of funds to keep her. Then they brought in someone else to take that job.[3]

One may wonder whether Charlie's and Jacqui's struggles were due to the lack of disclosure or diagnosis. But sadly, research has shown that disclosure does not always help.[4] Sometimes, diagnosis and disclosure provide yet more ammunition to those who would exclude and bully. Disclosure and diagnosis do not fix exclusionary environments.

 HUMAN HAPPENINGS

THE DRAWBACKS OF DISCLOSURE

Several years after the "just not be Jacqui" episode, Dr. Jacqui Wilmshurst was diagnosed, and she disclosed her neurodivergence to her new manager. She was immediately sent on a mandatory occupational health referral to reassess her ability to do the job. That was the job for which she had been through 11 interviews—after being invited to apply by the employer for her unusual thinking and innovative approach! After disclosure, Jacqui's manager said they needed a "playbook" to manage Jacqui, and only a doctor could provide that.

Jacqui ended up resigning and moving into a career focused on neurodiversity and consulting.

Jacqui's manager's desire for a "playbook" from a doctor is, unfortunately, not unique. The medical model, which is still very prevalent, often reduces individuals to a label; when people act on societal stereotypes, they also automatically reduce individuals to labels. Although there exist very general tips for working with neurodivergent employees that may fit some of the people some of the time, *the key tip for maximizing any human's performance is treating each person as a unique individual.*

Giving individualized consideration to each person is the central characteristic of leaders who effectively work with autistic employees; it is also one of the characteristics of leaders who positively influence employee well-being.[5,6] The idea of using a doctor's manual or playbook for managing a person based on a diagnostic label may seem like an appealing shortcut. But beware of the urge to simplify: when working with humans, any shortcut involves a very real danger of stereotyping.

Jacqui is Jacqui. And Charlie is Charlie. They might both be honest and hard-working people who just want to do a good job and be themselves. But beyond these similarities, they have their own personalities, strengths, and interests. When you've met one AuDHDer, then you've met one AuDHDer—and others will be different.

Leaders who want to unlock the talents of neurodivergent people—and people in general—will do best supporting everyone as one-of-a-kind human beings who just want to be themselves. And to be treated fairly.

 POINTS OF PRACTICE

FOCUS ON FAIRNESS

Bias enters into the process of performance management in many ways. Neurodivergent personality traits, where someone was born, what someone looks like—all these characteristics, although not related to performance, affect how people (or AI trained on the patterns and decisions of those people) perceive and evaluate human behavior and performance.[7]

Later in this chapter, we discuss a radical, deeply structural solution to improving performance management that requires a significant departure from traditional practices. But even in traditional organizations, managers and HR professionals can greatly improve the effectiveness of performance management and employee well-being by applying the principles of the Canary Code.

Employee Participation: Supporting employee participation can help leaders work with employee strengths. Most people, but especially neurodivergent individuals with their intense passions and areas of strong interest, perform better and are happier when work is aligned with intrinsic motivation. Human-centric managers seek employee input on job duties, performance goals, perceived wins and obstacles, and desired development opportunities. Job crafting to develop job roles, responsibilities, and career paths that align with employees' interests is likely to improve engagement and job satisfaction.

If Charlie had been offered professional development that aligned with her strengths and her love of people analytics and HR processes, she would not have developed depression, and her story would have been quite different. But she was thrust into a role that did not match her talents and required her to change who she was, and she suffered for it.

Focus on Outcomes: A focus on outcomes, in contrast to the typical focus on processes, presenteeism, and presentation, can benefit neurodivergent employees who may have unique and sometimes exceptionally effective ways of achieving goals. Setting clear, outcome-based performance objectives helps all employees understand what is expected of them and how their performance will be evaluated. With employee participation, managers can set objectives that align with organizational goals, as well as with an employee's career aspirations and intrinsically motivating areas of interest.

In general, making references to personality traits in performance evaluations is a poor practice fraught with bias and stereotyping.[8,9] As one example, women, particularly Black women in the US, are likely to be criticized for being "too aggressive" and men for being "too soft."[9,14] Behavioral evaluations are sometimes appropriate if they are directly related to performance; for example, a customer service representative must greet customers in a polite manner. However, behavioral feedback should be job-specific and identify an action that is within an individual's control. A neurodivergent designer who has difficulty focusing during long meetings but does their job well is unlikely to benefit from being told to pay attention.

In Jacqui's case, what her supervisor most likely meant by "playing a game" was "understand that the upper managers take things personally and are vengeful." Putting it this way is, of course, quite different from framing the situation as a "Jacqui problem."

Flexibility: Flexibility in terms of work schedules, tasks, and, if needed, accommodations can help neurodivergent employees perform to the best of their abilities. Understanding employees' interests, goals, and challenges can help align their responsibilities with their strengths, maximizing their performance, engagement, and job satisfaction.

Aligning Charlie's duties and schedule with what she is best at (deep work on analytics), rather than attending draining meetings, would have made for the best situation for Charlie and for her employer.

Organizational Justice: Treating employees fairly and equitably is the key to job satisfaction and performance. This is especially true for neurodivergent performers who tend to have a heightened sense of justice. Using performance management that is objective and based on measurable criteria, and allowing for redress if there are any issues, helps minimize the negative effects of personal biases and stereotypes.

When Jacqui's disclosure of a diagnosis resulted in a mandatory evaluation, her sense of justice was violated. And that resulted in her departure.

Transparency: Clear criteria and transparent procedures are crucial to employees' perception of organizational justice. Autistic employees in particular are negatively affected by the Byzantine complexities and unspoken rules that surround performance management and promotion practices in many organizations. This is both because these rules are hidden and hard to decipher, especially for many autistic people, and because autistic people are statistically more likely to prefer direct and authentic communication.[10,11] Thus, they are shocked and hurt when they are told to "just not be Jacqui."

Use of Valid Tools: Using valid and reliable tools to evaluate employee performance can ensure that the evaluation process is fair and unbiased. De-biasing performance management requires the development of measurements tied to specific essential tasks and skills. Joan Williams and her colleagues recommend modifying evaluation forms and training managers in bias interruption. Instead of open-ended prompts that invite subjective judgment, de-biased forms include specific, job-relevant competencies and require multiple pieces of evidence to back up ratings and promotion recommendations.[12]

Using de-biased tools is crucial to supporting equity and combating bias. Additional safeguards for ensuring objectivity include checking evaluations of all employees for consistency and statistically comparing evaluation averages for different groups of employees.

Finally, evaluation rubrics focused on key skills with clearly defined levels of skill development also support objectivity. De-biased performance management tools could have saved both Charlie and Jacqui from much stress by making their evaluations more objective.

DEEP DIVE

BIAS IN PERFORMANCE MANAGEMENT: THE BEST SOLUTIONS ARE STRUCTURAL

When supervisors evaluate stereotyped employees, preconceived ideas lead them to look for personal characteristics that either support those stereotypes or strongly disconfirm them. These characteristics, however, do not play a role in evaluating other employees. For example, a manager may scrutinize a dyslexic employee's written communication, even if most position-relevant communication occurs verbally, or remember every instance when someone who disclosed ADHD was late, even when other employees are more likely to be late.

Performance reviews of marginalized individuals are often influenced by the "tightrope" and "prove-it-again" biases.[12] Although their effects have been established in gender-focused research, these biases are also likely to affect neurodivergent experience.

The **"tightrope"** metaphor refers to the narrow range of behavior seen by society as acceptable for people from nondominant and stigmatized groups. Meanwhile, those from dominant groups enjoy much more leeway. In a classic example, women aspiring to leadership are expected to be "strong" but never "aggressive." Women walk the tightrope because the range of acceptable behavior is almost impossibly narrow.

What is seen as "assertive" in men is interpreted as "aggressive" in women.[13] But err just a bit toward agreeableness, and a woman is seen as a "pushover" and "not leadership material." Meanwhile, an agreeable man will be seen as kind and generous. Women of color must navigate an even narrower tightrope, and other intersectionalities—including neurodivergence—make the range of acceptable behaviors even smaller. Each intersectionality may leave individuals with fewer and fewer behavioral options that do not risk some form of social penalty.

Let's say an employee disclosed ADHD and received help with organization and time management. If that person stays supremely organized and always prepared by putting in extra effort, the supervisor may conclude that perhaps the person does not, in fact, have ADHD and is instead playing the system. However, if that person shows any sign of less-than-perfect organization, those instances are likely to be scrutinized and selectively remembered, probably affecting their performance evaluation. If employees belong to an ethnically, religiously, or otherwise stigmatized group, additional stereotypes are likely to leave them even fewer options.[21]

Catina Burkett describes just how narrow the tightrope got for her as a Black autistic woman in the US:[14]

When I am inflexible, I am sometimes called unfriendly, insubordinate, lazy, aggressive or uncontrollable. When I need to process a situation before I respond to it, some describe my quietness as a ticking bomb that may go off at any time. . . . Even when I do not validate the negative assumptions people make about me, they find a way to demonize my compliance.

Even though Catina Burkett received "90 percent exceeds expectations" on her performance review, a white female supervisor still indicated that she should adjust her demeanor with different people. That caused Burkett significant anxiety: "*I could not understand how to change who I am. I just focused on doing my job while being me. But my supervisor grew bitter and the work environment became hostile. Eventually, I had to quit.*"

"Doing my job while being me": Why is it so hard for our organizations to meet such a foundational human need? Does the ideal worker have to be a clone? The diversity promise will not be realized if we are not allowed to be ourselves.

"Prove-it-again" is another bias that strongly affects neurodivergent and other employees stereotyped as "less competent." For example, it may cause supervisors to expect autistic employees to demonstrate performance and even a "desirable" personal attribute over and over again before they receive credit for it or are recommended for a raise or promotion. This dynamic may set back marginalized employees' career progressions by years or even decades, significantly reducing their lifetime earnings.

For example, an autistic creative industry professional who chooses to identify here as Louise Belmonte demonstrated over and over again the ability to manage a team. Yet, instead of being promoted, she was offered more "opportunities to prove herself" through increasingly complex and time-consuming project management work with no additional salary. The problem was exacerbated by a revolving door of managers, who one after another wanted Louise to keep proving herself "for just one more year." This added up to a decade of lost years and a house's worth of stolen earnings.

Benevolent ableism, along with **hostile ableism**, can significantly harm neurodivergent workers.[15] *Hostile ableism* is manifested in blatant attempts to exclude individuals from specific roles and is motivated by dislike or mistrust (this parallels hostile sexism toward women). *Benevolent ableism* is a patronizing, infantilizing attitude parallel to benevolent sexism that prevents employees from fully exercising their abilities under the guise of protection. For example, decision makers may convince themselves they're protecting a neurodivergent individual from hardship by not promoting them or by making decisions for them. Ensuring fairness in the face of benevolent ableism requires careful assumption checking.

Just because someone with Tourette Syndrome has to deal with stares and sneers from others in reaction to their tics does not mean they would rather not take on a leadership position—or excel in such a position. And just because a person is dyslexic does not mean they can't write a dissertation or a book—let alone quarterly department reports. People should not be held back by someone else's presumption to make decisions for them.

Paternalistic bias can also result in unsolicited, offensive advice. In one case, Burnett Grant, a highly experienced Black autistic lab technician from the US, was advised by their supervisor "to get on disability benefits and clean houses for extra money under the table."[16] Burnett was a high performer and didn't ask for advice, which leaves little explanation for this unsolicited guidance other than stereotypes.

Supervisory training may address some of the issues with bias. Using valid tools, such as objective forms for performance evaluation tied to outcomes and supported by data, can greatly help curtail opportunities for bias to affect evaluations. However, the stressors and hustle of organizational life often prevent people from doing their best thinking and push them toward mental shortcuts—including the reliance on stereotypes in day-to-day performance management. Suboptimal management may result in performance that is lower than the employee's potential. The best way to make performance management fair is to build fairness into systems that scaffold everyday work interactions.

 DEEPER DIVE

A RADICAL DEPARTURE

Annual performance evaluations were never meant to be synonymous with performance management. *Continuous* performance management is a developmental, incremental process of regular feedback with the goals of growth and mastery. But with the tyranny of the urgent in most organizations, the main form of performance management is often a cyclical evaluation that combines summary feedback with high-stakes decisions on pay, promotion, and employment.

In this high-stakes form, performance evaluation is a source of anxiety and frustration for both managers and employees.[8] Most employees feel that the process is unfair and inaccurate and that it undermines rather than benefits their performance. This is particularly true of performance evaluation systems based on forced rankings, which can be extremely damaging to individual and organizational morale.[17,18] This stress is intensified for marginalized and stigmatized employees who are more likely to experience biases in the evaluation process.[11,12,15,19]

When added to a lifetime of trauma, an acute awareness of discrimination in employment, observation of biases, and limited opportunities, the typical evaluation processes can be extremely stressful for neurodivergent workers—like Charlie Hart, Catina Burkett, Burnett Grant, or Jacqui Wilmshurst. Or me.

Not only are periodic performance evaluations stressful but they fail to facilitate performance. More and more companies are abandoning annual reviews with their heavy emphasis on rewards and punishments for past behavior at the expense of current performance development.[15] Instead, regular conversations about performance and development shift the focus to improving performance in real time. This builds the workforce needed for organizational competitiveness—today and in the future. Such a change of focus supports productivity much better than annual evaluations.

 EMPLOYER EXCELLENCE

FIRING THE FEAR

Many companies test alternative methods of supporting employee growth. Deloitte, for example, experimented with getting rid of annual performance reviews for several years, with pilots eliminating them in various parts of the company until they were fully abandoned in favor of continuous improvement.[18] People check in with their managers once a week for a holistic conversation that goes beyond performance and includes a discussion of employee interests, strengths, and preferences. Work assignments are much more aligned with employee passions. As a result, employee engagement increased by more than 10 percent—likely because people have more opportunities to play to their strengths.

Patagonia built a system of skills-focused "regenerative performance" based on the understanding that people often grow in spurts.[20] Under this system, employees have both annual and quarterly goals, get regular feedback, and check in with managers or team leaders quarterly. At the end of the year, people can be rewarded in two ways: they receive bonuses based on attaining goals and an increase in base pay tied to their growth in market value. In other words, employees who develop new skills will make more money. This skills-focused system is not about promotion per se or a manager's control of an employee: it is an annual incentive to upskill.

As another example, Ultranauts experimented with its performance management practices, looking for the best trauma-informed way to provide regular feedback to its 75 percent autistic and largely neurodivergent workforce.[22,23] The task is complicated because trauma—including trauma stemming from abuse in previous positions—affects people in many different ways. Some anxiously seek frequent feedback. Others are frozen in fear and avoid any potentially triggering conversations. Yet others become so emotionally dysregulated and distraught in response to corrective feedback that it shakes up the employee and the entire team.

After trying the usual methods—training people to give and receive feedback—Ultranauts decided that there was no "one-size-fits-all" approach. They added a question about preferences for receiving feedback to their Biodex— the individual "user manual" all employees fill out. As expected, there was a great range of preferences. Some wanted the feedback immediately, others at the end of the day, or at the end of the week so they would have a chance to recover. Some wanted it in a conversation, others via email. Tailoring the feedback delivery to each individual was the solution that worked, and satisfaction with the ongoing feedback increased from 60 to 80 percent.

In addition to ensuring that continuous feedback was trauma-informed, Ultranauts decoupled rewards and promotions from performance feedback. This took several iterations. First, the company used a rather typical system with 360-degree evaluations. Most employees were OK with it, but some absolutely hated it. Perhaps there was a better way.

Ultranauts then invited the most vocal opponents to redesign the process to be more equitable and efficient. And they did. However, their suggestions indicated that the process was beyond repair. Performance reviews were not helping make informed promotion decisions or support meaningful career development. In search of a better way, Ultranauts developed a system of *community-driven promotions*.

The process is transparent and designed to ensure procedural justice. People understand how decisions are made and what steps they should take if they aim for promotions:

- All roles have clearly spelled-out benchmarks; for instance, noting the differences between a level 1 engineer and a level 2 engineer.
- To move to a higher level or role, employees must demonstrate the competencies outlined in the benchmarks for that role.

- Employees are responsible for documenting evidence of the competencies they believe demonstrate that they are meeting the standards of their desired position.
- The Learning and Development team collects this evidence and shares it with skilled endorsers specializing in each skill family.
- These expert endorsers evaluate the evidence and provide feedback on whether it meets the benchmark for that skill.

Promotions can be skip-level—as long as the competencies required for a level or role one has applied for are demonstrated and then endorsed by expert raters. Employees who receive expert endorsements for all the skills required for a position are considered ready for promotion. However, the management team must also consider business needs and whether the company can afford to support the promotion. In most cases, community-recommended promotions are approved. But if the management team at the quarterly meeting decides that a promotion is not possible—for example, the company has not had enough growth to support an additional manager or a senior engineer—it will provide direct feedback to the employee and outline the milestones that the company needs to meet before a promotion can be considered. This may not be what people want to hear, but it is transparent and equitably applied. This process helps ensure that promotions are based both on the readiness of the employee and the needs of the business—with justice and transparency.

Ultranauts' system helps alleviate the concern with bias and supports transparency and justice. The management team does *not* get to decide who gets promoted, which eliminates the potential for backdoor jousting that is so typical of most organizations.

The community-focused approach to promotion developed by Ultranauts is in some ways a more trauma-informed and transparent version of the traditional academic method of peers reviewing promotion portfolios. The Ultranauts' approach aims to reduce potential bias by safeguarding the process from being swayed or overturned by managers. The focus on making promotions as skills-focused and objective as possible helps Ultranauts both standardize and humanize a process that, across all industries, has been notoriously subjective[7] and, for many employees, heartbreakingly stressful.[24]

Fairness and compassion in the performance management process are not mutually exclusive. Especially for those who have been denied fair treatment for much of their lives, fairness is one of the key aspects of compassion. We don't expect to always get what we want. What matters is that in the process we are treated with dignity. Dignity, ultimately, is what we need.

Employers committed to developing innovative, caring, and trauma-informed approaches to neuroinclusion also commit to doing the hard work of crafting multiple iterations to the process, with employee participation and input. Ultranauts demonstrated exceptional commitment to doing this work of inclusion. In the next chapter, we learn more about the leadership and vision behind this commitment.

 KEY TAKEAWAYS

- *Personality-focused "performance management" is a major source of stress for neurodivergent people and a cause of talent loss for organizations. To create better systems:*
  - *Tailor the talent management approach to specific people: one size does not fit all.*
  - *Focus feedback and evaluation on outcomes and skills. Ensure that behavioral feedback is strictly tied to the role performance and behaviors within the individual's control. Do not attempt to change personalities or neurodivergent characteristics.*
  - *Separate continuous feedback from high-stakes evaluations.*
  - *Invite employee participation in developing goals.*
  - *Use trauma-informed and minimally stressful performance management to increase productivity.*

 DEVELOPMENTAL QUESTIONS

Personal processing:
- Have you suffered from a lack of sensitivity, humanity, and justice in the performance management process? I am truly sorry if you have. Does this experience still influence how you feel about the process? And how you might treat others?
- Have you been able to take steps toward breaking the cycle of pain that is sometimes connected to inappropriate performance management?
- Have you been able to release the weight of other people's choices from your shoulders—for example, through forgiveness—so that you are able to move on?

For employees:
- How (neuro)inclusive is performance management in your organization?
- Who could be your ally in helping introduce more inclusive practices?
- What resources could you share with these potential allies?

For managers/direct supervisors:
- How do you work with your direct reports to ensure high performance? Is this process neuroinclusive? Trauma-informed? Constructive?
- How could you better combine fairness and compassion to facilitate employee growth?

For HR and upper management:
- Is the system of performance management in your organization neuroinclusive? Trauma-informed? Constructive?
- How can examples in this chapter help you rethink or redesign your organization's career development and performance evaluation system?
- How might you reinvent your performance review system to better reward and encourage growth and contribution?
- What resources or training can help your people leaders better practice neuroinclusion?

PART IV

LEADERSHIP MATTERS

CHAPTER TEN

LEADING FOR INCLUSION

The Why

Managing our power wisely and honestly can happen only if we recognize the value and vulnerability of ourselves and others so that we do not abuse it.

—Donna Hicks

 EMPLOYER EXCELLENCE

THE WHY OF INCLUSION: ULTRANAUTS

In 2013 Ultranauts (then named Ultra Testing) was a pioneering company creating a majority-autistic workforce. Its cofounders Rajesh Anandan and Art Shectman were enthusiastic about the competitive advantage that would come from the strengths associated with autism. Many lauded their initiative.

Indeed, the company has done very well, largely due to the talents of its 75 percent neurodivergent workforce.[1] And yet, when I interviewed Rajesh Anandan 10 years later, in early 2023, the WHY of Ultranauts had developed well beyond the business case.[2] In fact, Rajesh realized that his early thinking reflected implicit ableism and that he was—and perhaps still is—an ableist CEO.

After getting to know his colleagues, Rajesh understood that describing autistic humans as a "competitive advantage" has disturbing implications. Some autistic people identify as disabled and others don't, but most deal with significant health and life challenges. Often, these challenges arise from traumatic experiences like bullying or abuse. But whether developmental or acquired, disability is not a competitive advantage. However, there is a *disadvantage* in not having diverse teams—and neurodivergence and disability are an important part of this diversity.

Rajesh is now also acutely aware of problems with generalized claims about "autistic superpowers." Yes, multiple studies show that autistic research participants, on average, are more likely to outperform others on tests of visual processing, search, and integration or creativity,[3,4] but just like with any group, these findings do not apply to every autistic person.[5] And they do not need to apply for every autistic human to be valuable.

"Superpowers" should not be a requirement for basic human dignity.

Rajesh no longer touts autistic "special talents" as the business case for hiring. Instead, he points out that, even though many of his colleagues at Ultranauts are exceptional, others are capable, conscientious performers, creative, and compassionate.[2] What more can someone ask of people?

 BRIDGING SCIENCE AND PRACTICE

THE WHY OF INCLUSION: BEYOND THE BUSINESS CASE

The business case for inclusion has produced much rhetoric that, at first glance, may sound well intended but is, in fact, dangerous. It is highly problematic to promote disability—or difference—as an opportunity for other people to take advantage of. This messaging happens, for example, when the autistic tendency to work without breaks (and to complete exhaustion) is promoted as part of the "business case" for hiring autistic professionals or when autistic loyalty is touted as something that makes retention efforts unnecessary.

More generally, the widespread practice of having to make a case for hiring people from marginalized groups, be it neurominorities or any other group, continues othering these people and perpetuates the power imbalance. Forcing the less privileged to keep justifying their existence to the more privileged is not a path to a fairer society. The best case for diversity might be just valuing humans—no justification needed.[6]

In a study of Fortune 500 companies, Oriane Georgeac and Aneeta Rattan found that 410 companies, or 82 percent, made a business case for diversity by linking it to their profit and bottom lines.[7] Fewer than 5 percent made a fairness case by linking diversity efforts to moral ideals. The remaining companies either did not list diversity as a value or did not provide any justification for it.

In follow-up experiments, Georgeac and Rattan found that making a business case for diversity was a turnoff for underrepresented job candidates. It signaled an instrumental, commodifying view of employees from underrepresented groups and heightened their concerns that they would be stereotyped and experience less belonging. The fairness case lowered such concerns by half. However, the "case" for diversity preferred by the candidates was no case at all.

Georgeac and Rattan's studies show that the best argument for diversity is valuing it as an absolute, with no argument needed. Making any type of a case for diversity "inherently implies that valuing diversity is up for discussion. You don't have to explain why you value innovation, resilience, or integrity. So why treat diversity any differently?"[8]

Another question we can ask is, Why is the business case for diversity required to include women but not men? Neurodivergent people but not neurotypical? Indeed, there is rarely a request to justify the dominance of the dominant group; instead, the burden of providing a business case is placed on those traditionally excluded. But is "because it's always been this way" enough of a business case for the exclusionary status quo?

 DEEPER DIVE

THE WHY OF INCLUSION: NON-ZERO-SUM

The human case for diversity appeals to members of marginalized groups. As a person, I am driven by the human case: upholding human dignity seems like the most natural thing to do. Yet, as an organizational professional, I am often asked to present a business case. The fact is, the language of the business case is the language taught in business schools and spoken in boardrooms, and learning a new language and a new mindset takes time and effort. Building communication requires finding something in common.

Perhaps choosing between the business case and the human case does not have to be a zero-sum game?

The human case for inclusion reflects moral and ethical arguments for creating diverse and inclusive environments. It emphasizes human dignity, equity, social justice, and the right of every individual to participate fully and meaningfully in an organization. The right to matter.

The business case for inclusion focuses on the tangible benefits to the organization, such as attracting diverse talent, increasing creativity, facilitating better decision making, improving reputation, and greater profitability.

The business case *can* be commodifying in its treatment of humans, but it does not have to be.

In my work with organizations, business-case arguments fall into two categories:

1. *A commodifying* business-case argument treats individuals as means to an end, rather than as intrinsically valuable. The focus is on how people can be used to achieve specific business goals, such as increasing profits or efficiency. Utility to the organization replaces human value. Commodifying could reflect a situation in which marginalized employees are hired because they are expected to work more for less until they are burned out and discarded without concern for their well-being ("autistic people don't take breaks" or "single women can work weekends"). It can also apply to situations when individuals are tokenized and used for organizational PR purposes whether they like it or not or are expected to serve as an "inspiration" or "motivation" for others (e.g., "if a disabled person can do this . . ."). The commodifying version of the business case is ethically problematic in many ways. But it is not the only version of the business case.

2. *A pragmatic* business-case argument recognizes the business benefits of human-centered organizations *and* respects the intrinsic value of individuals. It combines a focus on achieving organizational goals with a genuine commitment to individuals' well-being, growth, and dignity. Caring about productivity and organizational reputation can take the form of investing in human sustainability. For example, marginalized employees could be hired and supported in their growth and professional development to maximize their talents and build long-term careers—a win-win scenario for individuals and organizations.

Zero-sum thinking with mutually exclusive human and business cases is rooted in a fragmented understanding of how diversity and inclusion influence complex systems. By recognizing the interconnectedness of humans and organizational systems, we can let go of false dichotomies. When employees are diverse—and thrive—organizations and economies thrive.[9] This integrated approach, which I call **inclusive thriving**, upholds the inherent dignity and human value of employees while also recognizing that inclusion is a smart long-term organizational strategy.

Articulating the organizational why for inclusion helps bring coherence to strategies, planning, and collective action. And yet, for individual leaders, inclusive leadership requires a personal WHY. Because inclusive leadership is hard work.

For people used to traditional, one-size-fits-all management approaches and advice, switching to tailored, individual consideration and compassion-focused leadership is not easy—but it can be done.

 HUMAN HAPPENINGS

THE WHY OF INCLUSION: IT'S PERSONAL

Ultranauts, for example, went through several iterations of how to provide accurate, constructive feedback to employees in a trauma-informed way with minimal negative emotional impact. Originally, the company looked for a better "one-size-fits-all" solution before arriving at a highly individualized approach. So I asked Rajesh Anandan to tell me what drives this pursuit of continuous improvement, of doing inclusion better.

Rajesh does not tolerate intolerance, and there is a powerful reason for it.

He has seen the extremes of exclusion turning into hate and destruction. He has a *"fear of people fearing others"* and an *"intolerance of intolerance."*[2]

Growing up in the middle of a civil war in Sri Lanka, Rajesh saw what can happen when humans get tribal and intolerant of those who are not like them: it was brutal. To make matters worse, his family members were on opposite sides of the war. His dad's side of the family, the Tamil side, had to flee the country or face being killed. On his mom's Sinhalese side of the family, an uncle was deployed to fight against Rajesh's father's Tamil family.

When Rajesh was 10, the violence spread from the country's northern part to its south, where his family lived. Inflamed by the deaths of Sinhalese police troops in the north, ordinary citizens with no history of violence turned into mobs, sought out their Tamil neighbors, and burned them alive because of their Tamil last names. Rajesh's Tamil relatives crowded into the Anandan home seeking refuge because, even though they had the "wrong" last name, his mother's Sinhalese side of the family offered some protection. A family friend saved one of his uncles by dressing him in women's clothes and driving him to safety on a motorcycle.

This experience had a profound impact on how Rajesh Anandan sees the world. On the most fundamental level, he wants to change the underlying systems that play on human tribal instincts and result in fractured and polarized groups of humans, be it because of ethnicity, race, gender, ability, neurotype, or whatever difference. He wants to contribute to building systems that encourage more cohesive and supportive groups of humans.[2]

———————

Not everyone has a story this dramatic. Yet, if you got this far in this book, you probably have a personal WHY for at least exploring neuroinclusion and the roles of leaders in this work.

For many, the WHY is based on their life story: they may have neurodivergent children or a personal lived experience of neurodivergence. The discovery of one's children's differences often leads to a parent's realization that many of their personal "quirks" or struggles are best explained by neurodivergence. Connecting to the journeys of friends, family members, or colleagues or to our own story can be a powerful motivator to support neuroinclusion and create a more caring workplace culture.

Another powerful motivator might be a sense of social responsibility. Leaders may view neuroinclusion as a moral and ethical imperative and strive to reduce stigma and discrimination against neurodivergent individuals as part of their commitment to fairness, equity, and justice. And although the business case as a *sole* motivator is problematic, the bonus in talent acquisition, retention, and organizational reputation can be considerable.

Here are some additional personal testimonies for WHY both neurotypical and neurodivergent leaders have chosen to lead inclusively, even if it may seem to require some "extra" work of understanding someone very different from them.

There's a few reasons for me.

1. *There's creative genius in everyone. I love to see that unleashed.*
2. *I can't help myself and I get so much from creating spaces in which people can show up whole and thrive.*
3. *I know what it's like to not feel like I belong, am accepted, or am truly seen. I'm far from perfect at inclusion, but I try not to re-create what I have experienced that hasn't worked well for me or others.*

> Rashmir Balasubramaniam Strategic Thought Partner, Nsansa;
> Fellow, Royal Society for the Encouragement of Arts,
> Manufactures and Commerce, UK

I am blessed to be father of a young man who has a dual diagnosis of Down Syndrome and Autism. Ben is one of the most caring, affectionate, and insightful people I have ever met. For 30 years Ben has been teaching me to look beyond the surface and see the deep resources and revelatory humanity in every person, to see the gifts that every person has to share, and to make space for those gifts. That is my WHY.

> Jeff Hittenberger, PhD, School of Education Dean, Professor of
> Education, Vanguard University, Costa Mesa, California, US

When I can be there for other attorneys with disabilities to remove their own societal devastating "labels," I feel fulfilled. It is an active accomplishing an enormous 'mitzvah' (the Jewish concept of our joyous duty to be of service to others in our daily experience). Learning is so fundamental to my identity, heritage, and need for authenticity as a proud Jewish immigrant from Mexico: a dyslexic attorney who doesn't allow to be defined by prejudice.

> Salomon Chiquiar-Rabinovich, chair, Attorneys with
> Disabilities and their Allies Section Hispanic National Bar Association,
> Boston, Massachusetts, US

If someone tells you about their experience and you refuse to try and understand it or see your part in it, you do not have a relationship. So to not accommodate is to make an actual choice not to have a relationship with marginalized groups.

> Amanda Gibson, organizational development strategist,
> leadership advisor, Radix Strategy, LLC, Idaho, US

As a daughter of a German mother and a Japanese father growing up in London, I had the experience of being what is called a "third culture kid." At the time, the wounds of World War II must have been still fresh for a number of parents of my classmates as I was subjected to a number of racist tropes: Nazi salutes, "we remember Pearl Harbor," and children pulling their eyes slanted were some of them. Also as a female child of a Japanese father, I experienced the feeling of being a second-class child, especially when my younger brother came along. This sense of being an outsider was heightened when I decided to choose tech as a career since women are vastly underrepresented, especially in leadership roles. This feeling of things being profoundly unfair led me to found 2 DEI groups. The first was Women in Technology Employee Business Resource Group at my employer, Sony Pictures Entertainment. That was in 2014, and the group is flourishing and has spawned other chapters in India and Tokyo. The other group I founded the same year is Women in Technology: Hollywood, which has representation on our board from all the major studios and has grown to a list of 7,000 members.

Nadya Ichinomiya, VP, head of Agile Transformation, Enablement, & Operations Sony Pictures Entertainment, Los Angeles, California, US

Truly inclusive leadership is born of personal experience being excluded, a constructive optimism for a better future, as well as the reasoned conviction that inclusion is the best way to the best business outcomes, not just a nice thing to do.

Yuri Kruman, founder, HR, Talent & Systems, New York City, New York, US

Because I faced discrimination and know the effect it can have on person, group, community, I have made it a point to be more self-aware, educate myself and put together a system within the company that allows for inclusivity of all kinds: socio-economic background, ethnicity, culture, disability etc.

Neri Sillaman, founder of Moda Métiers, Paris, France

An organization that doesn't cultivate inclusive leadership is at the risk of burying its own talent. It takes a courageous mindset to embrace difference as a pathway to innovation and creativity. This requires fostering transparency and trust. Healthy change can often result from intrinsic motivation yielding a joyful flow of work in an organization.

I encourage our leaders to include marginalized voices and those quieter voices in an organization because they are often our buried gold—they have special insights into the operations and vision of their organizations; because of their cultural vulnerability in an organization, they often have insights into weaknesses and dysfunction. Finally, it's important for leaders to press through the fog of the culture wars to bring the buried talent to light. This is your organizational gold—that's undeveloped, untapped potential that could launch an organization into the future. Speaking again to vulnerability, those of us in the marginalized populations may experience the pressure points of the organization earlier or in a more intense manner than others in privileged spaces—we are the future in the present context. And this requires a type of leadership style with a loving approach, which takes time—but it is time well invested.

Karen An-hwei Lee, Provost and Professor of English, Wheaton College, Illinois, US

As a leader, I have a duty to model the behaviors I want to see. My progression to becoming a leader has been enabled by a few key allies in my career

who were of an inclusive mindset, who acknowledged the sometimes unconventional and creative approach I take to my work, and instead of trying to squash it encouraged me and nurtured it. An inspirational quote often cited on social media is "be the person you need." As a leader that is what I strive to be every day for those I lead, particularly those who may face additional challenges and feel misunderstood in their approach. It is a moral imperative for me to approach leadership in this spirit, as well as it being effective practice in motivating people to perform to the best of their ability.

Susannah Chambers, agile coach lead at LSEG (London Stock Exchange Group), Nottingham, England

As a leader, it's my job to serve others and care about people. As an inclusive leader, it's my job to understand each person's individual needs and flex my style and approach accordingly to provide them what they need to perform at their best. As a human leader, it's an honor and privilege to build relational connections with people, create an environment in which people can thrive, and ultimately grow and evolve to be their best human selves.

Jennifer Nash, author of *Be Human, Lead Human: How to Connect People and Performance*, founder and CEO, Jennifer Nash Coaching & Consulting, US

These personal testimonies provide insights into different perspectives on inclusion and experiences that might inspire inclusive leadership. Overarching themes extracted from these testimonies further illuminate the inclusive WHY:

1. **Empathy through Personal Experience:** Many inclusive leaders experienced discrimination, exclusion, or marginalization. These experiences shaped their understanding and compassion for others.
2. **Innovative Potential of Inclusion:** Inclusive leaders recognize the creative genius in everyone and believe that, by fostering an environment where people can be themselves, they are unlocking tremendous potential.
3. **Community and Relationship Building:** Inclusive leaders emphasize the importance of relationships and community. Inclusion is not merely a business strategy; it's about creating spaces where people feel seen, accepted, and part of a community.
4. **Combating Marginalization:** The understanding of struggles associated with marginalization has led some leaders to actively combat it. They also recognize that marginalized voices are valuable assets to the organization.

5. **Intrinsic Motivation and Ethical Responsibility:** Many leaders feel an ethical duty to be more inclusive. It's not just a strategy for better business outcomes but a conviction that inclusion is the right thing to do. Moreover, leaders find intrinsic joy in supporting other people.

6. **Inclusivity as a Business Advantage:** In addition to ethical and social considerations, leaders acknowledge the pragmatic business case for inclusivity. They believe that embracing differences and fostering trust and transparency help organizations find the "buried gold."

7. **Servant and Human-Centered Leadership:** Inclusive leaders see their jobs as much more than directing or managing. It's about serving others, understanding individual needs, and creating environments where people can grow, thrive, and be their best selves.

These themes paint a rich picture of the many personal "whys" behind leaders' investment in inclusion. Inclusion is a deeply human endeavor that connects to values, empathy, creativity, community, and the realization of human potential. A leader's recognition of the human potential of every person, coupled with a desire to create fair, productive, and compassionate environments, supports opportunities for inclusive thriving.

 KEY TAKEAWAYS

- *To sustain the work of inclusion, leaders must define their WHY.*
- *The WHY of inclusion should go beyond the business case. However, there are different types of business cases. The commodifying approach frames people as merely means to an end. A pragmatic business case upholds human dignity while also promoting organizational goals.*
- *The business case and the human case do not need to be a zero-sum game. They can be combined in an inclusive thriving case.*

 DEVELOPMENTAL QUESTIONS

For employees:
- Which WHYs for inclusion have you encountered?
- Which ones resonated with you, and which ones have not? What is your ideal WHY?

For people in organizational leadership/management positions:
- Did any of the WHYs particularly resonate with you?
- Has your leadership WHY evolved over time? How may it still need to evolve to support the inclusion of those who are different from you?
- Did any examples of WHY in this chapter resonate with you? Which life experiences—being excluded at school, living in a different culture, an exemplary leader in your life—might be relevant to your own why?

CHAPTER ELEVEN

LEADING FOR INCLUSION

The How

Rather than only focusing on key traits, we need to focus on clear actions individuals can take to be more inclusive leaders in the workplace.

—Mita Mallick

 HUMAN HAPPENINGS

THE HOW (NOT TO) OF INCLUSION

When Clare Kumar interviewed for her new job with a company in Canada, she disclosed her seasonal affective disorder and the need for natural light. Yet, when she came to work, she was pointed to a cubicle outside her boss's office that was about 30 feet away from a window.

There were several vacant desks near the windows, so Clare sat there until someone needed the spot. Her boss was not pleased. The tension only grew when Clare asked to work remotely about 50 percent of the time, particularly during the "dark" season, which she found hard to navigate. The manager told Clare that if she (the boss) were able to work in the office, so should Clare. This situation was not sustainable—Clare soon left and started her own consulting business.[22]

The irony was that the company that would not accommodate her remote work request sold equipment to enable people to work remotely.

DEEP DIVE

THE HOW OF PERSPECTIVE-TAKING: PERSONAL AND COLLECTIVE

Clare's boss illustrates a common way of thinking: I call it a "what works for me should work for you" fallacy. We probably all ran into people who felt others should function just like them. Most of us have likely been such people at some point. I once had a boss who insisted he needed only five hours of sleep and that this should be good enough for everyone else; it did not end well.

It is natural for us to assume that others appreciate the same things we do, and I made the same error when managing people. For example, I thrive with minimal supervision and maximal autonomy. Some of my employees also thrived with the same approach. Others needed what I would consider a demotivating level of micromanagement—but to them, what I would see as micromanagement meant attention. What worked for me was not working for them.

Even with a strong WHY, the HOW of neuroinclusion can be intimidating. Managers face many challenges and are not always prepared to deal with them. People are complex, and there is always more to learn about solving unique problems and creating better systems. However, the platinum rule[1] of treating people how they need to be treated—holistically, as human beings—goes a long way to ensuring the best outcomes. We are used to the golden rule—treating people how we want to be treated. But deep down, we want to be treated as unique individuals, not as someone else.

Inclusive leadership requires getting to know people and enabling them to work their best, even when their needs are very different from ours. Treating others as they need to be treated is not easy, intuitive, or automatic. Nevertheless, studies indicate that, with practice, people can develop a habit of perspective-taking. Perhaps more importantly, groups can create cultures that support and facilitate perspective-taking. A 2023 study indicated that it is possible to develop a system for supporting this practice in an organization.[2] Some steps for integrating perspective-taking into organizational habits include the following:

1. **Dedicating Time for Problem Solving:** Set aside protected time for individuals and groups to focus on discussing and addressing problems.
2. **Focusing on Understanding:** Promote efforts to understand the diverse experiences and viewpoints of others in the organization, in terms not only of knowledge but also of emotional and whole-person experience.

3. **Promoting Data and Evidence Sharing:** Encourage the sharing of data and evidence that can help individuals better understand different perspectives.

4. **Fostering a Multilevel Perspective:** Encourage people to shift between local and system-wide viewpoints, helping them understand different perspectives and how they contribute to the bigger picture. For example, if Clare's boss had been trained to focus on the organizational-level question of what outcomes need to be accomplished and then to consider whether the same outcomes could be accomplished with flexible work, the individual-level conversation with Clare might have been much more productive.

Cultures manifest through collective habits. Organizations that collectively implement these steps and integrate perspective-taking into daily practices and organizational habits can create a culture of improved understanding, collaboration, and flexibility. However, although organizational-level commitment to a culture of perspective-taking is my ideal, individual managers can make a difference in their units even if that higher-level change has not yet happened. Better still, making a difference and caring do not have to mean working harder.

 POINTS OF PRACTICE

THE HOW OF CARING SMARTER

Work life is often intense, and the pressure can be relentless. It is tempting to say that we don't have the time or energy to look for a unique approach for everyone. But being a considerate leader doesn't necessarily mean doing more; it could mean doing things differently and perhaps, rather than just adding new practices, discontinuing some old ones. Proactively supporting people can also help prevent time-consuming interpersonal or performance problems that may otherwise arise in the long run. Here are some principles for caring smarter:

1. **Mindset Shift:** Considerate leadership is more about a shift in mindset than adding to our to-do lists. It involves seeing our team members as individuals with unique strengths and needs. It could mean inviting people to codesign solutions rather than spending time developing, selling, and enforcing our plans. It could also mean spending a little more time explaining the work up front in ways that connect with people, rather than dealing with problems later.

2. **Quality Matters:** Being a considerate leader is not about working longer hours. It's about focusing on key experiences and being thoughtful in interactions with our teams. A short meeting where people feel heard is more effective than a long, laboriously developed presentation. A clear, concise, and kind email beats numerous emails.

3. **Listening over Talking:** Encouraging open, constructive communication prevents the shock of facing pent-up frustration. Regularly seeking feedback on our leadership and using it to improve can create connections that become leadership.

4. **Empowerment over Control:** Being considerate often means stepping back and allowing others to step up and develop self-leadership, a characteristic particularly important for hybrid and remote work.[3]

5. **Establishing Systems for a Considerate Climate:** Empathy means discovering how others want to be treated. It does not involve mind reading. A system can be as simple as asking people how they work best and acting on it. This is why Ultranauts' Biodex[4] is so effective: it tells us how others want to be treated in a simple and scalable way, and it can be implemented on the level of an entire organization or just within a small unit or a team.

In essence, being a considerate leader can be about working smarter, not harder. The initial effort to shift our mindsets and develop new habits can have a profound impact on our leadership—and on people's lives.

 HUMAN HAPPENINGS

THE HOW OF INCLUSION: MANAGEMENT MATTERS

Ben VanHook, an autistic self-advocate, community leader, and, at the time, a student, came to feel "incapable, stupid, and incompetent" at work.[5] At one point, he was actively searching for other jobs because he felt like a fraud, a burden on the organization who was not earning his pay.

Despite accomplishing results, Ben was constantly alerted to "deficiencies" in his process and yelled at for his "weaknesses." This kind of pressure is not good for anyone, and definitely not for someone who was left by his parents at a train station in northern China, adopted halfway around the world, and then bullied all through his time at school for being different. He had already dealt with way too many hits to his self-esteem.

And then his supervisor left the organization.

Ben's new supervisor let him know right away that, as long as the final product was good, he could do things in a way that aligned with his strengths. The feedback he received on his work came in the form of constructive conversations. His human needs and interests mattered.

It took a while to rebuild his confidence and trust, but this change in management helped Ben see what is possible and what he could do, rather than what he couldn't. Ben soared not just as an employee but also as a young leader within the Autistic community.

 POINTS OF PRACTICE

THE HOW OF INCLUSION: SYSTEMS OF SUPPORT

Leaders' focus on outcomes and participation made all the difference for Ben. And all Clare asked for was some flexibility.

Leaders carry a major responsibility for the well-being of their employees—neurodivergent or neurotypical. Leadership requires perspective-taking and understanding just how much power they have over their employees' lives. A 2023 study indicated that managers influence employee mental health as much as spouses.[6] Leadership practices have a major impact on the psychological climate, morale, trust, and inclusive practices in organizations.

At the same time, many managers are also stressed, lack training and support, and desperately need resources to do their jobs. If these managers are not supported, inclusion efforts are likely to fail. This means that line managers and supervisors, human resources/people operations leaders, and C-suite leaders all have important roles in creating organizations where people can thrive. Embedding the Canary Code principles across all levels and aspects of leadership can help create positive and high-performing environments. Table 1 provides practical steps leaders on all levels can take toward this goal. Although the focus is on neuroinclusion, the same principles can apply to supporting all employees.

At its core, neuroinclusive leadership is just good leadership. It calls for expanding the repertoire of communication, becoming better at perspective-taking and understanding others, using data and evidence, and, ultimately, creating a more robust and resilient organization.

Good leadership takes work. And it seems that with increasing complexity, this work can get even harder because it is increasingly hard to know where to focus. In stressful situations, some of us tend to focus on ourselves. But many remarkable things happen when we focus on others.

TABLE 1. The HOW of Inclusive Leadership

	Direct team leadership/people management	Human resources, DEI, Learning & Development, and other systemic support leadership	Systemic and organizational culture-shaping leadership
Focus on Outcomes	Focus on the outcomes of work. Facilitate achieving results in flexible ways that best support employee productivity.	Research and help develop strategies and tools to objectively assessing outcomes of work. Develop outcomes-focused policies and personnel forms, and support managers in their implementation.	Support the development of an outcomes-focused culture and procedures. This mindset shift can lead to higher performance and morale as employees accomplish goals with more autonomy.
Participation	Actively get to know your employees and their productivity needs. Encourage and facilitate the involvement of neurodivergent employees in decision-making processes related to their work. Support job crafting.	Support line managers in creating an environment for participation. Host focus groups in which neurodivergent employees can provide input on organizational inclusion practices and other aspects of the work environment. Collect and analyze data on belonging.	Champion the creation of procedures and norms to support effective employee participation in organizational life. Model participation by engaging in meaningful, two-way interactions with employees on a range of topics, such as neuroinclusion or flexible work arrangements.
Flexibility	Recognize that limiting work by time, place, workstyle, etc., limits the availability and diversity of talent an organization can attract and retain. Understand how one's own biases may influence the perception of flexibility for others.	Develop neuroinclusive policies for flexible work arrangements that support the unique strengths and workstyles of employees. This could include job matching, job crafting, job sharing, part-time options, and benefits that work for a wide range of needs.	Consider successful flexibility practices used by other organizations. Support flexibility in work arrangements, such as job crafting and job sharing. Support part-time options for employees who may need them. Model flexibility with your direct reports.

(continued)

TABLE 1. Continued

	Direct team leadership/people management	Human resources, DEI, Learning & Development, and other systemic support leadership	Systemic and organizational culture-shaping leadership
Focus on Organizational Justice	Use checks, balances, and transparency to ensure that employees are treated fairly. In particular, pay attention to the possibility that similar-to-me bias (the preference for those who share our characteristics) affects decisions.	Use data and best practices to ensure that neurodivergent (and all) employees are treated fairly in all aspects of their employment, from hiring to pay, benefits, promotion, and beyond. Develop a supportive system of accommodations. Organize training sessions on neuroinclusion.	Model the principles of justice in working with direct reports. For example, establish clear policies and procedures for promotions and rewards based on their performance and skills, rather than personal preferences or perceptions of "fit." Review data and follow up on evidence of whether neurodivergent employees are treated fairly.
Transparency and Clear Communication	Practice transparent communication in multiple formats. Hold yourself accountable by partnering with your team, HR, or others. Hold regular check-ins with employees to discuss their needs and concerns, actively solicit their input, create mechanisms for two-way communication, and actively follow up.	Ensure that there are clear and transparent guidelines for hiring, promotion, and performance evaluation. Monitor execution for clarity and transparency. Host regular check-ins and open forums where employees can voice their concerns and offer feedback.	Promote and model open and transparent communication within the organization via multiple channels (e.g., in-person, email, video, etc.). Make sure employees are informed of company decisions, policies, and changes in a clear and straightforward manner. Develop mechanisms for two-way communication with employees, and act on their input.
Valid Tools for Decision Making	Use evidence-based practices and tools to make decisions about hiring, promotion, and performance evaluations.	Ensure that personnel decisions are based on valid, work-related, outcomes-focused, and neuroinclusive approaches. Eliminate subjective practices that may systemically disadvantage neurodivergent employees. For example, establish a standard set of metrics for evaluating performance, and train managers to use these metrics fairly and consistently.	Understand principles of evidence-based practices. Ensure that managers consistently use evidence-based practices and objective measures in all personnel decisions. Model inclusive and evidence-based decision making.

HUMAN HAPPENINGS

THE HOW OF OTHER-FOCUS

In the early 2000s, Gil Winch, an industrial-organizational psychologist, had plenty to worry about. He was just diagnosed with an advanced-stage, incurable cancer. But he did not want to focus on cancer. He wanted to focus on living a meaningful life. So he decided to train for the half-marathon and figure out the root causes of disability unemployment.

After he did that, he focused on running a full marathon and fixing disability unemployment. Globally.

Gil's research had shown that the chronic unemployment of disabled people was not due to their disability but "to employers (and society at large) not understanding or addressing their true needs."[7] He was eager to make a difference by introducing his model of supporting "underdogs"—disabled and otherwise excluded employees like Arab-Israeli women and people older than 60—and proving that doing so was not just possible but also profitable.

Unfortunately, he could not find a company that would implement his ideas for employing and supporting underdogs. So in 2008, he cofounded Call Yachol, the first company of its kind in the world, which specializes in setting up outsourced call centers staffed mainly by people with disabilities and other "underdogs." By 2016, the company employed 200 people with physical, emotional, and sensory disabilities, making it the largest private employer of people with disabilities in Israel. As of 2023, Gil Winch and Call Yachol are going strong and sharing exemplary practices of facilitating disability employment worldwide.

———————

The story of Gil Winch and Call Yachol is truly exceptional. Yet, a substantial body of research highlights the benefits of kindness not only for personal health and well-being but also for professional success. Kind acts can improve longevity, reduce cardiovascular disease risk factors, and maintain vitality and cognitive function as people age. They can even relieve pain and promote happiness, resilience, and better relationships.[8]

Contrary to common beliefs, generous, caring, and agreeable individuals are more likely to succeed than selfish and manipulative individuals. However, the motive behind kindness matters. Strategic or forced acts of kindness do not yield the same results as genuine caring. Authentic altruism is key to the benefits of focusing on others.[9,10]

DEEPER DIVE

THE BEST LEADERSHIP?

In my consulting, people often ask me what is the best leadership style, both in working with neurodivergent people and in general. Now, that is a million-dollar question. Unfortunately, I don't think anyone is going to win that prize.

The leadership literature is immense. Over the years, there has been an avalanche in research and writing on leadership. In 1960, there were 499 peer-reviewed papers about leadership styles. In 2017, there were 31,339 papers.[11] In 2023, there were 53,221.[12]

To make things even more complicated, there is conceptual overlap in the definitions of many popular types of leadership, such as transformational, authentic, relational, participatory, servant-leadership on the "good" side and exploitive, toxic, and destructive on the "bad" side. The resulting confusion makes the "best style" question even trickier.[13,16]

A set of theories—for example, contingency and path-goal approaches[15]—proposed that the answer to "which is best" is "it depends." One cannot realistically hope to apply the same leadership behavior in different circumstances, with different people, and get the same result. The best leadership is flexible, other-focused, and situation-specific.

Research supports the idea that the "best" leadership depends on the desired outcome. The main correlations between leader behaviors and their outcomes as determined by a large-scale meta-analysis are as follows:[16]

1. **Job Performance:** Transformational, ethical, and servant leadership styles have a small to medium positive impact on job performance.
2. **Unit or Team Performance:** Servant leadership has a medium to large positive impact, whereas transformational, authentic, and ethical leadership have smaller positive effects.
3. **Organizational Citizenship Behaviors (voluntary positive behaviors):** Authentic leadership has the highest positive impact, whereas transformational, servant, and ethical leadership have no statistically discernible impact.
4. **Turnover Intentions:** Ethical and servant leadership styles reduce turnover intentions and increase retention rates, whereas transformational and authentic leadership have little or no consistent impact on turnover intentions.

Another meta-analysis focused on the impact of leadership on employee mental health and also revealed a rather complex pattern of relationships:[17]

Negative mental health (depression, burnout, poor health): *Psychological harm comes from destructive leadership and is ameliorated by transformational leadership, which also was the strongest predictor of overall mental health among followers.*

Positive mental health (well-being, empowerment): *The strongest predictors of positive mental health were relations-oriented and task-oriented leadership, followed by transformational leadership.*

The "best" leadership is also contingent on the characteristics of the person the leader is working with, and neurodivergence is an important aspect of those features. An important example is transformational leadership. For autistic employees, the *individual consideration* component of transformational leadership reduces anxiety and positively affects job performance and organizational commitment. However, the emotional intensity associated with the *inspirational motivation* component of the same style may increase anxiety and undermine work outcomes.[18]

Human complexity calls for leadership that can respond to individual needs and circumstances, such as the use of Biodex by Ultranauts to tailor communication, motivation, and performance management to each individual or Call Yachol's "fairness, kindness, and caring" approach that seeks to work with every employee's needs.[19] I like to call leadership based on caring and focused on others, in all their diversity, *platinum leadership*. And one way to develop such leadership is to think of leadership as diversity work by default.

 DEEP DIVE

ALL LEADERSHIP IS INTERCULTURAL

In my experience with global diversity, three characteristics consistently made a difference in determining a leader's success and failure: cultural humility, curiosity, and openness to learning. This observation is echoed by research on expatriate leaders (leaders working outside their home country): openness, cultural sensitivity, and nonjudgmental acceptance of cultural differences are some of the key factors in their performance.[20,21]

I find my global diversity and intercultural relations background immensely helpful in working with neurodiversity and all other types of diversity in organizations. In essence, in most modern settings, *all leadership is cross-cultural leadership*. Regional differences, ethnic cultures, socioeconomic backgrounds, and many other differences bring significant cultural diversity even to seemingly "local" workplaces. A culture-add approach helps support a collaborative and creative atmosphere in multinational settings, and it does the same for other types of diversity.

In many ways, neurodiversity is cultural diversity. For example, just like Deaf culture, Autistic culture has developed meanings and symbolism based on shared experience; there are Autistic art, literature, and scholarship.[14,25] Some scholars find that Autistic culture also has characteristics of a cultural group disadvantaged by societal power dynamics.[23] The neurodiversity movement can also be seen as a culture with its own systems of meaning, vocabulary, traditions, and celebrations.[24]

Expecting to encounter cultural differences can help people interpret differences through a cultural lens. Understanding neurodivergence as a culture can help managers, colleagues, and employees of neurodivergent people let go of the expectation of neuronormative sameness. Instead, it can facilitate an open-minded anticipation of differences that often occurs in cross-cultural interactions.[25]

Successful intercultural interactions require a good deal of cultural humility—a lifelong commitment to continuous cultural learning, with the understanding that our view of others' experiences is likely to always be incomplete.[26] Cultural humility promotes an other-oriented perspective and respect for the equal dignity of all individuals. It recognizes the value and complexity of their cultural backgrounds. The cultural humility perspective also calls for addressing power differentials and injustices.

In the workplace, applying cultural humility to neurodivergence could mean acknowledging the limitations of the neurotypical understanding of neurodivergent experience and learning from those who are experts on their own lives. Then, inviting their participation in creating work environments, rather than making decisions for them, is the most logical action.[27]

Cultural humility also includes an appreciation of different ways of thinking and communicating, rather than trying to change them. For example, through the lens of "different is less," autistic communication is seen as inferior, and autistic people are told to be less direct. However, national-level cultures also differ in their level of directness of communication.[28] From the perspective of cultural humility, different is not less. Neither the direct-communicating Dutch[29] nor the subtle Japanese[30] are broken: they are just different. Considering autistic communication from the cultural humility perspective makes it different, not less. Autistic people effectively communicate with other autistic people, and directness has the advantage of reducing the likelihood of misinterpretation in all contexts of communication.[31] Respecting Autistic communication from the perspective of cultural humility can make all interactions much more effective and enjoyable. In the same way, the cultural humility attitude makes working in a different country more effective and enjoyable.

Understanding neurodivergence as a cultural variation, coupled with cultural humility, can support skill development for neuroinclusive leaders in several ways:

1. **Building Empathy:** A deeper understanding of neurodivergence as a cultural variation stemming from a different social experience, even within the same society, can help leaders deepen their empathy toward neurodivergent individuals.
2. **Challenging Stereotypes:** Considering neurodivergence through a cultural lens can help leaders challenge stereotypes about neurodivergent individuals in the workplace using the same principles that are applied to other forms of diversity.
3. **Improving Collaboration:** Cultural humility can help leaders nurture a culture of collaboration where everyone's strengths are recognized and maximized.
4. **Creating Inclusive Policies:** Better understanding can help leaders collaboratively create inclusive policies that consider neurodivergent individuals' needs, such as flexible work or quiet spaces, leading to a more inclusive environment for all and improved productivity.
5. **Prioritizing Continuous Learning:** Cultural humility supports an ongoing commitment to learning and inclusive improvement.

Embracing cultural humility and applying it to neurodivergence, as well as to other dimensions of human differences, can help leaders develop a culture-add leadership style that can bring out the unique strengths and perspectives of all team members. It can help make organizations talent-rich environments where people belong and thrive.

POINTS OF PRACTICE

THE SHARED LEADERSHIP SOLUTION

In most organizations, leadership roles typically come with high expectations and demands.[32] Some would say that these are unreasonable demands. Employees hope for a wise superhero who can help them flourish, while executives and boards demand that leaders exceed performance targets and conserve resources.

Such expectations are a recipe for burnout. And indeed, many leaders are burned out. Middle managers are most affected: 42 percent report being "often stressed" out, compared to 42 percent of their team members and 35 percent of senior managers. And 25 percent say they are "often" or "always" burned out.[33]

A systemic, high-level solution to this widespread burnout is developing boards that consider long-term human sustainability in decision making. This usually means creating diverse and inclusive boards.[34]

There are also more immediate solutions. Some have proposed training managers to handle emotions and support others without burning out, which is a standard for clinicians.[35] Another, strengths–based solution, might be co-leadership by people with complementary talents.[36,37]

According to Josh Bersin, a leading thinker in HR and leadership, in modern organizations,

> *We still need leaders and managers. But their tasks, behaviors, and selection must change. The days of a boss sitting behind a desk, telling people what to do, and handing out annual appraisals have gone the way of the dinosaur. As I like to think about it, the role of a manager is to get work done, not to manage people.*
>
> *This means we have two types of managers in companies going forward— those who manage projects and work, and those who lead and coach people, or "people leaders." The job description of "manager" has changed, so companies now often use different language for the different roles.*[38]

In some companies, "people leaders" are called "sponsors," "career advisers," or "circle leaders," and although they don't tell people what to do, they help them grow and succeed.[38]

Co-leadership is not as easy as putting two people in charge of a group and reaping the rewards. As with any kind of teamwork, there are principles critical to the success of co leaders. Katrina Forrest and Catherine Patterson, co-executive directors of CityHealth, shared their six lessons on leading that organization together:[35]

1. **Communicate:** Understand each other's communication styles, use active listening, check assumptions, and be transparent about decision-making processes and direction.
2. **Make Space for Unique Strengths:** Appreciate individual leadership styles and strengths. Determine when each approach can best optimize team performance.
3. **Cocreate:** Stimulate creativity through collaboration, pushing each other outside their comfort zone.
4. **Recognize Each Other's Power:** Recognizing each other's expertise and power can build both coleaders.
5. **Embrace Differences:** As a Black woman and a White woman, Katrina and Catherine committed themselves to dissecting the ways in which race affects their lives. Embracing the diversity of perspectives can make coleadership more effective.
6. **Cultivate Self-Confidence:** Insecurity is a common struggle in the workplace. Take time to build confidence in yourself and each other so you can perform without feeling threatened.

There is not one perfect leadership style or perfect leader personality, and that is a good thing. A diverse workforce calls for leaders with a wide range of personalities and styles. The requirements for modern leadership are enormous. One way to meet them is to rely on diverse and neuroinclusive leadership teams, as described in the next chapter.

 KEY TAKEAWAYS

- *There is no perfect leadership style, but there are practical skills that support considerate, other-focused leadership.*
- *Becoming a more inclusive leader may not always mean doing more. Sometimes it may require that we stop some activities.*
- *A helpful way to develop leadership skills for a diverse world is to adopt a perspective of cultural humility.*
- *Leadership demands in modern organizations are enormous. One solution is shared leadership by people with complementary talents.*

DEVELOPMENTAL QUESTIONS

For employees:

- Which managerial practices in your organization are most neuroinclusive? Least neuroinclusive?
- Are there examples of neuroinclusive leadership that others could learn from?
- How could you share your knowledge or resources to support and encourage neuroinclusive leadership?

For people in all organizational leadership/management positions:

- What could you *stop* doing to be an inclusive leader? Which practices and approaches could you *replace* with more inclusive approaches?
- Is there a HOW problem you might be able to address by collaborating across the leadership levels to develop better systems? What about using skills associated with perspective-taking and cultural humility?
- Would you consider working with a co-leader? In what situations could this be a helpful solution?

CHAPTER TWELVE

LEADERSHIP PRACTICES

Breaking the Neuroexclusion Ceiling

One should waste as little effort as possible on improving areas of low competence. It takes far more energy and work to improve from incompetence to mediocrity than it takes to improve from first-rate performance to excellence.

—Peter Drucker

 NEURODIVERSITY NARRATIVES

NEUROEXCLUSION CEILING

"I want to be a better leader to autistic people."

That was one of the nice statements. Most said, "I want to know how to manage autistic workers."

When I started teaching and presenting on neurodiversity inclusion in the workplace, I kept seeing this statement as the reason for attendees' interest in my workshops. That statement did not just come from CEOs and managers leading neurodiverse teams. It just as often came from early career professionals in their first positions and from college students—people who had not yet managed anyone in their careers.

A few wanted to know how to be better peers and allies.

Nobody ever wondered how to best support a neurodivergent leader.

That kind of bias is as prevalent as it is concerning. In general, the stereotype that neurodivergent people are only a "fit" for entry-level jobs denies the tremendous range of their abilities and talents, as supported by many studies.[1,2] More personally, there I was, a PhD with decades of work experience, plus many things considered "impossible," on my resume. And yet, it seemed that the only way people would see me—even those with no work experience—was in the context of them managing me. The idea of neurodivergent people as highly accomplished leaders at work and in a larger society seemed to be baffling to many.

———————

In reality, there are more neurodivergent leaders than most people realize. Some are very vocal, like Virgin's founder Richard Branson, who forcefully championed his brand of dyslexic thinking for many years. Others, like the autistic Vice Admiral Nick Hine, took a more measured approach to disclosure.[3] But many are "in the closet"—and for a good reason. Neuroexclusion is no joke. Those who brave disclosure often pay the price: in pulled promotions, reduced pay, and bullying.

Still other neurodivergent leaders could not disclose if they wanted to because they were not aware of their neurodivergence until much later in life. They just work and lead and do their best—and offer fascinating leadership lessons that just might help improve all our organizations. This chapter is focused on lessons from several very different neurodivergent leaders.

 HUMAN HAPPENINGS

CHARLOTTE VALEUR: STRAIGHT TALK AND STRATEGY

Teachers at Charlotte Valeur's school in Copenhagen did not quite know what to do with her. Despite her photographic memory and the ability to see patterns, her grades were less than spectacular. She was quiet and preferred to spend time by herself. The school's bullies chose her as a target.[4]

Charlotte came out of school believing that she was stupid. But then she entered a career world of investment banking—and excelled, first in Copenhagen and then in London.

Some were taken aback by her direct, honest communication, devoid of the typical "micro lies" most people tell many times a day. For the most part, however, her direct style was an advantage in the banking world. So was her intense interest in economics. Her ability to think systemically and see risks and potential problems that others missed made her an excellent fit for corporate governance and boardroom positions.[5,6] She climbed to the top of the corporate world faster than most.

But along her way to corporate success, Valeur also found the demands for small talk exhausting, the hidden rules of the workplace baffling, and fitting in a grueling work. During some challenging times in her career, she felt that fitting in required things she really didn't want to do, such as social drinking or watching TV programs others seemed to want to talk about.[6] One day, a childhood friend wondered whether she was autistic. She took the tests—and yes, she was.

Looking back, she credits her autistic mind for her successful career: it was fueled by her ability to see patterns and the big picture of financial and economic trends. She now splits her time between continuing to serve on boards of directors and advocating for neuroinclusion in the workplace. She also teaches people how to be successful in executive, board, and strategic leadership positions, which she sees as quite different from direct people management roles.[7]

 HUMAN HAPPENINGS

AMAN ZAIDI: A PEOPLE PERSON

Aman Zaidi was anything but the best student in Pune, India. Despite his good ability scores, he was labeled distractable and inattentive. He just could not "get into" the standard schoolwork. He was, however, elected a school captain by his fellow students and relished in building relationships.

Aman was also ambitious, and after getting a degree in marketing, his workplace career took off. As a young corporate team leader, he developed a reputation as a manager everyone wanted to work with. People asked to be transferred to Aman's team because he was calm and fun, and he loved developing his people. He accepted promotion after promotion and seemed to be on a fast track to upper-level management.[8]

And then, a promotion sucked all the fun and joy out of his career.

Aman accepted a role as head of operations. The job came with an excellent salary and perks, but he lost all motivation to go to work. What used to be a source of joy was now a drag.

Aman realized that in his earlier positions he had worked directly with people. Focusing on their well-being, performance, and growth was energizing because it aligned with his natural strengths. He was always drawn to people, rather than abstract knowledge or processes. But his fancy new role was all about numbers, projects, and deadlines. It was draining. The misery was not worth the title or the perks.

Aman's understanding of his strengths and of the *importance* of using his strengths for a satisfying career led him to pivot into strengths-focused coaching and talent development. Focusing on improving human performance and well-being helped him get his mojo back. His paperwork-challenged, people-focused brain is happy. And he loves exploring psychology, neuroscience, and archaeology on the side.[9]

HUMAN HAPPENINGS

YURI KRUMAN: THE HR ANTHROPOLOGIST

Yuri Kruman graduated from his high school in Kentucky as a straight-A student. Then, he bombed in his first college ambition, pre-med. But he developed a passion for anthropology and excelled in it. Analyzing human systems was fascinating.

At the start of his career, he got promising positions in corporate and startup organizations. However, his penchant for anthropological analysis might have done him more harm than good on the lower rungs of organizational leadership (and undiagnosed ADHD probably did not help). He saw right through the corporate paper shuffling and fiefdoms, and he did not have much patience for it. Yuri was let go by several companies for seeing "too much" and being "too quick."

After being let go yet another time, Yuri started his own executive coaching company—and grew it into a six-figure business. Then he branched out into HR and learning and development consulting in the US, Israel, and globally. The HR world agreed with him—but then, much of HR is about human systems.

He returned for three successful stints in corporate life, serving as a chief HR officer (CHRO) and a chief learning officer, won numerous awards, wrote seven books, advised numerous companies, and became recognized as one of the "Top 5 Thought Leaders in Global HR." He now believes that ADHD was a huge competitive advantage after all. And thinking as an anthropologist was put to good use as well.[10]

HUMAN HAPPENINGS

KRISTINA MARSH: PICTURES AND PUZZLES

Kristina Marsh is a first-generation high school graduate with a rough childhood experience- turned MBA. She has always loved learning—and teaching. She delights in solving complex problems. She also thinks in pictures, and solutions come to her in a visual form. Problems are puzzles, with pieces laid out across the table of her mind's eye, motivating and exciting her to find the connections that pull the parts of the picture together.

She explains her solutions visually by drawing diagrams and illustrations. Colleagues would pop into her office to talk through ideas and roadblocks, and they would leave with a visual map to a solution. In addition, she has a knack for simplifying the complex. Once, she simplified global market planning for the corporation she worked for, condensing strategic plan documents from 100 pages to just 10 pages of common-sense strategy.

Despite Kristina's accomplishments, she seemed stuck in the middle rungs of leadership. She loved supporting and coaching others. But she was never a fan of conversations that felt contrived or of meetings for the sake of meetings that lacked a clear goal. Even her ability to solve complex problems quickly was, at times, seen as a negative. She was told that her vision and answers came too quickly and easily. Others felt uncomfortable, unable to contribute because she arrived at solutions too fast.

She left the corporate world to consult and teach, and she has been extremely successful. Ironically, the corporate world loves her style as a consultant. She is paid to train and lead company leaders. Her fast, visual, unique thinking style is an asset to her as an external consultant, even though it was not entirely welcomed while she worked inside corporations.[11]

 DEEP DIVE

ON PEOPLE AND PUZZLES

The differences between leaders like Charlotte, Aman, Yuri, and Kristina are not just in their "skill sets." These differences are embedded in one's entire way of being, in the core of our neurological functioning, in the natural direction of our focus and curiosity, in what energizes and drains us. A person energized by people and interactions can learn to spend hours poring over strategy documents, yet is that the best use of their talent? A person who relishes strategy and the complexities of risk management can master day-to-day people management, but is that the best use of their energy?

Strengths do not have to be mutually exclusive—they are just relative. A person may enjoy collegial interactions—but puzzles are irresistible to their mind, and solving puzzles is also where they shine the most. A person who gets human systems can also understand finance—but improving human systems is their "jam."

Being able to do something is not the same as being energized by it. A person who delights in solving strategic and systemic problems can be polished and pleasant when interacting with people. But if interaction requirements are so high that they limit the time for deep work and solving puzzles, the mismatch between their top strengths and position requirements will likely result in burnout. Yes, we all sometimes do things that do not align with our key strengths—and we can even be good at them. But if 80 percent of our work drains us and only 20 percent fills us up, then that is a very poor energy economy. For those who have physical vulnerabilities to stress, it is a *dangerous* energy economy.

Burning people out by placing them in roles where they spend most of their time fighting who they are instead of building on their strengths—even if they are successful—seems like a terrible waste. But typical organizational hierarchies seem to demand that people fit into predetermined boxes, regardless of what talents are cut off in the process. The result is people not working with their strengths, suboptimal organizational performance, and the exclusion of neurodivergent talent and our "spiky" gifts.

If there is more than one way to be a leader, then why do most organizations worldwide have only one leadership pathway? Why are people with great strategic minds told they are "not leadership material" just because they find small talk draining? Why are great people managers placed into planning and operations positions that don't match their social energy? Why do we punish—or fire—talented people for being "too much" for the jobs they are placed in, instead of placing them into jobs that are a better fit?

According to Josh Alan Dykstra, CEO and cofounder of #lovework, "*Building a workplace around what brings people strength and energy is the only way to make work WORK in the future. The more we collectively learn and understand things like neurodivergence, trauma, and mental health, the more we realize that alignment of individuality to daily tasks isn't a 'nice to have' but a categorical imperative for a functioning organization.*"[12]

To build a diverse, strengths-focused workplace and a diverse, strength-focused leadership, we must first get rid of several highly damaging myths.

 DEEPER DIVE

LEADERSHIP MYTHS THAT KEEP US MISERABLE

When we compare the stories of Charlotte, Aman, Yuri, Kristina, and many others, it seems obvious that the best way to support the diversity of talent—

and organizational success—is to develop multiple growth tracks in organizations. But doing so in practice requires letting go of three intertwined myths that limit opportunities for full-range talent development:

1. **The "ideal leader" myth:** The first myth is the idea that there is an ideal type of leader endowed with the right set of characteristics. It assumes that all leaders need the same skills, personality traits, and management style. Even people from different functional areas in the same organization are often expected to have the same style and energy.

But if we are honest, nobody fits the ideal. Every leadership appointment decision I've ever facilitated or supported involved trade-offs between interpersonal skills, strategic thinking, expertise, and ephemeral, subjective things like "gravitas" and "fit." Or, if people were honest, one's pedigree and connections.

Making talent trade-offs means that people in leadership positions often end up spending most of their time doing work that is not aligned with their strengths. The problem for the organization is multiplied if the entire leadership team has the same strengths profile. Ask yourself: Would you rather work for a company led by four Charlotte or Aman clones (as wonderful as they are) or a company that has leaders with different types of strengths, focusing on the work at which each is best?

The "Ideal Leader" myth ignores the wide range of leadership tasks, from dealing with external business pressures to leading research innovation, and from improving internal systems to directly managing people. It is a good thing, then, that people have unique strengths, talents, and perspectives that can be developed and leveraged to create more diverse and effective leadership teams.

2. **The "pipeline" myth:** The second myth perpetuates the idea that there is a linear career path or pipeline that all aspiring leaders should follow. It assumes that employees need to progress through a standard series of hierarchical positions to be shaped into "ideal" leaders.[13] However, this myth ignores the fact that employees may have a wide range of valuable skills and experience that can be leveraged much more effectively with a flexible approach to development.

Traditional factory-style career paths, which are carried over from the industrial age more than a century ago, are modeled in turn after ancient military practices. Neither the diversity of talent nor the need for agility in meeting complex challenges and uncertainties is well served by this model. Having different paths to different types of leadership makes a lot more sense in a complex world. As leading HR expert Josh Bersin has noted, "*The idea that we build 'general managers' who can do everything is just not true. The best leaders are specialists in something. They have deep domain expertise, and they bring it to their job.*"[14]

3. **The "culture-fit" myth:** The third myth is that all employees need to fit into a company's culture to contribute and succeed. It assumes that a single, monolithic culture is (a) possible and (b) beneficial. However, this myth ignores that a culture-add workplace can lead to greater innovation, creativity, and success.

These advantages of diverse leadership teams are well documented. Organizations led by teams rich in multiple dimensions of diversity unlock innovation by creating environments where creative ideas are heard and valued and innovative solutions are implemented.[15,16]

In practice, a "culture fit" often takes the form of decisions guided by the "similar to me" bias and the preference for certain personality traits and styles. That, in turn, perpetuates the marginalization of those who are different—including neurodivergent employees who could have contributed unique and crucially important perspectives.

For example, research suggests that autistic people are predisposed to think systemically and are less susceptible to bias.[17,18] ADHD is associated with higher levels of divergent thinking and lower levels of convergent thinking—a cognitive style that may facilitate "thinking outside the box."[19] A culture-add approach enriches the collective expertise and talent, and it supports justice.

A study published in 2017 by Deloitte showed that people who reached the C-suite were more likely to be big-picture thinkers than the general business population. They were also more competitive, more tolerant of conflict, and more likely to make quick decisions without worrying about the popularity of those choices.[20] The study also indicated that these characteristics did not necessarily produce the best organizational results: psychological homogeneity in the C-suite could rob organizations of the benefits of cognitive diversity.[20,21] Researchers noted that supporting and developing leaders with less flashy but productive styles is likely to bring gains in performance.

Drastic societal and business changes since the 2017 study further confirmed the need for human-centric and collaborative leadership.[22] Newer research demonstrating the benefits of compassion in business also strongly points to the importance of psychological diversity and of kinder, gentler leadership to organizational resilience.[23]

In an increasingly complex world, organizational survival calls for busting the limiting leadership myths and supporting diversity in leadership styles. Recognizing each individual's unique strengths and talents—including neurodivergent talent with their "spiky" profiles—can help organizations create more inclusive, innovative, and resilient systems. Drawing leadership from the broadest talent pool strengthens inclusion—and helps organizations thrive.

 POINTS OF PRACTICE

SUPPORTING THE STRENGTHS

As organizations confront increasingly complex problems, a one-size-fits-all approach to career development that leads to homogeneity in leadership is becoming increasingly ineffective. Standardized career paths intended to shape the "ideal company person" fail to maximize the potential of employees' unique talents and unique minds. Unlocking the full potential of those who are energized by people, systems, strategy, or ideas requires different growth paths. It requires different ways to climb toward different talent "peaks" of our spiky profiles. A leadership team, then, will have the advantage of bringing together different—and maximized—talents.

Here are a few examples of how organizations can implement multiple leadership pathways. They could be mixed, matched, and combined in different ways to maximize the potential of specific individuals and organizational results. These do not have to be rigid tracks: what is important is a good match to individual strengths and a complementary balance of strengths on a leadership team. Because most individuals have primary and secondary strengths, members of leadership teams could design one person's role to be 80 percent strategy and 20 percent people management and another person's role to be 80 percent people management and 20 percent strategy.

- **A people management and development** focus will likely be a primary interest of employees whose strengths are in people-focused roles. They may have exceptional interpersonal skills, emotional intelligence, and the desire to inspire, coach, and develop others. Development opportunities such as leadership training, a gradual increase in team leadership opportunities, mentoring, and coaching can help them maximize their skills and contributions.

- **A systems and processes leadership** focus is an excellent fit for employees who shine in roles that involve decision making based on data analysis, systems thinking, and process improvement. Those with strong analytical skills, attention to detail, and a passion for identifying and solving complex problems and improving processes may not want to focus on managing people but are likely to feel stagnant if they do not have increasingly complex puzzles to solve.

Old puzzles become boring, but if the hurdle to more exciting puzzles is people management, these brilliant thinkers might be lost to organizations. By offering the systems track and development opportunities focused on analytics and process improvement, organizations can help these employees unlock their full potential.

- **A strategy leadership** focus is a match for those who are particularly good at monitoring external trends and strategically mapping the organization's long-term course. They will likely thrive with increasing responsibilities in strategic leadership, including long-term planning and external risk management. Just like those who are more interested in systems, strategic thinkers may not necessarily be energized by spending much of their time focused on people management but could still enjoy having a small portion of their time dedicated to mentoring and developing talent.
- **An expert leadership** focus will work for people who love growing their expertise in specialized roles, such as legal, medical, creative, engineering, or research professionals. They might be more interested in becoming the top expert in the world than in policies and politics. These employees may have advanced degrees and deep technical expertise and excel at critical analysis and problem solving.

Unfortunately, many current organizational charts "freeze" these insatiable learners in individual contributor roles that may feel like dead ends, especially when managed by those with significantly less expertise. By offering professional growth and advancement tracks toward senior and lead expert roles, perhaps with a mentoring component that focuses on cocreation rather than traditional supervision, organizations can help these employees advance their skills—and are more likely to retain their expertise.

Depending on the organizational type and size, there might be other talent pathways:

- **A thought leadership** focus might be ideal for employees who love solving puzzles applicable outside the organization. These people excel in conceptual thinking, research, finding innovative solutions to wicked problems, and communicating these solutions in an engaging and influential way. Often, this type of talent "outgrows" development opportunities offered by organizations and exits.

Meanwhile, organizations might be paying PR firms to do "thought leadership" these employees could have done much more authentically. By providing opportunities to develop thought leadership through education, research, writing, and presenting, organizations can retain unique talent that will support organizational visibility in unique, hard-to-replicate ways.

For example, David Lancefield, the head of thought leadership in PwC/Strategy, realized that authentic thought leadership helped the firm cut through "noise" to develop distinctive positions on topics that mattered. Thought leadership developed by people immersed in solving problems and substantiated by robust research compels people to act—it has to lead to an outcome, not just sit there as a report or an article. Smart organizations see thought leadership as something far more than a side hustle, a hobby, or a luxury to be enjoyed only after you have met your targets. Rather, they *"position thought leadership as central to their reputation and commercial (or public service) outcomes. In practice, this means leaders investing the time to create, share, and use thought leadership to open up new dialogues, develop new relationships, and enable new outcomes. It requires courage to tackle issues that are not necessarily in the mainstream, part of conventional wisdom, or current interest."*[24]

- **A global leadership** focus will be a draw to employees relishing roles that involve working across cultures, languages, and borders. These employees may have high levels of openness to experience, global professional acumen, and the capacity to navigate complex cultural landscapes. By offering development such as language training, international assignments, and global leadership opportunities, organizations can help these employees grow their skills while advancing global collaborations.
- **A creative ideation and problem-solving** focus might be of interest to people who excel in roles that involve creativity, innovation, and design

thinking. These employees may combine a strong creative streak with a willingness to take risks. By offering creativity tracks, organizations can stay ahead of the field while helping these employees maximize their potential.

Of course, these are only some examples in which organizations can help talent grow. Much depends on the industry and the size of the organization. Further, as society and technology develop rapidly, new ways of deploying talent may emerge. For example, around 2020, there was an increase in Well-being Officer roles.[25] In 2023, Ethics Officers and AI Ethics Officers became sought after.[26] It is likely that future societal changes will create new leadership roles and call for talent that is anything but typical. The need to support and grow unique talent ready to step into unique and emerging roles is yet another argument in favor of strength-based and neuroinclusive leadership development.

The next chapter shows what support and success look like for neurodivergent leaders and how they can lead authentically in the face of stigma and discrimination.

 KEY TAKEAWAYS

- *Neurodiversity in leadership is rarely discussed. However, studying examples of neurodivergent leaders can help us develop a deeper understanding of different types of leadership.*
- *There are more neurodivergent leaders than most people realize. Many neurodivergent leaders have developed unique ways to use their talents for effective leadership and meaningful impact.*
- *Myths and stereotypes, such as the "ideal leader," "pipeline," and "culture fit," interfere with the advancement of neurodivergent leaders.*
- *There are no "ideal" leaders. There are many different leadership strengths that can enrich neurodiverse leadership teams and organizations.*
- *Optimizing leadership teams may require developing diverse leadership talents in ways aligned with individual strengths.*

DEVELOPMENTAL QUESTIONS

For employees:

- Is the approach to leadership in your organization culture-fit or culture-add? How does this influence the employee experience?
- Are there forms of leadership you might not have considered before but now might want to try in the workplace or in different settings, such as in the community or volunteering? Are there forms of leadership you might have exercised without thinking of it as leadership?
- How could you support or encourage neurodivergent leaders or emerging leaders?

For managers/direct supervisors:

- When you look for emerging leadership talent, do you inadvertently pay more attention to those who are similar to you? How could some of the leadership myths have influenced your thinking?
- How could the leadership development in your organization be more neuroinclusive?
- When you think about your own growth, is there a form of leadership that is most appealing to you? Least appealing?

For HR and upper management:

- How (neuro)inclusive is your leadership development system? Is it focused on fitting people into boxes or on tailored growth pathways? Culture-fit or culture-add?
- How could you make leadership development opportunities more neuroinclusive?
- When you think about your own growth, is there a form of leadership that is most appealing to you? Least appealing?

CHAPTER THIRTEEN

LEADERSHIP PRACTICES

Leading While Stigmatized

The biggest barriers are prejudice and fear.

—Judith Heumann

 NEURODIVERSITY NARRATIVES

ON ARMOR AND VULNERABILITY

How do you lead in a world where 50 percent of managers don't even want to hire people like you?[1] How do you lead in a world that stereotypes, misunderstands, and even hates you?

This is the question Jerry Gidner, a long-time US federal executive, writer, and Tourette Syndrome inclusion leader, had to wrestle with, as he shared with me:[2]

> *I have experienced the pity, the stigma, the hushed whispers, the condescending attitudes, the daily insults—some large, some small, and the invisibility that comes from having a brain that works differently from theirs. I have also experienced the hostility. People hate what they fear and they fear what they don't understand. In some cases, that "thing" they hate and fear is me and my condition. . . . Owning my own story—I have Tourette's—was the biggest factor in my success as a leader.*

Tourette Syndrome, a neurological condition characterized by motor and vocal tics, is not easy to hide. The hardest lesson Jerry has learned: don't hide it. *"Leaders need to be authentic and vulnerable,"* and you can't do that *"if you are trying to conceal or deny one of the core things that makes you who you are."*

Jerry Gidner describes what many neurodivergent leaders face every day. The ever-present prejudice forces us to make some hard choices. And many neurodivergent leaders agree that despite the stigma and even hate, we must lead with authenticity—even when this authenticity comes at a price. In Jerry's words, *"Many people will assume you are "less" because you are neurodivergent. In my experience, most people who are neurotypical, whether they are leaders or employees, automatically assume they are superior to those of us who are not."*

I definitely felt this. And it feels like a gut punch every time. My autism disclosure brought out the worst in some people: the hate, the fear, the bullying, and the destructiveness. Even in those who had known me for years. Even in those who previously expressed admiration for my work.

The struggle with stigma is no joke.

I had to probe Jerry's thinking further. How do you cope with condescension and hostility? What is the internal step that you take from seeing the hate and fear in people to still doing your best, even for (or with) these people? How do we give from the heart when people aim for our hearts?

"It is hard. It is an everyday existential battle," he continued, *"and people in this situation can take every insult to heart—those who hurl them are aiming for your heart, after all. So you can charge into that world and absorb the blows, or you can withdraw into yourself and build an armor that is impenetrable. Ironically, once you do the latter, it is much easier to do the former."*

The armor and authenticity are not mutually exclusive. We can only be transparent and vulnerable when we are armed with knowing who we are and what we stand for. And what we can contribute to the world. In other words, our WHY.

WHY do we lead? Do we do it for the position and the satisfaction of power over people? The desire to see "underlings" toiling under our direction? Or are we motivated by the desire to serve and work with people to create a world with more justice, safety, and flourishing? To me, it is the latter that makes it worth the effort. And it is the latter that allows us to go beyond self-consciousness and worry about how others might perceive us.

Mockery seems less of an issue when you are on a mission.

> This chapter is focused on how neurodivergent leaders overcome—not their conditions—but the stigma and discrimination experienced because of these conditions.

DEEP DIVE

DOING LEADERSHIP DIVERGENTLY

The old ways of thinking are not working for solving the world's problems, from ethical dilemmas surrounding artificial intelligence to gaping economic disparities and climate disasters.[3,4] Humanity needs a new perspective on complex questions.[5] It needs more neurodivergent leaders—even if it is not ready for it.[6] Differently wired brains bring unique ways of knowing and problem solving. To survive in complex modern environments, humanity must draw leadership talent from the full range of human diversity.

Unfortunately, old biases get in the way of diversifying leadership.

The romanticized notion of the "ideal" leader clouds most people's ability to perceive the reality that effective leadership can be embodied in many forms and by people with different abilities. The less someone matches the socially formed representation of the "ideal" leader, the more likely it is that people will resent and resist their leadership.[7,8,9] Moreover, the traditional view of leadership, with its emphasis on hierarchy and leader-centricity, often favors those from traditionally privileged groups, potentially excluding others from leadership roles. The neuroableist version of this bias stems from the assumption that successful leadership can only be performed by those who fit a conventional, often narrow, notion of neuronormativity.

However, the evolving understanding of leadership embraces a broader, more inclusive perspective. For neurodivergent and disabled people, "doing" successful leadership might mean leveraging their unique experiences and perspectives to foster empathy, inclusivity, and resilience in their teams and formal or informal organizations. It might involve challenging traditional norms and expectations and advocating for more accessible, equitable workplaces. As Christina Ryan, founder of the Disability Leadership Institute in Canberra, Australia, has put it, "*Being more inclusive might be a specific skill of disability leaders. It seems to be about the understanding of others' struggles that marginalization brings, along with the commitment to community that being a person with leadership responsibility in that community invokes.*"[10]

The importance of representation in leadership is rarely challenged in discussions of most forms of diversity, although it is still not easy to accomplish. But disability and neurodiversity? Deep-seated ableism makes many people equate any limitation with the absence of any and all ability.[10,11] The implicit sense of superiority makes others react to disabled people in leadership with resentment, even anger.

As if external barriers to neurodivergent leadership emergence were not enough, internalized ableism can also make us limit our own aspirations.

The first step to overcoming the ableist and neuroableist systems is addressing our internal ableism.

 HUMAN HAPPENINGS

PERFECTLY IMPERFECT

Luis Velasquez is a father, a family man, an adviser and coach to CEOs, a published author, and a regular contributor to *Fast Company* and *Harvard Business Review*.

But getting to that place took some doing.

Luis 1.0 was an assistant professor of fungal genetics at Michigan State University, happily married. Coming from humble beginnings in Guatemala, he was proud of his achievements and the hard work he had to do to get where he was. His identity was tied to his academic success, publishing papers, getting promoted, and making his family proud and financially secure.

Then, something did not feel right. Something was really, really not right. A brain tumor.

Luis 2.0 was lost. After his brain surgery, he went back to work, and people were very accommodating and supportive. But he could not focus, analyze data, or, most notably, perform simple calculations. He couldn't—and still can't—calculate the amount of a tip without pen and paper, something Luis 1.0. could do easily. He could no longer hear instructions and execute them: he had to have all the instructions in writing. He also lost the ability to pay attention to detail and finish projects. Luis 2.0 had *"the attention and focus of a toddler in the middle of a toy store."*

He tried to persist with science and academia. But he kept making mistakes in his experiments, mistakes that terribly embarrassed him. It just was not going to work.

The loss of his professional identity was devastating. He considered himself broken goods. Worthless. He kept comparing himself with the person that he was, but that person didn't exist anymore. He could not meet professional expectations. He could not meet his family's expectations. This caused problems in his marriage as well.

At one point, Luis considered suicide. But he could not do that to his mother. So, he resolved to get better.

Luis 3.0 started running. He became an ultramarathoner and Ironman triathlete. Getting fit helped with his emotions and his sense of self-worth. His cognition improved—never to the level it was before, but he is now OK with that. He reinvented himself, got an MBA, became a consultant, and then an executive coach.

These dramatic changes happened as a result of two things. First, the acceptance that he is not the same person he was pre-surgery. He no longer saw the tumor as something foreign that got in the way of his perfect life. Once he accepted his new self, tumor included, he gave himself permission to not be perfect. Second, once he gave himself permission to be imperfect, he could be bolder and try new things, take more risks, and see what else he could do. He made peace with himself as a *"perfectly imperfect human."*

Luis also works differently. First, he is much more open to being wrong and is relentless in seeking feedback and suggestions to get better. He does not have to know everything as long as he can keep learning. Second, he is much more open to collaboration. He seeks out people with complementary abilities. Working with others really helps with his writing projects—and with his neurodivergent way of leading and helping others lead better.[12]

The way Luis talks about being perfectly imperfect and rebuilding himself reminds me of the Japanese art of kintsugi. Those practicing this art repair broken pottery, but they do not hide the cracks as if nothing had ever happened. Instead, they accentuate the seams with gold or other precious metals. The once-shattered cup or bowl is not quite its former self—but it proudly displays its history of struggle and strength. Its value transcends the mere addition of gold; it lies in the care and the lessons of restoration.[13]

Neurodivergent leaders face adversity. Sometimes we crack. But we also expand our capacity to mend the fractures within ourselves and the world around us. This mending can take the form of championing our communities and developing deeper connections. The gold of our mending is our compassion toward others and ourselves. We can turn our struggle with internalized stigma into fighting for a stigma-free world.

Openness about our struggles can be one of the best tools for helping create a better world. And organizational environments that welcome and support such openness can greatly multiply our impact.

EMPLOYER EXCELLENCE

NEURODIVERGENT LEADERS WELCOMED

Philips, a healthcare technology company headquartered in Amsterdam, has an over 130-year history of commitment to innovation. It is also a company that appreciates and supports neurodivergent talent and neurodivergent leadership. Tristan Lavender, an autistic founder and a chair of the 550-strong employee resource group, has built collaborative relationships across the organization.[14] With the participation of several openly neurodivergent leaders, Philips has created an environment where neurodivergent employees can be both themselves and successful.[15,16]

For example, Ben Gorissen built a 35-year career with Philips; he is currently the product safety risk management leader for MRI Systems. For most of this time, he was undiagnosed and struggled with sensory overwhelm and making transitions. The autism diagnosis helped him get the clarity and support he needed and to further develop as a leader. But he was not expected to change his way of being: he feels accepted as he is, authentically. Ben Gorissen also believes that in some ways, his autistic traits make him a more effective leader: "*Because of my personal need for order, I have always been keen to put structure in place when I started in a new role. This has helped me create focus and clarity for others as well, making me a more effective leader and colleague.*"[15]

Rokus Harder, MRI Service Innovation director and career coach at Philips, is a published author proving negative stereotypes about dyslexia wrong. He uses his creative thinking in leading a team of 30 professionals around the world to develop better ways of keeping MRI equipment in optimal condition. Rokus Harder also believes that managers should support the environment of psychological safety for people who struggle with dyslexia: "*I think the best thing you can do as a leader is to focus on people's strengths. This makes them feel valued for who they are. It also makes it easier to have conversations about support that people may need in areas that don't come naturally to them.*"[16]

Tristan Lavender both supports Philips's organizational thought leadership efforts and is a thought leader in his own right. Tristan is a fantastic example of an autistic leader thriving on the thought leadership track discussed in the previous chapter and making a difference both in his organization and the larger world. The supportive environment for neurodivergent leaders created by Philips has a positive impact outside the company.

Unfortunately, there are not enough companies like Philips. In most organizations, neurodivergent leaders struggle mightily to do their best and to be who they are.

 NEURODIVERSITY NARRATIVES

A CAREER CONUNDRUM

I coached many neurodivergent leaders and interviewed many more for this book. There seems to be a clear pattern in the careers of many autistic and multiply neurodivergent leaders—autistic + ADHD, autistic + dyslexic, and especially twice-exceptional (2E)—gifted with neurodivergent traits. Not every neurodivergent leader's career follows this pattern, of course, but it does seem to be a common story for many.

- First, there is a struggle with entry-level positions that do not allow independent thinking.
- Next comes rapid progress to midlevel positions of either elite individual contributors, high-level project managers, or midlevel managers.
- After that, a seemingly endless cycle of "prove-it-again" and doing high-responsibility work without matching titles or pay leaves individuals with a moral injury and a sense of organizational betrayal.[17]
- Finally, there is a move into consulting or thought leadership careers.

Kirsten Gural Howley, a business consultant from Virginia, in the US, has an interesting perspective on this phenomenon.

 HUMAN HAPPENINGS

THE ERUDITE NEED NOT APPLY: THE US EDITION

As a child, Kirsten was labeled as gifted. However, her intelligence masked her dyslexia, dyscalculia, and anxiety disorder, which remained unidentified until adulthood. Kirsten was able to develop self-coping mechanisms for her reading comprehension and number-switching issues. These mechanisms worked—but also delayed her diagnosis by decades.

As a business analyst, she worked in visuals, mapping out ideas and seeing "whole solutions." Others perceived her work ethic and dedication as "perfectionism," although she never felt like a perfectionist. Ironically, people also often attributed her great results to "luck" because she worked "too fast."

Kirsten was told she had CEO potential but that her perfectionist approach might be alienating and others might perceive her as too "erudite." She was also expected to wait and "pay her dues"; yet the promised promotions never came, and she finally left corporate life. She started her own consulting business helping clients analyze their business, marketing, and content strategy and develop their messaging. As an independent consultant, she is valued by her clients for the same fast and original thinking that was punished by her managers. Kirsten thinks that "*if you're a consultant, you're rewarded and hired to think outside the box, but within the corporate structure, you need to fit into the box.*"[18]

That seems like a great talent loss if organizations truly want innovation.

 HUMAN HAPPENINGS

THE ERUDITE NEED NOT APPLY: THE UK EDITION

There are other stories eerily similar to Kirsten's. Across the Atlantic, autistic leader Justin Donne worked in the UK for governmental organizations and in continental Europe for private companies like Disneyland in Paris. He served on many boards as well.[19] Like Kirsten, he was seen as "too much." He accomplished in hours what would take his colleagues days. So, he was told he was too fast and needed to slow down. Oh, and stop being so erudite in his emails.

In one of his roles, Justin broke organizational records for key performance indicators, facilitated fundraising windfalls, and developed award-winning programs. Then, he was placed under a micromanager who wanted to control everything Justin did and how he did it. That was the end of Justin's career with that organization and the end of the organization's record of success.

Why would organizations pay consultants to think outside the box but punish employees for doing the same?

DEEP DIVE

GET THE SMARTY PANTS

The struggles of many neurodivergent high achievers might be related to the "get the smarty pants" phenomenon, also known as bullying and victimization of top performers.[20] This phenomenon is well documented in the workplace and in school: it is driven by others' envy and concern with how they would look in comparison to the high achiever. Outstanding performance and the resulting coworker envy are likely to contribute to bullying and the holding back of neurodivergent performers.[21] In the case of autistic performers, the focus on work rather than socializing can also be perceived as a negative. Other "strikes" against autistic performers include their blunt communication style, which may be perceived as a lack of agreeableness, and simply being different.

Such perceptions have been stumbling blocks for many neurodivergent careers. Some advisers suggest that if neurodivergent performers want to succeed, they should put on a mask, moderate their "spiky" performance, hold back so as to not be more "average," and project the expected "persona." This sounds very similar to the advice I received early in my career—that "a girl should not be smarter than her boss." And it is just as depressing.

However, there might be another, better way. Instead of changing ourselves, we can help others reframe how they interpret our behavior. "Quiet" can be seen as "aloof" or "thoughtful." "Active" can be interpreted as " frantic" or "driven."

HUMAN HAPPENINGS

THE GREAT RE-FRAME

Luis Velasquez tells the story of his client identified here as John.

John is brilliant. He worked for some of the best and most-known companies in Silicon Valley: Facebook, Google, Uber, and Twitter.

John was identified as a potential leader in his organization and matched with a coach Luis. When Luis interviewed John's manager and several of his peers, the feedback was harsh. They said that John seemed unengaged, absent, and even aloof in team meetings. When Luis probed for detail, they said, "In meetings, *he sits in the back of the room* or at the end of the table, he rarely speaks, he doesn't engage much in small talk." John's manager said the only reason John is in this program is that he gets things done, but he won't go further if he doesn't engage with his peers and "add value to the team."

In contrast, John's direct reports loved him. They described him as a great manager, a person who would allow people to take responsibility; he always made himself available to explain and coach, and they felt empowered by him. "He is not a micromanager, which I appreciate" was a common comment among people in his unit. They did, however, want to do even more to increase their own visibility.

Luis explained to John this visibility problem. John was happy to bring his team to meetings and give them the visibility they wanted.

After some time, the managers who used to be skeptical about John were raving about him and the "change" he had undergone. They told Luis that he was taking real steps to "build the bench" (develop his direct reports). When Luis asked them what he does, his manager said that John *sits in the back of the room, and he lets his people shine*. He makes room for them and intercedes only when there is something important that they left out or if they didn't have the answer to a question.

John still sat quietly at the back of the room. But the interpretation was completely different. He did not have to change his personality. Just the framing.[12]

 DEEP DIVE

LEADING THROUGH INFLUENCE

Leadership may look like a mysterious art, but it is also a craft with a toolbox of approaches, and some of these tools might be particularly effective when we are imperfect and authentic. If the true goal of leadership is motivating people to achieve goals and effect change, the old model of using positional authority may never have been the most effective one.

We could also benefit from reframing our leadership by separating it from positions of management and formal authority—even when we are in positions of formal authority in our organizations. Often, we can lead as if we were leading without formal authority. Formal authority is a bonus that can make leadership easier—but it does not guarantee it. I delved into the dynamics of power and influence in one of my *Fast Company* articles.[22]

Social psychologists John French and Bertram Raven described five bases of interpersonal power, or the ability to effect change, back in 1959.[23] They disagreed on the sixth—informational power.[24] French believed that information produced influence but not power. Raven, in contrast, argued that informational influence *is* power and included it in his solo work.

It appears that Raven was right. As the workplace changed drastically, with remote and knowledge work limiting the usefulness of other power sources, informational influence is becoming an increasingly important power.

Here is the six-element version of the framework:

1. **Legitimate power** is positional power. A supervisor's job title signals the legitimate authority to be in charge. This often works because legitimate power typically comes with two other power sources: rewards and punishments.

2. **Reward power** is based on the ability to award bonuses, raises, promotions, and privileges.

3. **Coercive power** is supported by the ability to punish via demotion, undesirable scheduling, inferior workspace, or termination. People often resist coercive power, which may limit its effectiveness. Another limitation is that reward and coercive forms of power require *surveillance* and the continued use of positional authority, rewards, and punishments. In contrast, the remaining sources of power are not constrained by surveillance or the need to exert power nonstop. They are also not tied to the position of formal authority.

4. **Referent power** stems from our identification with leaders and the intrinsic desire to follow their example.

5. **Expert power** stems from our belief that the leader has a deeper understanding of relevant topics. The leader "knows best."

6. **Informational influence/power** goes beyond expert power by adding an element of learning. Not only does the leader know best but the follower is also developing an advanced *understanding* of why something is "best." As a result, followers experience a change of mind and know the *reason* for action. Raven called this a "socially independent change," which might have been initiated by the leader but continues without further leadership effort. People may not even remember who initiated the change.

In organizations, some people hold management positions and can exercise legitimate, reward, and coercive power—but they may or may not be able to use referent, expert, or informational power.

Referent, expert, and informational power are powers of leadership. Informal leaders who are not in a managerial position can exercise these powers. Those who are managers become leaders when they successfully use these powers.

Positional leaders still can—and sometimes need to—use legitimate, reward, and even coercive power. But as work becomes increasingly cognitive and emotional, the importance of referent, expert, and informational leadership powers will continue to grow, while the power of managerial levers will likely diminish. Moreover, younger employees and all who seek purpose and meaning in their work tend to be unimpressed by positional authority.[25]

Stigma and prejudice have forced many neurodivergent leaders to accomplish their work with little to no positional power. Although this is taxing, it also may result in developing skills of using influence without coercion or rewards—an invaluable skill in leading in remote and hybrid situations and in leading social action.

In fact, leading without positional power is a highly transferrable skill. I learned it as a teenager while organizing the community to protect local wetlands and lakes. Much later, it came in handy in leading a university accreditation process without having formal power over most of the units that needed to take action and provide information crucial to this work. It is also most handy in supporting neurodivergent communities via thought leadership.

 DEEPER DIVE

LOVE, NOT LORDING: LEADING WITH REFERENT, EXPERT, AND INFORMATIONAL INFLUENCE

Referent power is about leading by example. Aspiring leaders and those retooling for the relational future of work can develop their referent power if they model transparency and authenticity, listen, and act with compassion.[26]

Alan Robinson, who held leadership positions at several major technology companies in the US and UK and who identifies as an ADHDer with dyslexia and dysgraphia, believes in the benefits of *"utilizing a form of radical transparency—a kind of extreme openness in order to develop deeper, stronger, and more trusting relationships on the team and in a fraction of the time. Trust is the key ingredient of any successful relationship."*[27]

In addition to authenticity, listening to and understanding others are key to human connections. Relationships are much more intrinsically motivating than transactional rewards and punishments. Even before the COVID-19 pandemic brought considerate leadership to the forefront of workplace discussions, 78 percent of employees were willing to switch jobs to be in a more empathetic culture. And 77 percent were willing to give more work hours to an empathetic employer.[22] With many employees feeling the effects of stress and burnout, managers' compassion is increasingly important. Embracing a compassionate approach recognizes that employees are human beings with complex lives and emotional needs; it helps increase the sense of belonging. In the long run, compassionate leadership can lead to higher employee engagement, lower turnover, and more resilient and cohesive teams.

Listening can take many forms: it involves much more than using one's ears and may range from a basket of home-baked goods to poetry. Dr. Karen Anhwei Lee, provost and professor of English at Wheaton College in Illinois, shares her listening recipe: *"For twenty years, I've brought around a "gratitude basket" filled with home-baked goods to spend time with people and get to know them in the organizations where I serve. In a way, I believe that this basket operates as my organizational stethoscope—by spending time with people, I can better listen to the organizational pulse, the internal heartbeat, through the various in-person, impromptu conversations."*[28] But when COVID-19 interrupted in-person gatherings, writing and sharing poetry became her stethoscope and a way to connect with people on a deep, emotional level.

For many decades, **expert power** was demonstrated by hanging one's college diploma on the wall. Credential inflation and the emphasis on staying current require that leaders demonstrate expertise in many other ways, from advanced certifications to high-quality writing and speaking. But it does not mean a sole focus on academic expertise or being a know-it-all. First, knowing it all is increasingly impossible, and second, what people care about is that you listen and pay attention to what matters to them—and then find solutions to problems that matter. For example, Danny Combs and other leaders of TACT (Teaching Autism Community Trades) in Colorado teach autistic young people skilled trades—carpentry, auto mechanic work, welding, and other in-demand skills.[29] This is much-needed, likely life-changing work and an example of applying expertise to solve problems that matter. Spearheading this work is a superb application of leadership.

Using our work to encourage and support others through writing, speaking, and otherwise contributing to developing knowledge and thinking has elements of both expert and **informational power**. Done well, it can help both establish our expertise and support informational influence. And although the term "thought leadership" can be lofty, the core skills associated with it—connecting, changing people's minds, and inspiring at a distance—are crucial for the future of work.[30] Hybrid and remote work and the focus on continuous learning and creativity increasingly call for those in organizational leadership roles to inspire at a distance.

Leadership can no longer rely on control and command. Inclusive leadership is about love, not lording over people. To draw on referent, expert, and informational power, leadership must be cocreated around a shared purpose and genuine connection—from anywhere. In this approach, earning trust through transparency and authenticity is not optional but foundational.

The importance of authenticity in their work is stressed by many neurodivergent leaders I talked to.

Kelly Bron Johnson, an autistic and hard-of-hearing inclusion professional from Montreal, developed her leadership approach with the focus of staying true to herself:[31]

> My own approach is to help others understand that we might lead differently, but we're still leading. I am happy to "lead from behind," so to speak, and let others shine.
>
> I feel it's important that whatever style of leadership you choose, it has to be authentic to you and your nature. Don't try to work in ways that aren't authentic.
>
> The rest of the world can judge me as they please, but I am true to myself and can sleep at night. And eventually people pick up on my authenticity, how genuine and passionate I am, and they trust that and want to work with me *because* of those traits.

Charlotte Valeur, a Denmark-born neurodivergent business leader living in England and a director of the Neurodiversity Institute, put it this way: "*I have studied many leaders and found that the ones who come across mostly as themselves are the ones I relate most to. This has led me to hold on to myself as a leader and work hard to stay my authentic self even when it is hard to do so.*"[32]

Leading is never easy. Leading while neurodivergent can be excruciatingly hard. But we can lead authentically, with a commitment to our mission as our armor. We don't have to sacrifice who we are; we can frame our authentic approach in ways that resonate with others. And we can lead by building influence whether or not the world is ready to see us in positions of power.

I am encouraged and inspired by the many who are making a difference, whether in formal organizational leadership roles or in community leadership. The next and final chapter focuses on how we can all lead—from any position—in creating a neuroinclusive future of work and a more inclusive world.

KEY TAKEAWAYS

- *Neurodivergent leaders experience a unique set of barriers due to ableism, stigma, and neuromarginalization.*
- *In most cases, we are not overcoming our "conditions." We are overcoming discrimination on the basis of our differences and the resulting internalized stigma.*
- *A focus on authenticity and vulnerability is a common thread in the accounts of many neurodivergent leaders.*
- *Neurodivergent leaders can use the tools of influence to lead without coercion, regardless of their hierarchical positions.*

DEVELOPMENTAL QUESTIONS

For employees/job seekers:
- Have you felt like you need armor to deal with the world? How do you negotiate the need for armor and the need for authenticity? Is there a mission that has served or can serve as your armor?
- How can you make a positive difference, with or without positional authority?
- How could reframing help you work with others and be seen as a leader without giving up your authenticity?
- How could you develop your informational influence?

For managers/direct supervisors:
- Does your organization support leadership emergence among neurodivergent employees?
- Have you observed the "get the smarty pants" phenomenon and other biases that may particularly harm neurodivergent talent? How could you address these?
- In what ways might your leadership need to change to align more closely with the needs of the modern workplace?

For HR and upper management:

- Does your organization support leadership emergence among neurodivergent employees? In what way could your processes, procedures, and culture be supporting or hindering this emergence?
- Have you observed the "get the smarty pants" phenomenon and other biases that may particularly harm neurodivergent talent? How could you systemically address these?
- In what ways might your leadership need to change to align more closely with the needs of the modern workplace? In what ways might the system of leadership development and advancement need to change to ensure all forms of diversity, including neurodiversity, in the talent pipeline?

CONCLUSION

Every Changemaker

I alone cannot change the world, but I can cast a stone across the waters to create many ripples.

—Mother Teresa

 NEURODIVERSITY NARRATIVES

AYIRA'S NEURO SOUL CAFÉ

Ayira's Neuro Soul Café is much more than a café. It is a place where employees are young neurodivergent people, where neurodivergent neighbors and their families are welcome to come and interact with each other, and where guests can also attend workshops on topics of neurodiversity. The café is slowly becoming known in Nairobi, the capital of Kenya.[1]

The founder, Diana Ayoo, explains her inspiration behind the café: "*Ayira is named after my 6-year-old daughter called Ayira. She has a very unique condition called Primrose syndrome together with autism. As a mother and in this part of the world, I know that the neurodivergent are stigmatized and they are not really taken care of. I wanted to show the world that . . . they can be given a chance in society and contribute.*"

The café meets a need even if many people are not fully aware of that need. Ayoo "*noticed . . . that when people come to the restaurant and when you talk to them and explain to them what we do and who our people are, someone will always say, 'I have a brother, I had a sister, I have a cousin, I have a niece, I have a neighbor.' So this means that it touches people. . . . It is just that the awareness has not been so much out there for people to be able to know and accept and, you know, just understand the different conditions.*"

Diana Ayoo cannot employ every neurodivergent young person who needs opportunities. When I connected with her in the fall of 2023, she had six employees. Some come and volunteer or simply to check in, even though she does not yet have enough business to pay them. Just coming to work can give someone a powerful sense of participating in something meaningful; a sense of mattering.

For those who are paid staff, working at Ayira's Neuro Soul Café has been life changing.

Twenty-five-year-old Simon Njuki says that at the café, he feels accepted and loved, even though the larger society rejects people with dyslexia. The love Diana Ayoo extends to her employees gives Simon Njuki *"an opportunity to go further."*[1]

An opportunity to go further and make meaningful contributions is something that many neurodivergent people, all over the world, long for. And the larger society needs the contributions of neurodivergent people, even if it is not quite aware of it.

How can we all make a difference?

Large corporations like Microsoft, Dell, or Deloitte have the kind of resources that most of us might not be able to fathom. Their neuroinclusion work helps improve lives, and I would love to see it expand and deepen.

Innovative smaller and midsized companies like Legalite, Call Yachol, and Ultranauts show us what is possible with a radical, company-wide approach to inclusion.

And people like Diana Ayoo show us what is possible if just one person puts their mind and a loving heart into a mission. Positive change happens. Maybe not a perfect, "in the ideal world" change, but it is the most meaningful change for people like Simon Njuki.

Much more change is needed. Many Simons are still knocking at closed doors and looking for an opportunity to go further. Addressing the unemployment gaps faced by neurodivergent people requires a comprehensive approach, a 360° approach to inclusion, with governments, CEOs, HR professionals, managers, and everyday humans all playing essential roles. Systemic and lasting change involves changing nation-level structures and legislation, organizational structures and processes, as well as social norms and individual attitudes. This means that many people, with and without the power of the office, can play significant roles in facilitating the change. The cycle of change can start from any point.

POINTS OF PRACTICE

LEADERSHIP FROM THE TOP

Governmental and law-making entities establish the legal context of work. They have the authority and resources to create an environment where neuroinclusion and employee well-being are not just an occasional afterthought but are design principles for talent processes. Laws like the Americans with Disabilities Act (ADA) or Finland's Working Hours Act can improve the lives of millions and, if applied worldwide, billions of people.[2] Incentives can also effectively encourage organizations to hire and retain neurodivergent talent. Governments can improve accessibility standards in infrastructure and technology, as well as support awareness and education.

Within organizations, CEOs and board members have the leverage to effect change that others don't.[3] Prioritizing inclusion and holistic belonging in the company's mission, values, and everyday action can improve many lives. Using inclusion and well-being metrics like Ultranauts, humanizing interviews like Call Yachol, and customizing work, as shown by Lemon Tree and Legalite, can greatly improve neuroinclusivity at work. It can also create truly extraordinary and thriving organizations.

POINTS OF PRACTICE

OPERATIONAL LEADERSHIP

HR and people operations managers can organize training sessions to help debunk myths about neurodiversity and support a deeper understanding of the full range of human talents and differences. Making job descriptions more inclusive, establishing accessible application processes, and ensuring a fair pay and promotions system scaffold inclusion at work and support dignity and belonging for all. Providing accommodations and career development tailored to individual strengths is crucial to 360° degrees inclusion, and HR can support both by improving structures and processes and educating and supporting individuals one-on-one.

Team and department leaders and direct supervisors define the employee experience of inclusion—or exclusion. Inclusion succeeds when leaders push back against biases during the hiring, onboarding, and employee development process. Inclusion succeeds when they implement necessary adjustments or accommodations to ensure that team communication is accessible to all and that everyone is treated with dignity. Taking small daily steps toward continuous improvement in inclusion practices adds up to a major impact.

 POINTS OF PRACTICE

GRASSROOTS LEADERSHIP

We all have different strengths, and we can work with who we are to improve the world around us. The July 1990 Americans with Disabilities Act was passed by the US government, but its passage was prompted by many years of grassroots work by disability activists. This work included a dramatic visualization of how inaccessible environments affect people: in the March 1990 Capital Crawl, a group of disabled people, including eight-year-old Jennifer Keelan-Chaffins, left their wheelchairs and mobility aids and crawled up the steps of the US Capitol.[4] Without these disability advocates, this legislative change might have taken much longer. Change in large cultural systems tends to be slow, yet it does occur, and grassroots movements and individual changemakers can drive the difference. Smaller systems, such as teams or departments, can develop new social norms much faster.

As coworkers and team members, we can improve colleagues' experience and change group behavior by modeling support and bringing some of the Glastonbury crowd spirit to how we treat coworkers. Supporting each other with kindness and understanding that the needs of others might be different from ours can improve everyone's daily experience and, over time, can change social norms.

As organizational citizens, we can advocate for policies and procedures that will make work more accessible—for ourselves and for others. We can also help change organizational norms just by being an example: including transcripts with our videos, asking about and respecting colleagues' preferred forms of communication, considering sensory needs when planning events, and taking many other actions that are the heart of everyday inclusion.

Social change can start with one person. Someone in the Glastonbury crowd started singing first, and others followed the example. Experiments show that group norms reach a tipping point when change proponents make up 25 percent of group members.[5] By being an example and inspiring one-quarter of our colleagues—perhaps we could call it a Canary Coalition—we can create an inclusive environment because others are likely to follow our example.

As national and global citizens, we can use the same principle of the Canary Coalition to create societal-level change. A crucial part of this is normalizing disclosure and making invisible differences visible. I've had the Âû—for "autistic"—on my LinkedIn profile for years, and many others do the same. What would happen if more of us made our differences visible, reminding the world that neurodivergence is not rare, unusual, or something to hide? Sharing our stories and amplifying the stories of others may not be quite the visual equivalent of the Capitol Crawl, but many stories could combine into an impactful mental image.

Governments and CEOs have much power, but they may or may not be aware of the need for neuroinclusion in the workplace. Collectively, we can make the awareness happen. We live in a 360° connected, systemic world, and all types of contributions can make a difference Below are just a few examples of people starting where they are, with what resources they have, and making a difference.

Siena Castellon was a high school student in the UK when in 2018 she founded Neurodiversity Celebration Week to focus not just on the struggles but also on the talents and strengths of neurodivergent people.[6] Since then, Neurodiversity Celebration Week has become a tradition all over the world, helping correct misconceptions and advancing more equitable cultures not just at schools but also across many contexts.

Also in 2018, a group of five young neurodivergent people in Brazil started a podcast by autistic people, for autistic people, *Introvertendo*, or "Introverting." The much-needed Portuguese-language podcast has had 255 episodes as of summer 2023, has expanded to include a sign-language version, and has inspired others to start sharing neurodiversity messages in Portuguese.[7]

In 2021, an international group of nonspeaking autistics took part in the short educational film *Listen*,[8] helping change stereotypes about those who communicate via assistive technology. This free resource—along with longer documentaries like *This Is Not about Me*,[9] *The Reason I Jump*,[10] and *Spellers*[11]—challenges stereotypes about the widely misunderstood nonspeaking communities.

The ripples of unique and creative approaches to neuroinclusion can be seen all over the world. In 2023, in the UK, dyspraxic health economist Tumi Sotire and dyslexic public policy expert Charles Freeman saw how the science of economics could be used to address issues relevant to neurominorities and teamed up to create content and generate a dialogue on the role of economics in neuroinclusion and neuroequity.[12] Also in 2023, in Poland, Agnieszka Halikowska started a small NGO, Ponad Schematami (Beyond Labels) to support neurodivergent adults, with a focus on ADHD, and to debunk myths through the power of theater and neurodivergent art exhibitions.[13]

Change may or may not require organizing. Sometimes, thriving, creating beauty, and finding personal peace can be a powerful message of neurodiversity acceptance, as in the case of the neurodivergent artist and author Morgan Harper Nichols.[14] Fulfilling and creative lives have the power to dispel stereotypes.

We can use our talents to effect change in an infinite number of ways. Some can become entrepreneurs like Diana Ayoo. Some can start a podcast, create art, or raise capital. Most of us can also support colleagues with considerate communication, give another person the benefit of the doubt, and assume the best rather than the worst—and possibly change their lives. Our forms of contributing to the world with more belonging express our authenticity, and every changemaker counts. And if you are in a season of life when you need to put on your oxygen mask first, self-care counts too. Personal thriving counts. You can find additional suggestions and resources for supporting neuroinclusion and each other at thecanarycode.com.

———————

We influence the world every day, whether we know it or not, whether we expect it or not. Music fans in England inspired me, someone in California who constantly needs earplugs. Diana Ayoo inspires people who did not know they needed inspiration. You might inspire your neighbor, your boss, or someone on the other side of the world.

In a 360° interconnected world, every act of kindness and honoring human dignity can have a far-reaching ripple effect.

 KEY TAKEAWAYS

- *Changing the world and the workplace to become more neuroinclusive is a 360° process, and although people in positions of governmental and organizational power have critical levers of change, so do grassroots changemakers—especially, together.*
- *Grassroots changemakers can transform social norms. This does not require 100 percent support. Research indicates that the tipping point occurs with about 25 percent actively supporting change.*
- *There are many examples of single individuals and small groups starting successful change movements. Even a small action can create a major ripple effect.*

DEVELOPMENTAL QUESTIONS

- Which changemaker example, from this chapter, from the rest of the book, or from your other experiences, resonates with you the most?
- What kind of ripple effect would you like to create? What kind of baby steps could you take right now?
- Who could be in your 25 percent Canary Coalition?

SPOILER ALERT: ALL CHAPTER KEY TAKEAWAYS

INTRODUCTION

- *The Canary Code model is designed to help organizations remove barriers to work and success faced by neurodivergent talent.*
- *As canaries in the coal mine, many neurodivergent people are affected by unhealthy work environments before others are.*
- *The key Canary Code principles—participation, focusing on outcomes, flexibility, organizational justice, transparency, and using valid tools in decision making—can help improve the work experience for everyone.*
- *Unlocking neurodivergent abilities calls for developing inclusive talent systems that recognize different types of talent and can support everyone in working with their strengths.*
- *Designing inclusive systems requires an intersectional, comprehensive, and embedded approach informed by the perspective of the marginalized.*

CHAPTER 1

- *The neurodiversity perspective was born in the 1990s from the desire to reframe differences in neurobiology and their psychological expression (e.g., dyslexic or ADHD thinking, autistic focus, sensory differences) as an essential aspect of human diversity rather than a pathology.*
- *It was informed by the disability rights movement and the social model of disability, focused on fixing the environment rather than the person.*
- *The dominance of the pathology perspective still affects the everyday experience of neurodivergent people, including work opportunities. It is reflected in the language used to describe neurodivergent experiences and people, which can sometimes be dehumanizing.*
- *The movement toward neuroinclusion in the workplace aims to create flexible organizational systems that can support a wide range of talent and productivity styles.*

CHAPTER 2

- *People do their best work when they are supported in feeling and being their best.*
- *Holistic neuroinclusion means social, cognitive, emotional, and physical/sensory inclusion.*
- *A holistic approach to inclusion is likely to be the key to belonging for everyone—and belonging is the key to retention, productivity, and engagement.*
- *Organizational statements and PR cannot "create" belonging because it is processed on deep emotional and embodied levels.*

CHAPTER 3

- *Organizations that exemplify key principles of the Canary Code—participation, focusing on outcomes, flexibility, organizational justice, transparency, and the use of valid tools in decision making—push inclusion boundaries in ways previously thought impossible.*
- *Neuroinclusion principles help all employees thrive and support organizational outcomes.*
- *Organizations can start implementing neuroinclusion in many ways, from baby steps to system-wide.*
- *Companies such as Call Yachol, Legalite, and Ultranauts illustrate the win-win nature of systemic intersectional inclusion and the consideration of different employee needs for individuals and organizations.*
- *Using the Canary Code approach may also help develop broader support for inclusive practices and systemic change.*

CHAPTER 4

- *Selection practices are rapidly evolving. On the one hand, there is a promise that AI will help eliminate human bias in selection. On the other hand, automated screening systems may instead multiply this bias.*
- *Technology and data are no guarantee of unbiased evaluations—especially for groups that had been excluded from the workplace to the extent that there is not enough data on their performance to train the AI.*
- *Most of the data we currently have predicts success in organizations that are not neuroinclusive, which limits the usefulness of that data.*
- *Some of the most promising instruments for creating neuroinclusive selection are mini-work samples and skills tests tailored to specific positions.*

CHAPTER 5

- *To create a strong foundation for belonging, organizational pre-boarding and onboarding practices should consider individual differences and intersectional inclusion needs. One size does not fit all.*
- *New employee training should include multiple instructional methods and pacing options. Do not make assumptions about employee learning needs; ask if any accommodations are needed, and support all with flexible learning systems.*
- *Mentorship and support in navigating the new social environment might be appreciated even by the most outgoing employees.*
- *Provide new employees with performance-focused, clear, actionable feedback. Do not try to change their personalities.*
- *Creating neuroinclusive environments requires training for all employees. This training should help dispel myths and stereotypes.*
- *Accommodations for non-apparent differences are not "catering to preferences." They are essential for providing individuals with a fair opportunity to succeed.*
- *Neurodivergence-related pay gaps should be addressed in the same data-informed ways as gender or race pay gaps.*

CHAPTER 6

- *Physical work environments significantly affect well-being and productivity.*
- *Some inflexible aspects of the environment disadvantage or even exclude neurodivergent people.*
- *Inclusion requires flexible workspaces designed with substantial participation from employees.*
- *The "open office collaboration advantage" is a myth. Research shows that open offices undermine collaboration and overall productivity for all employees. They are particularly exclusionary to neurodivergent employees.*
- *It is a myth that supporting frontline workers with good spaces and flexibility is not possible. Remote and hybrid work is more available to frontline workers than many believe.*

CHAPTER 7

- *Purposeful planning of work is essential for ensuring that all activity is productive.*

- *Productivity is best facilitated by flexibility; a focus on outcomes helps eliminate "productivity theater."*
- *Schedule, workload, and continuity flexibility are increasingly used around the world to support employee productivity and well-being. These are also vital for neuroinclusion.*
- *To support productivity, organizations should monitor for and eliminate collaboration overload, such as unnecessary meetings.*
- *The use of asynchronous collaboration tools can help track contributions for fair performance evaluation without invasive monitoring.*

CHAPTER 8

- *Research revealed the five main attributes of toxic cultures—disrespectful, noninclusive, unethical, cutthroat, and abusive. All of these also threaten neuroinclusion.*
- *In addition, neuroinclusion is often hindered by highly political work environments.*
- *Unethical organizational practices may result in moral injury. Organizational recovery after moral breaches may require amends.*
- *Bullying is a behavior of opportunity, and much of it could be prevented by systemic safeguards.*
- *Applying the Canary Code principles and developing trauma-informed cultures can help prevent and address toxic buildup in organizations.*
- *Both positional and grassroots leaders can contribute to creating anti-toxic—actively kind and intentionally helpful environments.*

CHAPTER 9

- *Personality-focused "performance management" is a major source of stress for neurodivergent people and a cause of talent loss for organizations. To create better systems, do the following:*
  - *Tailor the talent management approach to specific people: one size does not fit all.*
  - *Focus feedback and evaluation on outcomes and skills. Ensure that behavioral feedback is strictly tied to the role performance and behaviors within the individual's control. Do not attempt to change personalities or neurodivergent characteristics.*
  - *Separate continuous feedback from high-stakes evaluations.*
  - *Invite employee participation in developing goals.*
  - *Use trauma-informed and minimally stressful performance management to support wellbeing and productivity.*

CHAPTER 10

- *To sustain the work of inclusion, leaders must define their WHY.*
- *The WHY of inclusion should go beyond the business case. However, there are different types of business cases. The commodifying approach frames people as merely means to an end. A pragmatic business case upholds human dignity while also promoting organizational goals.*
- *The business case and the human case do not need to be a zero-sum game. They can be combined in an inclusive thriving case.*

CHAPTER 11

- *There is no perfect leadership style, but there are practical skills that support considerate, other-focused leadership.*
- *Becoming a more inclusive leader may not always mean doing more. Sometimes it may require that we stop some activities.*
- *A helpful way to develop leadership skills for a diverse world is to adopt a perspective of cultural humility.*
- *Leadership demands in modern organizations are enormous. One solution is shared leadership by people with complementary talents.*

CHAPTER 12

- *Neurodiversity in leadership is rarely discussed. However, studying examples of neurodivergent leaders can help us develop a deeper understanding of different types of leadership.*
- *Many neurodivergent leaders have developed unique ways to use their talents for effective leadership.*
- *Myths and stereotypes, such as the "ideal leader," "pipeline," and "culture fit," interfere with the advancement of neurodivergent leaders.*
- *There are no "ideal" leaders. There are many different leadership strengths that can enrich neurodiverse leadership teams and organizations.*
- *Optimizing leadership teams may require developing diverse leadership talents in ways aligned with individual strengths.*

CHAPTER 13

- *Neurodivergent leaders experience a unique set of barriers due to ableism, stigma, and neuromarginalization.*
- *In most cases, we are not overcoming our "conditions." We are overcoming discrimination on the basis of our differences and the resulting internalized stigma.*

- *A focus on authenticity and vulnerability is a common thread in the accounts of many neurodivergent leaders.*
- *Neurodivergent leaders can use the tools of influence to lead without coercion, regardless of their hierarchical positions.*

CONCLUSION

- *Changing the world and the workplace to become more neuroinclusive is a 360° process, and although people in positions of governmental and organizational power have critical levers of change, so do grassroots changemakers—especially together.*
- *Grassroots changemakers can transform social norms. This does not require 100 percent support. Research indicates that the tipping point occurs with about 25 percent actively supporting change.*
- *There are many examples of single individuals and small groups starting successful change movements. Even a small action can create a major ripple effect.*

NEUROINCLUSIVE HIRING CHECKLIST

DEVELOPING A JOB DESCRIPTION

1. Make sure the job description accurately represents the role and its key responsibilities. Use job analysis to support your job requirements.
2. Clearly list only essential skills.
3. Avoid company jargon and noninclusive terminology.
4. Be clear and specific. Avoid vague and unnecessarily complex language.
5. Highlight that your value neurodiversity. Do not add a business case.

RECRUITMENT

1. Reach out to organizations and groups that work with neurodivergent individuals.
2. Train recruiters and hiring managers on neurodiversity to avoid bias in the recruitment process.
3. Use inclusive language in all recruitment communications.

APPLICATION PROCESS

1. Streamline the application process.
2. Offer alternative application methods—for example, video and audio—for those who may struggle with traditional written applications.
3. Make sure your application platform is accessible and user-friendly.

SCREENING AND SELECTION PROCESS

1. Check all screening methods for relevance and potential bias.
2. Consider incorporating work samples or skills demonstrations in the selection process, because traditional interviews might not fully capture a neurodivergent candidate's abilities.
3. If using interviews, do the following:
   a. Offer flexibility, such as the option for remote or in-person interviews.

    b. Provide detailed information ahead of the interview, including the format, estimated length, location with clear directions, who will be present, and what topics will be covered. Preferably, provide interview questions ahead of time. Ask whether the candidate has specific preferences and needs; for example, communicates via an assistive device, needs a quiet setting, and so on.

    c. Avoid tricking, psychologically pressuring, manipulating, and emotionally ambushing candidates with personal questions, unless this truly reflects the nature of the job. Conduct the interview in a manner most consistent with the actual work environment.

    d. Use structured interviews with predetermined questions and evaluation rubrics with clear criteria.

    e. If conducting in-person interviews, provide detailed instructions for how to get to the interview site. Whenever possible, meet the candidates by the entrance and accompany them to the interview location. Create a comfortable environment approximating the actual work environment.

4. After the test or interview, follow up as soon as you can to support a positive candidate experience.

NEUROINCLUSIVE MEETINGS CHECKLIST

FOR ALL TYPES OF MEETINGS

1. **Clear Agenda:** Always have a clear agenda and stick to it. This keeps the meeting focused and efficient. Distribute the agenda well in advance so everyone knows what to expect.

2. **Keep It Efficient:** Do preplanning to keep meetings as short as possible. However, for more complex work, one longer session may be more effective than a series of shorter meetings.

3. **Provide Pre-reads Well in Advance:** When there is necessary reading, provide it well in advance of the meeting to give everyone ample time to read and understand it. Avoid lengthy and complicated pre-reads or provide summaries and bullet points. Provide alternative forms of communication and access, and do not assume familiarity with the technology.

4. **Reasonable Adjustments:** Normalize conversation with your team members, including those who are neurodivergent, about their specific needs. Make appropriate adjustments to the meeting structure, environment, or materials to accommodate these needs.

5. **Use Plain Language:** Encourage everyone to use plain language, avoiding jargon, corporate-speak, or nuances that could confuse or alienate some participants.

6. **Encourage Participation:** Ensure that all participants understand that their contributions are valuable and their voices will be heard. This not only helps engage all participants but also supports the sharing of diverse ideas and perspectives.

7. **Provide Equal Speaking Opportunities:** Encourage turn-taking and waiting during discussions to prevent a few individuals from dominating the conversation. This ensures that everyone's voice is heard and promotes a balanced exchange of ideas. In some situations, using timed speaking or physical objects that can be passed to the next speaker can help create an inclusive structure.

8. **Promote a Sense of Psychological Safety:** Create an environment where team members, including neurodivergent individuals, feel comfortable expressing their needs, sharing their unique ideas, and exploring their strengths. This promotes inclusivity and fosters innovation.

9. **Value Learning over Perfection:** Make it clear that the aim of the meeting is to learn, grow, and solve problems, not to achieve perfection. Mistakes should be viewed as opportunities for learning and growth.

10. **Do Follow Up:** After the meeting, send out a summary of discussion points, decisions made, and the next steps. This helps ensure everyone is on the same page and aware of their responsibilities.

11. **Engage in Continuous Improvement:** Regularly review and seek feedback on your meeting practices. This can help identify any issues and allow you to make necessary improvements in a timely fashion, creating a more effective and inclusive environment for everyone.

FOR VIRTUAL MEETINGS

1. **Time Management:** Keep virtual meetings as short as possible. Limit meetings to a maximum of 60 minutes, if you can. A well-planned 15–20-minute meeting can be very effective. If there's a need for a longer session, make sure to schedule breaks.

2. **Considerate Scheduling:** Be mindful of different time zones and personal circumstances.

3. **Camera On or Off:** Normalize having cameras on or off, whichever makes individuals more comfortable.

4. **Asynchronous Brainstorming:** Consider using asynchronous methods for brainstorming sessions. Online tools allow people to add their ideas at their own pace, increasing inclusivity for individuals who might struggle with traditional brainstorming sessions.

5. **Session Recordings and Transcripts:** Whenever possible, record virtual meetings and provide transcripts. This ensures that those who couldn't attend or those who need to review the discussion can easily do so.

FOR FACE-TO-FACE MEETINGS

1. **Materials:** Have all necessary materials ready before the meeting starts.

2. **Environment:** Ensure the meeting room is comfortable and suitable for the number of participants. Keep the environment free of distractions, especially for neurodivergent individuals who may be sensitive to certain sensory stimuli. Consider a flexible seating arrangement where those who need to stand up and move about could do so without disturbing others.

3. **Inclusive Practices:** Share materials in accessible formats, providing alternative ways for participation, and respect individual communication preferences.
4. **Time for Breaks:** Provide scheduled breaks during longer meetings to allow for rest and processing time.

FOR HYBRID MEETINGS

1. **Equal Access:** Ensure that both remote and in-person participants have equal access to all meeting materials and can participate fully.
2. **Technology Setup:** Ensure all technology is set up correctly and is working properly before the meeting begins. This includes video conferencing equipment, presentation materials, and so on.
3. **Inclusive Practices:** Maintain an inclusive environment, considering the needs of both in-person and remote attendees. This might include providing meeting materials in accessible formats and ensuring clear communication for all participants.
4. **Clear Communication:** Keep lines of communication clear. Make sure both in-person and remote attendees can hear and see everything that's happening.
5. **Respect Time Zones:** If you're working with a global team, consider different time zones when scheduling hybrid meetings.
6. **Session Recordings and Transcripts:** Whenever possible, record hybrid meetings and provide transcripts. This ensures that those who couldn't attend or those who need to review the discussion can easily do so.

While business is not an excuse for a lack of inclusivity, planning and organizing quality meetings takes time and can be challenging in environments where overwork is expected and people have no margin. Leaders who aim to create inclusive environments must also create environments where employees have the time to do quality work without burning out, such as the 85 percent effort environment described by Greg McKeown.[1]

UNDERSTANDING ADULT DIAGNOSIS AND AVOIDING STEREOTYPING

While increasingly common, the late diagnosis of autism, ADHD, or learning differences such as dyslexia is still met by surprise.[1,2,3] In particular, many managers and HR personnel may wonder about a newly diagnosed employee, "How can this be? How did they get so far without being diagnosed? Is this for real?"

This book is filled with stories of late-diagnosed neurodivergent individuals, including myself. Here, I provide some additional resources that help understand this topic.[4,5]

Adult diagnosis of developmental differences is recognized and well documented. Numerous studies identify the reasons for late diagnosis. Generational differences, gender disparities in diagnosis, cultural factors, socioeconomic barriers, and masking all contribute to delayed identification of all neurodivergent conditions, although autism is the most researched at this time.

It is important to note that estimates of autism have changed with improved diagnostics. While older estimates suggested that autism occurs in approximately 1 percent of the population, modern estimates are close to 3 percent.[6] However, the diagnosis is very unevenly distributed among different demographics due to the historical and current lack of diagnostic opportunities for some groups. Research highlights the underdiagnosis of people from older generations, women, and those from less privileged cultural, racial, ethnic, linguistic, and socioeconomic backgrounds.

DIAGNOSIS, DEMOGRAPHICS, AND DISPARITIES

Generational Differences. Diagnostic criteria and awareness have evolved over time, leading to better recognition of neurodivergent conditions in younger generations.[7] However, individuals from older generations have grown up without the same understanding and resources, leading to missed or delayed diagnoses or misdiagnoses of depression, anxiety, and other conditions.[8,9,10]

The Gender Gap. One significant aspect influencing late diagnosis is the gender gap. Historically, autism has been predominantly associated with male presentation, and few clinicians are familiar with the female autism profile, resulting in missed or delayed diagnoses for women.[11,12] The presentation of autism in girls and women can differ from the stereotypical male traits. In some cases, suspicion of autism has been dismissed based on the false belief that "only boys have it." As a result, many girls and women go undiagnosed until later in life, hindering their access to appropriate support.

Females who are diagnosed in childhood experience more severe autistic difficulties and greater cognitive and behavioral problems compared to males. Because females are not "seen" as autistic, teachers are less likely to notice and report autistic traits in their female students. Women are also often diagnosed with depression or anxiety rather than autism. Ineffective treatment can contribute to feelings of personal failure.

A similar gendered dynamic exists with ADHD—females are less likely to be identified and referred for treatment than males.[13,14] The referral bias may have influenced the researchers' ability to separate the possible gender differences in ADHD presentation from the effects of the lack of referral in females.[15]

Cultural Perspectives. Cultural factors and varying ways of explaining psychological phenomena within different communities can impact diagnosis rates.[16] This may often result in national and ethnic disparities.

Character Attributions. In cultural contexts and families with limited neurodiversity awareness, people may attribute behaviors related to developmental differences to laziness, "not paying attention," or "being bad" on purpose.[9,17] This may result in the mistreatment of children, as well as the mistreatment of parents by other adults for their supposed "bad parenting." Individual and family psychological suffering may create significant trauma dynamics, further complicating a diagnosis.

Racial, Ethnic, and Cultural Bias in Diagnosis. A stereotypical autistic person is a white boy. Hence, children and adults from Black and Brown communities traditionally have been less likely to receive an autism diagnosis. Black boys might be misdiagnosed with ADHD or a conduct disorder rather than autism.[18] Ethnically and linguistically different immigrant groups may also be impacted by the effectiveness of diagnostic instruments for these populations, as documented by a study of dyslexia diagnosis in immigrant, bilingual populations in the Netherlands.[19]

Class Disparities and Access to Resources. Socioeconomic factors play a significant role in late diagnosis.[20] People from less privileged socioeconomic backgrounds may face barriers in accessing diagnostic services due to limited financial resources or inadequate healthcare systems.[21] This lack of access can contribute to delayed identification and intervention, prolonging the journey to diagnosis and sometimes completely excluding individuals from diagnostic opportunities.

Intelligence and Giftedness. Individuals who are highly intelligent or gifted are likely to be missed in ADHD, autism, dyslexia, dyscalculia, nonverbal learning disability, and other related diagnoses because their abilities mask or compensate for their challenges.[22,23,24,25,26] Their neurodivergence manifestations may also be attributed to being "bad."[9] In a misinformed dynamic that adds to psychological trauma, when gifted autistics are bullied, they are often blamed for "provoking" the bullies, leading to internalized blame, shame, and a sense of brokenness.[9]

Masking. The pressure to fit in and the pain of social rejection can trigger largely unconscious masking or camouflaging.[27] This is especially likely in females and those with higher intelligence.[11] An ADHDer may force themselves to sit still, and an autistic person may force themselves to make eye contact, despite the discomfort.[28] Generally, camouflaging is costly, unsustainable, and damaging.[29] It can also mask neurodivergent traits and delay diagnosis.[30]

There is growing recognition of the lasting impact of diagnostic delay on individuals. Late-diagnosed people often endure a lifetime of trauma resulting from their delayed understanding of self, challenges faced without appropriate support, and societal misconceptions and mistreatment—in addition to sensitivities associated with differences in neurological wiring.[10,11,31] This makes using trauma-informed management practices and fostering a supportive and inclusive work environment a must. Unfortunately, workplaces are often an additional source of trauma for undiagnosed and late-diagnosed neurodivergent people. In many cases, work-related stress is the "last straw," leading to a crisis that results in a diagnosis.

WHAT CAN TRIGGER AN ADULT DIAGNOSIS

Stories of many late-diagnosed adults show similar patterns. Autism, as well as ADHD, is often identified in parents after it is identified in their children.[32] It may also show dramatically, such as in the form of autistic burnout, when individuals experience an increase in demands or challenges and their coping resources are drained.[33]

In many cases, challenges and changes that trigger an adult diagnosis can be work related.

From the perspective of the social model of disability, the struggle of developmental differences such as autism or ADHD often reflects a mismatch between an individual and the environment.[8,34] A change in the workplace context can create or increase the mismatch, exceeding individuals' coping capacity. This can even occur while someone is still in the same job. In the case of a long-term employee, it is possible that someone was thriving in their position until the organization changed their work environment or their job responsibilities. For example, all items below—and many others—substantially change one's work environment:[4]

- *Increase in the workload due to layoffs, unfilled vacancies, or otherwise taking on someone else's responsibilities (e.g., covering someone's parental leave)*
- *Change in responsibilities leading to increased social, political, or other demands idiosyncratically taxing to the individual (multitasking, interruptions, dealing with hidden agendas)[35]*
- *Reorganizations leading to new reporting lines and work responsibilities*
- *A new manager who is less flexible, empathetic, or competent*
- *Increased social demand from a new manager or a coworker*
- *Change in responsibilities requiring more customer contact*
- *Change in organizational climate, specifically an increase in political behavior or within-organization competition[35]*
- *Bullying or increased organizational permissiveness of bullying[36]*
- *Being moved from a private office into an open office, or into an otherwise taxing sensory environment (in my case, a move to a much colder building with no ability to regulate the temperature was one of the "last straws")[37]*

For many late-diagnosed individuals, diagnosis can bring on a range of emotions, from relief to regret. It may elicit strong emotions of grief or sadness and a sense that some of life's struggles could have been avoided. It is also often a time of increased self-awareness and self-acceptance. It can bring the realization that their experiences were not solely due to personal shortcomings but instead rooted in neurodivergent wiring that is different, not deficient.

Caring workplace support can help make the diagnosis the start of a positive chapter in one's life. While some benefit from accommodations or job crafting, the key aspect of this support is simply believing us.

Believing is an act of inclusion.

AVOIDING STEREOTYPING

Sometimes, the lack of belief may appear to be phrased "positively"—but in fact, it could be a microaggression based on stereotypes.[38] Here are some examples.

But you are so empathetic![5]

As a late-diagnosed autistic, I have heard it a lot. The "autistic lack of empathy" stereotype is a major misconception, however.[5,39,40]

The relationship between empathy and autism is complex.[40,42] Autistic people differ in empathy—just like everyone else. Most desire relationships just as much as allistic (nonautistic) people, and many are extremely caring.[41,42] Autistic people can experience empathy and other emotions intensely, to the point of feeling overwhelmed.[43] This empathy often extends not only to other people but also to animals and global issues. Some, however, may struggle with expressing empathy—about 50 percent of autistic people have alexithymia, a difficulty with identifying and labeling emotions they experience.[44]

The disconnect in interactions with neuromajority individuals often labeled "autistic lack of empathy" is not an "autistic deficit" but a dual empathy problem.[45] Experiments show that autistic people have a better rapport with other autistic people. Additionally, people who are not autistic often lack empathy toward autistic individuals. This can lead to automatic biased behaviors. For example, they might avoid conversations, dismiss attempts by autistic people to connect socially, exclude them from activities, and bully them. The resulting disconnect, however, is attributed to "autistic lack of empathy."[46,47]

But you are so organized!

ADHD manifests in many ways, often without stereotypical hyperactivity or the lack of organization. Research shows that many individuals also use compensation strategies that could mask ADHD.[48] These include using checklists and reminder apps, delegating, and getting help with organization. Some structure their lives in extremely rigid and predictable ways because they feel that otherwise they will not be able to stay on track. Others put extra care and effort into ensuring that they are punctual.

Many ADHDers also develop strategies—consciously or subconsciously—to manage distractions. Some work in low-stimulus environments, such as at night or in isolated spaces. Some make sure to restrict appointments to one-on-one only to make sure they focus on one person.

But you are so talented/successful/accomplished/eloquent![5]

Highly intelligent or gifted neurodivergent (or 2E, twice-exceptional) people are likely to receive diagnosis late because talents can mask challenges. But talent does not mean there is no struggle. Coping strategies are usually high cost and high effort, even if the performance seems effortless from the outside.

Observers do not see the struggle or compensating and masking, but it does not mean that those struggles are not real.[49] Working with neurodivergent people requires adjusting mental models that do not take into account spiky ability profiles. When someone classified as an "achiever" struggles, do not assume they are being lazy or difficult on purpose. It is important to remember to control bias and to support neurodivergent performers in working with their strengths.

This appendix expands on earlier work.[4,5]

FLUENT IN FAIRNESS: DIVERSITY, EQUITY, INCLUSION, BELONGING, JUSTICE, AND ACCESSIBILITY TERMINOLOGY

The essence of inclusion work in organizations is fairness. However, the language we use to discuss the dimensions of fairness—not to mention the possible ways to achieve it—varies greatly within national cultures, and it has many different meanings globally. It is no wonder that there are many disagreements about the appropriate use of terms like "inclusion" or "equity."

In English-speaking contexts, fairness-focused efforts may be referred to by the acronyms D&I, DE&I, DEI, DEIB, DEIJ, JEDI, IDEA, ADI, DEIA, DE-IBA, or other similar acronyms. The *D* typically stands for *diversity, E* for *equity, I* for *inclusion, B* for *belonging, J* for *justice,* and *A* for *accessibility.* Preferences for specific language often indicate an approach to fairness stressed by the individual or the office/organization.[1]

Workplace *diversity* conversations tend to emphasize the representation of people with different backgrounds and identities in various departments or layers of the organization. Human differences manifest in many innate and acquired dimensions, such as age, sex, race, ethnicity, physical and mental abilities, neurobiology, culture, communication, migrant or local status, socioeconomic class, and may others.[1] The diversity focus reminds us of the profound impact of these differences on human experience, including the potential for unfair treatment. However, even though understanding the dimensions of diversity is crucial to ensuring fairness, diversity initiatives must be accompanied by creating systems that support inclusion and equity. Otherwise, an organizational focus on diversity at work, without inclusion and equity, may result in a subpar employee experience and high turnover among those who feel tokenized or excluded.[1,4,5]

Equity work creates procedures for fairness.[4] In contrast to *equality*, however, the equity approach does not require identical treatment of all people.[1,4] From the equity perspective, ensuring fairness calls for considering differences such as health status or economic resources. For example, providing disability accommodations, such as modified desks for wheelchair access or written communication options for nonspeaking individuals, enables the performance and productivity of employees who need such adjustments. These adjustments are fair and equitable even though they are not technically "equal." Not everyone needs a modified desk.

Inclusion reflects individual-level behaviors and organizational systems, policies, and practices that welcome or bar individuals' involvement in organizational life. Essential aspects of inclusion are honoring human dignity,[3] identity, and culture.[4,7]

Inclusive and equitable organizational cultures are likely to support a sense of *belonging*—a feeling of membership in the group.[1,4] A key to belonging is the perception that one's authentic identity is welcomed and supported. When "inclusion" is contingent on individuals' masking (such as concealing a disability or neurodivergent characteristics), cultural code-switching (downplaying one's cultural characteristics), or otherwise suppressing aspects of one's true self, the appearance of "inclusion" is in fact *assimilation*, and a sense of belonging is unlikely to result.[2]

Justice is the presence of processes, systems, and norms supporting fairness. It can manifest via fair outcomes, policies, and practices; transparent information sharing; and dignified interpersonal treatment. The most recent addition to justice considerations is *contributive* justice: the opportunity to fully engage and make an impact.[6]

Accessibility is focused on ensuring that physical, psychological, procedural, and digital aspects of work do not present barriers for people with varying abilities and health-related needs. The following misconceptions regarding accessibility often create confusion and even obstacles to disability inclusion:[1]

- *Accessibility = disability accommodation. This is incorrect. Although accommodations (or, in the UK, "adjustments") support specific populations or people, accessibility benefits everyone. Ramps help not only wheelchair users but also people transporting suitcases and bicycles, and closed captioning is now used by people with many different needs and backgrounds. Accommodations*

are also very prevalent for nondisabled people, such as caregivers and those needing religious accommodations.
- *Accessibility = disability inclusion. This is also incorrect. Although accessibility and, in some cases, accommodation support disability inclusion, they are not sufficient. Workplaces might be physically and digitally accessible, but coworkers may still avoid, bully, and discriminate against disabled employees, and structural "ceilings" to professional growth may still limit career opportunities.*

The language of fairness is in flux and sometimes controversial.[1,7] For example, the term "inclusion," although popular, communicates some problematic meanings. Specifically, it normalizes the implicit power differential between the "includers" and those "being included." It may even codify the authority of those born into dominant societal groups to decide which, when, and whether to include othered groups.[2] This form of "inclusion" can turn into assimilation, with loss of authenticity as "the price of admission."[2] Although this power differential is a fact of life in most organizations and societies, the prevalence of such power differentials does not make them ethically right. In this book, I use the term "inclusion" with an understanding of these complex power dynamics and the need to address them for true fairness to be achieved.

In addition to the more traditional D&I vocabulary, I also use the term "*dignity*," defined by the dignity expert Donna Hicks as the inherent value we are all born with, something we all have unconditionally, and something we don't need to earn or ask anyone for.[3] In a way, dignity precedes inclusion. If individuals and societies recognize the inherent dignity of every person, it sets a foundation for inclusive practices without requiring people to change or assimilate.

Another important addition to the language of fairness is *mattering*, which in the workplace builds on dignity by adding a sense of purpose and the significance of one's contributions. Mattering is linked to mental health and well-being.[4] Some consider mattering to be a more potent and crucial aspect of workplace fairness than belonging; its absence can be particularly harmful, especially for people from marginalized communities.[5]

In adding "dignity" and "mattering" to the traditional elements of diversity conversations, here is what I came up with. Honoring dignity (*D*) is a foundation of inclusion (*I*). Accessibility (*A*) is necessary for diversity (*D*). And when diversity is accompanied by equitable opportunities (*E*), mattering (*M*) is likely to arise. Together, they form the acronym DIADEM, which is quite easy to remember. An organization can support fairness and create conditions for belonging if it aims to be a DIADEM.

The language of fairness in the workplace is far from perfect, and there is no doubt it will continue to develop. But the need to clarify terminology should not slow down the work of removing unfair barriers. Fluency in fairness does not have to require words at all—it can take the form of creating an accessible physical or digital environment or eliminating a discriminatory promotion requirement. Ultimately, doing fairness is much more important than talking fairness.

This appendix expands on earlier work.[1,2]

GLOSSARY

Ableism: A prejudiced attitude toward disabled or neurodivergent people; a system that places value on people's bodies and minds based on societally constructed ideas of normalcy, intelligence, attractiveness, and/or productivity.

Accessibility: The "ability to access" the functionality, system, or entity. The concept of accessible design ensures both "direct access" (i.e., unassisted) and "indirect access" (i.e., compatibility with a person's assistive technology—for example, computer screen readers).

Accommodation (US) or Adjustment (UK): A modification to various aspects of work to meet employee needs. Reasonable accommodation considers employers' resources in providing accommodation.

ADHD: A neurodivergent condition/difference, "Attention-Deficit/Hyperactivity Disorder." It manifests in many ways, such as notably inconsistent attention or impulsive behaviors, with some people also being highly active or stimulation-seeking.

Alexithymia: Difficulty in identifying, labeling, and describing one's feelings. Often co-occurs with autism and other neurodivergent conditions.

Allistic: A person who is not autistic but could still be neurodivergent.

Allyship: Active support for the equal treatment and rights of a minority or marginalized group without being a member.

Asperger's Syndrome: A previously used diagnosis term that described people with autism-like characteristics. Since the 2013 publication of *The Diagnostic and Statistical Manual of Mental Disorders (DSM-5)*, it is now part of a broad category called autism spectrum disorder (ASD).

AuDHD: A combination of autism and ADHD in a person. They may prefer to be called an "AuDHDer."

Autism: Also known as autism spectrum disorder (ASD), it is a neurodivergent condition/difference characterized by differences in social skills and communication, repetitive behavior, and intense interests, among other traits that can vary widely from person to person.

Belonging: The act or need to be an accepted member of a group to accomplish something greater than when alone.

Bias: A preference or prejudice in favor of or against a person, group, idea, or thing. Some examples are the following:

Prove-It-Again Bias: A bias resulting in the need for marginalized employees to prove themselves again and again in their careers.

Proximity Bias: A preference for people who are familiar to us due to physical proximity and the resulting familiarity.

Similarity Bias (Similar-to-Me Bias): A preference for people who share important demographic, cultural, and other characteristics with us.

Tightrope Bias: The narrow range of behavior seen by society as acceptable for people from nondominant and stigmatized groups.

Unconscious Bias: Unconscious assumptions about and attitudes toward different groups. These learned mental shortcuts affect how we perceive and respond to people.

Burnout: A response to chronic workplace stress characterized by physical, mental, or emotional exhaustion, mental detachment from work, and reduced professional efficacy.

Disability: A limitation in performing physical, mental, or emotional activities due to an underlying condition, social disablement, or both.

Disclosure: In the context of disabilities, it is the idea of telling another person or group about difficulties performing certain functions or a diagnosis.

Diversity: The fact that people have different characteristics and abilities. A diverse group of people contains different types of people.

Dyscalculia: A neurodivergent condition/difference marked by difficulties in performing math.

Dysgraphia: A neurodivergent condition/difference marked by difficulties in writing.

Dyslexia: A neurodivergent condition/difference marked by difficulties in reading.

Dyspraxia: A neurodivergent motor condition/difference affecting fine and gross motor skills, motor planning, and coordination. People with dyspraxia may have trouble with balance and movement.

Culture-Add Approach: a form of valuing diversity in which hiring and professional development aims not to match but to expand and complement the existing strengths, perspectives, cultural, and personal styles of teams and organizations. This does not preclude hiring for values-fit. However, the **culture-fit approach** has become a catchall justification for exclusion, reflecting hiring managers' personal preferences and biases and limiting organizational talent pools.

Equity: The idea that not all people start with the same resources and abilities and that adjustments need to be made to ensure that we all have the same opportunities to perform.

Hyperfocus: Complete absorption in a task, to a point where a person appears to ignore or tune out everything else. Often discussed as a pattern in the context of autism and ADHD, it can also be experienced by neurotypical people.

Inclusion: The idea of a person being welcomed in a group or an organization.

Intersectionality: Coined by Kimberle Crenshaw in 1989, intersectionality is the notion that understanding everyone's experiences of discrimination and oppression must consider multiple interacting factors that can marginalize people (gender, race, disability, class, neurodivergence, education, and so on).

Job Analysis: A systematic process of gathering and analyzing information about the outcomes, contexts, activities, and human requirements of jobs. It should be the foundation for selection decisions and other personnel processes.

Job Satisfaction: The attitude of an employee toward their job, which may include liking or disliking the work itself, the context (working conditions, colleagues, managers), and its rewards (pay, promotions, recognition).

Leadership: The act or abilities of a person or people to influence and guide other people, such as members of an organization, society, team, or other group.

Autocratic Leadership: Autocratic leaders maintain strong control over all decisions, with little input from team members. They dictate all the work methods and processes and make decisions unilaterally.

Charismatic Leadership: Charismatic leaders use their personality and charm to inspire and motivate their teams. They create enthusiasm and can significantly influence their teams, but this leadership style can risk focusing too much on the leader as an individual, rather than the team or organization.

Democratic/Participative Leadership: This style involves leaders sharing decision-making responsibilities with team members, promoting participation, collaboration, and individual creativity. Democratic leaders value team feedback and involve team members in planning and policymaking.

Ethical Leadership: Ethical leaders prioritize values and morals in their decision-making process. They lead by example, promote transparency, and foster an ethical culture within their teams. They take responsibility for their actions and encourage their teams to do the same.

Inclusive Leadership: Inclusive leaders strive to overcome personal biases to welcome, effectively work with, and support people who are different from them, and create systems that ensure justice and equity.

Servant Leadership: Servant leaders seek to enhance the personal growth, empowerment, and well-being of those they lead. They often have a holistic approach to work, promoting a sense of community and shared decision making.

Transactional Leadership: Transactional leaders operate on the basis of exchanges with their team members. They set clear expectations and goals, and team members receive rewards for achieving these goals or face consequences for failing to meet them.

Transformational Leadership: This leadership style involves leaders inspiring and motivating their team members to go beyond their own individual performance goals and achieve a shared vision. Transformational leaders encourage innovation, creativity, and personal development in their team.

Marginalization: The conscious or unconscious act of placing a person or thing in a position of lesser importance, influence, or power; the state of being placed in such a position.

Masking (aka "Camouflaging"): The suppression of aspects of self and identity to fit in or pass as a neurotypical using conscious (e.g., rehearsing "small talk") or unconscious (e.g., unknowingly suppressing sensory needs) means.

Moral Injury: Injury to an individual's moral conscience resulting from committing or witnessing a moral transgression.

Neuro-ableism/Neuroableism/NeuroAbleism (Julia Feliz; http://www.neuroableism.com/): The specific type of ableism experienced by neurodivergent people due to the dominant expectations of neuronormativity.

Neurobiology: The combination of a person's brain, nervous system, spinal cord, and related body systems.

Neurodivergent: A person or people whose neurobiological development or functioning diverges from the range conventionally seen as typical.

Neurodiversity: The idea that people experience and interact with the world around them in many different ways. There is no one right way of thinking, learning, and behaving, and differences are not viewed as deficits.

Neuroinclusion: Inclusion of people with a focus on differences in neurobiology.

Neurominority: A population of marginalized people sharing an innate form of neurodivergence.

Neuronormative: A set of ideals, actions, and functions seen as "normal" by prevailing cultural and societal standards.

Neurotypical: A person or people whose neurodevelopment falls within the range conventionally seen as typical by prevailing cultural standards and is enabled by their society for a given period.

Nonverbal Learning Disability/Difference (NVLD): Difficulties in visual-spatial ability or a discrepancy between visual-spatial and verbal ability, accompanied by problems in math calculation but not basic reading or spelling skills. In addition, difficulties in function of visual-spatial memory, attention, visual executive functioning, fine-motor skills, and social skills are often present.

Organizational Justice: The presence of processes, systems, and norms supporting fairness of procedures and outcomes in an organizaiton. Also, employee perceptions of how fair an organization is.

Contributive Justice: Opportunities to contribute to the organization through meaningful work and instrumental voice.

Distributive Justice: Perceptions of the fairness of outcomes that employees receive.

Informational Justice: The clarity of explanations provided for procedures and outcomes.

Interpersonal Justice: The degree to which people are treated with politeness and dignity.

Procedural Justice: Fairness of the procedures used in distributing these outcomes.

Pay Gap: The difference in pay for equal work performed by the more privileged compared to the less privileged; for example, the difference in pay between neurotypical and neurodivergent people.

Psychological Safety: An environment where team members, including neurodivergent individuals, feel comfortable sharing their unique ideas and suggestions, expressing their needs, and exploring their strengths, without negative repercussions.

Self-Fulfilling Prophecy: A process through which an expectation leads to its own confirmation (e.g., treating someone as if they were talented/incapable/dangerous or the like evokes the response confirming the expectation).

Sensory: Related to the senses, sensation, or to a part or all of the neural apparatus involved in any of these.

Sensory Disability: A significant limitation in the ability to process information via one or more senses (e.g., blindness).

Sensory Sensitivity: A characteristic of being more acutely sensitive to sensory input. Being overwhelmed at times by sensory input is to be **hypersensitive**. This may result in **sensory avoidance**. It is also possible to be **hyposensitive**, which may lead to **sensory-seeking** behavior. Some individuals can be both sensory-seeking and sensory-avoidant (e.g., avoiding noise but seeking tactile stimulation).

Spiky Profile: The observation that neurodivergent people have much more significant differences ("peaks and valleys") in their strengths and weaknesses than neurotypical people.

Spoon Theory: A way to explain the amount of energy that a disabled or chronically ill person has available to perform tasks, with each task requiring a certain number of spoons. If the person does not have enough spoons available, then a seemingly "easy" task may be very difficult or impossible to perform.

Tourette Syndrome: A neurodivergent condition/difference that may cause people to experience sudden, repetitive tics such as sounds, twitches, or other movements that cannot be or are very difficult to control.

Twice-Exceptional (2E): A person who is gifted and has at least one other specific neurodivergent condition.

NOTES

PRELUDE AND DEDICATION

1. Aisha Nozari, "Lewis Capaldi's Glastonbury Set Makes Mum of Teenage Boy with To-urette's Cry," *Metro*, June 25, 2023, https://metro.co.uk/2023/06/25/lewis-capaldis -glastonbury-set-makes-mum-of-teen-with-tourettes-cry-19011317.
2. Shivani Chaudhari, "Lewis Capaldi's Glastonbury Performance Gets Support from Community," *Worcester News*, June 26, 2023, https://www.worcesternews.co.uk/news /23614726.lewis-capaldis-glastonbury-performance-gets-support-community.
3. "Half of All Leaders and Managers Would Not Employ a Neurodivergent Person," In-stitute of Leadership, accessed August 9, 2023, https://leadership.global/resourceLibrary /half-of-all-leaders-and-managers-would-not-employ-a-neurodivergent-person1.html.

PREFACE

1. Miriam Harmens, Felicity Sedgewick, and Hannah Hobson, "The Quest for Acceptance: A Blog-Based Study of Autistic Women's Experiences and Well-Being during Autism Identification and Diagnosis," *Autism in Adulthood* 4, no. 1 (2022): 42–51, https://doi .org/10.1089/aut.2021.0016.
2. Kristen Gillespie-Lynch, Emily Hotez, Matthew Zajic, Ariana Riccio, Danielle DeNi-gris, Bella Kofner, Dennis Bublitz, Naomi Gaggi, and Kavi Luca, "Comparing the Writ-ing Skills of Autistic and Nonautistic University Students: A Collaboration with Autistic University Students," *Autism: The International Journal of Research and Practice* 24, no. 7 (2020): 1898–912, https://doi.org/10.1177/1362361320929453.
3. Sarah Bargiela, Robyn Steward, and William Mandy, "The Experiences of Late-Diagnosed Women with Autism Spectrum Conditions: An Investigation of the Female Autism Phe-notype," *Journal of Autism and Developmental Disorders* 46, no. 10 (2016): 3281–94, https://doi.org/10.1007/s10803-016-2872-8.
4. Eric Patton, "Autism, Attributions and Accommodations: Overcoming Barriers and In-tegrating a Neurodiverse Workforce," *Personnel Review* 48, no. 4 (2019): 915–34, https:// doi.org/10.1108/PR-04-2018-0116.
5. Timo Lorenz, Cora Frischling, Raphael Cuadros, and Kathrin Heinitz, "Autism and Overcoming Job Barriers: Comparing Job-Related Barriers and Possible Solutions in and outside of Autism-Specific Employment," *PLOS ONE* 11, no. 1 (2016), https://doi.org /10.1371/journal.pone.0147040.
6. Benjamin Wen, Henriette van Rensburg, Shirley O'Neill, and Tony Attwood, "Autism in the Australian Workplace: The Employer Perspective," *Asia Pacific Journal of Human Resources* 61, no. 1 (2023): 146–67, https://doi.org/10.1111/1744-7941.12333.

7. Fabian Frank, Martina Jablotschkin, Tobias Arthen, Andreas Riedel, Thomas Fangmeier, Lars P. Hölzel, and Ludger Tebartz van Elst, "Education and Employment Status of Adults with Autism Spectrum Disorders in Germany—a Cross-Sectional-Survey," *BMC Psychiatry* 18 (March 2018): article 75, https://doi.org/10.1186/s12888-018-1645-7.

INTRODUCTION

1. "1986: Coal Mine Canaries Made Redundant," On This Day, BBC, December 30, 1986, http://news.bbc.co.uk/onthisday/hi/dates/stories/december/30/newsid_2547000/2547587.stm.
2. Ludmila Praslova, "To Build a Healthy Workplace, You Need a Toxic Culture Alarm," *Fast Company*, March 14, 2022, https://www.fastcompany.com/90730688/to-build-a-healthy-workplace-you-need-a-toxic-culture-alarm.
3. "The Device Invented to Resuscitate Canaries in Coal Mines (circa 1896)," Open Culture, May 29, 2018, https://www.openculture.com/2018/05/the-device-invented-to-resuscitate-canaries-in-coal-mines-circa-1896.html.
4. "Who We Are," Autistic Doctors International, accessed August 12, 2023, https://autisticdoctorsinternational.com/about-us.
5. Carrero Yesenia, "The Center for Neurodiversity and Employment," University of Connecticut Werth Institute for Entrepreneurship and Innovation, September 29, 2021, https://entrepreneurship.uconn.edu/neurodiversitycenter-2.
6. Nikola Tesla, "Tesla Speech for the Institute of Immigrant Welfare," *New York Times*, May 12, 1938, https://teslauniverse.com/nikola-tesla/articles/tesla-speech-institute-immigrant-welfare.
7. J. Harold Byers, "The Miracle Mind of Nikola Tesla," *Fate*, July 1949, https://teslauniverse.com/nikola-tesla/articles/miracle-mind-nikola-tesla.
8. Molly Brown, "Nikola Tesla Predicted Smartphones in 1926 like a Boss," *GeekWire*, July 6, 2015, https://www.geekwire.com/2015/nikola-tesla-predicted-smartphones-in-1926-like-a-boss.
9. "Was Nikola Tesla Autistic?," Applied Behavior Analysis, September 5, 2017, https://www.appliedbehavioranalysisedu.org/was-nikola-tesla-autistic.
10. Susan Borowski, "The Brilliant and Tortured World of Nikola Tesla," *Scientia* (blog), American Association for the Advancement of Science (AAAS), May 29, 2012, https://www.aaas.org/brilliant-and-tortured-world-nikola-tesla.
11. Maria Milojković, "17 Weird Facts about Nikola Tesla, the Man Who Invented the 20th Century," Medium, *Lessons from History* (blog), December 6, 2022, https://medium.com/lessons-from-history/17-weird-facts-about-nikola-tesla-the-man-who-invented-the-20th-century-c18d103fbf01.
12. Temple Grandin, "Autism and Visual Thought," in *Thinking in Pictures: My Life with Autism* (New York: Vintage Press), 3–32.
13. Joseph S. Roucek, "The Image of the Slav in U.S. History and in Immigration Policy," *American Journal of Economics and Sociology* 28, no. 1 (1969): 29–48, https://www.jstor.org/stable/3485555.
14. Brian Lisi, "Thomas Edison's Shocking History of Electrocuting Dogs, Horses and People," *New York Daily News*, February 12, 2017, https://www.nydailynews.com/news/national/thomas-edison-history-electrocuting-dogs-horses-people-article-1.2969425.

15. Marc Seifer, *Wizard: The Life and Times of Nikola Tesla: Biography of a Genius* (New York: Kensington Publishing, 2016).

16. Reuters Fact Check, "Fact Check—Lewis Latimer Invented a Longer Lasting Filament for Lightbulbs, Not the Lightbulb Itself," *Reuters*, March 5, 2021, https://www.reuters .com/article/factcheck-lightbulbs-latimer-idUSL2N2L3237.

17. Randall E. Stross, *The Wizard of Menlo Park: How Thomas Alva Edison Invented the Modern World* (New York: Three Rivers Press, 2007).

18. Charles Oliver, "George Westinghouse: Problem-Solver," Foundation for Economic Education, September 1, 2002, https://fee.org/articles/george-westinghouse-problem-solver.

19. Kathy Joseph, "Why Nikola Tesla Is So Famous (and Westinghouse Is Not)," Kathy Loves Physics, *History of Science* (blog), November 23, 2022, https://kathylovesphysics.com /why-nikola-tesla-is-so-famous-and-westinghouse-is-not.

20. "Working Conditions," Library of Congress, accessed August 12, 2023, https://www.loc .gov/collections/films-of-westinghouse-works-1904/articles-and-essays/the -westinghouse-world/working-conditions.

21. Katie Blackley, "Westinghouse's Bertha Lamme Was the Nation's First Female Mechanical Engineer," 90.5 WESA, January 29, 2019, https://www.wesa.fm/arts-sports-culture /2019-01-29/westinghouses-bertha-lamme-was-the-nations-first-female-mechanical -engineer.

22. Elzbieta Sikorska-Simmons, "Predictors of Organizational Commitment among Staff in Assisted Living," *The Gerontologist* 45, no. 2 (2005): 196–205, https://doi.org/10.1093 /geront/45.2.196.

23. Gary Hoover, "George Westinghouse: Servant Leader, Inventor, Captain of Industry," American Business History Center, February 27, 2019, https://americanbusinesshistory .org/george-westinghouse-servant-leader-inventor-captain-of-industry.

24. "Tesla—Master of Lightning: Harnessing Niagara," PBS, accessed August 12, 2023, https://www.pbs.org/tesla/ll/ll_niagara.html.

25. "Neurodiversity in the Workplace | Statistics | Update 2023," MyDisabilityJobs, October 14, 2022, https://web.archive.org/web/20230315021851/https://mydisabilityjobs .com/statistics/neurodiversity-in-the-workplace/.

26. "Government Must Tackle the Autism Employment Gap," National Autistic Society, October 27, 2016, https://www.autism.org.uk/what-we-do/news/government-must-tackle -the-autism-employment-gap.

27. "Are 85 Percent of Autistic College Grads Unemployed?," Skeptics, December 29, 2020, https://skeptics.stackexchange.com/questions/50092/are-85-of-autistic-college-grads -unemployed.

28. Amy-Jane Griffiths, Cristina M. Giannantonio, Amy E. Hurley-Hanson, and Donald N. Cardinal, "Autism in the Workplace: Assessing the Transition Needs of Young Adults with Autism Spectrum Disorder," *Journal of Business and Management* 22, no. 1 (2016): 5–22.

29. Alexandra Ossola, "Neurodiverse Applicants Are Revolutionizing the Hiring Process," *Quartz*, March 26, 2021, https://qz.com/work/1981466/neurodiverse-applicants-are -revolutionizing-the-hiring-process.

30. David Kushner, "Serving on the Spectrum: The Israeli Army's Roim Rachok Program Is Bigger than the Military," *Esquire*, April 2, 2019, https://www.esquire.com/news-politics /a26454556/roim-rachok-israeli-army-autism-program.

31. Ben Flanagan, "Who Wants to Be a Millionaire?," *The Observer*, October 4, 2003, https://www.theguardian.com/uk/2003/oct/05/benflanagan.theobserver.

32. Jane Ann Sedgwick, Andrew Merwood, and Philip Asherson, "The Positive Aspects of Attention Deficit Hyperactivity Disorder: A Qualitative Investigation of Successful Adults with ADHD," *ADHD Attention Deficit and Hyperactivity Disorders* 11, no. 3 (2019): 241–53, https://doi.org/10.1007/s12402-018-0277-6.

33. "50 Percent Employers Admit They Won't Hire Neurodivergent Talent," Fair Play Talks, November 3, 2020, https://www.fairplaytalks.com/2020/11/03/50-employers-admit-they-wont-hire-neurodivergent-talent-reveals-ilm-study.

34. Angela Marie Mai, "Hiring Agents' Beliefs: A Barrier to Employment of Autistics," *SAGE Open* 9, no. 3 (2019): 2158244019862725, https://doi.org/10.1177/2158244019862725.

35. Elizabeth Morey, "6 Ways Companies Could Be Exploiting Employees on the Autism Spectrum," *Autism Site News*, July 13, 2018, https://blog.theautismsite.greatergood.com/workplace-exploitation.

36. Nicole Lyn Pesce, "Most College Grads with Autism Can't Find Jobs: This Group Is Fixing That," MarketWatch, April 2, 2019, https://www.marketwatch.com/story/most-college-grads-with-autism-cant-find-jobs-this-group-is-fixing-that-2017-04-10-5881421.

37. Ludmila N. Praslova, "Autism Doesn't Hold People Back at Work: Discrimination Does," *Harvard Business Review*, December 13, 2021, https://hbr.org/2021/12/autism-doesnt-hold-people-back-at-work-discrimination-does.

38. Donald Sull, Charles Sull, and Ben Zweig, "Toxic Culture Is Driving the Great Resignation," *MIT Sloan Management Review*, January 11, 2022, https://sloanreview.mit.edu/article/toxic-culture-is-driving-the-great-resignation.

39. "Employee App: 7 Reasons Why Your Company Needs One Today," *Firstup* (blog), June 24, 2022, https://firstup.io/blog/employee-app-seven-reasons-why-your-company-needs-one-today.

40. "Highlights: Workplace Stress & Anxiety Disorders Survey," Anxiety and Depression Association of America (ADAA), accessed August 12, 2023, https://adaa.org/workplace-stress-anxiety-disorders-survey.

41. "Workplace Stress Continues to Mount," Korn Ferry, accessed August 12, 2023, https://www.kornferry.com/insights/this-week-in-leadership/workplace-stress-motivation.

42. Ludmila N. Praslova, "Research Is In: Work Stress Is Not 'Just in Your Head,'" *Positively Different* (blog), Psychology Today, June 27, 2023, https://www.psychologytoday.com/us/blog/positively-different/202301/research-is-in-work-stress-is-not-just-in-your-head.

43. Workforce Institute at UKG, "Mental Health at Work: Managers and Money," UKG Inc., accessed November 17, 2023, https://www.ukg.com/resources/article/mental-health-work-managers-and-money.

44. Ludmila N. Praslova, "7 Dos and Don'ts of Inclusion by Design," *The SHRM Blog* (blog), February 11, 2021, https://blog.shrm.org/blog/7-do-s-and-don-ts-of-inclusion-by-design.

45. Emma Goldberg, "Do We Know How Many People Are Working from Home?," *New York Times*, March 30, 2023, sec. Business, https://www.nytimes.com/2023/03/30/business/economy/remote-work-measure-surveys.html.

46. Zach Winn, "Leveraging the Power of Neurodiversity," *MIT News*, December 1, 2020, https://news.mit.edu/2020/ultranauts-neurodiversity-1201.

47. Max Roser, "Talent Is Everywhere, Opportunity Is Not: We Are All Losing out because of This," Our World in Data, July 2023, https://ourworldindata.org/talent-is-everywhere -opportunity-is-not.

48. Matt Gonzales, "Remote Work Helps People with Disabilities Land Jobs," SHRM, October 21, 2022, https://www.shrm.org/resourcesandtools/hr-topics/behavioral-com petencies/global-and-cultural-effectiveness/pages/remote-work-helps-people-with -disabilities-land-jobs.aspx.

49. Ludmila N. Praslova, "3 Things That Might Be Missing from Your Inclusion Efforts," *Fast Company*, November 1, 2021, https://www.fastcompany.com/90690568/3-things -that-might-be-missing-from-your-inclusion-efforts.

50. Ludmila N. Praslova, "Defeat Diversity Derailers: Inclusion by Design," *The SHRM Blog* (blog), February 10, 2021, https://blog.shrm.org/blog/defeat-diversity-derailers-inclusion -by-design.

51. Kimberle Crenshaw, "Demarginalizing the Intersection of Race and Sex: A Black Feminist Critique of Antidiscrimination Doctrine, Feminist Theory and Antiracist Politics," *University of Chicago Legal Forum* 1 (1989): 139–67.

52. Ludmila N. Praslova, "An Intersectional Approach to Inclusion at Work," *Harvard Business Review*, June 21, 2022, https://hbr.org/2022/06/an-intersectional-approach-to -inclusion-at-work.

CHAPTER ONE

1. Keri Opai, "Te Reo Hapai Launches Its New Website," Te Pou, September 14, 2020, https://www.tepou.co.nz/stories/te-reo-hapai-launches-its-new-website.

2. "Browse English» Te Reo Māori," Te Reo Hāpai, accessed July 22, 2023, https://www .tereohapai.nz/Browse/Terms/en-NZ?q=A.

3. Connor Tom Keating, Lydia Hickman, Joan Leung, Ruth Monk, Alicia Montgomery, Hannah Heath, and Sophie Sowden, "Autism-Related Language Preferences of English-Speaking Individuals across the Globe: A Mixed Methods Investigation," *Autism Research* 16, no. 2 (2023): 406–28, https://doi.org/10.1002/aur.2864.

4. Naomi Williams, "'Kura Urupare' Is the Maori Word for Autism and It Means 'Gift/ Treasure in around Your Head,'" *Inclusive Solutions* (blog), October 4, 2022, https:// inclusive-solutions.com/blog/takiwatanga-is-the-maori-word-for-autism-and-it-means -in-their-own-time-and-space.

5. Krista L. Best, W. Ben Mortenson, Zach Lauzière-Fitzgerald, and Emma M. Smith, "Language Matters! The Long-Standing Debate between Identity-First Language and Person First Language," *Assistive Technology: The Official Journal of RESNA* 34, no. 2 (2022): 127–28, https://doi.org/10.1080/10400435.2022.2058315.

6. Monique Botha, Jacqueline Hanlon, and Gemma Louise Williams, "Does Language Matter? Identity-First versus Person-First Language Use in Autism Research: A Response to Vivanti," *Journal of Autism and Developmental Disorders* 53, no. 2 (2021): 870–78, https://doi.org/10.1007/s10803-020-04858-w.

7. Nick Walker, "Neurodiversity: Some Basic Terms & Definitions," Neuroqueer, August 1, 2021, https://neuroqueer.com/neurodiversity-terms-and-definitions.

8. Judy Singer, *NeuroDiversity: The Birth of an Idea* (self-published, 2016).

9. Judy Singer, "Neurodiversity: Definition and Discussion," Reflections on the Neurodiversity Paradigm, accessed July 10, 2023, https://neurodiversity2.blogspot.com/p/what.html.

10. Elizabeth Pellicano and Jacquiline den Houting, "Annual Research Review: Shifting from 'Normal Science' to Neurodiversity in Autism Science," *Journal of Child Psychology and Psychiatry* 63, no 4 (2021): 381–96, https://doi.org/10.1111/jcpp.13534.

11. Robert Chapman, "What Does 'Neurotypical' Even Mean?," *Critical Neurodiversity* (blog), May 26, 2022, https://criticalneurodiversity.com.

12. Martin Silvertant, "Neurotypical & Neurodivergent," *Embrace Autism* (blog), August 14, 2018, https://embrace-autism.com/neurotypical-and-neurodivergent.

13. Nick Walker, *Neuroqueer Heresies: Notes on the Neurodiversity Paradigm, Autistic Empowerment, and Postnormal Possibilities* (Fort Worth: Autonomous Press, 2021).

14. Lori Nishiura Mackenzie and Melissa V. Abad, "Are Your Diversity Efforts Othering Underrepresented Groups?," *Harvard Business Review*, February 5, 2021, https://hbr.org/2021/02/are-your-diversity-efforts-othering-underrepresented-groups.

15. Howard Timberlake, "Why There Is No Such Thing as a 'Normal' Brain," *BBC*, October 10, 2019, https://www.bbc.com/future/article/20191008-why-the-normal-brain-is-just-a-myth.

16. José Luis Velázquez Pérez and Roberto Galán, "Information Gain in the Brain's Resting State: A New Perspective on Autism," *Frontiers in Neuroinformatics* 7, no. 37 (2013), https://www.frontiersin.org/articles/10.3389/fninf.2013.00037.

17. Adam Teitelbaum, Jason Belkas, and Jose Luiz Pérez Velázquez, "Distinct Patterns of Cortical Coordinated Activity in Autism," in *Autism Spectrum Disorders: New Research*, ed. C. E. Richardson and R. A. Wood (Hauppauge: Nova Publishers, 2012), 95–112.

18. Henry Markram, Tania Rinaldi, and Kamila Markram, "The Intense World Syndrome—An Alternative Hypothesis for Autism," *Frontiers in Neuroscience* 1, no. 1 (2007): 77–96, https://doi.org/10.3389/neuro.01.1.1.006.2007.

19. Chunyan Meng, Chao Huo, Hongxin Ge, Zuoshan Li, Yuanyan Hu, and Jing Meng, "Processing of Expressions by Individuals with Autistic Traits: Empathy Deficit or Sensory Hyper-reactivity?," *PLOS ONE* 16, no. 7 (2021): e0254207, https://doi.org/10.1371/journal.pone.0254207.

20. Yang Hu, Alessandra M. Pereira, Xiaoxue Gao, Brunno M. Campos, Edmund Derrington, Brice Corgnet, Xiaolin Zhou, Fernando Cendes, and Jean-Claude Dreher, "Right Temporoparietal Junction Underlies Avoidance of Moral Transgression in Autism Spectrum Disorder," *Journal of Neuroscience* 41, no. 8 (2021): 1699–715, https://doi.org/10.1523/JNEUROSCI.1237-20.2020.

21. Uta Frith and Chris Frith, "Reputation Management: In Autism, Generosity Is Its Own Reward," *Current Biology* 21, no. 24 (2011): R994–95, https://doi.org/10.1016/j.cub.2011.11.001.

22. Etan Smallman, "Pioneering Neuroscientists Uta and Chris Frith on Autism, Anti-Vaxxers & Their 55-Year Marriage," Inews, February 22, 2022, https://inews.co.uk/news/long-reads/uta-chris-frith-neuroscientist-couple-interview-autism-anti-vaxxers-marriage-1473644.

23. Autistic Science Person [pseud.], "Bias in Autism Research and the Neurotypical Advantage," NeuroClastic, May 14, 2019, https://neuroclastic.com/autism-research.

24. Autistic Science Person [pseud.], "Autistic People Care Too Much, Research Says," NeuroClastic, November 7, 2020, https://neuroclastic.com/autistic-people-care-too -much-research-says.

25. Peter Crosbie, "Autistics: Less Biased. Researchers?," Autism Advantage, 2016, https:// autism-advantage.com/autistics-less-biased.-researchers.html.

26. Laurent Mottron, "The Power of Autism," *Nature* 479, no. 7371 (2011): 33–35, https:// doi.org/10.1038/479033a.

27. Rachel Nuwer, "Meet the Autistic Scientists Redefining Autism Research," *Spectrum*, June 10, 2020, https://www.spectrumnews.org/features/deep-dive/meet-the-autistic -scientists-redefining-autism-research.

28. Monique Botha and Eilidh Cage, "'Autism Research Is in Crisis': A Mixed Method Study of Researcher's Constructions of Autistic People and Autism Research," *Frontiers in Psychology* 13 (2022), https://www.frontiersin.org/articles/10.3389/fpsyg.2022.1050897.

29. *Smarter Faster*, Axios Studios, accessed August 13, 2023, https://www.jpmorganchase .com/news-stories/smarter-faster-autism-at-work.

30. Darelyn Pazdel, "Viewpoint: How to Become a Champion for Employees with Autism," SHRM, accessed April 27, 2023, https://www.shrm.org/resourcesandtools/hr-topics /behavioral-competencies/global-and-cultural-effectiveness/pages/viewpoint-how-to -become-a-champion-for-employees-with-autism.aspx.

31. Lindsay C. Peters and Rachel H. Thompson, "How Teaching Perspective Taking to In- dividuals with Autism Spectrum Disorders Affects Social Skills: Findings from Research and Suggestions for Practitioners," *Behavior Analysis in Practice* 11, no. 4 (2018): 467– 78, https://doi.org/10.1007/s40617-018-0207-2.

32. Tiffany L. Hutchins, "A Review of the Nature and Development of Lying and Deception and Considerations for Teaching Prosocial Lying to Autistic Persons," *Seminars in Speech and Language* 43, no. 4 (2022): 316–30, https://doi.org/10.1055/s-0042-1750350.

33. Pier Jaarsma, Petra Gelhaus, and Stellan Welin, "Living the Categorical Imperative: Au- tistic Perspectives on Lying and Truth Telling—Between Kant and Care Ethics," *Medicine, Health Care, and Philosophy* 15, no. 3(2012): 271–77, https://doi.org/10.1007 /s11019-011-9363-7.

34. Yonason Goldson, "This Is the Secret to Healing a Toxic Culture," *Fast Company*, ac- cessed April 16, 2023, https://www.fastcompany.com/90881819/this-is-the-secret-to -healing-a-toxic-culture.

35. Chris Bailey, *Hyperfocus: How to Be More Productive in a World of Distraction* (New York: Viking, 2018).

36. Annie Dupuis, Piyumi Mudiyanselage, Christie L. Burton, Paul D. Arnold, Jennifer Crosbie, and Russell J. Schachar, "Hyperfocus or Flow? Attentional Strengths in Autism Spectrum Disorder," *Frontiers in Psychiatry* 13 (2022): 886692, https://doi.org/10.3389 /fpsyt.2022.886692.

37. Jane Ann Sedgwick, Andrew Merwood, and Philip Asherson, "The Positive Aspects of Attention Deficit Hyperactivity Disorder: A Qualitative Investigation of Successful Adults with ADHD," *ADHD Attention Deficit and Hyperactivity Disorders* 11, no. 3 (2018): 241–53, https://doi.org/10.1007/s12402-018-0277-6.

38. Brandon K. Ashinoff and Ahmad Abu-Akel, "Hyperfocus: The Forgotten Frontier of At- tention," *Psychological Research* 85 (February 2021): 1–19, https://doi.org/10.1007 /s00426-019-01245-8.

39. Sebastian Charles Keith Shaw and John Leeds Anderson, "Doctors with Dyslexia: A World of Stigma, Stonewalling and Silence, Still?," MedEdPublish, February 2017, https://doi.org/10.15694/mep.2017.000029.

40. Eleanor Walker, Sebastian C. K. Shaw, Malcolm Reed, and John L. Anderson, "The Experiences of Foundation Doctors with Dyspraxia: A Phenomenological Study," *Advances in Health Sciences Education* 26, no. 3 (2021): 959–74, https://doi.org/10.1007/s10459-021-10029-y.

41. Anselm B. M. Fuermaier, Lara Tucha, Janneke Koerts, Anna K. Mueller, Klaus W. Lange, and Oliver Tucha, "Measurement of Stigmatization towards Adults with Attention Deficit Hyperactivity Disorder," *PLOS ONE* 7, no. 12 (2012): e51755, https://doi.org/10.1371/journal.pone.0051755.

42. Lynda R. Matthews, Lynne M. Harris, Alison Jaworski, Ashraful Alam, and Gokcen Bozdag, "Function, Health and Psychosocial Needs in Job-Seekers with Anxiety, Mood, and Psychotic Disorders Who Access Disability Employment Services," *Work* 49, no. 2 (2014): 271–79, https://doi.org/10.3233/WOR-131660.

43. Joseph A. Himle, Addie Weaver, Deborah Bybee, Lisa O'Donnell, Sarah Vlnka, Wayne Laviolette, Edward Steinberger, Zipora Golenberg, and Debra Siegel Levine, "Employment Barriers, Skills, and Aspirations among Unemployed Job Seekers with and without Social Anxiety Disorder," *Psychiatric Services* 65, no. 7 (2014): 924–30, https://doi.org/10.1176/appi.ps.201300201.

44. Liana Bernard, Stefanie Fox, Kay Kulason, Alex Phanphackdy, Xander Kahle, Larry Martinez, Ludmila Praslova, and Nicholas A. Smith, "Not Your 'Typical' Research: Inclusion Ethics in Neurodiversity Scholarship," *Industrial and Organizational Psychology* 16, no. 1 (2023): 50–54, https://doi.org/10.1017/iop.2022.100.

45. "Half of All Leaders and Managers Would Not Employ a Neurodivergent Person," Institute of Leadership, accessed July 11, 2023, https://leadership.global/resourceLibrary/half-of-all-leaders-and-managers-would-not-employ-a-neurodivergent-person1.html.

46. Ari Ne'eman and Elizabeth Pellicano, "Neurodiversity as Politics," *Human Development* 66, no. 2 (2022): 149–57, https://doi.org/10.1159/000524277.

47. Monique Botha and Kristen Gillespie-Lynch, "Come as You Are: Examining Autistic Identity Development and the Neurodiversity Movement through an Intersectional Lens," *Human Development* 66, no. 2 (2022): 93–112, https://doi.org/10.1159/000524123.

48. Michael Oliver, *Social Work with Disabled People* (Basingstoke: Macmillan, 1983).

49. Jim Sinclair, "Don't Mourn for Us," *Autonomy, the Critical Journal of Interdisciplinary Autism Studies* 1, no. 1 (2012), https://philosophy.ucsc.edu/SinclairDontMournForUs.pdf.

50. angryautie [pseud.], "The Institute for the Study of the Neurologically Typical," *Angry Autie* (blog), June 24, 2013, https://angryautie.wordpress.com/2013/06/24/the-institute-for-the-study-of-the-neurologically-typical.

51. Monicca Leseyane, Peter Mandende, Mary Makgato, and Madoda Cekiso, "Dyslexic Learners' Experiences with Their Peers and Teachers in Special and Mainstream Primary Schools in North-West Province," *African Journal of Disability* 7 (2018): 363, https://doi.org/10.4102/ajod.v7i0.363.

52. Yi Guo, Xiao Tan, and Qiu-jin Zhu, "Chains of Tragedy: The Impact of Bullying Victimization on Mental Health through the Mediating Role of Aggressive Behavior and

Perceived Social Support," *Frontiers in Psychology* 13 (2022): 988003, https://doi.org/10
.3389/fpsyg.2022.988003.

53. Emily Sohn, "How Abuse Mars the Lives of Autistic People," *Spectrum*, February 5, 2020,
https://www.spectrumnews.org/features/deep-dive/how-abuse-mars-the-lives-of
-autistic-people.

54. Harvey Blume, "Neurodiversity: On the Neurological Underpinnings of Geekdom," *The
Atlantic*, September 30, 1998, https://www.theatlantic.com/magazine/archive/1998/09
/neurodiversity/305909.

55. Steve Silberman, *Neurotribes: The Legacy of Autism and the Future of Neurodiversity*, repr.
ed. (New York: Avery, 2016).

56. Edith Sheffer, "The Problem with Asperger's," *Scientific American Blog Network*, May 2,
2018, https://blogs.scientificamerican.com/observations/the-problem-with-aspergers.

57. Zoë Corbyn, "'They Tried to Wipe It Out': The Problem with Talking about Asperger's," *The Guardian*, April 16, 2023, https://www.theguardian.com/society/2023/apr/16
/they-tried-to-wipe-it-out-the-problem-with-talking-about-aspergers.

58. Damian Milton, *So What Exactly Is Autism?* (London: Autism Education Trust, 2012).

59. Damian Milton, Emine Gurbuz, and Beatriz López, "The 'Double Empathy Problem':
Ten Years On," *Autism* 26, no. 8 (2022): 1901–3, https://doi.org/10.1177/13623613
221129123.

60. William Dodson, "ADHD and the Epidemic of Shame," *ADDitude*, August 24, 2022,
https://www.additudemag.com/slideshows/adhd-and-shame.

61. Eric Garcia, "The School That Uses Shock Therapy on Autistic Students," *The Independent*,
July 16, 2021, US edition, https://www.independent.co.uk/voices/autism-shock-therapy
-trump-biden-b1885595.html.

62. Dan Habib, dir., *See Us. Hear Us.—Jordyn Zimmerman* (Communication First, 2022),
https://www.youtube.com/watch?v=_qkndlGznCw.

63. Sara Luterman, "Jordyn Zimmerman Is Redefining Communication as a Nonspeaking
Advocate for Disability Rights," The 19th, April 19, 2023, https://19thnews.org/2023
/04/jordyn-zimmerman-nonspeaking-autistic-advocate-communication.

CHAPTER TWO

1. Mary McConner, founder, Inclusive Excellence Consulting, in discussion with the author, July 2023.

2. Jenna, "Autism Interview #187: Jessica Jahns on Late Diagnosis, Disclosure, and the
Workplace," *Learn from Autistics* (blog), December 29, 2021, https://learnfromautistics
.com/autism-interview-187-jessica-jahns-on-late-diagnosis-disclosure-and-the-workplace.

3. Henry Markram, Tania Rinaldi, and Kamila Markram, "The Intense World Syndrome—
An Alternative Hypothesis for Autism," *Frontiers in Neuroscience* 1, no. 1 (2007): 77–96,
https://doi.org/10.3389/neuro.01.1.1.006.2007.

4. Chunyan Meng, Chao Huo, Hongxin Ge, Zuoshan Li, Yuanyan Hu, and Jing Meng,
"Processing of Expressions by Individuals with Autistic Traits: Empathy Deficit or Sensory Hyper-reactivity?," *PLOS ONE* 16, no. 7 (2021): e0254207, https://doi.org/10
.1371/journal.pone.0254207.

5. Yongtao Xie, Xuping Gao, Yiling Song, Xiaotong Zhu, Mengge Chen, Li Yang, and Yu-
anchun Ren, "Effectiveness of Physical Activity Intervention on ADHD Symptoms: A

Systematic Review and Meta-Analysis," *Frontiers in Psychiatry* 12 (2021), https://www.frontiersin.org/articles/10.3389/fpsyt.2021.706625.

6. Jacki Edry, *Moving Forward: Reflections on Autism, Neurodiversity, Brain Surgery, and Faith* (self-pub., Jacki Edry, 2021).

7. Jerry Gidner, US federal executive, in discussion with the author, February 2022.

8. Steve Lohr, "Remote but Inclusive for Years, and Now Showing Other Companies How," *New York Times*, October 18, 2020, https://www.nytimes.com/2020/10/18/technology/ultranauts-remote-work.html.

9. Ultranauts, *The Biodex—A User Manual for Every Teammate*, March 2020, https://ultranauts.co/wp-content/uploads/2020/03/Ultranauts-Tools-BioDex.pdf.

10. Ming Zhang, Yuqi Zhang, and Yazhuo Kong, "Interaction between Social Pain and Physical Pain," *Brain Science Advances* 5, no. 4 (2019): 265–73, https://doi.org/10.26599/BSA.2019.9050023.

11. "Our Values," Twilio, accessed July 27, 2023, https://www.twilio.com/en-us/company/values.

12. Alison Reynolds and David Lewis, "Teams Solve Problems Faster When They're More Cognitively Diverse," *Harvard Business Review*, March 30, 2017, https://hbr.org/2017/03/teams-solve-problems-faster-when-theyre-more-cognitively-diverse.

13. Ludmila N. Praslova, "7 Dos and Don'ts of Inclusion by Design," *The SHRM Blog* (blog), February 11, 2021, https://blog.shrm.org/blog/7-do-s-and-don-ts-of-inclusion-by-design.

14. Ludmila N. Praslova, "Today's Most Critical Workplace Challenges Are about Systems," *Harvard Business Review*, January 10, 2023, https://hbr.org/2023/01/todays-most-critical-workplace-challenges-are-about-systems.

15. Ludmila N. Praslova, "Productivity, Wellbeing, and Mental Health," *The SHRM Blog* (blog), May 20, 2021, https://blog.shrm.org/blog/productivity-wellbeing-and-mental-health.

16. Carmen L. A. Zurbriggen, Martin Venetz, Susanne Schwab, and Marco G. P. Hessels, "A Psychometric Analysis of the Student Version of the Perceptions of Inclusion Questionnaire (PIQ)," *European Journal of Psychological Assessment: Official Organ of the European Association of Psychological Assessment* 35, no. 5 (2019): 641–49, https://doi.org/10.1027/1015-5759/a000443.

17. Danielle Miller, Jon Rees, and Amy Pearson, "'Masking Is Life': Experiences of Masking in Autistic and Nonautistic Adults," *Autism in Adulthood: Challenges and Management* 3, no. 4 (2021): 330–38, https://doi.org/10.1089/aut.2020.0083.

18. Jean Decety and Keith J. Yoder, "Empathy and Motivation for Justice: Cognitive Empathy and Concern, but Not Emotional Empathy, Predict Sensitivity to Injustice for Others," *Social Neuroscience* 11, no. 1 (2016): 1–14, https://doi.org/10.1080/17470919.2015.1029593.

19. David De Cremer and Kees van den Bos, "Justice and Feelings: Toward a New Era in Justice Research," *Social Justice Research* 20, no. 1 (2007): 1–9, https://doi.org/10.1007/s11211-007-0031-2.

20. Jann Ingmire, "Brain Scans Link Concern for Justice with Reason, Not Emotion," *University of Chicago News*, March 27, 2014, https://news.uchicago.edu/story/brain-scans-link-concern-justice-reason-not-emotion.

21. Ludmila N. Praslova, "Practice Emotional Inclusion at Work, Not Toxic Positivity," *Psychology Today* (blog), June 29, 2022, https://www.psychologytoday.com/us/blog/positively-different/202206/practice-emotional-inclusion-at-work-not-toxic-positivity.

22. Vinesh G. Oommen, Mike Knowles, and Isabella Zhao, "Should Health Service Managers Embrace Open Plan Work Environments? A Review," *Asia Pacific Journal of Health Management* 3, no. 2 (2008): 37–43.

23. Annie Reneau, "Oregon Hospital Workers Smash Plates to Relieve Stress," Upworthy, August 24, 2021, https://www.upworthy.com/healthcare-heroes-throwing-plates-at-walls.

24. "Why Every Office Should Have a Crying Room," *Glamour*, March 10, 2017, https://www.glamour.com/story/why-every-office-should-have-a-crying-room.

25. Robert P. Vecchio, "Negative Emotion in the Workplace: Employee Jealousy and Envy," *International Journal of Stress Management* 7, no. 3 (2000): 161–79, https://doi.org/10.1023/A:1009592430712.

26. Ludmila N. Praslova, "Are There Limits to Authenticity at Work?," *Psychology Today* (blog). September 2022, https://www.psychologytoday.com/us/blog/positively-different/202209/are-there-limits-to-authenticity-at-work.

27. *The U.S. Surgeon General's Framework for Workplace Mental Health & Well-Being* (Washington, DC: Office of the U.S. Surgeon General, 2022), 25, https://www.hhs.gov/sites/default/files/workplace-mental-health-well-being.pdf.

28. "Disability and Health Inclusion Strategies," Centers for Disease Control and Prevention, September 15, 2020, https://www.cdc.gov/ncbddd/disabilityandhealth/disability-strategies.html.

29. Michael Oliver, *Social Work with Disabled People*, Practical Social Work Series (Basingstoke: Macmillan, 1983).

30. Michael Oliver, *The Politics of Disablement* (London: Macmillan Education, 1990).

31. Michael Oliver, *Social Work: Disabled People and Disabling Environments* (London: J. Kingsley Publishers, 1991).

32. Barbara Ruth Saunders, writer, editor, in discussion with the author, February 2023.

33. Evan W. Carr, Andrew Reece, Gabriella Rosen Kellerman, and Alexi Robichaux, "The Value of Belonging at Work," *Harvard Business Review*, December 16, 2019, https://hbr.org/2019/12/the-value-of-belonging-at-work.

34. Colleen Bordeaux, Betsy Grace, and Naina Sabherwal, "Why Does Belonging Matter in the Workplace?," *Capital H: Human Capital Blog* (blog), November 23, 2021, https://www2.deloitte.com/us/en/blog/human-capital-blog/2021/what-is-belonging-in-the-workplace.html.

35. Holly Althof, "Viewpoint: Belonging Is the Missing Piece in the Fight for Inclusion," SHRM, August 21, 2020, https://www.shrm.org/resourcesandtools/hr-topics/behavioral-competencies/global-and-cultural-effectiveness/pages/viewpoint-belonging-is-the-missing-piece-in-the-fight-for-inclusion.aspx.

36. Jena McGregor, "First There Was 'Diversity,' Then 'Inclusion': Now HR Wants Everyone to Feel like They 'Belong,'" *Washington Post*, December 30, 2019, https://www.washingtonpost.com/business/2019/12/30/first-there-was-diversity-then-inclusion-now-hr-wants-everyone-feel-like-they-belong.

37. Daniel Kahneman, *Thinking, Fast and Slow*, 1st ed. (New York: Farrar, Straus and Giroux, 2013).

38. Jessica E. Dinh, Robert G. Lord, and Ernest Hoffman, "Leadership Perception and Information Processing: Influences of Symbolic, Connectionist, Emotional, and Embodied Architectures," in *The Oxford Handbook of Leadership and Organizations*, ed. David V. Day (New York: Oxford University Press, 2014), 305–30.

39. Robert G. Lord, and Jessica E. Dinh, "What Have We Learned That Is Critical in Understanding Leadership Perceptions and Leader-Performance Relations?," *Industrial and Organizational Psychology* 7, no. 2 (2014): 158–77, https://doi.org/10.1111/iops.12127.

40. Jaak Panksepp, "The Riddle of Laughter: Neural and Psychoevolutionary Underpinnings of Joy," *Current Directions in Psychological Science* 9, no. 6 (2000): 183–86, https://doi.org/10.1111/1467-8721.00090.

41. Joshua M. Ackerman, Christopher C. Nocera, and John A. Bargh, "Incidental Haptic Sensations Influence Social Judgments and Decisions," *Science* 328, no. 5986 (2010): 1712–15, https://doi.org/10.1126/science.1189993.

42. Antonio Damasio and Hanna Damasio, "Consciousness Begins with Feeling, Not Thinking," Institute of Art and Ideas, April 20, 2023, https://iai.tv/articles/consciousness-begins-with-feelings-hanna-damasio-auid-2462.

CHAPTER THREE

1. "Resource Library," Disability:IN, accessed November 17, 2023, https://disabilityin.org/resources/.

2. Boston Consulting Group (BCG), "Companies Are Drastically Underestimating How Many of Their Employees Have Disabilities," Cision PR Newswire, May 10, 2023, https://www.prnewswire.com/news-releases/companies-are-drastically-underestimating-how-many-of-their-employees-have-disabilities-301820285.html.

3. Ludmila N. Praslova, "An Intersectional Approach to Inclusion at Work," *Harvard Business Review*, June 21, 2022, https://hbr.org/2022/06/an-intersectional-approach-to-inclusion-at-work.

4. REL Midwest, "What Does the Research Say about the Relationship of Visual, Public Behavior Management Displays (e.g., Clip Charts or Behavior Management Charts) and Student Well-Being (e.g., Psychological Impact of Public Shaming or Praise)?," Regional Educational Laboratory Program (REL), January 1, 2018, https://ies.ed.gov/ncee/rel/Products/Region/midwest/Ask-A-REL/10190.

5. Genevieve Shaw Brown, "Teacher's Post on Why Her Neurotypical Classroom Looks like a Special Education One Goes Viral," *Good Morning America*, October 8, 2020, https://www.goodmorningamerica.com/gma/story/teachers-viral-post-neurotypical-classroom-special-education-73473843.

6. Joan C. Williams, Marina Multhaup, and Sky Mihaylo, "Why Companies Should Add Class to Their Diversity Discussions," *Harvard Business Review*, September 5, 2018, https://hbr.org/2018/09/why-companies-should-add-class-to-their-diversity-discussions.

7. Christine Exley and Judd Kessler, "Why Don't Women Self-Promote as Much as Men?," *Harvard Business Review*, December 19, 2019, https://hbr.org/2019/12/why-dont-women-self-promote-as-much-as-men.

8. Clément Bosquet, Pierre-Philippe Combes, and Cecilia García-Peñalosa, "Gender and Promotions: Evidence from Academic Economists in France," *Scandinavian Journal of Economics* 121, no. 3 (2019): 1020–53, https://doi.org/10.1111/sjoe.12300.

9. Muriel Niederle and Lise Vesterlund, "Do Women Shy Away from Competition? Do Men Compete Too Much?," *Quarterly Journal of Economics* 122 (2007): 1067–1101, https://doi.org/10.1162/qjec.122.3.1067.

10. Delroy L. Paulhus, Bryce G. Westlake, Stryker S. Calvez, and P. D. Harms, "Self-Presentation Style in Job Interviews: The Role of Personality and Culture," *Journal of Applied Social Psychology* 43, no. 10 (2013): 2042–59, https://doi.org/10.1111/jasp.12157.

11. Ludmila N. Praslova, "Workplace Bullying of Autistic People: A Vicious Cycle," *Specialisterne* (blog), April 24, 2022. https://us.specialisterne.com/workplace-bullying-of-autistic-people-a-vicious-cycle.

12. Samantha Fuld, "Autism Spectrum Disorder: The Impact of Stressful and Traumatic Life Events and Implications for Clinical Practice," *Clinical Social Work Journal* 46, no. 3 (2018): 210–19, https://doi.org/10.1007/s10615-018-0649-6.

13. Daniel W. Hoover and Joan Kaufman, "Adverse Childhood Experiences in Children with Autism Spectrum Disorder," *Current Opinion in Psychiatry* 31, no. 2 (2018): 128–32, https://doi.org/10.1097/YCO.0000000000000390.

14. Mallory E. Bowers and Rachel Yehuda, "Intergenerational Transmission of Stress in Humans," *Neuropsychopharmacology* 41, no. 1 (2016): 232–44, https://doi.org/10.1038/npp.2015.247.

15. Ludmila N. Praslova, Ron Carucci, and Caroline Stokes, "How Bullying Manifests at Work—and How to Stop It," *Harvard Business Review*, November 4, 2022, https://hbr.org/2022/11/how-bullying-manifests-at-work-and-how-to-stop-it.

16. Donald Sull, Charles Sull, and Ben Zweig, "Toxic Culture Is Driving the Great Resignation," *MIT Sloan Management Review*, January 11, 2022, https://sloanreview.mit.edu/article/toxic-culture-is-driving-the-great-resignation.

17. Ludmila N. Praslova, "To Build a Healthy Workplace, You Need a Toxic Culture Alarm," *Fast Company*, March 14, 2022, https://www.fastcompany.com/90730688/to-build-a-healthy-workplace-you-need-a-toxic-culture-alarm.

18. Craig Johnson, "Enron's Ethical Collapse: Lessons for Leadership Educators," *Journal of Leadership Education* 2, no. 1 (2003), https://doi.org/10.12806/V2/I1/C2.

19. Ludmila N. Praslova, "Today's Most Critical Workplace Challenges Are about Systems," *Harvard Business Review*, January 10, 2023, https://hbr.org/2023/01/todays-most-critical-workplace-challenges-are-about-systems.

20. Rebecca Bondü and Günter Esser, "Justice and Rejection Sensitivity in Children and Adolescents with ADHD Symptoms," *European Child & Adolescent Psychiatry* 24, no. 2 (2015): 185–98, https://doi.org/10.1007/s00787-014-0560-9.

21. Thomas Schäfer and Thomas Kraneburg, "The Kind Nature behind the Unsocial Semblance: ADHD and Justice Sensitivity—A Pilot Study," *Journal of Attention Disorders* 19, no. 8 (2015): 715–27, https://doi.org/10.1177/1087054712466914.

22. Chunyan Meng, Chao Huo, Hongxin Ge, Zuoshan Li, Yuanyan Hu, and Jing Meng, "Processing of Expressions by Individuals with Autistic Traits: Empathy Deficit or Sensory Hyper-reactivity?," *PLoS ONE* 16, no. 7 (2021): e0254207, https://doi.org/10.1371/journal.pone.0254207.

23. Amelia Hill, "'Clients Say It Feels like We've Always Known Each Other': The Mental Health Experts Who Believe Their Autism Has Turbocharged Their Work," *The Guardian*, February 3, 2022, https://www.theguardian.com/society/2022/feb/03/clients-say-it

-feels-like-weve-always-known-each-other-the-mental-health-experts-who-believe-their
-autism-has-turbocharged-their-work.

24. Yang Hu, Alessandra M. Pereira, Xiaoxue Gao, Brunno M. Campos, Edmund Derrington, Brice Corgnet, Xiaolin Zhou, Fernando Cendes, and Jean-Claude Dreher,
"Right Temporoparietal Junction Underlies Avoidance of Moral Transgression in Autism Spectrum Disorder," *Journal of Neuroscience* 41, no. 8 (2021): 1699–1715, https://
doi.org/10.1523/JNEUROSCI.1237-20.2020.

25. Pier Jaarsma, Petra Gelhaus, and Stellan Welin, "Living the Categorical Imperative: Autistic Perspectives on Lying and Truth Telling—Between Kant and Care Ethics," *Medicine, Health Care, and Philosophy* 15, no. 3 (2012): 271–77, https://doi.org/10.1007
/s11019-011-9363-7.

26. Marianne Sunderland, "Dyslexia Success Story: Erin Brockovich," *Homeschooling with
Dyslexia* (blog), May 7, 2016, https://homeschoolingwithdyslexia.com/dyslexia-success
-story-erin-brockovich.

27. Tameir Yeheyes, "Olympic & Disability Champion Simone Biles Makes History while
Mesmerizing Many," RespectAbility, *Fellows Blog Series*, February 11, 2018, https://www
.respectability.org/2018/02/olympic-disability-champion-simone-biles-makes-history
-mesmerizing-many.

28. Rebecca Shabad, "'We Have Been Failed': Simone Biles Breaks down in Tears Recount-
ing Nassar's Sexual Abuse," *NBC News*, September 15, 2021, https://www.nbcnews.com
/politics/congress/we-have-been-failed-simone-biles-breaks-down-tears-recounting
-n1279255.

29. Nicole Strah and Deborah E. Rupp, "Are There Cracks in Our Foundation? An Integrative Review of Diversity Issues in Job Analysis," *Journal of Applied Psychology* 107, no. 7
(2022): 1031–51, https://doi.org/10.1037/apl0000989.

30. Q. Roberson and W. Scott, "Contributive Justice: An Invisible Barrier to Workplace Inclusion," *Journal of Management*, online first (August 2022), https://doi.org/10.1177
/01492063221116089.

31. Ludmila N. Praslova, "Neurodiversity at Work: 'Unique Approaches' or Best Talent Practices?," in *Evidence-Based Organizational Practices for Diversity, Inclusion, Belonging and
Equity*, ed. Ludmila N. Praslova (Tyne, England: Cambridge Scholars, 2023).

32. Ludmila N. Praslova, "Defeat Diversity Derailers: Inclusion by Design," *The SHRM Blog*,
(blog), February 10, 2021, https://blog.shrm.org/blog/defeat-diversity-derailers-inclusion
-by-design.

33. Ann Heylighen and Andy Dong, "To Empathise or Not to Empathise? Empathy and Its
Limits in Design," *Design Studies* 65 (2019): 107–24, https://doi.org/10.1016/j.destud
.2019.10.007.

34. Tony Ho Tran, "How to Design for the Margins," Dscout, accessed August 13, 2023,
https://dscout.com/people-nerds/christina-harrington.

35. Seval Gündemir, Astrid C. Homan, and Lindred (Lindy) Greer, "Overcoming the Inclusion Facade," *MIT Sloan Management Review*, March 21, 2023, https://sloanreview
.mit.edu/article/overcoming-the-inclusion-facade.

36. Richard D. Rosenberg and Eliezer Rosenstein, "Participation and Productivity: An Empirical Study," *ILR Review* 33, no. 3 (1980): 355–67, https://doi.org/10.1177
/001979398003300306.

37. David Martinez, data analyst, Deloitte, in discussion with the author, March 2023.

38. Ludmila N. Praslova and Satoris Howes, "Employing a Neurodiverse Workforce: Considerations for Human Resource Management," in *Research in Human Resource Management*, ed. Brian Murray and Deanna Stone (Charlotte, NC: Information Age Publishing, forthcoming).

39. Holger Reisinger and Dane Fetterer, "Forget Flexibility: Your Employees Want Autonomy," *Harvard Business Review*, October 29, 2021, https://hbr.org/2021/10/forget-flexibility-your-employees-want-autonomy.

40. Carolyn Moore, "We Need to Talk about How the New Way to Work Is about Outcomes, Not Hours," *Fast Company*, May 14, 2021, https://www.fastcompany.com/90634884/we-need-to-talk-about-how-the-new-way-to-work-is-about-outcomes-not-hours.

41. Homepage, MarisaHamamoto.com, accessed August 13, 2023, https://www.marisahamamoto.com.

42. TEDx Talks, *Serving Others Starts with This | Marisa Hamamoto | TEDxDelthorneWomen*, 2023, https://www.youtube.com/watch?v=FC3zZlSEWw4.

43. Kate Hogan, "Marisa Hamamoto Is Shattering Stereotypes about Dancers: 'We're Changing the Narrative around Disability,'" *People*, March 5, 2021, https://people.com/human-interest/marisa-hamamoto-infinite-flow-inclusive-dance-company.

44. "Indicator: Employee Engagement," Gallup, accessed August 13, 2023, https://www.gallup.com/394373/indicator-employee-engagement.aspx.

45. Shevonne Joyce, head of business strategy and innovation at Legalite, in discussion with the author, July 2023.

46. Robert Evert Cimera, Paul Wehman, Michael West, and Sloane Burgess, "Do Sheltered Workshops Enhance Employment Outcomes for Adults with Autism Spectrum Disorder?," *Autism* 16, no. 1 (2012): 87–94, https://doi.org/10.1177/1362361311408129.

47. Gerald S. Leventhal, *What Should Be Done with Equity Theory? New Approaches to the Study of Fairness in Social Relationships* (Detroit: Wayne State University, 1976), https://eric.ed.gov/?id=ED142463.

48. Gil Winch, *Winning with Underdogs: How Hiring the Least Likely Candidates Can Spark Creativity, Improve Service, and Boost Profits for Your Business* (Kindle, 2022).

49. Rajesh Anandan, CEO of Ultranauts, in discussion with the author, March 2023.

50. Digital Agency Development Team, "Universal Workplace," Ultranauts, accessed August 13, 2023, https://ultranauts.co/universal-workplace.

51. Adrián Díaz Barragán, Jimena Y. Ramírez Marín, and Francisco J. Medina Díaz, "The Irony of Choice in Recruitment: When Similarity Turns Recruiters to Other Candidates," *M@n@gement* 22, no. 3 (2019): 466–86, https://doi.org/10.3917/mana.223.0466.

52. Angela Marie Mai, "Hiring Agents' Beliefs: A Barrier to Employment of Autistics," *SAGE Open* 9, no. 3 (2019): 2158244019862725, https://doi.org/10.1177/2158244019862725.

53. Strah and Rupp, "Are There Cracks in Our Foundation?"

54. "A Look inside Our Neurodiversity Hiring Program," Dell Technologies, July 14, 2022. https://jobs.dell.com/Dells-Neurodiversity-Hiring-Program.

55. Ludmila N. Praslova, "7 Dos and Don'ts of Inclusion by Design," *The SHRM Blog* (blog), February 11, 2021, https://blog.shrm.org/blog/7-do-s-and-don-ts-of-inclusion-by-design.

56. John P. Kotter, "Winning at Change," *Leader to Leader* 10 (1998): 27–33, https://doi.org/10.1002/ltl.40619981009.

CHAPTER FOUR

1. Caroline Stokes, founder of Forward, in discussion with the author, April 2023.
2. Timothy J. Luke, "Lessons from Pinocchio: Cues to Deception May Be Highly Exaggerated," *Perspectives on Psychological Science* 14, no. 4 (2019): 646–71, https://doi.org/10.1177/1745691619838258.
3. Alliyza Lim, Robyn L. Young, and Neil Brewer, "Autistic Adults May Be Erroneously Perceived as Deceptive and Lacking Credibility," *Journal of Autism and Developmental Disorders* 52, no. 2 (2022): 490–507, https://doi.org/10.1007/s10803-021-04963-4.
4. Maury Hanigan, "Candidates Don't Trust You . . . and They Shouldn't," *SparcStart* (blog), February 3, 2022, https://www.sparcstart.com/candidates-dont-trust-you.
5. Peter Cappelli, "Your Approach to Hiring Is All Wrong," *Harvard Business Review*, May 1, 2019, https://hbr.org/2019/05/your-approach-to-hiring-is-all-wrong.
6. Cynthia Measom, "How to Spot Fake Glassdoor Reviews: 7 Key Signs," Yahoo!, December 16, 2022, https://www.yahoo.com/now/spot-fake-glassdoor-reviews-7-190023847.html?guccounter=1.
7. ContractRecruiter, *Why 81% of New Hires Fail*, accessed February 5, 2023, https://www.contractrecruiter.com/wp-content/uploads/2023/02/5-Why-81-Percent-of-New-Hires-Fail.pdf.
8. Michael Moffa, "Type I, II Errors in Recruiting," Recruiter.com, accessed July 17, 2023, https://www.recruiter.com/recruiting/type-i-ii-errors-in-recruiting.
9. Skye Schooley, "How to Handle a Bad Hire," business.com, May 26, 2020, https://www.business.com/articles/cost-of-a-bad-hire/.
10. Arlene S. Hirsch, "Should You Trust Your Gut in Hiring Decisions?," SHRM, May 1, 2018, https://www.shrm.org/resourcesandtools/hr-topics/talent-acquisition/pages/trust-your-gut-hiring-decisions.aspx.
11. Tomas Chamorro-Premuzic, "Why Do So Many Incompetent Men Become Leaders?," *Harvard Business Review*, August 22, 2013, https://hbr.org/2013/08/why-do-so-many-incompetent-men.
12. Justin, Carrero, Anna Krzeminska, and Charmine E. J. Härtel, "The DXC Technology Work Experience Program: Disability-Inclusive Recruitment and Selection in Action," *Journal of Management & Organization* 25, no. 4 (2019): 535–42, https://doi.org/10.1017/jmo.2019.23.
13. Michał T. Tomczak, Joanna Maria Szulc, and Małgorzata Szczerska, "Inclusive Communication Model Supporting the Employment Cycle of Individuals with Autism Spectrum Disorders," *International Journal of Environmental Research and Public Health* 18, no. 9 (2021): 4696, https://doi.org/10.3390/ijerph18094696.
14. Nicole Strah and Deborah E. Rupp, "Are There Cracks in Our Foundation? An Integrative Review of Diversity Issues in Job Analysis," *Journal of Applied Psychology* 107, no. 7 (2022): 1031–51, https://doi.org/10.1037/apl0000989.
15. Krystin E. Mitchell, George M. Alliger, and Richard Morfopoulos, "Toward an ADA-Appropriate Job Analysis," *Human Resource Management Review* 7, no. 1 (1997): 5–26, https://doi.org/10.1016/S1053-4822(97)90003-6.
16. Ludmila N. Praslova and Satoris Howes, "Employing a Neurodiverse Workforce: Considerations for Human Resource Management," in *Research in Human Resource Management*,

ed. Brian Murray and Deanna Stone (Charlotte, NC: Information Age Publishing, forthcoming).

17. Tara Sophia Mohr, "Why Women Don't Apply for Jobs Unless They're 100% Qualified," *Harvard Business Review*, August 25, 2014, https://hbr.org/2014/08/why-women -dont-apply-for-jobs-unless-theyre-100-qualified.

18. EARN, "Including Neurodivergent Workers: Job Descriptions and Interviewing," Employer Assistance and Resource Network on Disability Inclusion, accessed July 17, 2023, https://askearn.org/page/neurodiversity-job-descriptions-and-interviewing.

19. Oriane A. M. Georgeac and Aneeta Rattan, "The Business Case for Diversity Backfires: Detrimental Effects of Organizations' Instrumental Diversity Rhetoric for Underrepresented Group Members' Sense of Belonging," *Journal of Personality and Social Psychology* 124, no. 1 (2023): 69–108, https://doi.org/10.1037/pspi0000394.

20. Ludmila N. Praslova, "The 'Talent Shortage' Problem Is a Diversity Problem," ERE, accessed July 16, 2023, https://www.ere.net/articles/the-talent-shortage-problem-is-a -diversity-problem.

21. Veronica Combs, "Autistic People Succeed in IT Jobs When Companies Hire for Capabilities Not Credentials," *TechRepublic*, February 23, 2021, https://www.techrepublic .com/article/people-with-autism-succeed-in-it-jobs-when-companies-hire-for -capabilities-not-credentials.

22. Karen S. Markel and Brittany Elia, "How Human Resource Management Can Best Support Employees with Autism: Future Directions for Research and Practice," *Journal of Business and Management* 22, no. 1 (2016): 71–86.

23. Wilma Wake, Eric Endlich, and Robert S. Lagos, *Older Autistic Adults: In Their Own Words: The Lost Generation* (Shawnee, KS: AAPC Publishing, 2021).

24. Ludmila N. Praslova, Eric Rodriguez, and Jeff Hittenberger, "Inclusive Thriving: Diversity for the Better Normal," keynote address presented at the Creating Healthy Organizations Conference, Costa Mesa, CA, October 17, 2020.

25. Eric Sydell, EVP for Innovation at Modern Hire, in discussion with the author, March 23, 2023.

26. Dave Zielinski, "Is Your Applicant Tracking System Hurting Your Recruiting Efforts?," *Harvard Business Review*, March 8, 2022, https://www.shrm.org/hr-today/news/hr -magazine/spring2022/pages/are-applicant-tracking-systems-working.aspx.

27. Zielinski, "Is Your Applicant Tracking System Hurting Your Recruiting Efforts?"

28. Cheryl Simpson and Jenna Arcand, "3 Ways to Age-Proof Your Resume & LinkedIn Profile," Work It Daily, accessed January 5, 2023, https://www.workitdaily.com/resume -linkedin-profile-age-proof/how-do-you-age-proof-your-resume-and-linkedin-profile.

29. Robin Madell, "Should Older Workers Leave Dates off Resumes?," *FlexJobs* (blog), accessed July 17, 2023, https://www.flexjobs.com/blog/post/should-older-workers-leave -dates-off-resumes-v2.

30. Jade Davies, Brett Heasman, Adam Livesey, Amy Walker, Elizabeth Pellicano, and Anna Remington, "Access to Employment: A Comparison of Autistic, Neurodivergent and Neurotypical Adults' Experiences of Hiring Processes in the United Kingdom," *Autism*, January (2023): 13623613221145376, https://doi.org/10.1177/13623613221145377.

31. Temple Grandin, "When Great Minds Don't Think Alike," *Harvard Business Review*, May 23, 2023, https://hbr.org/2023/05/when-great-minds-dont-think-alike.

32. Wayne Cascio, *Managing Human Resources*, 11th ed. (New York: McGraw Hill, 2018).

33. Mikaela Finn, Rebecca L. Flower, Han Ming Leong, and Darren Hedley, "'If I'm Just Me, I Doubt I'd Get the Job': A Qualitative Exploration of Autistic People's Experiences in Job Interviews," *Autism*, February 16, 2023, https://doi.org/10.1177/13623613 231153480.

34. Emeric Kubiak, "Why We Shouldn't Rely on Intuition When Hiring," *HR Director*, June 3, 2022, https://www.thehrdirector.com/features/hr-in-business/shouldnt-rely -intuition-hiring.

35. Eric Patton, "Autism, Attributions and Accommodations: Overcoming Barriers and Integrating a Neurodiverse Workforce," *Personnel Review* 48, no. 4 (2019): 915–34, https://doi.org/10.1108/PR-04-2018-0116.

36. James Richards, "Examining the Exclusion of Employees with Asperger Syndrome from the Workplace," *Personnel Review* 41, no. 5 (2012): 630–46, https://doi.org/10.1108 /00483481211249148.

37. Noah J. Sasson, Daniel J. Faso, Jack Nugent, Sarah Lovell, Daniel P. Kennedy, and Ruth B. Grossman, "Neurotypical Peers Are Less Willing to Interact with Those with Autism Based on Thin Slice Judgments," *Scientific Reports* 7, no. 1 (2017): 40700, https://doi.org/10.1038/srep40700.

38. Rebecca L. Flower, Louise M. Dickens, and Darren Hedley, "Barriers to Employment: Raters' Perceptions of Male Autistic and Non-Autistic Candidates during a Simulated Job Interview and the Impact of Diagnostic Disclosure," *Autism in Adulthood: Challenges and Management* 3, no. 4 (2021): 300–309, https://doi.org/10.1089/aut.2020 .0075.

39. Martin Oscarsson, Martina Nelson, Alexander Rozental, Ylva Ginsberg, Per Carlbring, and Fredrik Jönsson, "Stress and Work-Related Mental Illness among Working Adults with ADHD: A Qualitative Study," *BMC Psychiatry* 22 (2022): 751, https://doi.org/10 .1186/s12888-022-04409-w.

40. Grant S. Shields, Matthew A. Sazma, and Andrew P. Yonelinas, "The Effects of Acute Stress on Core Executive Functions: A Meta-analysis and Comparison with Cortisol," *Neuroscience and Biobehavioral Reviews* 68 (2016): 651–68, https://doi.org/10.1016/j .neubiorev.2016.06.038.

41. Gil Winch, *Winning with Underdogs: How Hiring the Least Likely Candidates Can Spark Creativity, Improve Service, and Boost Profits for Your Business* (McGraw Hill, 2022).

42. Geoff Tuff, Steve Goldbach, and Jeff Johnson, "When Hiring, Prioritize Assignments over Interviews," *Harvard Business Review*, September 27, 2022, https://hbr.org/2022 /09/when-hiring-prioritize-assignments-over-interviews.

43. Damian Milton, *So What Exactly Is Autism?* (London: Autism Education Trust, 2012).

44. Patti Waldmeir, "Overlooked Workers Gain Appeal in Challenging Times," *Financial Times*, March 17, 2020, https://www.ft.com/content/ea9ca374-6780-11ea-800d -da70cff6e4d3.

45. David Martinez, data analyst, Deloitte, in discussion with the author, March 2023.

46. Ludmila N. Praslova, "The Radical Promise of Truly Flexible Work," *Harvard Business Review*, August 15, 2023, https://hbr.org/2023/08/the-radical-promise-of-truly-flexible -work.

CHAPTER FIVE

1. Arlene S. Hirsch, "Reducing New Employee Turnover among Emerging Adults," SHRM, June 2, 2016, https://www.shrm.org/resourcesandtools/hr-topics/employee-relations/pages/reducing-new-employee-turnover-among-emerging-adults.aspx.

2. Ron Carucci, "To Retain New Hires, Spend More Time Onboarding Them," *Harvard Business Review*, December 3, 2018, https://hbr.org/2018/12/to-retain-new-hires-spend-more-time-onboarding-them.

3. Jennifer Payne, "Pre-boarding and the Importance of Human Connection in the Workplace—A Q&A with #SHRM18 Speaker Cecile Alper-Leroux," *The SHRM Blog* (blog), May 1, 2018, https://blog.shrm.org/blog/pre-boarding-and-the-importance-of-human-connection-in-the-workplace-a-qa-w.

4. Payne, "Pre-boarding and the Importance of Human Connection in the Workplace."

5. "Education and Socioeconomic Status," American Psychological Association, 2017, https://www.apa.org/pi/ses/resources/publications/education.

6. Harry Badger, autistic journalist, in discussion with the author, February 2023.

7. Alexandra Ossola, "Neurodiverse Applicants Are Revolutionizing the Hiring Process," *Quartz*, March 26, 2021, https://qz.com/work/1981466/neurodiverse-applicants-are-revolutionizing-the-hiring-process.

8. Mohammad Hossein Keshavarz and Asegul Hulus, "The Effect of Students' Personality and Learning Styles on Their Motivation for Using Blended Learning," *Advances in Language and Literary Studies* 10, no. 6 (2019): 78–88, https://doi.org/10.7575/aiac.alls.v.10n.6p.78.

9. David Martinez, solutions analyst, Deloitte, in discussion with the author, March 2023.

10. Malcolm S. Knowles, Elwood F. Holton III, and Richard A. Swanson, *The Adult Learner: The Definitive Classic in Adult Education and Human Resource Development*, 6th ed. (Burlington, VT: Elsevier, 2005).

11. Amy E. Margolis, Jessica Broitman, John M. Davis, Lindsay Alexander, Ava Hamilton, Zhijie Liao, Sarah Banker, et al., "Estimated Prevalence of Nonverbal Learning Disability among North American Children and Adolescents," *JAMA Network Open* 3, no. 4 (2020): e202551, https://doi.org/10.1001/jamanetworkopen.2020.2551.

12. Anna L. (confidential) in communication with the author, May 2023.

13. American Psychiatric Association, *Diagnostic and Statistical Manual of Mental Disorders*, 5th ed. (Washington, DC: American Psychiatric Publishing, 2013).

14. Julia Phelan, "Designing Inclusive Onboarding through a Learning Engineering Lens," in *Evidence-Based Organizational Practices for Diversity, Inclusion, Belonging and Equity*, ed. Ludmila N. Praslova (Tyne, England: Cambridge Scholars, 2023), 172–213.

15. Richard K. Wagner, Fotena A. Zirps, Ashley A. Edwards, Sarah G. Wood, Rachel E. Joyner, Betsy J. Becker, Guangyun Liu, and Bethany Beal, "The Prevalence of Dyslexia: A New Approach to Its Estimation," *Journal of Learning Disabilities* 53, no. 5 (2020): 354–65, https://doi.org/10.1177/0022219420920377.

16. Andrew Hughes, "Tips to Avoid Cognitive Overload in Employee Training Programs," ELearning Industry, December 12, 2019, https://elearningindustry.com/avoid-cognitive-overload-in-employee-training-programs.

17. Amanda Gibson, strategist, Radix Strategy, LLC, in discussion with the author, April 2023.

18. June L. Chen, Connie Sung, and Sukyeong Pi, "Vocational Rehabilitation Service Patterns and Outcomes for Individuals with Autism of Different Ages," *Journal of Autism*

and Developmental Disorders 45, no. 9 (2015): 3015–29, https://doi.org/10.1007/s10803
-015-2465-y.

19. Anna Melissa Romualdez, Zachary Walker, and Anna Remington, "Autistic Adults' Experiences of Diagnostic Disclosure in the Workplace: Decision-Making and Factors Associated with Outcomes," *Autism & Developmental Language Impairments* 6 (2021): 23969415211022956, https://doi.org/10.1177/23969415211022955.

20. Melissa Scott, Ben Milbourn, Marita Falkmer, Melissa Black, Sven Bölte, Alycia Halladay, Matthew Lerner, Julie Lounds Taylor, and Sonya Girdler, "Factors Impacting Employment for People with Autism Spectrum Disorder: A Scoping Review," *Autism* 23, no. 4 (2019): 869–901, https://doi.org/10.1177/1362361318787789.

21. Patti Waldmeir, "Overlooked Workers Gain Appeal in Challenging Times," *Financial Times*, March 17, 2020, https://www.ft.com/content/ea9ca374-6780-11ea-800d
-da70cff6e4d3.

22. Ludmila N. Praslova, "Why Autism Inclusion at Work Matters, and Why We Are Not There Yet," *The SHRM Blog* (blog), April 2, 2021, https://blog.shrm.org/blog/why-autism
-inclusion-at-work-matters-and-why-we-are-not-there-yet.

23. Hari Srinivasan, "Dignity Remains Elusive for Many Disabled People," *Giving Voice* (blog), Psychology Today, July 13, 2023, https://www.psychologytoday.com/us/blog
/giving-voice/202307/dignity-remains-elusive-for-many-disabled-people.

24. Lionel Standing, Danny Lynn, and Katherine Moxness, "Effects of Noise upon Introverts and Extroverts," *Bulletin of the Psychonomic Society* 28, no. 2 (1990): 138–40, https://
doi.org/10.3758/BF03333987.

25. G. Belojevic, V. Slepcevic, and B. Jakovljevic, "Mental Performance in Noise: The Role of Introversion," *Journal of Environmental Psychology* 21, no. 2 (2001): 209–13, https://
doi.org/10.1006/jevp.2000.0188.

26. Gianna Cassidy and Raymond A. R. MacDonald, "The Effect of Background Music and Background Noise on the Task Performance of Introverts and Extraverts," *Psychology of Music* 35, no. 3 (2007): 517–37, https://doi.org/10.1177/0305735607076444.

27. K. MacLennan, S. O'Brien, and T. Tavassoli, "In Our Own Words: The Complex Sensory Experiences of Autistic Adults," *Journal of Autism and Developmental Disorders* 52, no. 7 (2022): 3061–75, https://doi.org/10.1007/s10803-021-05186-3.

28. Sarah Deweerdt, "Unseen Agony: Dismantling Autism's House of Pain," *Spectrum*, May 21, 2015, https://www.spectrumnews.org/features/deep-dive/unseen-agony
-dismantling-autisms-house-of-pain.

29. Jason Landon, Daniel Shepherd, and Veema Lodhia, "A Qualitative Study of Noise Sensitivity in Adults with Autism Spectrum Disorder," *Research in Autism Spectrum Disorders* 32 (2016): 43–52, https://doi.org/10.1016/j.rasd.2016.08.005.

30. Marian Schembari, *A LITTLE LESS BROKEN* (New York: Flatiron Books, in press).

31. Damian Mellifont, "COVID-19 Related Factors Affecting the Experiences of Neurodivergent Persons in the Workplace: A Rapid Review," *Work* 71, no. 1 (2022): 3–12, https://
doi.org/10.3233/WOR-210811.

32. "Boosting Neurodiverse Employee Wellbeing Post Pandemic," JourneyHR, March 13, 2023, https://www.journeyhr.com/our-views/boosting-neurodiverse-employee-wellbeing
-post-pandemic.

33. Brennan Doherty, "The Pandemic Gave Some Neurodivergent Workers the Office They Need: Now, We're 'Going Backwards,'" *The Globe and Mail*, March 3, 2023, https://

www.theglobeandmail.com/business/careers/article-the-pandemic-gave-some
-neurodiverse-workers-the-office-they-need-now.

34. Charles Freeman, public policy consultant, in discussion with the author, August 2023.

35. Salomon Chiquiar-Rabinovich, attorney, in discussion with the author, August 2023.

36. Patrick Dorrian, "Dyslexic HUD Attorney Says He Was Wrongly Fired for Hiring Help," *Bloomberg Law*, July 20, 2020, https://news.bloomberglaw.com/daily-labor-report/dyslexic-hud-attorney-says-he-was-wrongly-fired-for-hiring-help.

37. Anne M., autistic manager, in discussion with the author, August 2023.

38. Christina Ryan, founder, Disability Leadership Institute, in discussion with the author, August 2023.

39. Allie Nawrat, "Autistic Workers Have the Largest Disability Pay Gap," UNLEASH, April 26, 2022, https://www.unleash.ai/diversity-equity-inclusion/autistic-workers-have
-the-largest-disability-pay-gap.

40. "Disability Pay Gaps in the UK: 2021," Office for National Statistics, April 25, 2022, https://www.ons.gov.uk/peoplepopulationandcommunity/healthandsocialcare/disability/articles/disabilitypaygapsintheuk/2021.

41. Jennifer Cheeseman Day and Danielle Taylor, "In Most Occupations, Workers with or without Disabilities Earn about the Same," US Census Bureau, March 21, 2019, https://www.census.gov/library/stories/2019/03/do-people-with-disabilities-earn-equal-pay.html.

42. Barbara Kornblau, Scott Robertson, and Sarah Mbiza, "Autistic Adults' Perceptions of Barriers to Work," *American Journal of Occupational Therapy* 73, no. S1 (2019).

43. Fabian Frank, Martina Jablotschkin, Tobias Arthen, Andreas Riedel, Thomas Fangmeier, Lars P. Hölzel, and Ludger Tebartz van Elst, "Education and Employment Status of Adults with Autism Spectrum Disorders in Germany—A Cross-Sectional-Survey," *BMC Psychiatry* 18, no. 1 (2018): 75, https://doi.org/10.1186/s12888-018-1645-7.

44. Henri V. Pesonen, Tarja Tuononen, Marc Fabri, and Minja Lahdelma, "Autistic Graduates: Graduate Capital and Employability," *Journal of Education and Work* 35, no. 4 (2022): 374–89, https://doi.org/10.1080/13639080.2022.2059455.

45. Vicky Caron, Nuria Jeanneret, Mathieu Giroux, Lucila Guerrero, Mélanie Ouimet, Baudouin Forgeot d'Arc, Isabelle Soulières, and Isabelle Courcy, "Sociocultural Context and Autistics' Quality of Life: A Comparison between Québec and France," *Autism* 26, no. 4 (2022): 900–913, https://doi.org/10.1177/13623613211035229.

46. June L. Chen, Geraldine Leader, Connie Sung, and Michael Leahy, "Trends in Employment for Individuals with Autism Spectrum Disorder: A Review of the Research Literature," *Review Journal of Autism and Developmental Disorders* 2, no. 2 (2015): 115–27, https://doi.org/10.1007/s40489-014-0041-6.

47. James Mahoney, "J. P. Morgan: Autism at Work," Vercida, accessed August 10, 2023, https://resources.vercida.com/jpmorgan-autism-at-work.

48. Martin Silvertant, "Autistics Work Hard," *Embrace Autism* (blog), March 2, 2023, https://embrace-autism.com/autistics-work-hard.

49. Robert D. Austin and Gary P. Pisano, "Neurodiversity as a Competitive Advantage," *Harvard Business Review*, May 1, 2017, https://hbr.org/2017/05/neurodiversity-as-a
-competitive-advantage.

50. Elizabeth Morey, "6 Ways Companies Could Be Exploiting Employees on the Autism Spectrum," *Autism Site News*, July 13, 2018, https://blog.theautismsite.greatergood.com/workplace-exploitation.

51. Shirin Ali, "Workers with Disabilities Could Be Paid Higher Wages with Biden's Build Back Better Plan," *Changing America* (blog), The Hill, December 13, 2021, https://thehill.com/changing-america/respect/accessibility/585591-workers-with-disabilities-could-be-paid-higher-wages.

52. Amii Barnard-Bahn, "How to Identify—and Fix—Pay Inequality at Your Company," *Harvard Business Review*, November 3, 2020, https://hbr.org/2020/11/how-to-identify-and-fix-pay-inequality-at-your-company.

53. Emilio J. Castilla, "Accounting for the Gap: A Firm Study Manipulating Organizational Accountability and Transparency in Pay Decisions," *Organization Science* 26, no. 2 (2015): 311–33, https://doi.org/10.1287/orsc.2014.0950.

54. Daniel Laurison and Sam Friedman, "The Class Pay Gap in Higher Professional and Managerial Occupations," *American Sociological Review* 81, no. 4 (2016): 668–95, https://doi.org/10.1177/0003122416653602.

CHAPTER SIX

1. Alan Bainbridge, "How BBC's Cardiff Building Considers Neurodiversity in Creating an Inclusive Workplace," *Architects' Journal*, June 3, 2019, https://www.architectsjournal.co.uk/news/opinion/how-bbcs-cardiff-building-considers-neurodiversity-in-creating-an-inclusive-workplace.

2. Ike Ijeh, "Projects: New Broadcasting House, BBC Cymru Wales, Cardiff," *Building*, February 19, 2020, https://www.building.co.uk/buildings/projects-new-broadcasting-house-bbc-cymru-wales-cardiff/5104374.article.

3. Tristan Lavender, senior content strategist, founder and chair of the Philips Employee Resource Group, in discussion with the author, June 2023.

4. Thomas Parkinson, Stefano Schiavon, Richard de Dear, and Gail Brager, "Overcooling of Offices Reveals Gender Inequity in Thermal Comfort," *Scientific Reports* 11, no. 1 (2021): 23684, https://doi.org/10.1038/s41598-021-03121-1.

5. Tom Y. Chang and Agne Kajackaite, "Battle for the Thermostat: Gender and the Effect of Temperature on Cognitive Performance," *PLOS ONE* 14, no. 5 (2019): e0216362, https://doi.org/10.1371/journal.pone.0216362.

6. Boris Kingma and Wouter van Marken Lichtenbelt, "Energy Consumption in Buildings and Female Thermal Demand," *Nature Climate Change* 5, no. 12 (2015): 1054–56, https://doi.org/10.1038/nclimate2741.

7. Ed Dupree, business data analyst, in discussion with the author, April 2023.

8. Ethan S. Bernstein and Stephen Turban, "The Impact of the 'Open' Workspace on Human Collaboration," *Philosophical Transactions of the Royal Society B: Biological Sciences* 373, no. 1753 (2018): 20170239, https://doi.org/10.1098/rstb.2017.0239.

9. Christina Bodin Danielsson, "Office Type's Association to Employees' Welfare: Three Studies," *Work* 54, no. 4 (2016): 779–90, https://doi.org/10.3233/WOR-162361.

10. Jungsoo Kim and Richard de Dear, "Workspace Satisfaction: The Privacy-Communication Trade-Off in Open-Plan Offices," *Journal of Environmental Psychology* 36 (2013): 18–26, https://doi.org/10.1016/j.jenvp.2013.06.007.

11. Vinesh Oommen, Mike Knowles, and Isabella Zhao, "Should Health Service Managers Embrace Open Plan Work Environments? A Review," *Asia Pacific Journal of Health Management* 3, no. 2 (2008): 37–43.

12. Morlagh Shafiee Masoud, Rostam Golmohammadi, Mohsen Aliabadi, Javad Faradmal, and Akram Ranjbar, "Empirical Study of Room Acoustic Conditions and Neurophysiologic Strain in Staff Working in Special Open-Plan Bank Offices," *Acoustics Australia* 46, no. 3 (2018): 329–38, https://doi.org/10.1007/s40857-018-0143-x.

13. Libby (Elizabeth) Sander, "The Research on Hot-Desking and Activity-Based Work Isn't So Positive," *The Conversation*, April 11, 2017, http://theconversation.com/the-research -on-hot-desking-and-activity-based-work-isnt-so-positive-75612.

14. Alena Maher and Courtney von Hippel, "Individual Differences in Employee Reactions to Open-Plan Offices," *Journal of Environmental Psychology* 25, no. 2 (2005): 219–29, https://doi.org/10.1016/j.jenvp.2005.05.002.

15. Tonya Smith-Jackson, Rodney Middlebrooks, John Francis, Tiara Gray, Kaleb Nelson, Briana Steele, Kionda Townsend, and Cedric Watlington, "Open Plan Offices as Sociotechnical Systems: What Matters and to Whom?," *Work* 54, no. 4 (2016): 807–23, https://doi.org/10.3233/WOR-162362.

16. American Psychiatric Association, *Diagnostic and Statistical Manual of Mental Disorders*, 5th ed. (Washington, DC: American Psychiatric Publishing, 2013).

17. Monique Botha and David M. Frost, "Extending the Minority Stress Model to Understand Mental Health Problems Experienced by the Autistic Population," *Society and Mental Health* 10, no. 1 (2020): 20–34, https://doi.org/10.1177/2156869318804297.

18. Jin-Ha Yoon, Jong-Uk Won, Wanhyung Lee, Pil Kyun Jung, and Jaehoon Roh, "Occupational Noise Annoyance Linked to Depressive Symptoms and Suicidal Ideation: A Result from Nationwide Survey of Korea," *PLoS ONE* 9, no. 8 (2014): e105321, https:// doi.org/10.1371/journal.pone.0105321.

19. S. M. Barreto, A. J. Swerdlow, P. G. Smith, and C. D. Higgins, "Risk of Death from Motor-Vehicle Injury in Brazilian Steelworkers: A Nested Case-Control Study," *International Journal of Epidemiology* 26, no. 4 (1997): 814–21, https://doi.org/10.1093/ije /26.4.814.

20. Anne Cosgrove, "Revived Breakroom Makes a Splash with Employees," Facility Executive Magazine, *FacilityBlog* (blog), March 22, 2018, https://facilityexecutive.com/revived -breakroom-makes-a-splash-with-employees.

21. Michael Quine, "Zappos, 'Tanked' Crew Come up Big with Nap Room in Las Vegas," *Las Vegas Review-Journal*, December 22, 2017, https://www.reviewjournal.com/business /zappos-tanked-crew-come-up-big-with-nap-room-in-las-vegas.

22. David Putrino, Jonathan Ripp, Joseph E. Herrera, Mar Cortes, Christopher Kellner, Dahlia Rizk, and Kristen Dams-O'Connor, "Multisensory, Nature-Inspired Recharge Rooms Yield Short-Term Reductions in Perceived Stress among Frontline Healthcare Workers," *Frontiers in Psychology* 11 (2020), https://www.frontiersin.org/articles/10.3389 /fpsyg.2020.560833.

23. Fortesa Latifi, "Spoon Theory: What It Is and How I Use It to Manage Chronic Illness," *Washington Post*, January 14, 2023, sec. Well+Being Body, https://www.washingtonpost .com/wellness/2023/01/14/spoon-theory-chronic-illness-spoonie.

24. Baylee Kalmbach, "A COVID Silver Lining? How Telework May Be a Reasonable Accommodation after All," *University of Cincinnati Law Review* 90, no. 4 (2022): 1294–1321.

25. Cevat Giray Aksoy, Jose Maria Barrero, Nicholas Bloom, Steven J. Davis, Mathias Dolls, and Pablo Zarate, "Time Savings When Working from Home," *AEA Papers and Proceedings* 113 (2023): 597–603, https://doi.org/10.1257/pandp.20231013.

26. Gleb Tsipursky, "The Forced Return to the Office Is the Definition of Insanity," *Fortune*, June 26, 2023, https://fortune.com/2023/06/26/forced-return-to-office-is-the-definition-of-insanity-remote-hybrid-work-careers-gleb-tsipursky.

27. Kessler Foundation, "NTIDE August 2022 Jobs Report: Employment Indicators Virtually Unchanged for People with Disabilities despite Concerns about Recession," August 2022, https://kesslerfoundation.org/press-release/ntide-august-2022-jobs-report-employment-indicators-virtually-unchanged-people.

28. Brennan Doherty, "The Pandemic Gave Some Neurodivergent Workers the Office They Need: Now, We're 'Going Backwards,'" *The Globe and Mail*, March 1, 2023, https://www.theglobeandmail.com/business/careers/article-the-pandemic-gave-some-neurodiverse-workers-the-office-they-need-now.

29. Jane Thier, "Flexibility, Not the Office, Improves Culture and Productivity at Work," *Fortune*, February 15, 2023, https://fortune.com/2023/02/15/remote-work-culture-productivity-slack-future-forum/?queryly=related_article.

30. Tapas K. Ray and Regina Pana-Cryan, "Work Flexibility and Work-Related Well-Being," *International Journal of Environmental Research and Public Health* 18, no. 6 (2021): 3254, https://doi.org/10.3390/ijerph18063254.

31. McKinsey & Company, "Americans Are Embracing Flexible Work—and They Want More of It," June 23, 2022, https://www.mckinsey.com/industries/real-estate/our-insights/americans-are-embracing-flexible-work-and-they-want-more-of-it.

32. Pamela Hinds and Brian Elliott, "WFH Doesn't Have to Dilute Your Corporate Culture," *Harvard Business Review*, February 1, 2021,

33. Weronika Niemczyk, "4 Ways Remote Work Has Improved Company Culture," Enterprisers Project, December 2, 2022, https://enterprisersproject.com/article/2022/12/remote-work-improve-company-culture.

34. Mark C. Bolino and Corey Phelps, "Case Study: Should Some Employees Be Allowed to Work Remotely Even If Others Can't?," *Harvard Business Review*, January 2023,

35. Emma Goldberg, "How Remote Work Connected Employees Making $19 an Hour and $80,000 a Year," *New York Times*, May 31, 2023, sec. Business, https://www.nytimes.com/2023/05/31/business/work-home-return-office-amazon.html.

36. Sarah Chaney Cambon and Andrew Mollica, "Remote Work Sticks for All Kinds of Jobs," *Wall Street Journal*, July 4, 2023, sec. Economy, https://www.wsj.com/articles/remote-work-sticks-for-all-kinds-of-jobs-db9786ee.

37. Gleb Tsipursky, "Newsflash: Even Frontline Employees Can Reap the Benefits of Remote Work," *Fast Company*, April 19, 2023, https://www.fastcompany.com/90883362/frontline-employees-remote-work.

38. Christine Sinsky, Lacey Colligan, Ling Li, Mirela Prgomet, Sam Reynolds, Lindsey Goeders, Johanna Westbrook, Michael Tutty, and George Blike, "Allocation of Physician Time in Ambulatory Practice: A Time and Motion Study in 4 Specialties," *Annals of Internal Medicine* 165, no. 11 (2016): 753–60, https://doi.org/10.7326/M16-0961.

39. Bernie Monegain, "Survey Shows Nurses Spend Most of Their Time on Paperwork," *Healthcare IT News*, March 9, 2010, https://www.healthcareitnews.com/news/survey-shows-nurses-spend-most-their-time-paperwork.

40. Stephen Hansen, Peter John Lambert, Nicholas Bloom, Steven J. Davis, Raffaella Sadun, and Bledi Taska, "Remote Work across Jobs, Companies, and Space," Working Paper, National Bureau of Economic Research, 2023, https://doi.org/10.3386/w31007.

41. Erin Ney, Michael Brookshire, and Joshua Weisbrod, "A Treatment for America's Health-care Worker Burnout," Bain & Company, October 11, 2022, https://www.bain.com/insights/a-treatment-for-americas-healthcare-worker-burnout.

42. Arlene S. Hirsch, "Preventing Proximity Bias in a Hybrid Workplace," SHRM, March 22, 2022, https://www.shrm.org/resourcesandtools/hr-topics/employee-relations/pages/preventing-proximity-bias-in-a-hybrid-workplace.aspx.

43. Gleb Tsipursky, "What Is Proximity Bias and How Can Managers Prevent It?," *Harvard Business Review*, October 4, 2022, https://hbr.org/2022/10/what-is-proximity-bias-and-how-can-managers-prevent-it.

44. Gloria Martin-Lowery, "How Proximity Bias May Be Secretly Cutting into Your Career Advancement," *Fast Company*, August 27, 2022, https://www.fastcompany.com/90781064/how-proximity-bias-may-be-secretly-cutting-into-your-career-advancement.

45. Kimberly D. Elsbach, Dan M. Cable, and Jeffrey W. Sherman, "How Passive 'Face Time' Affects Perceptions of Employees: Evidence of Spontaneous Trait Inference," *Human Relations* 63, no. 6 (2010): 735–60, https://doi.org/10.1177/0018726709353139.

46. Nicholas A. Bloom, James Liang, John Roberts, and Zhichun Jenny Ying, "Does Working from Home Work? Evidence from a Chinese Experiment," *Quarterly Journal of Economics* 130, no. 1 (2014): 165–218, https://doi.org/10.1093/qje/qju032.

47. Edmund L. Andrews, "The Pandemic Blew Up the American Office—For Better and Worse," Stanford Graduate School of Business, June 3, 2023, https://www.gsb.stanford.edu/insights/pandemic-blew-american-office-better-worse.

48. Enda Curran, "Work from Home to Lift Productivity by 5% in Post-pandemic U.S.," Bloomberg.com, April 22, 2021, https://www.bloomberg.com/news/articles/2021-04-22/yes-working-from-home-makes-you-more-productive-study-finds.

49. Timothy D. Golden and Kimberly A. Eddleston, "Is There a Price Telecommuters Pay? Examining the Relationship between Telecommuting and Objective Career Success," *Journal of Vocational Behavior* 116 (Part A, 2020): 103348, https://doi.org/10.1016/j.jvb.2019.103348.

50. Ioana C. Cristea and Paul M. Leonardi, "Get Noticed and Die Trying: Signals, Sacrifice, and the Production of Face Time in Distributed Work," *Organization Science* 30, no. 3 (2019): 552–72, https://doi.org/10.1287/orsc.2018.1265.

51. Joan C. Williams, Rachel M. Korn, and Mikayla Boginsky, "Don't Lose the Democratizing Effect of Remote Work," *Harvard Business Review*, August 4, 2021, https://hbr.org/2021/08/dont-lose-the-democratizing-effect-of-remote-work.

52. Shane McFeely and Ben Wigert, "This Fixable Problem Costs U.S. Businesses $1 Trillion," Gallup, March 13, 2019, https://www.gallup.com/workplace/247391/fixable-problem-costs-businesses-trillion.aspx.

CHAPTER SEVEN

1. Caroline Stokes, founder of Forward, in discussion with the author, April 2023.

2. W. Edwards Deming, *Out of the Crisis*, repr. ed. (Cambridge, MA: MIT Press, 2018).

3. Ellen Ernst Kossek, Patricia Gettings, and Kaumudi Misra, "The Future of Flexibility at Work," *Harvard Business Review*, September 28, 2021, https://hbr.org/2021/09/the-future-of-flexibility-at-work.

4. Ludmila N. Praslova, "Flexibility in the Workplace and Unlocking Neurodiversity Inclusion," *Specialisterne* (blog), March 27, 2023, https://ca.specialisterne.com/flexibility-in-the-workplace-and-unlocking-neurodiversity-inclusion.

5. Lockton Global Compliance, "New Remote Working Legislation around the World," Lockton Global Benefits, June 28, 2023, https://globalnews.lockton.com/new-remote-working-legislation-around-the-world.

6. Maddy Savage, "Why Finland Leads the World in Flexible Work," *BBC Worklife*, August 8, 2019, https://www.bbc.com/worklife/article/20190807-why-finland-leads-the-world-in-flexible-work.

7. Anna Sophie Hahne, *The Impact of Teleworking and Digital Work on Workers and Society—Case Study on Finland (Annex III)* (Luxembourg: Policy Department for Economic, Scientific and Quality of Life Policies, European Parliament, 2021), https://www.europarl.europa.eu/RegData/etudes/STUD/2021/662904/IPOL_STU(2021)662904(ANN01)_EN.pdf.

8. "Federal Employees—Flexible Work Schedules," US Office of Personnel Management, accessed July 20, 2023, https://www.opm.gov/policy-data-oversight/pay-leave/work-schedules/fact-sheets/alternative-flexible-work-schedules.

9. "Lockheed Martin Reviews: What Is It Like to Work at Lockheed Martin?," Glassdoor, September 7, 2022, https://www.glassdoor.com/Reviews/Lockheed-Martin-Reviews-E404.htm. Glassdoor is an anonymous review site on which employees or former employees can rate their organizations.

10. "Life at Lockheed Martin," Lockheed Martin, accessed July 20, 2023. https://www.lockheedmartin.com/en-gb/careers/life-at-lockheed-martin.html.

11. "100-80-100™," 4 Day Week Global, accessed July 20, 2023, https://www.4dayweek.com/100-80-100.

12. Bill Chappell, "4-Day Workweek Boosted Workers' Productivity by 40%, Microsoft Japan Says," *NPR*, November 4, 2019, https://www.npr.org/2019/11/04/776163853/microsoft-japan-says-4-day-workweek-boosted-workers-productivity-by-40.

13. Steve Glaveski, "The Case for the 6-Hour Workday," *Harvard Business Review*, December 11, 2018, https://hbr.org/2018/12/the-case-for-the-6-hour-workday.

14. Giulia Carbonaro, "Are Six-Hour Workdays the New Four-Day Workweek?," *Euronews*, August 4, 2022, https://www.euronews.com/next/2022/07/27/is-the-6-hour-workday-the-answer-to-a-better-work-life-balance.

15. Rajesh Anandan, CEO, Ultranauts, in discussion with the author, March 2023.

16. Amy Bach, "The Zoom Revolution Largely Benefited Men: Is Job Sharing the Way Forward for Women's Workplace Flexibility?," *The Guardian*, January 15, 2023, sec. Opinion, https://www.theguardian.com/commentisfree/2023/jan/16/the-zoom-revolution-largely-benefited-men-is-job-sharing-the-way-forward-for-womens-workplace-flexibility.

17. Ludmila N. Praslova, "The Great Win-Win: Supporting Neurodivergent Employees in Job Crafting," *Specialisterne* (blog), February 23, 2023, https://us.specialisterne.com/the-great-win-win-supporting-neurodivergent-employees-in-job-crafting.

18. "Global Survey: The Workplace Is Failing a Major Demographic," Alludo, accessed July 20, 2023, https://www.alludo.com/en/newsroom/news/data-insights/neurodiversity-at-work-report.

19. "Alludo Survey: Neurodivergent Workers Significantly Enrich Companies' Capacity for Innovation, Problem-Solving, Yet Remain Overlooked by Employers," Alludo,

March 30, 2023, https://www.alludo.com/en/newsroom/press-releases/20230330
-neurodivergent-workers.

20. Natalie Marchant, "Zurich Added These 6 Words to Job Adverts and More Women Applied," World Economic Forum, December 8, 2020, https://www.weforum.org/agenda
/2020/12/zurich-flexible-working-women-diversity.

21. "Zurich Sees Leap in Women Applying for Senior Roles," Zurich UK, November 17, 2020, https://www.zurich.co.uk/media-centre/zurich-sees-leap-in-women-applying-for
-senior-roles-after-offering-all-jobs-as-flexible.

22. "Maternity Leave by Country 2023," World Population Review, 2023, https://
worldpopulationreview.com/country-rankings/maternity-leave-by-country.

23. Kira Schabram, Matt Bloom, and DJ DiDonna, "Research: The Transformative Power of Sabbaticals," *Harvard Business Review*, February 22, 2023, https://hbr.org/2023/02
/research-the-transformative-power-of-sabbaticals.

24. Kellie Scott and Matt Ryan, "Adult Gap Year: 'I'd Slipped into the Monotony of the Daily Grind,'" *ABC Everyday*, updated August 26, 2019, https://www.abc.net.au
/everyday/taking-a-career-break-for-an-adult-gap-year/9938100.

25. Country Herald National, "Are You Suffering from Burnout? Here's How Germany's Policies Could Help Americans," *Country Herald*, March 14, 2023, https://www
.countryherald.com/news/health/are-you-suffering-from-burnout-heres-how-germanys
-policies-could-help-americans.

26. Beth Winegarner, "'The Battery's Dead': Burnout Looks Different in Autistic Adults," *New York Times*, October 14, 2021, https://www.nytimes.com/2021/09/03/well/live
/autistic-burnout-advice.html.

27. Dora M. Raymaker, Alan R. Teo, Nicole A. Steckler, Brandy Lentz, Mirah Scharer, Austin Delos Santos, Steven K. Kapp, Morrigan Hunter, Andee Joyce, and Christina Nicolaidis, "'Having All of Your Internal Resources Exhausted beyond Measure and Being Left with No Clean-Up Crew': Defining Autistic Burnout," *Autism in Adulthood Knowledge Practice and Policy* 2, no. 2 (2020): 132–43, https://doi.org/10.1089/aut.2019.0079.

28. Shevonne Joyce, head of business strategy and innovation, in discussion with the author, June 2023.

29. Jeremy N. Bailenson, "Nonverbal Overload: A Theoretical Argument for the Causes of Zoom Fatigue," *Technology, Mind, and Behavior* 2 (2021), https://doi.org/10.1037
/tmb0000030.

30. John Lacy, "Slack and Zoom Were Distracting Our Teams: Here's How We Regained Focus," *Fast Company*, January 5, 2021, https://www.fastcompany.com/90588307/slack
-and-zoom-were-distracting-our-teams-heres-how-we-regained-focus.

31. Christina Rouvalis, "Neurodiverse Employees May Need Accommodations for Remote Work," SHRM, June 12, 2020, https://www.shrm.org/resourcesandtools/hr-topics
/employee-relations/pages/neurodiverse-employees-may-need-accommodations-for
-remote-work.aspx.

32. Adam Grant, "Your Email Does Not Constitute My Emergency," *New York Times*, April 13, 2023, sec. Opinion, https://www.nytimes.com/2023/04/13/opinion/email
-time-work-stress.html.

33. Ben Laker, Vijay Pereira, Pawan Budhwar, and Ashish Malik, "The Surprising Impact of Meeting-Free Days," *MIT Sloan Management Review*, January 18, 2022, https://
sloanreview.mit.edu/article/the-surprising-impact-of-meeting-free-days.

34. John Rampton, "The Psychological Price of Meetings," *Productivity Center* (blog), May 7, 2019, https://www.calendar.com/blog/the-psychological-price-of-meetings.

35. Oshin Vartanian, Sidney Ann Saint, Nicole Herz, and Peter Suedfeld, "The Creative Brain under Stress: Considerations for Performance in Extreme Environments," *Frontiers in Psychology* 11 (2020), https://www.frontiersin.org/articles/10.3389/fpsyg.2020 .585969.

36. Alludo, *Neurodivergent at Work Survey Report*, 2023, https://www.alludo.com/static/all /pdfs/newsroom/data-insights/neurodiversity-at-work-report/neurodivergent-at-work -survey-report.pdf.

37. Chunyan Meng, Chao Huo, Hongxin Ge, Zuoshan Li, Yuanyan Hu, and Jing Meng, "Processing of Expressions by Individuals with Autistic Traits: Empathy Deficit or Sensory Hyper-reactivity?," *PLOS ONE* 16, no. 7 (2021): e0254207, https://doi.org/10 .1371/journal.pone.0254207.

38. Florence Neville, "Reacting, Retreating, Regulating and Reconnecting: Summary of Study Findings," *Autism HWB* (blog), February 18, 2022, https://autismhwb.com /reacting-retreating-regulating-and-reconnecting.

39. Steve Glaveski, "Remote Work Should Be (Mostly) Asynchronous," *Harvard Business Review*, December 1, 2021, https://hbr.org/2021/12/remote-work-should-be-mostly -asynchronous.

40. Gloria Mark, Shamsi T. Iqbal, Mary Czerwinski, Paul Johns, Akane Sano, and Yuliya Lutchyn, "Email Duration, Batching and Self-Interruption: Patterns of Email Use on Productivity and Stress," in *Proceedings of the 2016 CHI Conference on Human Factors in Computing Systems* (San Jose, CA: ACM, 2016), 1717–28, https://doi.org/10.1145 /2858036.2858262.

41. Dovico, "Time Management Facts and Figures," *Dovico Blog*, March 6, 2018, https:// www.dovico.com/blog/2018/03/06/time-management-facts-figures.

42. Steve Glaveski, "10 Quick Tips for Avoiding Distractions at Work," *Harvard Business Review*, December 18, 2019, https://hbr.org/2019/12/10-quick-tips-for-avoiding -distractions-at-work.

43. Susan M. Hayward, Keith R. McVilly, and Mark A. Stokes, "Challenges for Females with High Functioning Autism in the Workplace: A Systematic Review," *Disability and Rehabilitation* 40, no. 3 (2016): 249–58, https://doi.org/10.1080/09638288.2016 .1254284.

44. Cal Newport, *Deep Work: Rules for Focused Success in a Distracted World* (London: Piatkus Books, 2016).

45. Ludmila N. Praslova, "Life Should Come First in Life-Work Balance," *Psychology Today*, January 13, 2022, https://www.psychologytoday.com/us/blog/positively-different /202201/life-should-come-first-in-life-work-balance.

46. Nir Eyal, "Managers, Stop Distracting Your Employees," *Harvard Business Review*, January 12, 2023, https://hbr.org/2023/01/managers-stop-distracting-your-employees.

47. Ludmila N. Praslova, "From Frazzled to Flow: Neurodiversity, Inclusion, and Enabling the Best Work," *Specialisterne* (blog), April 19, 2023. https://ca.specialisterne.com/from -frazzled-to-flow-neurodiversity-inclusion-and-enabling-the-best-work.

48. Kathryn Moody, "One Company Canceled All Meetings for a Month: Employees Felt More Productive," *HR Dive*, January 13, 2023, https://www.hrdive.com/news/one -company-canceled-all-meetings-employees-more-productive/640383.

49. Ludmila N. Praslova, "An Intersectional Approach to Inclusion at Work," *Harvard Business Review*, June 21, 2022, https://hbr.org/2022/06/an-intersectional-approach-to-inclusion-at-work.

50. Ryan Wong, "'Productivity Theater' Is Officially out of Control at Work: Here's How to Prevent It," *Fast Company*, April 21, 2023, https://www.fastcompany.com/90884412/productivity-theater-is-officially-out-of-control-at-work-heres-how-to-prevent-it.

51. David Allen and Justin Hale, "7 Ways Managers Can Help Their Team Focus," *Harvard Business Review*, January 24, 2023, https://hbr.org/2023/01/7-ways-managers-can-help-their-team-focus.

52. Greg McKeown, "To Build a Top Performing Team, Ask for 85% Effort," *Harvard Business Review*, June 8, 2023, https://hbr.org/2023/06/to-build-a-top-performing-team-ask-for-85-effort.

53. Karina Nielsen, Morten B. Nielsen, Chidiebere Ogbonnaya, Marja Känsälä, Eveliina Saari, and Kerstin Isaksson, "Workplace Resources to Improve Both Employee Well-Being and Performance: A Systematic Review and Meta-analysis," *Work & Stress* 31, no. 2 (2017): 101–20, https://doi.org/10.1080/02678373.2017.1304463.

54. Aruna Ranganathan, "Research: Asynchronous Work Can Fuel Creativity," *Harvard Business Review*, April 17, 2023, https://hbr.org/2023/04/research-asynchronous-work-can-fuel-creativity.

55. John Shumway, "Rethinking How We Work: ROWE or 'Results Only Work Environments' Beginning to Pop Up," CBS News, August 31, 2022, https://www.cbsnews.com/pittsburgh/news/rethinking-how-we-work-rowe-or-results-only-work-environments-beginning-to-pop-up.

56. Sean Peek, "Is a Results-Only Workplace Right for Your Business?," Business.Com, March 23, 2023, https://www.business.com/articles/do-results-only-workplaces-really-work.

57. Kathryn Vasel, "These Employers Don't Care When or Where You Work," CNN Business, October 18, 2019, https://www.cnn.com/2019/10/18/success/results-only-work-place/index.html.

58. Ludmila N. Praslova, "Today's Most Critical Workplace Challenges Are about Systems," *Harvard Business Review*, January 10, 2023, https://hbr.org/2023/01/todays-most-critical-workplace-challenges-are-about-systems.

59. Rob Cross, Reb Rebele, and Adam Grant, "Collaborative Overload," *Harvard Business Review*, January 1, 2016, https://hbr.org/2016/01/collaborative-overload.

60. Amanda Crowell, "There's One Kind of Employee Who Is Vastly Under-appreciated in Most Modern Offices," *Quartz*, March 21, 2017, https://qz.com/938169/introverts-are-the-secret-weapons-of-the-modern-office.

61. Ludmila N. Praslova, "2 Things Most People Get Wrong about Autistic Talent," *Fast Company*, March 30, 2023, https://www.fastcompany.com/90872761/things-people-get-wrong-autistic-talent.

62. Ludmila N. Praslova, "Autism Doesn't Hold People Back at Work: Discrimination Does," *Harvard Business Review*, December 13, 2021, https://hbr.org/2021/12/autism-doesnt-hold-people-back-at-work-discrimination-does.

63. Eilidh Cage and Zoe Troxell-Whitman, "Understanding the Reasons, Contexts and Costs of Camouflaging for Autistic Adults," *Journal of Autism and Developmental Disorders* 49, no. 5 (2019): 1899–1911, https://doi.org/10.1007/s10803-018-03878-x.

64. Ludmila N. Praslova, "Feeling Distressed at Work? It Might Be More than Burnout," *Fast Company*, January 14, 2022, https://www.fastcompany.com/90712671/feeling -distressed-at-work-it-might-be-more-than-burnout.

65. Ludmila N. Praslova, "Moral Injury at Work and Neurodiversity: Are There Additional Risk Factors?," *Specialisterne* (blog), February 1, 2022, https://ca.specialisterne.com/moral -injury-at-work-and-neurodiversity-are-there-additional-risk-factors.

66. Yang Hu, Alessandra M. Pereira, Xiaoxue Gao, Brunno M. Campos, Edmund Der- rington, Brice Corgnet, Xiaolin Zhou, Fernando Cendes, and Jean-Claude Dreher, "Right Temporoparietal Junction Underlies Avoidance of Moral Transgression in Autism Spectrum Disorder," *Journal of Neuroscience* 41, no. 8 (2021): 1699–1715, https://doi .org/10.1523/JNEUROSCI.1237-20.2020.

67. "How to Stop People from Dominating Meetings," Kellogg School of Management, June 26, 2014, https://www.kellogg.northwestern.edu/news_articles/2014/06262014 -video-thompson-brainwriting.aspx.

68. "Nurturing Original Ideas at the Workplace: The Importance of Brainwriting and Re- fining," Moneycontrol, accessed July 20, 2023, https://www.moneycontrol.com/europe /news/trends/lifestyle-trends/nurturing-original-ideas-at-the-workplace-the -importance-of-brainwriting-and-refining-9156481.html.

69. Heather Gilmartin, Emily Lawrence, Chelsea Leonard, Marina McCreight, Lynette Kel- ley, Brandi Lippmann, Andrew Coy, and Robert E. Burke, "Brainwriting Premortem," *Journal of Nursing Care Quality* 34, no. 2 (2019): 94–100, https://doi.org/10.1097/NCQ .0000000000000360.

70. Association for Psychological Science, "There's a Better Way to Brainstorm," March 15, 2016, https://www.psychologicalscience.org/news/minds-business/theres-a-better-way-to -brainstorm.html.

71. Gleb Tsipursky, "Why Virtual Brainstorming Is Better for Innovation," *Harvard Busi- ness Review*, February 3, 2022, https://hbr.org/2022/02/why-virtual-brainstorming-is -better-for-innovation.

72. Tomas Chamorro-Premuzic, "Why Brainstorming Works Better Online," *Harvard Busi- ness Review*, April 2, 2015, https://hbr.org/2015/04/why-brainstorming-works-better -online.

73. Alexandra Samuel, "Collaborating Online Is Sometimes Better than Face-to-Face," *Har- vard Business Review*, April 1, 2015, https://hbr.org/2015/04/collaborating-online-is -sometimes-better-than-face-to-face.

74. Deming, *Out of the Crisis*, 101.

CHAPTER EIGHT

1. Shivani Chaudhari, "Lewis Capaldi's Gladstonbury Performance Gets Support from Community," *Worcester News*, June 26, 2023, https://www.worcesternews.co.uk/news /23614726.lewis-capaldis-glastonbury-performance-gets-support-community.

2. Aisha Nozari, "Lewis Capaldi's Glastonbury Set Makes Mum of Teenage Boy with To- urette's Cry," *Metro*, June 25, 2023, sec. Entertainment, https://metro.co.uk/2023/06 /25/lewis-capaldis-glastonbury-set-makes-mum-of-teen-with-tourettes-cry-19011317.

3. Donald Sull, Charles Sull, William Cipolli, and Caio Brighenti, "Why Every Leader Needs to Worry about Toxic Culture," *MIT Sloan Management Review*, March 16, 2022, https://sloanreview.mit.edu/article/why-every-leader-needs-to-worry-about-toxic-culture.

4. Janice Mandel, president of String Communications, Toronto, in discussion with the author, August 2023.

5. Tonya Eckert, "Managers Impact Our Mental Health More than Doctors, Therapists—and Same as Spouses," UKG, January 24, 2023, https://www.ukg.com/about-us/newsroom/managers-impact-our-mental-health-more-doctors-therapists-and-same-spouses.

6. Samantha Fuld, "Autism Spectrum Disorder: The Impact of Stressful and Traumatic Life Events and Implications for Clinical Practice," *Clinical Social Work Journal* 46, no. 3 (2018): 210–19, https://doi.org/10.1007/s10615-018-0649-6.

7. Linda Roloff, disability support professional, in discussion with the author, August 2023.

8. Donald Sull and Charles Sull, "How to Fix a Toxic Culture," *MIT Sloan Management Review*, September 28, 2022. https://sloanreview.mit.edu/article/how-to-fix-a-toxic-culture.

9. Ludmila N. Praslova, "Today's Most Critical Workplace Challenges Are about Systems," *Harvard Business Review*, January 10, 2023, https://hbr.org/2023/01/todays-most-critical-workplace-challenges-are-about-systems.

10. Ludmila N. Praslova, Ron Carucci, and Caroline Stokes, "How Bullying Manifests at Work—and How to Stop It," *Harvard Business Review*, November 4, 2022, https://hbr.org/2022/11/how-bullying-manifests-at-work-and-how-to-stop-it.

11. Ludmila N. Praslova, Ron Carucci, and Caroline Stokes, "What to Do When a Direct Report Is Bullying You," *Harvard Business Review*, December 8, 2022, https://hbr.org/2022/12/what-to-do-when-a-direct-report-is-bullying-you.

12. Becca Lory Hector, founder of Truly Inclusive Leadership, in discussion with the author, August 2023.

13. "What Is an Organizational Ombuds?," International Ombuds Association, accessed August 14, 2023, https://www.ombudsassociation.org/what-is-an-ombuds-.

14. Wouter Wolf, Jacques Launay, and Robin I. M. Dunbar, "Joint Attention, Shared Goals and Social Bonding," *British Journal of Psychology* 107, no. 2 (2016): 322–37, https://doi.org/10.1111/bjop.12144.

15. Muzafer Sherif, "Superordinate Goals in the Reduction of Intergroup Conflict," *American Journal of Sociology* 63, no. 4 (1958): 349–56.

16. J. Yo-Jud Cheng and Boris Groysberg, "Research: What Inclusive Companies Have in Common," *Harvard Business Review*, June 18, 2021, https://hbr.org/2021/06/research-what-inclusive-companies-have-in-common.

17. Holger Reisinger and Dane Fetterer, "Forget Flexibility: Your Employees Want Autonomy," *Harvard Business Review*, October 29, 2021, https://hbr.org/2021/10/forget-flexibility-your-employees-want-autonomy.

18. Michele McGovern, "The Problems with 'Culture Cliques'—and 5 Ways to Fix Them," HRMorning, February 28, 2023. https://www.hrmorning.com/articles/culture-cliques.

19. Ludmila N. Praslova and Satoris Howes, "Employing a Neurodiverse Workforce: Considerations for Human Resource Management," in *Research in Human Resource Management*, ed. Brian Murray and Deanna Stone (Charlotte, NC: Information Age Publishing, forthcoming).

20. Toni Schmader, Tara C. Dennehy, and Andrew S. Baron, "Why Antibias Interventions (Need Not) Fail," *Perspectives on Psychological Science* 17, no. 5 (2022): 1381–403, https://doi.org/10.1177/17456916211057565.

21. Mark Abadi, "When CEO Satya Nadella Took over Microsoft, He Started Defusing Its Toxic Culture by Handing Each of His Execs a 15-Year-Old Book by a Psychologist," *Business Insider*, October 7, 2018, https://www.businessinsider.com/microsoft-satya -nadella-nonviolent-communication-2018-10.

22. Marshall B. Rosenberg, *Nonviolent Communication: A Language of Life: Life-Changing Tools for Healthy Relationships*, 3rd ed. (Encinitas, CA: PuddleDancer Press, 2015).

23. Ludmila N. Praslova, "Facts and Feelings: Alternatives to Non-Violent Communication and I-Statements in Diverse Workplaces," *Specialisterne* (blog), October 31, 2022, https://ca.specialisterne.com/facts-and-feelings-alternatives-to-non-violent -communication-and-i-statements-in-diverse-workplaces.

24. Jonathan Shay, "Moral Injury," *Psychoanalytic Psychology* 31, no. 2 (2014): 182–91, https://doi.org/10.1037/a0036090.

25. Wendy Dean, Simon Talbot, and Austin Dean, "Reframing Clinician Distress: Moral Injury Not Burnout," *Federal Practitioner* 36, no. 9 (2019): 400.

26. Ludmila N. Praslova, "Feeling Distressed at Work? It Might Be More than Burnout," *Fast Company*, January 14, 2022, https://www.fastcompany.com/90712671/feeling -distressed-at-work-it-might-be-more-than-burnout.

27. Ludmila N. Praslova, "Moral Injury at Work and Neurodiversity: Are There Additional Risk Factors?," *Specialisterne* (blog), February 1, 2022, https://ca.specialisterne.com/moral -injury-at-work-and-neurodiversity-are-there-additional-risk-factors.

28. Ludmila N. Praslova, "The Moral Injury: Coping, Healing, and Post-traumatic Growth," *Specialisterne* (blog), March 25, 2022, https://ca.specialisterne.com/the-moral-injury -coping-healing-and-post-traumatic-growth.

29. Autistic Science Person [pseud.], "Autistic People Care Too Much, Research Says," NeuroClastic, November 7, 2020, https://neuroclastic.com/autistic-people-care-too-much -research-says.

30. Center for Ethical Organizational Cultures, *Volkswagen Cleans up Reputation after Emissions Scandal* (Auburn, AL: Auburn University, n.d.), https://harbert.auburn.edu/binaries /documents/center-for-ethical-organizational-cultures/cases/vw.pdf.

31. "US Outdoor Clothing Brand Patagonia Wins UN Champions of the Earth Award," UN Environment Programme, September 24, 2019, http://www.unep.org/news-and-stories /press-release/us-outdoor-clothing-brand-patagonia-wins-un-champions-earth-award.

32. Douglas Cumming, Chris Firth, John Gathergood, and Neil Stewart, "Work-from-Home and the Risk of Securities Misconduct," *European Financial Management*, May 2023, https://doi.org/10.1111/eufm.12426.

33. David L. Dickinson and David Masclet, "Unethical Decision Making and Sleep Restriction: Experimental Evidence," *Games and Economic Behavior* 141 (2023): 484–502, https://doi.org/10.1016/j.geb.2023.07.004.

34. John Lampton, "Transparency Is the Bedrock of Ethics," *SF Strategic Finance*, September 1, 2019, https://www.sfmagazine.com/articles/2019/september/transparency-is-the -bedrock-of-ethics.

35. Jeffrey Pfeffer and Robert I. Sutton, *The Knowing-Doing Gap: How Smart Companies Turn Knowledge into Action* (Cambridge, MA: Harvard Business Review Press, 2000).

36. Jaclyn M. Jensen, Pankaj C. Patel, and Jana L. Raver, "Is It Better to Be Average? High and Low Performance as Predictors of Employee Victimization," *Journal of Applied Psychology* 99, no. 2 (2014): 296–309, https://doi.org/10.1037/a0034822.

37. *ScienceDaily*, "Children with Autism More Likely to Be Bullied at Home and at School, Study Finds," July 22, 2019, https://www.sciencedaily.com/releases/2019/07/190722085822.htm.

38. Tiffany D. Johnson and Aparna Joshi, "Dark Clouds or Silver Linings? A Stigma Threat Perspective on the Implications of an Autism Diagnosis for Workplace Well-Being," *Journal of Applied Psychology* 101, no. 3 (2016): 430–49, https://doi.org/10.1037/apl0000058.

39. National Autistic Society, *The Autism Employment Gap: Too Much Information in the Workplace* (London: NAS, 2016), https://www.basw.co.uk/system/files/resources/basw_53224-4_0.pdf.

40. Eugene Kim and Theresa M. Glomb, "Get Smarty Pants: Cognitive Ability, Personality, and Victimization," *Journal of Applied Psychology* 95, no. 5 (2010): 889–901, https://doi.org/10.1037/a0019985.

41. Eugene Kim and Theresa Glomb, "Victimization of High Performers: The Roles of Envy and Work Group Identification," *Journal of Applied Psychology* 99, no. 2 (2014), https://doi.org/10.1037/a0035789.

42. Gary Namie, "The Challenge of Workplace Bullying," *Employment Relations Today* 34, no. 2 (2007): 43–51, https://doi.org/10.1002/ert.20151.

43. Christine Porath, "How to Avoid Hiring a Toxic Employee," *Harvard Business Review*, February 3, 2016, https://hbr.org/2016/02/how-to-avoid-hiring-a-toxic-employee.

44. Ludmila N. Praslova, "Workplace Bullying of Autistic People: A Vicious Cycle," *Specialisterne* (blog), April 24, 2022, https://us.specialisterne.com/workplace-bullying-of-autistic-people-a-vicious-cycle.

45. Justin Donne, autistic leader, in discussion with the author, April 2023.

46. Workplace Bullying Institute, *2021 WBI U.S. Workplace Bullying Survey* (Utica, NY: WBI, April 2021).

47. Christina Ryan, founder, Disability Leadership Institute, in discussion with the author, August 2023.

48. Steve Glaveski, "Remote Work Should Be (Mostly) Asynchronous," *Harvard Business Review*, December 1, 2021, https://hbr.org/2021/12/remote-work-should-be-mostly-asynchronous.

49. Brent, "The Autistic Traits That Got Me Fired: These Employees Share Their Stories," *Ammok*, July 28, 2022, https://www.ammok.com.au/autism-workplace-challenges-that-got-me-fired-12-autistic-employees-shared-their-stories.

50. Chu-Hsiang Chang, Christopher C. Rosen, and Paul E. Levy, "The Relationship between Perceptions of Organizational Politics and Employee Attitudes, Strain, and Behavior: A Meta-Analytic Examination," *Academy of Management Journal* 52, no. 4 (2009): 779–801, https://doi.org/10.5465/amj.2009.43670894.

51. Jennifer P. Wisdom and Mira Brancu, *Millennials' Guide to Workplace Politics: What No One Ever Told You about Power and Influence* (New York: Winding Pathway Books, 2021).

52. Ing-Chung Huang, Chih Hsun Jason Chuang, and Hao-Chieh Lin, "The Role of Burnout in the Relationship between Perceptions of Organizational Politics and Turnover Intentions," *Public Personnel Management* 32, no. 4 (2003): 519–31, https://doi.org/10.1177/009102600303200404.

53. Tomas Chamorro-Premuzic and Abhijit Bhaduri, "How Office Politics Corrupt the Search for High-Potential Employees," *Harvard Business Review*, October 19, 2017, https://hbr.org/2017/10/how-office-politics-corrupt-the-search-for-high-potential-employees.

54. Perry, "Office Politics," *The Autism Community* (Forum), 2020, https://community
.autism.org.uk/f/adults-on-the-autistic-spectrum/18720/office-politics.

55. Madeleine Wyatt and Elena Doldor, "Office Politics Don't Have to Be Toxic," *Harvard
Business Review*, May 30, 2022, https://hbr.org/2022/05/office-politics-dont-have-to-be
-toxic.

56. Kate Mackenzie Davey, "Women's Accounts of Organizational Politics as a Gendering
Process," *Gender, Work & Organization* 15, no. 6 (2008): 650–71, https://doi.org/10
.1111/j.1468-0432.2008.00420.x.

57. Joan C. Williams, Marina Multhaup, and Sky Mihaylo, "Why Companies Should Add
Class to Their Diversity Discussions," *Harvard Business Review*, September 5, 2018,
https://hbr.org/2018/09/why-companies-should-add-class-to-their-diversity-discussions.

58. Michelle King, David Denyer, and Emma Parry, "Is Office Politics a White Man's Game?,"
Harvard Business Review, September 12, 2018, https://hbr.org/2018/09/is-office-politics
-a-white-mans-game.

59. Shevonne Joyce, head of business strategy and innovation at Legalite, in discussion with
the author, July 2023.

60. Han Yi, Po Hao, Baiyin Yang, and Wenxing Liu, "How Leaders' Transparent Behavior
Influences Employee Creativity: The Mediating Roles of Psychological Safety and Ability to Focus Attention," *Journal of Leadership & Organizational Studies* 24, no. 3 (2017):
335–44, https://doi.org/10.1177/1548051816670306.

61. Erik Berggren and Rob Bernshteyn, "Organizational Transparency Drives Company
Performance," *Journal of Management Development* 26, no. 5 (2007): 411–17, https://
doi.org/10.1108/02621710710748248.

62. "Transparency Is Key to Inclusive Employment and Government Integrity," World Economic Forum, April 25, 2019, https://www.weforum.org/agenda/2019/04/trans
parency-is-key-to-inclusive-employment-and-government-integrity.

63. Rajesh Anandan, CEO of Ultranauts, in discussion with the author, March 2023.

64. Ludmila N. Praslova, "Trauma-Informed Workplace: Kindness Works Better," *The SHRM
Blog* (blog), March 23, 2021, https://blog.shrm.org/blog/trauma-informed-organizational
-behavior-kindness-works-better.

65. "Infographic: 6 Guiding Principles to a Trauma-Informed Approach," Centers for Disease Control and Prevention, September 17, 2020, https://www.cdc.gov/orr/infographics
/6_principles_trauma_info.htm.

CHAPTER NINE

1. Charlie Hart, "Struggling through Education and Work Oblivious to My Autism (Updated)," *Ausome Charlie Neurodiversity Advocate* (blog), April 20, 2021, https://web
.archive.org/web/20230129165127/https://alicewhatsthematterblog.wordpress.com
/2021/04/20/struggling-through-education-and-work-oblivious-to-my-autism-updated.

2. Susan M. Hayward, Keith R. McVilly, and Mark A Stokes, "'I Would Love to Just Be
Myself': What Autistic Women Want at Work," *Autism in Adulthood* 1, no. 4 (2019):
297–305, https://doi.org/10.1089/aut.2019.0020.

3. Jacqui Wilmshurst, neurodivergent consultant, in discussion with the author, July 2023.

4. Tiffany D. Johnson and Aparna Joshi, "Dark Clouds or Silver Linings? A Stigma Threat
Perspective on the Implications of an Autism Diagnosis for Workplace Well-Being," *Journal of Applied Psychology* 101, no. 3 (2016): 430–49, https://doi.org/10.1037/apl0000058.

5. Alissa D. Parr and Samuel T. Hunter, "Enhancing Work Outcomes of Employees with Autism Spectrum Disorder through Leadership: Leadership for Employees with Autism Spectrum Disorder," *Autism: The International Journal of Research and Practice* 18, no. 5 (2014): 545–54, https://doi.org/10.1177/1362361313483020.

6. Diego Montano, Joyce Elena Schleu, and Joachim Hüffmeier, "A Meta-analysis of the Relative Contribution of Leadership Styles to Followers' Mental Health," *Journal of Leadership & Organizational Studies* 30, no. 1 (2023): 90–107, https://doi.org/10.1177/15480518221114854.

7. Leonardo Nicoletti and Dina Bass, "Humans Are Biased: Generative AI Is Even Worse," *Bloomberg*, May 31, 2023, https://www.bloomberg.com/graphics/2023-generative-ai-bias.

8. Lori Nishiura Mackenzie, JoAnne Wehner, and Shelley J. Correll, "Why Most Performance Evaluations Are Biased, and How to Fix Them," *Harvard Business Review*, January 11, 2019, https://hbr.org/2019/01/why-most-performance-evaluations-are-biased-and-how-to-fix-them.

9. Shelley J. Correl, Katherine R. Weisshaar, Alison T. Wynn, and JoAnne Delfino Wehner, "Inside the Black Box of Organizational Life: The Gendered Language of Performance Assessment," *American Sociological Review* 85 no. 6 (2020): 1022–50, https://doi.org/10.1177/0003122420962080.

10. Tiffany L. Hutchins, "A Review of the Nature and Development of Lying and Deception and Considerations for Teaching Prosocial Lying to Autistic Persons," *Seminars in Speech and Language* 43, no. 4 (2022): 316–30, https://doi.org/10.1055/s-0042-1750350.

11. Pier Jaarsma, Petra Gelhaus, and Stellan Welin, "Living the Categorical Imperative: Autistic Perspectives on Lying and Truth Telling—Between Kant and Care Ethics," *Medicine, Health Care, and Philosophy* 15, no. 3 (2012): 271–77, https://doi.org/10.1007/s11019-011-9363-7.

12. Joan C. Williams, Denise Lewin Loyd, Mikayla Boginsky, and Frances Armas-Edwards, "How One Company Worked to Root out Bias from Performance Reviews," *Harvard Business Review*, April 21, 2021, https://hbr.org/2021/04/how-one-company-worked-to-root-out-bias-from-performance-reviews.

13. Kieran Snyder and Aileen Lee, "No More 'Abrasive,' 'Opinionated,' or 'Nice': Why Managers Need to Stop Giving Women and People of Color Feedback on Their Personality," *Fortune*, June 15, 2022, https://fortune.com/2022/06/15/performance-reviews-bias-gender-race-language-textio-kieran-snyder-aileen-lee.

14. Catina Burkett, "'Autistic while Black': How Autism Amplifies Stereotypes," *Spectrum*, January 21, 2020, https://www.spectrumnews.org/opinion/viewpoint/autistic-while-black-how-autism-amplifies-stereotypes.

15. Ludmila N. Praslova and Satoris Howes, "Employing a Neurodiverse Workforce: Considerations for Human Resource Management," in *Research in Human Resource Management*, ed. Brian Murray and Deanna Stone (Charlotte, NC: Information Age Publishing, forthcoming).

16. Burnett Grant, autistic professional, in discussion with the author, February 2023.

17. Peter Cappelli and Anna Tavis, "The Performance Management Revolution," *Harvard Business Review*, October 2016, https://hbr.org/2016/10/the-performance-management-revolution.

18. Kathleen Doheny, "Annual Performance Review Bows Out," SHRM, January 12, 2021, https://www.shrm.org/resourcesandtools/hr-topics/people-managers/pages/ditching -the-annual-performance-review-.aspx.

19. Joan C. Williams, *Bias Interrupted: Creating Inclusion for Real and for Good* (Cambridge, MA: Harvard Business Review Press, 2021).

20. Chris Mason, "Patagonia's Journey into a New Regenerative Performance Approach," *People & Strategy* 40, no. 3 (2017): 30–34.

21. Ludmila N. Praslova, "Taming the Tightrope Bias," Specialisterne (blog), August 29, 2022, https://ca.specialisterne.com/taming-the-tightrope-bias/.

22. Vickie Choitz and Stacey Wagner, *A Trauma-Informed Approach to Workforce: An Introductory Guide for Employers and Workforce Development Organizations* (Washington, DC: National Fund for Workforce Solutions, 2021), https://nationalfund.org/wp-content /uploads/2021/04/A-Trauma-Informed-Approach-to-Workforce.pdf.

23. Rajesh Anandan, CEO of Ultranauts, in discussion with the author, April 2023.

24. Lan Nguyen Chaplin, "How to Disrupt a System That Was Built to Hold You Back," *Harvard Business Review*, March 8, 2021, https://hbr.org/2021/03/how-to-disrupt-a -system-that-was-built-to-hold-you-back.

CHAPTER TEN

1. Zach Winn, "Leveraging the Power of Neurodiversity," *MIT News*, December 1, 2020, https://news.mit.edu/2020/ultranauts-neurodiversity-1201.

2. Rajesh Anandan, CEO of Ultranauts, in discussion with the author, March 2023.

3. Anna M. Remington, John G. Swettenham, and Nilli Lavie, "Lightening the Load: Perceptual Load Impairs Visual Detection in Typical Adults but Not in Autism," *Journal of Abnormal Psychology* 121, no. 2 (2012): 544–51, https://doi.org/10.1037 /a0027670.

4. Anat Kasirer and Nira Mashal, "Verbal Creativity in Autism: Comprehension and Generation of Metaphoric Language in High-Functioning Autism Spectrum Disorder and Typical Development," *Frontiers in Human Neuroscience* 8 (August 2014): 615, https:// doi.org/10.3389/fnhum.2014.00615.

5. Ludmila N. Praslova, "Autistic Strengths, Human Value, and Human Uniqueness: Untangling the Strengths-Based Approach from Stereotypes and Simplifications," *Specialisterne*, October 15, 2021, https://ca.specialisterne.com/autistic-strengths-human-value -and-human-uniqueness-untangling-the-strengths-based-approach-from-stereotypes -and-simplifications.

6. Ludmila N. Praslova, "Disability at Work: The Forgotten Diversity," *Positively Different* (blog), Psychology Today, June 30, 2023, https://www.psychologytoday.com/us/blog /positively-different/202306/disability-at-work-the-forgotten-diversity.

7. Oriane A. M. Georgeac and Aneeta Rattan, "The Business Case for Diversity Backfires: Detrimental Effects of Organizations' Instrumental Diversity Rhetoric for Underrepresented Group Members' Sense of Belonging," *Journal of Personality and Social Psychology* 124, no. 1 (2023): 69–108, https://doi.org/10.1037/pspi0000394.

8. Oriane Georgeac and Aneeta Rattan, "Stop Making the Business Case for Diversity," *Harvard Business Review*, June 15, 2022, https://hbr.org/2022/06/stop-making-the -business-case-for-diversity.

9. Ludmila N. Praslova, "Thriving at Work While Autistic, Introverted, Shy, and Otherwise Different: Part 4," *Neuroclastic* (blog), September 21, 2020, https://neuroclastic.com/thriving-at-work-while-autistic-introverted-shy-and-otherwise-different-part-4/.

CHAPTER ELEVEN

1. Tony Alessandra and Michael O'Connor, *The Platinum Rule: Discover the Four Basic Business Personalities and How They Can Lead You to Success* (New York, NY: Grand Central Publishing, 1996).

2. Thomas Calvard, Emily Cherlin, Amanda Brewster, and Leslie Curry, "Building Perspective-Taking as an Organizational Capability: A Change Intervention in a Health Care Setting," *Journal of Management Inquiry* 32, no. 1 (2023): 35–49. https://doi.org/10.1177/10564926211039014.

3. Kirsi Sjöblom, Soile Juutinen, and Anne Mäkikangas, "The Importance of Self-Leadership Strategies and Psychological Safety for Well-Being in the Context of Enforced Remote Work," *Challenges* 13, no. 1 (2022): 14, https://doi.org/10.3390/challe13010014.

4. Ultranauts, *The Biodex—A User Manual for Every Teammate*, March 2023, https://ultranauts.co/wp-content/uploads/2020/03/Ultranauts-Tools-BioDex.pdf.

5. Ben VanHook, autistic self-advocate, in discussion with the author, March 2023.

6. Workforce Institute at UKG, *Mental Health at Work: Managers and Money*, 2023, https://www.ukg.com/resources/article/mental-health-work-managers-and-money.

7. Gil Winch, *Winning with Underdogs: How Hiring the Least Likely Candidates Can Spark Creativity, Improve Service, and Boost Profits for Your Business* (McGraw Hill, 2022), 271.

8. Stephen Trzeciak, Anthony Mazzarelli, and Emma Seppälä, "Leading with Compassion Has Research-Backed Benefits," *Harvard Business Review*, February 27, 2023, https://hbr.org/2023/02/leading-with-compassion-has-research-backed-benefits.

9. Netta Weinstein and Richard M. Ryan, "When Helping Helps: Autonomous Motivation for Prosocial Behavior and Its Influence on Well-Being for the Helper and Recipient," *Journal of Personality and Social Psychology* 98, no. 2 (2010): 222–44, https://doi.org/10.1037/a0016984.

10. Winch, *Winning with Underdogs*, 210.

11. David Wilkinson, "There Are Too Many Leadership Concepts . . . but Which Ones Are Redundant?," *Oxford Review* (blog), March 29, 2019, https://oxford-review.com/leadership-concepts.

12. Author's search of Vanguard University databases, July 19, 2023.

13. Hamed Dehghanan, Fatemeh Gheitarani, Saeed Rahimi, and Khaled Nawaser, "A Systematic Review of Leadership Styles in Organizations: Introducing the Concept of a Task-Relationship–Change Leadership Network," *International Journal of Innovation and Technology Management* 18, no. 7 (2021): 2130007, https://doi.org/10.1142/S021987702130007X.

14. John Bruni, "Talking Heads, Fear of Music, and the 'Different Thinking' of David Byrne," *Ought: The Journal of Autistic Culture* 4, no. 2 (2023), https://doi.org/10.9707/2833-1508.1124.

15. John Levine and Michael Hogg, eds., "Contingency Theories of Leadership," in *Encyclopedia of Group Processes & Intergroup Relations* (Thousand Oaks: SAGE Publications, 2010), 152–55.

16. Julia E. Hoch, William H. Bommer, James H. Dulebohn, and Dongyuan Wu, "Do Ethical, Authentic, and Servant Leadership Explain Variance above and beyond Transformational Leadership? A Meta-analysis," *Journal of Management* 44, no. 2 (2018): 501–29, https://doi.org/10.1177/0149206316665461.

17. Diego Montano, Joyce Elena Schleu, and Joachim Hüffmeier, "A Meta-analysis of the Relative Contribution of Leadership Styles to Followers' Mental Health," *Journal of Leadership & Organizational Studies* 30, no. 1 (2023): 90–107, https://doi.org/10.1177/15480518221114854.

18. Alissa D. Parr, Samuel T. Hunter, and Gina Scott Ligon, "Questioning Universal Applicability of Transformational Leadership: Examining Employees with Autism Spectrum Disorder," *The Leadership Quarterly* 24, no. 4 (2013): 608–22, https://doi.org/10.1016/j.leaqua.2013.04.003.

19. Winch, *Winning with Underdogs*, 210.

20. Joe Jordan and Sue Cartwright, "Selecting Expatriate Managers: Key Traits and Competencies," *Leadership & Organization Development Journal* 19, no. 2 (1998): 89–96, https://doi.org/10.1108/01437739810208665.

21. Kelly Ross, "Characteristics of Successful Expatriates: Unleashing Success by Identifying and Coaching on Specific Characteristics," Northwestern University, School of Education & Social Policy, March 2011, https://www.sesp.northwestern.edu/masters-learning-and-organizational-change/knowledge-lens/stories/2013/characteristics-of-successful-expatriates-unleashing-success-by-identifying-and-coaching-on-specific-characteristics.html.

22. Clare Kumar, president, Streamlife Ltd., in discussion with the author, April 2023.

23. Pier Jaarsma and Stellan Welin, "Autism as a Natural Human Variation: Reflections on the Claims of the Neurodiversity Movement," *Health Care Analysis* 20, no. 1 (2012): 20–30, https://doi.org/10.1007/s10728-011-0169-9.

24. Ken Gobbo and Solvegi Shmulsky, "Should Neurodiversity Culture Influence How Instructors Teach?," *Academic Exchange Quarterly* 23, no. 4 (2019), http://rapidintellect.com/AEQweb/ed-5971.pdf.

25. Ludmila N. Praslova, "Embracing Autism as Culture: How Leaders and Allies Can Foster a More Inclusive Workplace," *Specialisterne* (blog), May 30, 2023, https://ca.specialisterne.com/embracing-autism-as-culture-how-leaders-and-allies-can-foster-a-more-inclusive-workplace.

26. Melanie Tervalon and Jann Murray-García, "Cultural Humility versus Cultural Competence: A Critical Distinction in Defining Physician Training Outcomes in Multicultural Education," *Journal of Health Care for the Poor and Underserved* 9, no. 2 (1998): 117–25, https://doi.org/10.1353/hpu.2010.0233.

27. Ludmila N. Praslova, "An Intersectional Approach to Inclusion at Work," *Harvard Business Review*, June 21, 2022, https://hbr.org/2022/06/an-intersectional-approach-to-inclusion-at-work.

28. US Department of State, "Dimensions of Culture," in *"So You're an American?" A Guide to Answering Difficult Questions Abroad*, https://www.state.gov/courses/answeringdifficultquestions/assets/m/resources/DifficultQuestions-Dimensions-V2.pdf.

29. Naqui Shaikh, "Communicating the Dutch Way," Veem, January 12, 2018, https://www.veem.com/library/communicating-the-dutch-way.

30. "High Context Countries 2023," World Population Review, accessed August 7, 2023, https://worldpopulationreview.com/country-rankings/high-context-countries.

31. Catherine J. Crompton, Danielle Ropar, Claire V. M. Evans-Williams, Emma G. Flynn, and Sue Fletcher-Watson, "Autistic Peer-to-Peer Information Transfer Is Highly Effective," *Autism* 24, no. 7 (2020): 1704–12, https://doi.org/10.1177/1362361320919286.

32. Dina Denham Smith and Alicia A. Grandey, "The Emotional Labor of Being a Leader," *Harvard Business Review*, November 2, 2022, https://hbr.org/2022/11/the-emotional-labor-of-being-a-leader.

33. Ludmila N. Praslova, "Research Is In: Work Stress Is Not 'Just in Your Head,'" *Positively Different* (blog), Psychology Today, June 27, 2023, https://www.psychologytoday.com/us/blog/positively-different/202301/research-is-in-work-stress-is-not-just-in-your-head.

34. Simran Jeet Singh, "Boards Need Real Diversity, Not Tokenism," *Harvard Business Review*, August 31, 2021, https://hbr.org/2021/08/boards-need-real-diversity-not-tokenism.

35. Joshua J. Baugh and Ali S. Raja, "Six Lessons on Fighting Burnout from Boston's Biggest Hospital," *Harvard Business Review*, February 10, 2021, https://hbr.org/2021/02/six-lessons-on-fighting-burnout-from-bostons-biggest-hospital.

36. Katrina Forrest and Catherine Patterson, "6 Lessons We've Learned from Our First Year of Co-Leadership," CityHealth, September 29, 2021, https://www.cityhealth.org/resource/lessons-from-co-leadership.

37. Manfred Kets de Vries, "Two CEOs, No Drama: Ground Rules for Co-leadership," INSEAD Knowledge, June 30, 2021, https://knowledge.insead.edu/leadership-organisations/two-ceos-no-drama-ground-rules-co-leadership.

38. Josh Bersin, *Irresistible: The Seven Secrets of the World's Most Enduring, Employee-Focused Organizations* (Ideapress Publishing, 2022), 93–94.

CHAPTER TWELVE

1. Ludmila Praslova, "Neurodivergent People Make Great Leaders, Not Just Employees," *Fast Company*, December 15, 2021, https://www.fastcompany.com/90706149/neurodivergent-people-make-great-leaders-not-just-employees.

2. Ludmila Praslova, "Neurodiversity Is Critical for Innovation in the Workplace," *Fast Company*, August 26, 2022, https://www.fastcompany.com/90782113/neurodiversity-is-critical-for-innovation-in-the-workplace.

3. Katie Weston, "'Autism Made Me a Better Naval Officer': Second Sea Lord Vice Admiral Nick Hine Reveals He Is Autistic after Being Diagnosed 10 Years Ago and Says Military Needs More 'Neurodiversity,'" *The Daily Mail*, March 12, 2021, https://www.dailymail.co.uk/news/article-9354415/Second-Sea-Lord-Vice-Admiral-Nick-Hine-reveals-autistic-diagnosed-10-years-ago.html.

4. "Charlotte Valeur: 'My Autism Is My Strength,'" *CA Magazine*, February 24, 2021, https://www.icas.com/members/ca-magazine/ca-magazine-articles/charlotte-valeur-my-autism-is-my-strength.

5. Dynamic Boards, dir., *"Being Autistic Made My Career": An Interview with Charlotte Valeur*, 2021, YouTube video, https://www.everythingneurodiversity.com/post/being-autistic-made-my-career-an-interview-with-charlotte-valeur.

6. Simon Duke, "Autistic Pioneer Has Sights Set on a New Frontier for Diversity," *The Times* (UK), August 8, 2023, sec. Business, https://www.thetimes.co.uk/article/autistic-pioneer -has-sights-set-on-a-new-frontier-for-diversity-skv2k8szz.

7. Charlotte Valeur and Claire Fargeot, eds., *Effective Directors: The Right Questions to Ask* (New York: Routledge, 2022).

8. TEDx Talks, dir., *Towards A Strengths-Based Education System | Aman Zaidi | TEDxElpro-IntlSchool*, YouTube video, 2021, https://www.youtube.com/watch?v=nVWEPGIuvRs.

9. Aman Zaidi, founder, Fortius, in discussion with the author, April 2023.

10. Yuri Kruman, fractional CHRO, author, professor, in discussion with the author, April 2023.

11. Kristina Marsh, business and marketing consultant, in discussion with the author, April 2023.

12. Josh Alan Dykstra, CEO of #lovework, in discussion with the author, April 2023.

13. "Developing Employee Career Paths and Ladders," SHRM, https://www.shrm.org /resourcesandtools/tools-and-samples/toolkits/pages/developingemployeecareerpathsan dladders.aspx.

14. Josh Bersin, *Irresistible: The Seven Secrets of the World's Most Enduring, Employee-Focused Organizations* (Ideapress Publishing, 2022), 92.

15. Sylvia Ann Hewlett, Melinda Marshall, and Laura Sherbin, "How Diversity Can Drive Innovation," *Harvard Business Review*, December 1, 2013, https://hbr.org/2013/12/how -diversity-can-drive-innovation.

16. Lindsay Dodgson, "Why Diverse Companies Turn Higher Profits and Reap Rewards," World Economic Forum, March 15, 2017, https://www.weforum.org/agenda/2017/03 /why-diverse-companies-turn-higher-profits-and-reap-rewards.

17. Simon Baron-Cohen, Emma Ashwin, Chris Ashwin, Teresa Tavassoli, and Bhismadev Chakrabarti, "Talent in Autism: Hyper-systemizing, Hyper-attention to Detail and Sensory Hypersensitivity," *Philosophical Transactions of the Royal Society B: Biological Sciences* 364, no. 1522 (2009): 1377–83, https://doi.org/10.1098/rstb.2008.0337.

18. Joseph M. Moran, Eshin Jolly, and Jason P. Mitchell, "Spontaneous Mentalizing Predicts the Fundamental Attribution Error," *Journal of Cognitive Neuroscience* 26, no. 3 (2014): 569–76, https://doi.org/10.1162/jocn_a_00513.

19. Holly A. White and Priti Shah, "Uninhibited Imaginations: Creativity in Adults with Attention-Deficit/Hyperactivity Disorder," *Personality and Individual Differences* 40, no. 6 (2006): 1121–31, https://doi.org/10.1016/j.paid.2005.11.007.

20. "Business Chemistry in the C-Suite," Deloitte United States, March 2017, https:// www2.deloitte.com/us/en/pages/consulting/articles/c-suite-business-chemistry-cxo -research.html.

21. Kim Christfort, "Pioneers and Drivers: Dominant Personality Traits in the C-Suite," *Wall Street Journal*, March 30, 2017, https://deloitte.wsj.com/cfo/2017/03/30/pioneers-and -drivers-dominant-personality-traits-in-the-c-suite.

22. David Green, "Rethinking Leadership for the Future of Work (Interview with Heather McGowan)," Digital HR Leaders Podcast, June 27, 2023, https://www.myhrfuture.com /digital-hr-leaders-podcast/rethinking-leadership-for-the-future-of-work.

23. Stephen Trzeciak, Anthony Mazzarelli, and Emma Seppälä, "Leading with Compassion Has Research-Backed Benefits," *Harvard Business Review*, February 27, 2023, https://hbr.org/2023/02/leading-with-compassion-has-research-backed-benefits.

24. David Lancefield, head of Thought Leadership at PwC/Strategy, in discussion with the author, April 2023.

25. Colleen Reilly, "The Rise of the Chief Wellbeing Officer," *Forbes*, July 7, 2020, https://www.forbes.com/sites/colleenreilly/2020/07/07/the-rise-of-the-chief-wellbeing-officer.

26. Sarah Hallam, "The Rise of the Chief AI Ethics Officer," The Org, April 5, 2023, https://theorg.com/iterate/the-rise-of-the-chief-ai-ethics-officer.

CHAPTER THIRTEEN

1. "50% Employers Admit They Won't Hire Neurodivergent Talent," *Fair Play Talks* (blog), November 3, 2020. https://www.fairplaytalks.com/2020/11/03/50-employers-admit-they-wont-hire-neurodivergent-talent-reveals-ilm-study.

2. Jerry Gidner, US federal executive, in discussion with the author, February 2022.

3. Ludmila N. Praslova, "Does ChatGPT Mean the End of 'Thought Leaders'?," *Fast Company*, February 3, 2023, https://www.fastcompany.com/90842966/chatgpt-end-thought-leaders.

4. Caroline Stokes, "It Is Time for the Game Industry to Lead on Environmental, Social, Governance," *VentureBeat*, April 6, 2023, https://venturebeat.com/games/it-is-time-for-the-game-industry-to-lead-on-environmental-social-governance.

5. Ludmila N. Praslova, "Today's Most Critical Workplace Challenges Are about Systems," *Harvard Business Review*, January 10, 2023, https://hbr.org/2023/01/todays-most-critical-workplace-challenges-are-about-systems.

6. Ludmila N. Praslova, "Neurodivergent People Make Great Leaders, Not Just Employees," *Fast Company*, December 15, 2021, https://www.fastcompany.com/90706149/neurodivergent-people-make-great-leaders-not-just-employees.

7. David E. Rast III, Michael A. Hogg, and Georgina Randsley de Moura, "Leadership and Social Transformation: The Role of Marginalized Individuals and Groups," *Journal of Social Issues* 74, no. 1 (2018): 8–19, https://doi.org/10.1111/josi.12253.

8. Robert Lord and Rosalie Hall, "Identity, Leadership Categorization, and Leadership Schema," in *Leadership and Power: Identity Processes in Groups and Organizations*, ed. Daan Van Knippenberg and Michael A. Hogg (London: Sage Publications, 2023), 48–64, https://doi.org/10.4135/9781446216170.

9. Robert G. Lord and Sara J. Shondrick, "Leadership and Knowledge: Symbolic, Connectionist, and Embodied Perspectives," *Leadership Quarterly* 22, no. 1 (2011): 207–22, https://doi.org/10.1016/j.leaqua.2010.12.016.

10. Christina Ryan, founder of the Disability Leadership Institute, in discussion with the author, August 2023.

11. Caroline Casey, "Why Elevating Leaders with Disabilities Is so Crucial to Disability Inclusion," *Fast Company*, July 9, 2022, https://www.fastcompany.com/90764817/why-elevating-leaders-with-disabilities-is-so-crucial-to-disability-inclusion.

12. Luis Velasquez, founder, managing partner, Velas Coaching LLC, experiential facilitator, Stanford University Graduate School of Business, in discussion with the author, April 2023.

13. Ludmila N. Praslova, "How to Heal from Stress and Trauma: Lessons from Kintsugi," *Psychology Today, Positively Different* (blog), March 23, 2022, https://www .psychologytoday.com/us/blog/positively-different/202203/how-heal-stress-and -trauma-lessons-kintsugi.

14. Tristan Lavender, senior content strategist; founder and chair of the Philips Employee Resource Group, in discussion with the author, June 2023.

15. Tristan Lavender, "Building a Meaningful Career with Autism—Ben's Story," Philips, March 3, 2023, https://www.careers.philips.com/emea/en/blogarticle/building-a -meaningful-career-with-autism?.

16. Tristan Lavender, "Thriving with Dyslexia—Meet Rokus," Philips, July 20, 2023, https://www.careers.philips.com/emea/en/blogarticle/thriving-with-dyslexia-meet -rokus.

17. Ludmila N. Praslova, "Feeling Distressed at Work? It Might Be More than Burnout," *Fast Company*, January 14, 2022, https://www.fastcompany.com/90712671/feeling -distressed-at-work-it-might-be-more-than-burnout.

18. Kirsten Gural Howley, business owner and consultant, in discussion with the author, April 2023.

19. Justin Donne, autistic leader, in discussion with the author, April 2023.

20. Eugene Kim and Theresa M. Glomb, "Get Smarty Pants: Cognitive Ability, Personality, and Victimization," *Journal of Applied Psychology* 95, no. 5 (2010): 889–901, https://doi .org/10.1037/a0019985.

21. Eugene Kim and Theresa M. Glomb, "Victimization of High Performers: The Roles of Envy and Work Group Identification," *Journal of Applied Psychology* 99, no. 4 (2014), https://doi.org/10.1037/a0035789.

22. Ludmila N. Praslova, "We're in the Midst of a Fundamental Shift in Leadership," *Fast Company*, June 30, 2022, https://www.fastcompany.com/90764849/were-in-the-midst -of-a-fundamental-shift-in-leadership.

23. John R. P. French and Bertram Raven, "The Bases of Social Power," in *Studies in Social Power*, ed. Dorwin Cartwright (Ann Arbor: University of Michigan, 1959), 150–67.

24. Bertram H. Raven, "The Bases of Power and the Power/Interaction Model of Interpersonal Influence," *Analyses of Social Issues and Public Policy* 8, no. 1 (2008): 1–22, https:// doi.org/10.1111/j.1530-2415.2008.00159.x.

25. Ali B. Mahmoud, Leonora Fuxman, Iris Mohr, William D. Reisel, and Nicholas Grigoriou, "'We Aren't Your Reincarnation!' Workplace Motivation across X, Y and Z Generations," *International Journal of Manpower* 42, no. 1 (2021): 193–209, https://doi.org/10 .1108/IJM-09-2019-0448.

26. Laura Macpherson, "8 Examples of Transparent Leaders to Follow," Front, February 5, 2021, https://front.com/blog/8-examples-of-transparent-leaders-to-follow.

27. Alan Robinson, vice president, Legal Solutions, Gulfstream Legal Group, LLC, in discussion with the author, April 2022, August 2023.

28. Karen An-hwei Lee, provost and professor of English at Wheaton College, in discussion with the author, August 2023.

29. "The Team," Build with TACT, accessed August 8, 2023, https://www.buildwithtact.org /team.

30. Denise Brosseau, "6 Characteristics Great Thought Leaders Share," *Entrepreneur*, January 10, 2014, https://www.entrepreneur.com/growing-a-business/6-characteristics-great-thought-leaders-share/230696.

31. Kelly Bron Johnson, founder, Completely Inclusive, in discussion with the author, April 2022.

32. Charlotte Valeur, director of Neurodiversity Institute, in discussion with the author, April 2022.

CONCLUSION

1. "The Kenyan Café Welcoming People with Cognitive Disorders," *Africanews*, May 5, 2023, https://www.africanews.com/2023/05/05/the-kenyan-cafe-welcoming-people-with-cognitive-disorders.

2. Maddy Savage, "Why Finland Leads the World in Flexible Work," *BBC Worklife*, August 8, 2019, https://www.bbc.com/worklife/article/20190807-why-finland-leads-the-world-in-flexible-work.

3. Donald Sull and Charles Sull, "How to Fix a Toxic Culture," *MIT Sloan Management Review*, September 28, 2022, https://sloanreview.mit.edu/article/how-to-fix-a-toxic-culture.

4. Becky Little, "When the 'Capitol Crawl' Dramatized the Need for Americans with Disabilities Act," *History*, October 5, 2023, https://www.history.com/news/americans-with-disabilities-act-1990-capitol-crawl.

5. Toni Schmader, Tara C. Dennehy, and Andrew S. Baron, "Why Antibias Interventions (Need Not) Fail," *Perspectives on Psychological Science* 17, no. 5 (2022): 1381–1403, https://doi.org/10.1177/17456916211057565.

6. "Neurodiversity Celebration Week," Neurodiversity Week, accessed November 5, 2023, https://www.neurodiversityweek.com.

7. Marina Martinez, "Creating an Autistic-Led and Neurodiverse-Friendly Media in Brazil," International Journalists' Network, August 23, 2022, https://ijnet.org/en/story/creating-autistic-led-and-neurodiverse-friendly-media-brazil.

8. *LISTEN* (CommunicationFirst, 2021), https://communicationfirst.org/LISTEN/.

9. Marco Niemeijer, dir., *This Is Not about Me* (2021), https://thisisnotaboutme.film/.

10. Jerry Rothwell, dir., *The Reason I Jump* (2020), https://thereasonijumpfilm.com/.

11. Pat Notaro, dir., *Spellers* (2023), https://spellersthemovie.com.

12. Tumi Sotire, "The Economics of Neurodiversity—Introduction," LinkedIn, September 8, 2023, https://www.linkedin.com/pulse/economics-neurodiversity-introduction-tumi-sotire/.

13. Fundacja Ponad Schematami, homepage, accessed November 5, 2023, https://ponadschematami.org/.

14. *Prioritizing Peace with Morgan Harper Nichols*, YouTube video, 2023, https://www.youtube.com/watch?v=xyvpdG-LGzQ.

APPENDIX C

1. Greg McKeown, "To Build a Top Performing Team, Ask for 85% Effort," *Harvard Business Review*, June 8, 2023, https://hbr.org/2023/06/to-build-a-top-performing-team-ask-for-85-effort.

APPENDIX D

1. Yunhe Huang, Samuel R. C. Arnold, Kitty-Rose Foley, and Julian N Trollor, "Diagnosis of Autism in Adulthood: A Scoping Review," *Autism* 24, no. 6 (2020): 1311–27, https://doi.org/10.1177/1362361320903128.

2. James J. McGough and Russell A. Barkley, "Diagnostic Controversies in Adult Attention Deficit Hyperactivity Disorder," *American Journal of Psychiatry* 161, no. 11 (2004): 1948–56, https://doi.org/10.1176/appi.ajp.161.11.1948.

3. Andrea Sadusky, Andrea E. Reupert, Nerelie C. Freeman, and Emily P. Berger, "Diagnosing Adults with Dyslexia: Psychologists' Experiences and Practices," *Dyslexia* 27, no. 4 (2021): 468–85, https://doi.org/10.1002/dys.1689.

4. Ludmila Praslova, "Supporting Late-Diagnosed Neurodivergent Employees," *Specialisterne* (blog), June 9, 2023, https://ca.specialisterne.com/supporting-late-diagnosed-neurodivergent-employees/.

5. Ludmila N. Praslova, "Adult, Accomplished, Autistic: The Late Diagnosis Diaries," *Positively Different* (blog), *Psychology Today*, August 5, 2023, https://www.psychologytoday.com/us/blog/positively-different/202306/adult-accomplished-autistic-the-late-diagnosis-diaries.

6. "Autism Prevalence Higher, According to Data from 11 ADDM Communities," Centers for Disease Control and Prevention, March 23, 2023, https://www.cdc.gov/media/releases/2023/p0323-autism.html.

7. Melissa Rudy, "ADHD Numbers Rise in the U.S., Especially among Women: Study," *New York Post*, April 5, 2023, https://www.foxnews.com/health/adhd-numbers-climbing-dramatically-us-especially-among-women-says-study.

8. Wilma Wake, Eric Endlich, and Robert S. Lagos, *Older Autistic Adults: In Their Own Words: The Lost Generation* (Shawnee, KS: AAPC Publishing, 2021).

9. Marina Sarris, "A Lost Generation: Growing Up with Autism before the 'Epidemic,'" Kennedy Krieger Institute, July 25, 2017, https://www.kennedykrieger.org/stories/interactive-autism-network-ian/lost-generation-growing-up-autism-before-epidemic.

10. Steven D. Stagg and Hannah Belcher, "Living with Autism without Knowing: Receiving a Diagnosis in Later Life," *Health Psychology and Behavioral Medicine* 7, no. 1 (2019): 348–61, https://doi.org/10.1080/21642850.2019.1684920.

11. Dori Zener, "Journey to Diagnosis for Women with Autism," *Advances in Autism* 5, no. 1 (2019): 2–13, https://doi.org/10.1108/AIA-10-2018-0041.

12. Sarah Bargiela, Robyn Steward, and William Mandy, "The Experiences of Late-Diagnosed Women with Autism Spectrum Conditions: An Investigation of the Female Autism Phenotype," *Journal of Autism and Developmental Disorders* 46, no. 10 (2016): 3281–94, https://doi.org/10.1007/s10803-016-2872-8.

13. Julia J. Rucklidge, "Gender Differences in Attention-Deficit/Hyperactivity Disorder," *Psychiatric Clinics of North America* 33, no. 2 (2010): 357–73, https://doi.org/10.1016/j.psc.2010.01.006.

14. Ortal Slobodin and Michael Davidovitch, "Gender Differences in Objective and Subjective Measures of ADHD among Clinic-Referred Children," *Frontiers in Human Neuroscience* 13 (2019), https://doi.org/10.3389/fnhum.2019.00441.

15. M. Gaub and C. L. Carlson, "Gender Differences in ADHD: A Meta-analysis and Critical Review," *Journal of the American Academy of Child and Adolescent Psychiatry* 36, no. 8 (1997): 1036–45, https://doi.org/10.1097/00004583-199708000-00011.

16. Raphael Bernier, Alice Mao, and Jennifer Yen, "Psychopathology, Families, and Culture: Autism," *Child and Adolescent Psychiatric Clinics of North America* 19, no. 4 (2010): 855–67, https://doi.org/10.1016/j.chc.2010.07.005.

17. "Do I Have ADHD . . . or Am I Just Lazy?," *Amen Clinics* (blog), March 25, 2021, https://www.amenclinics.com/blog/do-i-have-adhdor-am-i-just-lazy/.

18. David S. Mandell, Richard F. Ittenbach, Susan E. Levy, and Jennifer A. Pinto-Martin, "Disparities in Diagnoses Received Prior to a Diagnosis of Autism Spectrum Disorder," *Journal of Autism and Developmental Disorders* 37, no. 9 (2007): 1795–802, https://doi.org/10.1007/s10803-006-0314-8.

19. Anick Verpalen, Fons Van de Vijver, and Ad Backus, "Bias in Dyslexia Screening in a Dutch Multicultural Population," *Annals of Dyslexia* 68, no. 1 (2018): 43–68, https://doi.org/10.1007/s11881-018-0155-0.

20. Jess Joho, "Privilege Plays a Huge Role in Getting an ADHD Diagnosis," PennState Social Science Research Institute, June 28, 2021, https://ssri.psu.edu/news/privilege-plays-huge-role-getting-adhd-diagnosis.

21. Brandon S. Aylward, Diana E. Gal-Szabo, and Sharief Taraman, "Racial, Ethnic, and Sociodemographic Disparities in Diagnosis of Children with Autism Spectrum Disorder," *Journal of Developmental and Behavioral Pediatrics* 42, no. 8 (2021): 682–89, https://doi.org/10.1097/DBP.0000000000000996.

22. Maureen Neihart, "Gifted Children with Asperger's Syndrome," *Gifted Child Quarterly* 44, no. 4 (2000): 222–30, https://doi.org/10.1177/001698620004400403.

23. Susan G. Assouline, Megan Foley Nicpon, Nicholas Colangelo, and Matthew O'Brien, *The Paradox of Giftedness and Autism: Packet of Information for Professionals (PIP)—Revised (2008)* (Iowa City: University of Iowa, 2008).

24. Juliette François-Sévigny and Mathieu Pilon, "Gifted Children with ADHD, and the Challenges Their Parents Face," *The Conversation*, October 6, 2021, http://theconversation.com/gifted-children-with-adhd-and-the-challenges-their-parents-face-168644.

25. "Gifted and Dyslexic: Identifying and Instructing the Twice Exceptional Student Fact Sheet," International Dyslexia Association, October 11, 2014, https://dyslexiaida.org/gifted-and-dyslexic-identifying-and-instructing-the-twice-exceptional-student-fact-sheet/.

26. Else Beckmann and Alexander Minnaert, "Non-cognitive Characteristics of Gifted Students with Learning Disabilities: An In-Depth Systematic Review," *Frontiers in Psychology* 9 (April 2018): 504, https://doi.org/10.3389/fpsyg.2018.00504.

27. Eilidh Cage and Zoe Troxell-Whitman, "Understanding the Reasons, Contexts and Costs of Camouflaging for Autistic Adults," *Journal of Autism and Developmental Disorders* 49, no. 5 (2019): 1899–911, https://doi.org/10.1007/s10803-018-03878-x.

28. Ludmila N. Praslova, "Autism Doesn't Hold People Back at Work. Discrimination Does," *Harvard Business Review*, December 13, 2021, https://hbr.org/2021/12/autism-doesnt-hold-people-back-at-work-discrimination-does.

29. Jonathan S. Beck, Rebecca A. Lundwall, Terisa Gabrielsen, Jonathan C. Cox, and Mikle South, "Looking Good but Feeling Bad: 'Camouflaging' Behaviors and Mental Health in Women with Autistic Traits," *Autism* 24, no. 4 (2020): 809–21, https://doi.org/10.1177/1362361320912147.

30. Franchine Russo, "The Costs of Camouflaging Autism," *Spectrum*, February 21, 2018, https://www.spectrumnews.org/features/deep-dive/costs-camouflaging-autism/.

31. Vanessa Hughes, "Best Day of My Life ~ Late Diagnosis," *ADHD and Women* (blog), August 23, 2021, https://adhd-women.eu/blog/best-day-of-my-life-late-diagnosis/.

32. Jen Malia, "My Daughter and I Were Diagnosed with Autism on the Same Day," *New York Times*, April 15, 2020, https://www.nytimes.com/2020/04/15/parenting/autism -mom.html.

33. Beth Winegarner, "'The Battery's Dead': Burnout Looks Different in Autistic Adults," *New York Times*, October 14, 2021, https://www.nytimes.com/2021/09/03/well/live /autistic-burnout-advice.html.

34. Hirotaka Kosaka, Toru Fujioka, and Minyoung Jung, "Symptoms in Individuals with Adult-Onset ADHD Are Masked during Childhood," *European Archives of Psychiatry and Clinical Neuroscience* 269, no. 6 (2019): 753–55, https://doi.org/10.1007/s00406 -018-0893-3.

35. Ludmila Praslova, "Workplace Politics and Inclusive Organizations: Thinking like an Autistic," *Specialisterne* (blog), September 30, 2022, https://ca.specialisterne.com/workplace -politics-and-inclusive-organizations-thinking-like-an-autistic/.

36. Ludmila N. Praslova, Ron Carucci, and Caroline Stokes, "How Bullying Manifests at Work—and How to Stop It," *Harvard Business Review*, November 4, 2022, https://hbr .org/2022/11/how-bullying-manifests-at-work-and-how-to-stop-it.

37. Ludmila Praslova, "Sensory Safety: A Must of Neurodiversity Inclusion in the Workplace," *Specialisterne* (blog), January 18, 2023, https://ca.specialisterne.com/sensory-safety -a-must-of-neurodiversity-inclusion-in-the-workplace/.

38. Ella F. Washington, "Recognizing and Responding to Microaggressions at Work," *Harvard Business Review*, May 10, 2022, https://hbr.org/2022/05/recognizing-and -responding-to-microaggressions-at-work.

39. "Adults with Autism Can Read Complex Emotions in Others," *ScienceDaily*, January 7, 2019, https://www.sciencedaily.com/releases/2019/01/190107112947.htm.

40. Ido Shalev, Varun Warrier, David M. Greenberg, Paula Smith, Carrie Allison, Simon Baron-Cohen, Alal Eran, and Florina Uzefovsky, "Reexamining Empathy in Autism: Empathic Disequilibrium as a Novel Predictor of Autism Diagnosis and Autistic Traits," *Autism Research: Official Journal of the International Society for Autism Research* 15, no. 10 (2022): 1917–28, https://doi.org/10.1002/aur.2794.

41. Megan C. Tobin, Kathryn D. R. Drager, and Laura F. Richardson, "A Systematic Review of Social Participation for Adults with Autism Spectrum Disorders: Support, Social Functioning, and Quality of Life," *Research in Autism Spectrum Disorders* 8, no. 3 (2014): 214–29, https://doi.org/10.1016/j.rasd.2013.12.

42. Sue Fletcher-Watson and Geoffrey Bird, "Autism and Empathy: What Are the Real Links?," *Autism* 24, no. 1 (2020): 3–6, https://doi.org/10.1177/1362361319883506.

43. Amber-Sophie Dugdale, Andrew R. Thompson, Alexandra Leedham, Nigel Beail, and Megan Freeth, "Intense Connection and Love: The Experiences of Autistic Mothers," *Autism* 25, no. 7 (2021): 1973–84, https://doi.org/10.1177/13623613211005987.

44. Potheini Vaiouli and Georgia Panayiotou, "Alexithymia and Autistic Traits: Associations with Social and Emotional Challenges among College Students," *Frontiers in Neuroscience* 15 (2021), https://doi.org/10.3389/fnins.2021.733775.

45. Peter Mitchell, Elizabeth Sheppard, and Sarah Cassidy, "Autism and the Double Empathy Problem: Implications for Development and Mental Health," *British Journal of Developmental Psychology* 39, no. 1 (2021): 1–18, https://doi.org/10.1111/bjdp.12350.

46. Noah J. Sasson, Daniel J. Faso, Jack Nugent, Sarah Lovell, Daniel P. Kennedy, and Ruth B. Grossman, "Neurotypical Peers Are Less Willing to Interact with Those with Autism Based on Thin Slice Judgments," *Scientific Reports* 7, no. 1 (2017): article 40700, https://doi.org/10.1038/srep40700.

47. Jessica H. Schroeder, Catherine Cappadocia, James M. Bebko, Debra J. Pepler, and Jonathan A. Weiss, "Shedding Light on a Pervasive Problem: A Review of Research on Bullying Experiences among Children with Autism Spectrum Disorders," *Journal of Autism and Developmental Disorders* 44, no. 7 (2014): 1520–34, https://doi.org/10.1007/s10803-013-2011-8.

48. Carlos Canela, Anna Buadze, Anish Dube, Dominique Eich, and Michael Liebrenz, "Skills and Compensation Strategies in Adult ADHD—a Qualitative Study," *PLoS ONE* 12, no. 9 (2017): e0184964, https://doi.org/10.1371/journal.pone.0184964.

49. Julia Cook, Laura Hull, Laura Crane, and William Mandy, "Camouflaging in Autism: A Systematic Review," *Clinical Psychology Review* 89 (November 2021): 102080, https://doi.org/10.1016/j.cpr.2021.102080.

APPENDIX E

1. Ludmila N. Praslova, "Diversity, Equity, Inclusion and Belonging at Work: The Focus on Fairness," in *Evidence-Based Organizational Practices for Diversity, Inclusion, Belonging and Equity*, ed. Ludmila N. Praslova (Newcastle, UK: Cambridge Scholars, 2023).

2. Ludmila N. Praslova, "Dancing with Diversity: From Inclusion Illusion to Authentic Belonging," *The SHRM Blog* (blog), November 30, 2020, https://blog.shrm.org/blog/dancing-with-diversity-from-inclusion-illusion-to-authentic-belonging.

3. Donna Hicks, *Leading with Dignity: How to Create a Culture That Brings Out the Best in People* (New Haven: Yale University Press, 2018).

4. *The U.S. Surgeon General's Framework for Workplace Mental Health & Well-Being* (Washington, DC: Office of the U.S. Surgeon General, 2022), https://www.hhs.gov/sites/default/files/workplace-mental-health-well-being.pdf.

5. Gordon L. Flett, "An Introduction, Review, and Conceptual Analysis of Mattering as an Essential Construct and an Essential Way of Life," *Journal of Psychoeducational Assessment* 40, no. 1 (2022): 3–36, https://doi.org/10.1177/07342829211057640.

6. Q. Roberson and W. Scott, "Contributive Justice: An Invisible Barrier to Workplace Inclusion," *Journal of Management*, online first (August 2022), https://doi.org/10.1177/01492063221116089.

7. Seval Gündemir, Astrid C. Homan, and Lindred (Lindy) Greer, "Overcoming the Inclusion Facade," *MIT Sloan Management Review*, March 21, 2023, https://sloanreview.mit.edu/article/overcoming-the-inclusion-facade.

ACKNOWLEDGMENTS

How do I express my gratitude for the journey of a lifetime and for the hundreds of other life journeys distilled into this book?

I am deeply humbled by the trust of every wonderful human who shared their stories with me and the world. Thank you for sharing your heart, your life, and your hard-earned lessons. Thank you for your vulnerability and passion for creating a better future of work. Thank you for being uniquely you.

My neurodivergent community, thank you for being the inspiration and the WHY of this book. Thank you for persevering, learning, teaching, doing your best with what you have, and managing to have fun in the face of all the challenges. Thank you for your insatiable curiosity and for telling me to keep going.

My heartfelt appreciation to the terrific team at Berrett-Koehler Publishers. Lesley Iura, thank you for believing in this book. It truly would not have been here without you. Jeevan Sivasubramaniam, thank you for your wisdom and patience. Ashley Ingram, thank you for working with me through all the iterations of the cover, and Sarah Nelson, for all the iterations of the marketing copy!

Thank you to my reviewers Alexis Woodcock, Eileen Hammer, and Sara Jane Hope for their thorough and generous feedback.

My writing process would have been very lonely without amazing editors who contributed their big-picture perspective, incredible attention to detail, and enthusiasm for this book: Gee Abraham, Elizabeth Borcia, Ruth-Anne Eisler, Barbara Ruth Saunders, and Kellyn Standley. My heartfelt gratitude to Vanguard University of Southern California for supporting Elizabeth's work on this book and for being a place where I've met incredible, inclusive, and brilliant colleagues who bless me in countless ways and keep me focused on what truly matters.

INDEX

Note: Page numbers followed by *f* and *t* refer to figures and tables.

ABOUT THE AUTHOR

Dr. Ludmila Praslova started working in global diversity as a starry-eyed college student intent on creating vibrant, culture-add organizational systems. Since then, she had experienced the good, the bad, and the unspeakable of work life. She developed a passion for doing better than organizational approaches to inclusion that focused on just one aspect of who we are, leaving many people unincludable.
After several years of working in global diversity, she earned a PhD in industrial-organizational psychology, searching for ways to create lasting, positive organizational change and support systemic inclusion that would embrace all dimensions of human difference.

As she continued her career in academia and consulting, she was shocked by the statistic that 85 percent of autistic college graduates in the US were unemployed and underemployed. The realization both of the extent of neurodiversity exclusion in the workplace and of her own neurodivergent identity prompted the development of her approach to total, multi-intersectional inclusion: systems designed to support the most excluded can support all.

Dr. Praslova is a Professor of Graduate Industrial-Organizational Psychology at Vanguard University of Southern California. Her consulting is focused on creating human-centric organizational systems and providing neuroinclusion training and support to organizations such as Amazon, Bank of America, and MIT. She regularly writes for *Harvard Business Review* and *Fast Company* and is the first person to have published in *Harvard Business Review* from an autistic perspective.

Dear reader,

Thank you for picking up this book and welcome to the worldwide BK community! You're joining a special group of people who have come together to create positive change in their lives, organizations, and communities.

What's BK all about?

Our mission is to connect people and ideas to create a world that works for all.

Why? Our communities, organizations, and lives get bogged down by old paradigms of self-interest, exclusion, hierarchy, and privilege. But we believe that can change. That's why we seek the leading experts on these challenges—and share their actionable ideas with you.

A welcome gift

To help you get started, we'd like to offer you a **free copy** of one of our bestselling ebooks:

www.bkconnection.com/welcome

When you claim your **free ebook**, you'll also be subscribed to our blog.

Our freshest insights

Access the best new tools and ideas for leaders at all levels on our blog at ideas.bkconnection.com.

Sincerely,

Your friends at Berrett-Koehler